Supremely American

Popular Song in the 20th Century: Styles and Singers and What They Said about America

Nicholas Tawa

THE SCARECROW PRESS, INC.
Lanham, Maryland • Toronto • Oxford
2005

SCARECROW PRESS, INC.

Published in the United States of America
by Scarecrow Press, Inc.
A wholly owned subsidiary of
The Rowman & Littlefield Publishing Group, Inc.
4501 Forbes Boulevard, Suite 200, Lanham, Maryland 20706
www.scarecrowpress.com

PO Box 317
Oxford
OX2 9RU, UK

British Library Cataloguing in Publication Information Available

Library of Congress Cataloging-in-Publication Data

Tawa, Nicholas E.
   Supremely American : popular song in the 20th century : styles and singers and
what they said about America / Nicholas Tawa.
       p. cm.
   Includes bibliographical references and index.
   ISBN 0-8108-5295-0 (pbk. : alk. paper)
   1. Popular music—United States—History and criticism. I. Title.
ML3477.T39 2005
782.42164'0973'0904—dc22   2004022882

⊗™ The paper used in this publication meets the minimum requirements of
American National Standard for Information Sciences—Permanence of Paper
for Printed Library Materials, ANSI/NISO Z39.48-1992

Contents

Acknowledgments

Introduction

Five of my previously published books paid close attention to popular song from colonial times to 1910.[1] In all of them primary considerations were the general political, social, and economic changes that took place, the public affected by these changes, and the popular song that provided entertainment and expressed people's feelings, values, and sense of beauty as these changes took effect. In this study of popular song of the 20th century, I have continued my examination and brought it to the beginning of the year 2004. I keep in mind that whatever the popular music, it exists only because a huge assembly of listeners selects and supports it, however much the "music industry" tries to manipulate tastes and the aesthetically sensitive set deplores its lack of artistic quality.

To me, entertainment has two aspects that I apply to song: one is amusement and diversion, the other is recreation—that is to say, the "creating anew" of the spirits. I have not concentrated on a technical analysis and explication of the songs; Alec Wilder and many others have already done exceptional musical analyses of Tin Pan Alley and Broadway songs; numerous books and articles offer explanations of the songs from country, rhythm and blues, rock, and so on. Nor do I go exhaustively into the music business for its own sake, a subject amply covered by Russell and David Sanjek. Nor is it my purpose to engage in academic dissections, debates, and comparisons. Academic research, while sometimes sterile, does offer certain insights into popular culture. However, this is not the route I wish to take. I wish to address the general reader with little or no formal training in music and with an approach meaningful to him.

In addition, it is not a part of my study to include every songwriter, singer, and instrumentalist. Many fine musicians were omitted from this history. Although many songs first appeared in staged musicals, especially in the 1920s, '30s, and '40s, I maintain that much of their popularity was owing to their detachability, their ability to take on a life of their own apart from a show. My focus is usually on the songs themselves as separable entities. For the most part, I leave the discussion of musicals and the way songs work in them to others.

Unfortunately, much as I may try, my words cannot convey the magic of a fine melody, bouncy rhythm, memorable harmony, or their fascinating combination to the general reader. Nor does the insertion of brief examples of the music in the text help when a person cannot read music. Besides, a few notes fail to suggest the delight that a listener may derive from an entire composition. In an important sense, the lines that the lyricist devises after the composer writes the music or vice versa (and normally, especially in the first half of the century, the music was created first) are in themselves an interpretation of the music's meaning. That is one of the givens when I discuss lyrics.

It is the way popular music—words and music—concerned American life that interests me: what it was and why and how it existed; how its songs fitted within the context of the larger 20th-century society; why musical styles changed and what were the new styles that emerged were. I hope to be straightforward, even informal, in my language and respond directly to what the music and the times tell me. My aim is to engage the interest of the intelligent music lover who wants to know more about popular music. Those expecting a different approach are forewarned.

In my discussion of the songs of the Jazz Age and the Swing Era, years when stylistic homogeneity more or less prevailed, the music is considered primarily in terms of song types and their relationship to the times. This procedure does not work after the first half of the century, when a multitude of different styles and variations within each style arose. At any rate, songs frequently became closely identified with particular singers and performing groups. For these reasons, the attention will shift to the styles that emerged and the singers identified with each style and the songs they purveyed and to which they gave distinction.

A brief survey of song history can serve to orient the reader and indicate the scope of my study. During the earliest years of our history, the popular music heard in America was mostly imported from the British Isles. However, American songwriters and performers gradually emerged to become a strong force by the 1850s. What they wrote and what they performed was in direct response to their American audience. As a result, the subject of their lyrics, their use of harmony, and the shape of their tunes began to take on an American character—simple, direct, and democratically focused. These attributes would apply to song throughout the next century. A distinctive American genre, minstrel song, emerged that was musically indebted to traditional ditties and dances of boatmen, woodsmen, lumberjacks, and so on. Although a "black" dialect entered and ostensibly "black" subjects were treated, any resemblance to African-Americans was, for the most part, coincidental, with one or two exceptions.

Adolescents took the greatest interest in song during the 19th century, although songs were produced for and did satisfy all age groups. Romantic expression was paramount in the lyrics, as was the celebration of ordinary persons in everyday speech. The great devotion of adolescents to sentimental song, however redefined, and the use of informal language are found to be a characteristic of songs in all periods—19th and 20th century.

My first concern in this book was to try to understand what alterations took place in the United States when the balance was tipped toward an industrial and urban society infused with a large immigrant population. Americans needed and sought something fresh with which to express themselves.[2] After the turn of the century, strikingly new sounds were in the air; strikingly new rhythms (ragtime, Charleston, fox trot, etc.) propelled the steps and swayed the bodies of the public. African-American innovators and white songwriters, most of them recent Jewish immigrants or their offspring, fashioned fresh danceable songs to satisfy the demand. Melody grew more syncopated, more chromatic, and harmony grew more complex. New rhythmic configurations were introduced. Lyrics became more colloquial, even slangy, more concerned with the here and now, and more the embodiment of the modernity that was redefining society. From the early 19th century on, American song mostly centered on the individual, the "I." After the turn of the century, lyrics increasingly underlined an individual's enjoyment and contentment as the chief good in life and reflected the view that all behavior is motivated by the pursuit of pleasure or the avoidance of pain.

World War I and the decade after accelerated the process. On hand were songwriters of exceptional ability, Berlin, Kern, Gershwin, Arlen, Rodgers, and others, who provided music for the "Jazz Age," capturing its energized and emotional atmosphere in their melodies, harmonies, and rhythms. So also did literate and sophisticated lyricists like Ira Gershwin and Hammerstein in their song lyrics. These composers and lyricists were professional craftsmen, in part inspired, in part trying to create a product that would satisfy a wide public, young and old. Much of their vocal music, it is true, initially existed as part of staged musicals, but most Americans who cultivated the songs never attended the musicals and depended on radio, recordings, player pianos, and stock arrangements employed by local bands and singers to gain familiarity with the latest pieces. It was with the songs that people's allegiance lay—not with the composers, or lyricists, or musicals. Later, radio and movies would play a large part in familiarizing the public with songs. Microphones and electrical amplification entered, as did the crooner, as a new kind of vocalist conveying an intimate message. Singers altered the ways they projected their voices. Instrumentalists altered the ways they produced tones.

Songwriters studied what was succeeding with audiences. They produced down-to-earth torch songs, love ditties, and novelty numbers in accord with public taste and the "modern" point of view. None was interested in getting ahead of their audience—for that meant an end to him or her as a songwriter. A Jerome Kern might make noises in the direction of "art," but for the most part it was Berlin's attitude that prevailed—do your best to write a fine piece, yes, but always keep the public happy, because that's where the money is. During the first half of the century the songwriter was still distinct from performer, and songs were sometimes tailored to suit particular voices.

In 1929 came the Great Depression, then the slow recovery period of the late thirties, and the ominous gathering of war clouds in Europe. Interestingly, most popular song lyrics did not mirror the desolation and apprehensions of the times. Much of the music did not wail in loud complaint. People, for the most part, wanted psychological relief from their everyday burdens. The Swing Era began, with its dynamic bands and singers and with composers like Porter who reflected the new character of pop. If anything, the lyrics, rhythms, and harmonies grew even more sophisticated. Not drastic but subtle changes took place in song.

Soon the performer as a dominant figure begins to emerge, and command an adulatory young audience—Bing Crosby and Frank Sinatra to name two. Favorite singers became idolized as musical personalities, and more and more did their individual voices shape the creation of new songs. The era of the passionately dedicated teenage music fanatic had also become a reality. The pictures of the zoot-suiter and the frenzied, swooning bobby-soxer, in the shape of an adolescent girl, grew ubiquitous.

World War II, the drafting of band players, the curtailment of travel, and the Petrillo ban on recordings by union members all helped to usher out the swing bands. The repeated airing of old recordings, which stood in the place of new ones, became tiresome. Record companies began turning to nonunion musicians in order to continue recording. Most of these musicians came from country and western or rhythm and blues venues. White urban music lovers were being allowed to taste a "forbidden fruit" to which they became addicted. The era of the swing band was over, as were the songs the period had inspired.

Our attention turns next to the 1950s. With these years came a postwar population boom and greater affluence for many. Also evident was a rootlessness caused by families looking for the "good life" in a suburbia of newly constructed homes or by families having to move wherever a company sent them. The latchkey boy or girl was a new phenomenon. These were children of working parents who came home from school and had to spend afternoons at home unsupervised. Wives and mothers had aided the war effort by taking over their men's jobs and were reluctant to take up again their roles as housewives. For many of them work was a necessity. At the same time, conformity and political right thinking took over. The atom bomb, Cold War, the Korean War, and McCarthyism infected much of the American populace with hatred, distrust, and profound unease. Considerable numbers of the public found McCarthy's unjust allegations and fascistic investigative techniques repugnant but panicked when it came to expressing their opinions openly and frankly. Witch hunts sought out the persons who refused to conform to established attitudes and prejudices. Disillusion with many aspects of American society was inevitable and would percolate down to the young. Song grew sensitive to all of this insanity and anxiety. It would be reflected in music and lyrics.

With social instability came a division into two mutually opposed groups, adults and their children—not all adults and children, to be sure, but enough so that the estrangement would have an impact on society. The reasons for this division have everything to do with the novel trends that would take place in music. Americans had always been infatuated with the idea of youth—the appearance, vigor, and attitudes characteristic of the young. Now the under-twenty age group was growing at a rapid rate. At the same time this group had money to spend and desired to make its own presence known, especially through dress and conduct at variance with what had gone before. There was a burning desire to discover forms of expression to represent them and not their parents. Recent technical innovations helped them realize their goals: television and recordings—whether cassette, LP, or CD. Electrified and electronic instruments provided a new sound alternative that many boys and girls found attractive.

To give birth to the new, the Tin Pan Alley and Broadway styles gave way to the blending of country and western with rhythm and blues, which produced rock 'n' roll. Young songwriters and performers like Little Richard and Elvis Presley, guided by astute producers, proposed a different popular idiom that addressed itself to the needs and desires of the under-twenty crowd. The novel idiom grew enormously in popularity, although it did not entirely supplant the earlier mainstream song style. At the same time, a folk-music revival grew in importance—a celebration of what seemed a more honest, sincere, and natural way of living (Seeger). Then, too, there was "protest," the making of music that criticized the "Establishment" (Dylan). Folk eventually produced folk-rock.

In the sixties came the highly unpopular Vietnam War, civil-rights protests, demonstrations, marches, and riots. White hippie, black militant, and liberated feminist loomed large in the society. Battles against established values, morals, and cultural expression ensued. Drugs and sexual freedom were essential parts of a growing counterculture. Folk-rock, psychedelic rock, progressive rock, soul and funk, and new directions for country and western captured the moods of the decade. In addition an extraordinary British invasion took place, beginning with the Beatles, who synthesized several of the American rock styles and gave them fresh expression.

The 1970s found many fans turning away from a rock idiom that they saw as getting tame and losing its incisive rhythms. In addition America's much touted prosperity was excluding large numbers of the working class who found it hard to make ends meet; and America's much lauded racial enlightenment had not benefited many black Americans who still suffered social and economic discrimination. Reggae, disco, heavy metal, and punk became the new movements and the desired correctives to what had gone before in rock music. In the eighties, further developments took place, stretching rock music to its extremes—from grunge and garage rock, hardcore, and hip-hop to rap and gangsta rap. Outrage gave way to outrageousness.

Throughout the postfifties decades there were always individual singers who resisted the trend and remained with a more melodious and mellifluent sort of song, Barbra Streisand to name one. Tony Bennett continued as a holdover from Tin Pan Alley. In addition there were performers who did not adhere to any one style yet became widely popular: Madonna, Michael Jackson, and Mariah Carey to name three. In significant ways, their songs pulled rock back to a dance focus, however showy their individual music presentations.

An inseparable connection came to exist between songwriter, producer, and performer. After the 1950s, few popular songs were conceivable without this tripartite input. Oftentimes, songwriter(s) and vocalist(s) and rock band were one. In addition, American popular music now turned truly intercontinental in its influence. Even when European songwriters and performers appeared (the Beatles, Rolling Stones), they had borrowed almost totally from American styles. "Authenticity" was coming to the fore. So as not to appear in a false light, performers needed to be authenticated by indisputable evidence. One important way for a singer to appear genuine was for him or her to participate in writing one's own songs. More than ever, the singer's persona was expected to saturate the song. The melody was not set forth as it might stand on paper. It had to change completely into a vehicle for self-expression. Melody was altered to encompass the singer's personal emotional agenda.

A mood of "outlaw" romanticism permeated rock lyrics. In them a person refused to be governed by the established rules and invested himself with a rebellious romantic character. Protest against the status quo appeared in song, much of it sincere, some of it superficial. Anomie, a rejection of social norms and values, loomed large in a youthful society. This condition when heard in song was accompanied by a sense of personal disorientation, anxiety, and social isolation.

Psychedelia, an aspect of anomie, was a component of the rock scene, starting in California. Popular music was linked with drugs (such as LSD) that produced abnormal psychic effects (as hallucinations) and that sometimes created psychic states resembling mental illness. Song lyrics directly referred to, even encouraged, the use of psychedelic drugs, in order to produce an intensified experience. Concerts imitated or reproduced the effects (as blurry or bizarre images or sounds) of drugs, within a calculated psychedelic musical performance. Violence and death were occasional components of the drug scene.

The popular-song world cultivated bizarreness in order to appear out of the ordinary and against conventional standards real or implied. Behavior and language often deviated from good taste and accepted standards. Calculated immaturity replaced sophistication. Performers dressed oddly, extravagantly, or eccentrically, as did some of their fans.

They set out to create situations that involved sensational contrasts, striking incongruities, and elements of the fantastic. Lasciviousness also came to the fore. Performers indulged in, and songs celebrated, free sexual activity. With the entry of rap, memorable melody was in abeyance; battering rhythms had taken over.

Now, after the turn of the century, all previous rock styles are being revived—as if following an imperative to reexamine the roads taken. Eclectic rock is to the fore, as songwriters and performers combine whatever styles they wish and think will go over with the public—from Tin Pan Alley and rockabilly to rap. Testing the musical waters is everywhere apparent. Increasing hints at reinstated melodiousness, harmoniousness, and even restraint are evident. A new category, quiet rock, has seen birth. In conclusion, at the beginning of the 21st century, there appears to be a consensus emerging that popular song needs renewal. Musicians are proposing all sorts of alternatives. What final shape that renewal will take, the public will decide, as has always been its prerogative. Nevertheless, first-rate and enjoyable songs have gone public in every year of the twentieth century. My hope is that the following pages will guide the reader to many of them.

NOTES

1. *Sweet Songs for Gentle Americans* (1980), *A Sound of Strangers* (1982), *A Music for the Millions* (1984), *The Way to Tin Pan Alley* (1990), and *High-Minded and Low-Down* (2000).

2. The changeover is carefully examined in two of my books: *A Sound of Strangers* (1982) and *The Way to Tin Pan Alley* (1990).

Chapter One

Preliminary Considerations

The term "popular song" has usually indicated a vocal composition that is easy to sing and remember. The piece of music is intended for as wide a distribution as possible. Designed to be immediately attractive, it normally remains in vogue for a relatively brief period—for a few years, two centuries ago; for a few months, a century ago; for a few weeks, today. However, an occasional song can exhibit a qualitative excellence and staying power that allow it to live indefinitely, decade after decade. To achieve success, songwriters cannot go it alone and express themselves only. They must observe and take note of their public, digest what they see and hear, mirror this knowledge in their writing, and offer up a composition devised for the public's enjoyment and the songwriter's profit. For many songs, first-rateness is verified by how widespread their following is.

Throughout its history, popular song has aimed at conforming to public needs and tastes. In the 1850s and '60s, George Root had written several hits, popular all over America. Friends urged him to write more ambitious pieces. He refused, saying the demand for them was nil. He preferred to address the needs of "tens of thousands of people" who responded to something uncomplicated and ear-catching to sing. Almost a century later, Alec Wilder observed, "I think that to [Irving] Berlin, as well as to many other song writers, a *good* song and a *hit* song are synonymous." The famous songwriter George Gershwin did not hesitate to say that he tried to cater to the public and give it simple, singable, melodious songs. He exploited the infectious rhythms and syncopations of jazz to boost the likeability of his songs; he resorted to repeated melodic phrases to etch the music in people's memories. Finally, knowledgeable writers observing the more recent rock scenes commented that accessibility was essential for making a rock song instantly appealing. They recommended danceable rhythms, and "most important . . . melodic emphasis." They said these were truisms recognized by Broadway, Tin Pan Alley, country-and-western songs, soul, and music of the Beatles and Motown. Punk and rap did not have as broad an appeal, they added, unless somebody like Dr. Dre vivified the rhythms with melodic pop hooks (appealing phrases that captured one's attention).[1]

Clearly, a new popular song needs to find an audience of some size—whether in the thousands or, the songwriter hopes, in the millions, whether spread out or gathered in urban centers. And it is the singer attuned to his or her listeners who finds it that audience. Like Bing Crosby and Frank Sinatra, Tony Bennett raised many a song to "hit" status because he sensed what pieces sung by him had a potential to please his public. This understanding, in large part, is behind his comment, "Talent isn't everything; it's really those entertainers who have empathy with their audience who are the most successful."[2] This observation would hold even truer in the rock 'n' roll period.

What is "excellence" in the popular world? Advanced aesthetic judgment does not readily enter the equation. It is true that arbiters of taste have often discovered evidence of bad taste in the music favored by the mass public. Academics in recent years have been exhaustively studying popular styles, individual artists, and individual songs and publishing their findings in university-press publications and journals like *Popular Music*, *American Music*, *Musical Quarterly*, and *Popular Music and Society*. Nevertheless, their opinions do not have the standing in the popular field that they would like to see. Their assessments tend to remain in the background.[3] Moreover, such evidence may fail to capture the vigor, openness, and catchy attractiveness of the musical offerings. What then is the primary criterion that identifies poor taste for a popular songwriter? In answer, I can rephrase the comment of Wilder: to Berlin, as well as to many other songwriters, a *bad* song and a *failed* song are synonymous. Even Jerome Kern, who aspired to artistic distinction, had to accept the public's verdict about which of his songs qualified to become hits.

When critics panned "I Can't Give You Anything but Love," lyric by Dorothy Fields, music by Jimmy McHugh, with the music commentator Gilbert Gabriel calling it "a sickly, puerile song," the public went ahead and bought over two and a half million recordings not caring what reviewers said of the music. When critics praised "Fools Fall in Love," by Irving Berlin, with Alec Wilder calling it "one of Berlin's most majestic melodies," the public ignored their assessment and refused to elevate the song into the circle of big hits.[4]

The commercial music business, if behaving as it should, does a valuable job of discovering talent and getting music to the public. On the other hand, what seems phony and deceitful in popular music can often be laid at its door—the greed and hunger to enlarge earnings. Likewise, the media, in its reviews, articles, and commentaries, provides important information about popular song and its performers. However, it may also misrepresent the news and thus abet whatever empty pretension exists in popular music. All too often, channels of mass communication and information buy into the music industry's calculated publicizing of events. They tolerate the puerile musical arrangements, the puffing of nubile and pretty-boy performers, and the vulgar showy exaggeration in some performances. The media's sins are compounded especially in those publications and broadcasts aimed at adolescents. Sometimes a song that otherwise would not have made it to the top achieves "hit" status through careful and astute promotion among the young. However, after it receives its fifteen minutes of fame, it disappears into the limbo of forgotten compositions.

Young people from the ages of ten to twenty have always played an important part in the nurturing of popular song. In addition, their likes and dislikes have usually carried over into their adult years. In a study of 18th- and 19th-century private sheet-music collections that I published in 1980,[5] I found that the most songs were purchased or came as gifts during adolescence. Around the beginning of the 20th century, George M. Cohan said knowledgeably, "What the fifteen-year old, clean faced, fresh minded, full of life American girl likes, the average American audience will like."[6] Closer to our time, the Carnegie Council on Adolescent Development (1995) reported that boys and girls, including preteens, spent several hours a day listening to music and purchased most of the recordings on the market. Why? The changeover from childhood to adulthood precipitated a conflict of emotions seeking expression through music. It was a period of restiveness, indecision, and stress resulting from irreconcilable inner urges. Music provided both a refuge and emotional outlet.

The young people were anxious over the emptiness caused by the giving up of intimacy they had as children close to their parents. The void needed filling. Confusion entered their minds as they tried to become self-sufficient and assert their individuality. To win independence, to gain freedom of action, and to realize their own personalities were their imperatives. They might yearn for something or someone new to love as an answer to loneliness—someone to whom they could relate. At the same time, they often had uncertain interactions with, or difficulty in relating to, others, even their peers. All too frequently the loneliness and difficulty relating to others continued through adulthood. Songs mirrored these states and helped them face their dilemmas. Asked about song's virtues, the songwriter Harold Arlen once said, "Words make you think and music makes you feel a feeling, but a song makes you feel a thought."[7] Song lovers, young and old, would have said *amen* to this conclusion.

THE 19TH CENTURY'S CLOSE

Popular-song styles continuously change as the public vacates an old and turns to a new mode of musical expression. However, a few years after the Civil War, song styles changed extensively. They were responding to an emerging new America that would require altered forms of expression by the century's end. Rapid extension of settlements into the trans-Mississippi territories and the hard scrabble for survival, the escalating presence of impoverished migrants on our shores and their joining the native factory and mill workers, and the relentless expansion of industry indifferent to the human toll it exacted were defining an America that had few precedents. The people from the countryside and foreign lands flocking to the American cities in search of work had limited financial means and a hunger to better themselves in whatever way they could. The country was becoming increasingly urbanized. By 1915 over 40 percent of all Americans lived in cities and worked for wages. A preoccupation with material, rather than idealized or spiritual, things could not help but enter the lyrics of songs. Among the fifteen million people who came to America in the decade before and after the 20th century began were eastern European Jews, Mediterranean peoples, Slavs, and Hungarians. They were excluded from high cultural pursuits owing to deficient education, lack of money, and real and imagined discrimination. The doors of popular culture, in contrast, stood wide open. The only test for entry was talent and the ability to please the multitudes.

The Jews in particular would have a major impact on American popular music. In the 1880s, about 19,000 a year were arriving here from eastern Europe; in the 1890s, around 37,000 a year; and in the first decade and a half of the new century, about 76,000 a year.[8] If they wished to enter the art-music world, most lacked the education and the ability to surmount the social and professional barriers in their way. On the other hand, the popular-music world was wide open to them. To succeed, all they had to do was reach, attract, persuade, and please the common people of America. They would set up music publishing firms specializing in popular songs (the Witmarks, Edward Marks, Shapiro-Bernstein, Joseph Stein), build chains of theaters in which to perform them, organize circuits of entertainers to service the theaters (the Shuberts, Adolph Zucker, Marcus Loewe), and contribute major performers (Sophie Tucker, Al Jolson, Fanny Brice) and songwriters (Jerome Kern, Irving Berlin, Vincent Youmans, Richard Rodgers, Harold Arlen, George Gershwin) to the American entertainment world. Many of them had started off with little money and no goods but then found a niche in show business. Rude, rough, and arrogant some of them may have been, but they also had a gut feeling about what entertainment the public wanted.[9]

By the eve of World War I, one out of every three Americans was an immigrant or a child of one.[10] Whether they were involved in the music business or part of the consuming public, they found the traditions and imagery of extant American song to be unfamiliar. Soon they composed an influential segment of the urban producers of and audiences for song and brought their preferences to bear—always melding their choices with those of the generality of Americans. Not for them earlier song's concentration mostly on bucolic scenes, and depiction of innocent girlhood and stalwart manhood strengthened by steadfast belief in a supreme being. Faith and strength they had, but they also experienced the different reality surrounding them, which they refused to ignore or reconcile with the will of a higher being.

The core of the post-Victorian songs was the portrayal of feelings that a person was powerless to manage, like senseless cruelty, powerful obsession, untrustworthy camaraderie, and the conditions they produced. One was alone; God was nowhere to help in many song lyrics; society was uninvolved. A new examination of what was right, what was wrong, and why was taking place. However, serious songs of sentiment on love of home and a beloved were still on request, and songwriters like Harry Kennedy ("Molly and I and the Baby," 1892), Paul Dresser ("On the Banks of the Wabash Far Away," 1897), and Ernest Ball ("Love Me, and the World Is Mine," 1906) were on hand to supply the demand. Yet, other serious songs, often from the same songwriters, were now far more troubled: note the worry in Ernest Ball's "Will You Love Me in December as You Do in May?" (1905) and the desolation behind Shelton Brooks's "Some of These

Days" (1910). A violence-ridden marriage invests "Don't Take Me Home" (Harry Von Tilzer, 1908). Survival of the fittest provides the subject of "Down in Jungle Town" (Theodore Morse, 1908). An abused woman pleads, "Bill Bailey, Won't You Please Come Home" (Hughie Cannon, 1902). Getting drunk can offer relief: "Budweiser's a Friend of Mine" (Seymour Furth, 1907). Sexiness is okay: "Betsy's the Belle of the Bathers" (Richard Carle, 1907). One is alone in this world: "Can't You See I'm Lonely" (Harry Armstrong, 1905). These were subjects rarely touched upon before the 1890s. The old America was left behind in songs about telephones ("Hello, Central, Give Me Heaven," Charles Harris, 1901), automobiles ("In My Merry Oldsmobile," Gus Edwards, 1905), baseball ("Take Me Out to the Ball Game," Albert Von Tilzer, 1908), and airplanes ("Come, Josephine, in My Flying Machine," Fred Fisher, 1910). A young woman stumbles along while trying to cope and speaks for many when she sings, "It's a great big world and it's new to me, /And I don't quite understand . . ."[11]

The introductory verse followed by a chorus, which had characterized popular song since the 1840s, continued, except that the melodic emphasis was on the chorus. The "chorus" (the label continued to occur in 20th-century songs) was no longer harmonized for four voices but had turned into a soloistic refrain carrying the burden of the song. Thus the terms "chorus" and "refrain" came to be used interchangeably. Some truth lurked in Edward Marks's claim, "The verse doesn't matter. Nobody ever remembered it anyhow."[12] More and more, people remembered the tune of the refrain only. Singers and band leaders were apt to cut the verse out altogether. What vocal harmonizing took place was in the form of barbershop and, later, doo-wop. Chromaticism, the use of tones foreign to the basic key, increased in order to enrich melody and harmony; so also did syncopations, the shifting of the regular metrical accent to an offbeat.

From the turn of the century on, contrasts in song genres were striking. On the one hand, the American waltz held sway for a while and sported negligible chromaticism, simple harmonies, and scarcely a syncopation. This three-quarter-time genre, imported from Europe, was given an American inflection in Charles Harris's extraordinarily popular "After the Ball" (1892), which was followed by other favored waltz pieces, like Charles Ward's "The Band Played On" (1895) and Leo Friedman's "Let Me Call You Sweetheart" (1910). Also coming from Europe were the operetta songs, which for several years were all the rage. Harmonies were richer than those of the waltz, melodies more demanding to sing, and lyrics usually devoid of American colloquialisms and subject matter. Victor Herbert's "Gypsy Love Song" (1898), "Kiss Me Again" (1905), and "Ah, Sweet Mystery of Life" (1910) are three examples.

Songs from the operettas of Herbert, Rudolph Friml, and Sigmund Romberg drew listeners who favored what was customary and predictable. Besides, the tunes were addictive. Quite a few of these men and women had also attended the operetta performances and had loved the magnificent stage productions with their picturesque costumes and quaint language. They came away singing Friml's "Only a Rose," "Rose Marie," and "Song of the Vagabonds," and Romberg's "Will You Remember?" and "Softly as in a Morning Sunrise." Operettas and their songs would be kept alive through the thirties, with the widely viewed movie versions starring Nelson Eddy and Jeannette MacDonald.

Opposing these songs were distinctly American productions. As precursors of what was to come, there were the confident marches of John Philip Sousa ("Washington Post," 1889, and "The Stars and Stripes Forever," 1897). They were famous as instrumental numbers, but words were put to some:

Hurrah for the flag of the free!
May it wave as our standard forever,
The gem of the land and the sea,
The banner of the right.

Also, there was the brash chortling of George M. Cohan ("Give My Regards to Broadway," 1904, and "The Yankee Doodle Boy," 1904):

I'm the kid that's all the candy,
I'm a Yankee Doodle Dandy,
I'm glad I am,
So's Uncle Sam.
I'm a real live Yankee Doodle,
Made my name and fame and boodle
Just like Mr. Doodle did
By riding on a pony.

And there was the bumptious assertiveness of Henry Sayers's "Ta-ra-ra-bom-der-e" (1891) and Theodore Metz's "A Hot Time in the Old Town" (1896).

Without question, the most American and un-European compositions were the rag songs—extremely syncopated, marchlike works that had descended from American marches, African-American cakewalks (black-slave caricature dances done to entertain white plantation owners), and pseudo-black minstrel songs (by way of "coon" songs). Here we can see some of the vital and long-lasting contributions that African-Americans had made (and would continue to make) to America's music. Ragtime piano compositions began appearing in the 1890s, played especially by roving black pianists or the black house pianists of bawdy houses. The respectable Scott Joplin, highly regarded as a composer, was the best-known of the black ragtime-piano musicians and creator of the fascinating ragtime opera *Treemonisha*. His death in 1917 would signal the close of the ragtime era. By the very end of the century lyrics were being put to rags. They proved popular with white Americans, who liked their bold and impudent approach toward life. Lyrics were slangy and often, like the earlier minstrel and coon songs, had pseudo-black subjects. In several instances, the language was racist and demeaned African-Americans. White songwriters were soon composing rag songs to satisfy the demand. Winning national followings were Joseph Howard's "Hello! Ma Baby" (1899) and "Goodbye, My Lady Love" (1904) and Hughie Cannon's "Bill Bailey, Won't You Please Come Home?" (1902).

Hello! Ma baby. Hello! Ma honey. Hello! Ma ragtime gal.
Send me a kiss by wire, baby, me heart's on fire!
If your refuse me, Honey, you'll lose me, then you'll be left alone;
Oh baby, telephone, and tell me I'm your own.
Hello! Hello! Hello! Hello there.

Also extremely favored was "Under the Bamboo Tree" (1902), written by black songwriters Bob Cole and J. Rosemond Johnson.

Down in the jungles lived a maid,
Of royal blood though dusky shade,
A marked impression once she made
Upon a Zulu from Matabooloo;
And ev'ry morning he would be
Down underneath a bamboo tree,
Awaiting there his love to see
And then to her he'd sing:

If you lak-a-me, lak I lak-a-you
And we lak-a-both the same,
I lak-a-say, this very day, I lak-a-change your name;

'Cause I love-a-you and love-a-you true
And if you-a love-a-me.
One live as two, two live as one
Under the bamboo tree.

Speaking for his generation, in an article published in the *Seven Arts Monthly* of July 1917, Hiram Motherwell wrote, "To me ragtime brings a type of musical experience which I can find in no other music. I like to think that it is the perfect expression of the American city, with its restless bustle and motion, its multitude of unrelated details, with its underlying rhythmic progress toward a vague Somewhere."[13]

The enthusiasm for rag quickly produced new types of social dancing. A mania for rag-dance competitions was one result. The European imports—polka, waltz, schottische, and the like—could no longer suffice for the younger Americans. They loved stepping out onto the dance floor but sought something more tuned into the contemporary zeitgeist. Rag for them was a liberating force. It gave them the freedom to sway, slide, glide, shake, walk, and rock more as they wished. Dancers, too, tried novel "animal" steps, like the grizzly bear, bunny hug, kangaroo hop, and camel walk. A couple of songs even gave instructions on how to execute the newer steps. In the unconstrained and mischievous "Ballin' the Jack" (1913), lyric by Jim Burris, music by Chris Smith, we are told:

First you put your two knees close up tight,
Then you sway 'em to the left,
Then you sway 'em to the right. . . .

Four years later, Shelton Brooks's ragged version of the two-step in "The Darktown Strutters' Ball" enticed people with its attention-gripping tune and tempting syncopated rhythms to fling themselves with abandon onto the dance floor.

A variety of animal and bird "trots" made their way into American dance floors after the turn of the century.[14] However, dancers eventually bestowed their greatest favor on the fox trot. One story goes that the fox trot originated in the Jardin de Danse, on the roof of the New York Theatre, where Harry Fox was doing trotting steps to ragtime music, in May 1914, which dancers at first referred to as "Fox's Trot." It developed into a dance that combined quick and slow steps, allowed flexibility of movement, and gave more dancing pleasure than the one-step and two-step.[15] Another story goes that the Vernon and Irene Castle dance team popularized the dance in 1914, inspired by their backup band, one established and led by an African-American, Jim Europe.[16] One day, during a rehearsal break, Europe's ensemble started to play Handy's "Memphis Blues" at an even, moderate 4/4 speed. The Castles liked what they were hearing and started to invent steps for the music. They then introduced these "fox trot" steps to Americans throughout the country. Before long the fox trot was clearly what dancers adhered to when a popular ballad was performed.[17] Seeking to please this dance crowd, up-to-date ballrooms opened in the major cities, some of them quite plushy in their trimmings. Two of the best known were New York's Palais de Dance and the Jardin de Danse. In addition, by 1915, Florenz Ziegfeld was establishing a fresh form of entertainment, the cabaret, when he introduced the *Midnight Frolics* at the New Amsterdam Theater—where one could eat, drink, and enjoy a newfangled floor show featuring plenty of pretty young women, singing, and dancing.[18]

Songwriters immediately bought into the new dancing trends. Irving Berlin's "Alexander's Ragtime Band" came in response to the growing dance craze. For the fox trot lovers, he provided "A Pretty Girl Is Like a Melody" and "Always." Berlin was an acute observer of popular taste and kept on the watch for the latest dance craze. In 1927, while he and his wife Ellin were in Palm Springs, Florida, she went to a local ballroom with Anita Loos to execute the steps for the recently invented Black Bottom, with sinuous hip movements and a rocking gait. This novel dance was then giving stiff competition to the Charleston.[19] Irving Berlin, of course, would have known of her going to dance the Black Bottom. He would certainly have discussed her and the ballroom crowd's response to it, and then weighed its possibilities as a vehicle for a new song.

THE AFRICAN-AMERICAN INPUT

Few among the millions of white song lovers of the turn of the century and after realized to what extent black music influenced all popular music and how many black composers made vital contributions to the general repertoire. Too often, black Americans were those "other people," to be ignored or maligned. Gary Giddins, in his biography of Bing Crosby, writes that scarcely any whites understood what black musicians had accomplished. Certainly the young Bing Crosby and his friends listened to white bands popularizing songs like "I Wish I Could Shimmy Like My Sister Kate,"

"Way Down in New Orleans," and "The Charleston" without knowing of their black origin. What they did love, as did the white public, were the memorable melodies, thrilling rhythms, and uncanny harmonies they were listening to.[20]

Also entering the popular consciousness were the blues of African-Americans, with their "bluesy" tones, bent pitches, shouts, and vocal cries telling of personal troubles. First appearing in the rural South, especially the Mississippi Delta, the blues migrated with African-Americans north to cities like Chicago and Detroit, where urban performers took them up. The first blues heard by whites were sung mainly by black women, like the famous Ma Rainey, Mamie Smith, and Bessie Smith. The stanzas to the blues were set to a customary rhythmic-harmonic structure normally of 12-bar length, although there was a great deal of flexibility. The most commercially renowned of the blues songs were W. C. Handy's "Memphis Blues" (1912) and "St. Louis Blues" (1914). Possibly the crossover from black to white was made easier because Handy shared a similar taste with whites, acquired when he worked in a steel mill in the 1890s. Speaking of himself and his white boss's son, Handy wrote, "We liked the same books and enjoyed singing the same popular songs of the day, *That Is Love*, *Down Went McGinty*, and *White Wings*."[21] It was Sophie Tucker, belting the "St. Louis Blues" out on the vaudeville circuit, who made it nationally well liked.

> I hate to see de ev'nin' sun go down,
> Hate to see de ev'nin' sun go down
> 'Cause ma baby, he done lef' dis town.

Then, too, there was the African-American religious music—the spirituals, hymns, and gospel songs. They, too, entered national consciousness. Perhaps the most famous, and of unknown origin, was the New Orleans funeral hymn "When the Saints Go Marching In," which Louis Armstrong often sang.

> Oh, when the saints go marching in,
> Oh, when the saints go marching in,
> Lord how I want to be in that number,
> When the saints go marching in.

The music of "jazz" left the black enclaves and entered the awareness of the general public early on in the 20th century. It was a uniquely rhythmic

American music, a musical style that grew out of black spirituals, gospel songs, blues, ragtime, and marches. Played by ensembles that usually included trumpet, clarinet, saxophone, bass, drums, and sometimes piano or guitar, jazz was characterized by extempore ad-libbing from the musicians, ceaselessly syncopated lines over steady rhythms, and ensemble playing featuring the simultaneous performance of the same melody with individual variations, by two or more performers. Also introduced were unusual melodic elements (blued notes, "bent" sounds, growls, and muted wah-wah bawling) in the instrumental performance that were borrowed from and paralleled the vocal techniques of black singers.

New Orleans was the originating center for much of the early jazz. The sound became widely known through the enthusiastically received recordings made by a white group, the Original Dixieland Jazz Band, beginning in 1917. It was not until 1923 that real black jazz began to be disseminated nationwide. In that year, King Oliver, who had traveled to Chicago from New Orleans, made his first recordings with his band, which had Louis Armstrong as a member. These disks, considered "race" records, were sold mostly in African-American markets, although some could not help but fall into white hands. Other "race" recordings followed, by musicians like Louis Armstrong fronting his own group, Duke Ellington and his orchestra, Jelly Roll on his piano, and Bessie Smith singing her blues selections. Meant to incite dancing, this music's catchy rhythms found their way into most black-American ballrooms and dance halls. Eventually jazz and blues broke through the race barriers to attract an appreciative white audience.

Popular dance music influenced by jazz (though it more often resembled an intensified ragtime) was played in the 1920s in a vigorous rhythmic manner by bands like those of Jean Goldkette, Paul Whiteman, Fletcher Henderson, and Isham Jones. To many men and women, the sounds coming from these bands symbolized an exciting America still in its youth, awakening from its years of isolation, and realizing its latent power for the first time.

Most white songwriters knew about jazz only at second and third hand, absorbing its "feel" because its sound was so much in the air and "the thing." One or two, Gershwin and Arlen come to mind, had empathy for black music and revealed this affinity in their songs. Directly or, usually, indirectly, jazz infused fresh rhythms, harmonies, and melodic contours into popular music. For example, it was behind Gershwin's strong and firm offerings, like those in the musical comedy *Lady, Be Good!* (1924)—"Oh, Lady, Be Good," "Fascinating Rhythm," "Little Jazz Bird," "The Half of

It, Dearie, Blues," "So Am I," and "Hang on to Me." Edward Jablonski has provided a proviso to this observation about Gershwin, writing that Americanisms such as his borrowed only in part from jazz. The rhythmic syncopations, blue notes, and chromatic harmonies in his music were also found in Jewish and Hungarian music.[22]

THE NEW BREED OF SONGWRITERS

Although the staged musical plays in urban theater were well attended, it was vaudeville, reaching almost every town, that supplanted earlier forms of entertainment from the 1880s on. Vaudeville really made huge numbers of Americans familiar with popular songs. It would remain the most popular entertainment for ordinary men and women until movies with sound tracks came along in the 1930s. Vaudeville offered light amusement contained in brief acts, with monologuists, comics, magicians, jugglers, acrobats, dancers, and, most of all, singers. From this perspective, the already-mentioned cabaret can be regarded as a modification of vaudeville. Also a close relative to vaudeville was the staged theater revue, a theatrical entertainment of little weight, consisting of sketches, songs, monologues, and prettily costumed young women. Audiences came expecting to find a jumble of songs, "living pictures," and dancing chorus girls.

Songwriters understood that most of the music they wrote would reach the major part of the public mainly via vaudeville or the revues, and later via recordings and radio. Broadway musicals with some semblance of plot, like Gershwin's *Lady, Be Good!* were beginning to appear. However, the story lines were very loose and barely held together productions that existed largely for the sake of song, dance, spectacle, and witty repartee. Besides, the songs that proved attractive to theatergoers quickly found their way into vaudeville, where singers and song-and-dance teams disseminated them to the mass audience.

Again and again, songwriters of the Jazz and Swing Eras tell us that they considered themselves professionals who had to turn out music without waiting for inspiration. Speaking for composers, Gershwin said, "Out of my entire annual output of songs, perhaps two—or, at the most, three—come as a result of inspiration. We can never rely on inspiration. When we most want it, it does not come. Therefore, the composer does not sit around and wait for an inspiration to walk up and introduce itself. What he substitutes for it is nothing more than talent plus his knowledge. If his endowment is great enough, the song is made to sound as if it were truly inspired." Speaking for lyricists, Oscar Hammerstein agreed that professionals had to get the job done and could not wait around for an inspiration. Lyricists, he said, had recourse to their memories and experiences, then worked hard to get the lyrics right.[23]

Very rarely, and normally as an afterthought, a songwriter might believe that an external influence acted directly and immediately upon his mind, in short, that inspiration was somehow involved. This, Hoagy Carmichael once thought as he listened to a playback of "Stardust" (1929). It sounded unfamiliar; it didn't seem his creation at all. He was troubled by the notion that the song was being attributed to him. "To lay my claims, I wanted to shout back at it, 'Maybe I didn't write you, but I found you.'"[24]

Nevertheless, whether inspiration was involved or not, whether composers and lyricists labored to turn out a commercially viable product or one tinged with personal feeling, the results could be inspiriting. Again and again, popular songs emerged that did achieve high artistic standards, take on the mantle of greatness, and remain meaningful over the years.

It was the nature of the game that composers and lyricists had to hone their instincts as to what would go over and what would fail. Instinct, professionals like Berlin, Kern, George and Ira Gershwin, and Oscar Hammerstein had decidedly. Nor did they rely only on their own opinions. They solicited those of others with practical knowledge of the song business, whose views they respected. Margaret Whiting, daughter of the songwriter Richard Whiting, recalls that Jerome Kern called her up soon after her father died, in 1938, saying that her father had told him she was a great judge of songs. He wanted to come over and let her hear a few new ones of his in order to find out what she thought about them. He came. She listened to the songs, among them "I'm Old Fashioned" and "Dearly Beloved," and assured him that they had promise. He went away satisfied. She also tells of how one night in Hollywood, in 1941, she, Judy Garland, Mickey Rooney, Martha Raye, and Mel Tormé were socializing at the Whiting house, when Harold Arlen and Johnny Mercer dropped in. They had just completed "Blues in the Night" and needed to try it out on others. The reaction? "Socko, boffo, *wham!* At one end of the room, Martha Rae almost passed out; for once she didn't have a funny line. Tormé was so knocked out by the musicianship, he just sat there. Mickey Rooney kept saying, 'My God, this is unbelievable!' And Judy and I raced to the piano to see which of us could learn the song first! You knew right away the song was so *important*."[25] Gershwin is said to have stood in the theater lobby at the premiere of his shows, gauging the reception of his tunes by observing how many men and women were humming them as they left for home. Berlin was known to stand in the rear of the auditorium and wait to measure the reaction to his songs at the end of a concert. He explained, "You gotta watch what they're humming when they come out," or else you will get nowhere.[26]

Melody came first. It might move effortlessly from note to note or jump about, but it had to be simple, easy to sing and remember, and agreeable to the ear. Richard Rodgers's "My Funny Valentine" (1937) provides an example of the former, scarcely ever taking a skip of any sort. The notes of his "My Favorite Things" (1959), on the other hand, do not stay put. Both succeeded with the public. When harmony was added to the melody, it was allowed discreet dissonances and some chromatic sliding about but had to enhance and not get in the way of the melody. Rhythm had to be firm, more a strong, bouncing two-beat pulsation in the twenties, a smoother, swinging four-beat pulsation later.

Keeping to fixed musical forms facilitated the conveyance of tunes from composer to listener. Expectations would not suffer defeat. Isaac Goldberg at the beginning of the 1930s opined, "The song of today is machine-made, machine-played, machine-heard. It is a formula, as surely as is the short story of the magazine, the crime fiction, the mystery tale."[27] Of course this is an exaggeration. The superior songwriter circumvented the "machine" labeling by adding something unique to the sound. Nevertheless, a piece did follow the conventions that seemed effective in popularizing a composition. Conventions helped the listener quickly to assimilate a tune. Often, though not always, the melody of the refrain was served up in a thirty-two measure length and divided into four phrases (sections) of eight measures each. There was almost always the repetition of a main tune-phrase, which we can call "A," and a different transitional tune-phrase, sometimes called a release or bridge, which we can call "B." The customary structure translated as AABA, as in Walter Donaldson's "My Blue Heaven" (1927), Richard Rodgers's "Blue Moon" (1934), and Harold Arlen's "Over the Rainbow" (1939). Commenting on Jerome Kern's "I Won't Dance" (1935), which had a hard-to-sing release, Alec Wilder said, "It is a theory of many song writers and publishers that as long as the main strain of a song is not beyond the capacity of the average untrained ear, the release can do whatever it pleases, particularly since the main strain will be the last thing heard."[28]

Of course, not all songs adhered to this formulation. Occasionally, a composer was more profligate with his tune-phrases, setting up, say, an

ABAC structure, as in Nat Herb Brown's "You Were Meant for Me" (1929). Or phrase lengths and repetition patterns could be far less predictable, as in the songs of Cole Porter and Harold Arlen. Porter's "Begin the Beguine" (1935), for example, has an extraordinary ABCDEFG phrase structure, with each phrase 16 measures in length, except for the last, which is in 8 measures—making the tune 104 measures long! Ira Gershwin said of Arlen that he was "no thirty-two bar man." Arlen's "Black Magic" had a length of 72 measures; "One for My Baby," 48 measures; "The Man That Got Away," 62 measures. One song, "Gotta [Have Me Go with You]" was out of the ordinary not only for its 24-measure verse and 48-measure refrain, but also because the first 8 measures of the verse music returns twice in the refrain.[29]

A majority of songs adhered to a *moderato* tempo, not too fast and not too slow, just right for singing or for dancing the fox trot. Performers understood that the indicated tempo was more a suggestion than an ironclad directive, subject to modification in order to accommodate different styles, vocalists, and situations.

Gershwin believed that, though formulaic, songs were also "a matter of invention aided and abetted by emotion." He maintained that it was always possible to create something that sounded fresh. A fine songwriter started with an idea for a song and contributed something personal and distinctive to it, which resulted in a tune that was original in some way.[30]

Expertise in constructing a song, they all had to have. Yet, this know-how could exist with or without knowledge of music theory and orchestration. What was most important was for songwriters to receive their initial training in the field. As a rule, this meant working as singers, instrumentalists, and band leaders or finding employment in music publishing houses—as staff composers writing what the marketplace dictated, song pluggers trying to put over unfamiliar songs, pianists demonstrating new music to entertainment-wise musicians, and arrangers preparing songs for sheet-music publication and adapting them for performance situations. They came away experienced professionals.

A composer like Jerome Kern or Richard Rodgers had received a thorough music education. On the other hand, Irving Berlin had received none, learning by looking around him and by doing and sharpening his musical skills as he went along. During his youth, Berlin went from street singer, to singing waiter, to song plugger, to stage performer—accumulating knowledge along the way. Technical music training was not part of the experience. It meant that as a songwriter he would be able to think up memorable melodies and affecting lyrics attuned to American music lovers—that was it. The rest was left to an amanuensis. His greatest strength was to feel as one with the man in the street and to know exactly what would please him. The result was that Berlin became one of the greatest American songwriters, some of his songs entering the realm of tradition—"Easter Parade" (1933), "God Bless America" (1939), "White Christmas" (1942), and "There's No Business Like Show Business" (1946). Ironically, though he sang of Easter and Christmas, he himself was Jewish. Yet, his lyrics, like his melodies, struck home.

Few composers tried to write their own lyrics, although every so often they came up with titles. Berlin and Porter were exceptions; they composed and poetized. Others left the task to professional lyricists who knew how to construct appropriate verses to fit a melody and, at the same time, push the right emotional buttons. One of the most successful writers, who teamed up with his celebrated brother, was Ira Gershwin. He said that mastering the trade of lyricist was a difficult undertaking. In order to endure, the lyricist had to be well read, well informed, and hardworking. This applied not only to him, "but for—in any order you like—[Cole] Porter, [Dorothy] Fields, [Irving] Berlin, [Johnny] Mercer, [Alan] Lerner, [Frank] Loesser, [Howard] Dietz, [P. G.] Wodehouse, [Betty] Comden and [Adolph] Green, [Oscar] Hammerstein, [Lorenz] Hart, [Erwin "Yip"] Harburg, and two or three others whose work I respect."[31] It should be added that the lyricists did not normally write the "book" (the script) for a musical show, only the lyrics for the songs. There were a few notable exceptions. Oscar Hammerstein wrote the book for Kern's seminal *Show Boat* and for the extraordinarily successful Broadway musicals he put together in collaboration with Richard Rodgers, beginning with *Oklahoma!* in 1943.

Almost always, the song's music was composed first and the lyric written later. Wodehouse thought that in this way songwriters achieved the best results. When the melody came first, the lyricist could locate the most important points in the music and invent proper words to fit them. Johnny Mercer felt strongly that composers made a mess of things when they tried putting a melody to a lyric. Oscar Hammerstein said that the custom arose because the European song composers who worked in the United States had no grasp of the language and so wrote the music alone, letting an American contribute the verses. In addition, with the songs of the 20th century, the abruptly changing rhythms of rag and the new dance steps did not permit standard meters. In order to achieve success, melodies had to be fine dance tunes—their creation had to come first in a songwriter's considerations. Thus, the lyricist had little choice but to fit words to a melody destined usually for dancing. It was not until the 1940s, when Hammerstein began working with Richard Rodgers, that he wrote the lyrics before the music.[32]

Lyrics did contain the more standard romantic feelings, with far less of the sentimentality that had prevailed in the previous century. Indeed, many of the lyrics exhibited a sense of effortlessness, a good-humored natural-ness of expression, an urbane handling of the subject, a familiar conversa-tional speech, and a succinct statement of ideas.[33] Writers were forever in search of a new way to say "I love you." They might say it fervently, charmingly, or comically, so long as they knew enough to steer clear of the unreal, syrupy language of operetta—as with Rudolph Friml's "Indian Love Call" that starts "Ooh! Ooh! Echoes of sweet love notes gently fall/Through the forest stillness,/As fond waiting Indian lovers call." Modern, up-to-date American lyricists had to have a smart new way of put-ting things. They could not follow the lead of the Europeans and expect to get anywhere with American audiences.

Instead of turning romantically sentimental, Handy's singer of the "St. Louis Blues" (1914) dwells in a real world. She gives vent to her feelings with dignity and straightforwardness stripped of exaggerated sentiment when she tells why she hates to see the sun go down. A fresh toughness of fiber shows through in "After You've Gone" (1918), lyric by Henry Creamer, music by Turner Layton. It is more a giving notice than a moan-ing over one's fate:

> After you've gone and left me cryin',
> After you've gone—there's no denyin',
> You'll feel blue, you'll feel sad,
> You'll miss the dearest pal you ever had.

Here is a different world from that of operetta song.

Loesser's lover croons to a Carmichael tune, "Heart and soul, I fell in love with you." He admits this is what "a fool would do"—falling in love "madly, because you held me tight." Porter's unconventional lover gets "no kick from champagne," and "mere alcohol doesn't thrill me at all," but "I get a kick out of you." Leo Robin and Ralph Rainger's flip lover sings, "Thanks for the memory," continues with, "You might have been a headache but you never were a bore," and concludes with "Awf'ly glad I met you, cheerio and toodleoo." None of this is stuff that operetta songs are made of.

We learn that Jerome Kern, for example, was sickened by the over-romanticizing in many operetta songs and especially disliked the overused word "cupid." Unsurprisingly, he prohibited the word from appearing in his songs. Following Kern's completion of the music for "Why Do I Love You?" in *Show Boat*, Hammerstein played an unfair trick on him. During the rehearsal, he introduced slyly the verse:

> Cupid knows the way.
> He is the naked boy
> Who can make you sway
> To love's own joy.
> When he shoots his little ar-row,
> He can thrill you to the mar-row.

Kern was horrified and not a little annoyed.[34] At the same time, Hammerstein's laugh-provoking interpolation underscored what was seen as *un-American* in lyrics.

All songwriters were expected, indeed needed, to have their finger constantly on the American pulse. Alan Lerner, a noted lyricist, was fond of sojourning in France with his French wife. However, he realized one day that he was lingering too long in Paris and losing his professional bearings. It wasn't long before he was saying, "Americans really can't work in Paris—or in any other country but his own. He begins to lose the national identity of his work. He can't tell if it's American. Once I asked Micheline [his wife] what she thought of something I had written. Her answer was: 'If you're no longer sure, it's time to go back home.'"[35] Back home he went.

In response to the new rhythms, lyricists were quick to capture the droll, arresting, or odd in contemporary life and to express it ingeniously and engagingly. They sometimes became extravagantly clever or excessively biting, when in pursuit of a novel approach. They also had to achieve a certain level of sophistication. Ira Gershwin asserts in song that what he does "is much more fun," because "I love to rhyme." Yes, "Mountaineers love to climb / Criminals love to crime"; however, "I love to rhyme." Or he slyly insinuates, "Honestly I thought you wouldn't / Naturally you thought you couldn't / And probably we shouldn't / But aren't you glad we did?" Whatever was written had to fuse naturally with the melody and remain singable—inserting places to breathe, giving open vowels to high notes, removing what might tie the tongue.

GOING AFTER THE PUBLIC

At least 95 percent of published American popular songs fall quickly into oblivion, with only 5 percent, or even less, making a real impression on listeners. First of all, to do well, some element, usually not readily identifiable, in the music or lyric must ignite listeners, viscerally and emotionally. Second, to succeed, popular songs have to prove their flexibility. If the vogue veered in a new direction, the proven songs were capable of doing the same. The most renowned compositions, whether by a one-song-hit composer or by a giant like Berlin, do allow varied readings. Whatever the designated speed on the printed material, it is not an iron-clad directive. In performance, songs go slower or faster, in whichever direction the public favors, and can be configured not just as fox trots, but if circumstances require it, as marches, waltzes, polkas, Latin dances, bouncy up-tempo or torchy down-tempo pieces, or what have you. Thirdly, familiar elements must be present to help listeners assimilate the composition—an easy flow of notes, an already familiar element incorporated into the sound and structure, a subtle reminiscence of a previously popular song. Complete originality only gets in the way of acceptance. Fourthly, even if a song integrates well into the plot of a Broadway musical or Hollywood movie, it still is addressing comparatively few listeners. In the twenties and thirties, thousands might attend a successful musical, but millions listened to the musical's songs on radio and recordings. The song had to be capable of living on its own, apart from its original surroundings, in order to enter the winner's circle. It revealed its attractiveness on the dance floor, as a recorded single, in vaudeville, in night clubs, in popular-band concerts, and at weddings and other domestic celebrations. Otherwise it failed to flourish. This Rodgers and Hammerstein recognized when they fitted their songs snugly into the stories of shows like *The Sound of Music*, *South Pacific*, and *Oklahoma!* but also tried to make certain their songs were detachable.

As a case in point, there was painstaking incorporation of the songs into the narrative of *Lady in the Dark* (1941), book by Moss Hart, music by Kurt Weill, and lyrics by Ira Gershwin. In addition, these writers kept formulas at a minimum. As a result, well regarded as the show was by critics, it produced no big hit. It was an exceptional "play with music," but also one whose very transcendence of formula had limited its appeal. When I attended a university production of the musical, put on for a conference of American-music scholars, I thoroughly enjoyed the presentation. The music was first-rate; the lyrics were apt; the story was fascinating. However, my colleagues and I went away humming hardly anything. "In more than fifty years, *Lady in the Dark*, one of Ira Gershwin's greatest contributions to the musical theater, has never had a major revival."[36]

Philip Furia makes an important observation about the trend in writing song lyrics for musicals in the 1940s. He comments that after the success of *Oklahoma!* (1943), Broadway began to shut out lyricists like Johnny Mercer, who "thought in terms of the song rather than the show." Hollywood, also, was making fewer original musicals. It would be one reason why Tin Pan Alley ceased to be "the center of the musical universe," eventually to be replaced by rhythm and blues, country and western, and rockabilly music.[37]

A Broadway musical had to have at least one hit song to make it memorable, as far as the public was concerned—in Kern's *Sally* (1920), it was "Look for the Silver Lining"; in Gershwin's *Oh, Kay!* (1926), it was "Someone to Watch over Me"; in Porter's *The Gay Divorce* (1932), it was "Night and Day"; and when Kern's *Roberta* (1933) was foundering, "Smoke Gets in Your Eyes" saved it.[38]

Modifications in the way popular music was rendered took place after World War I. The public was going for musical sounds in league with the developing hedonistic social behavior of the twenties. Strings disappeared, and the more assertive trumpets, trombones, clarinets, saxophones, pianos, guitars, and drums took over the popular instrumental ensembles. The well-trained and opulent voices of operetta were less in demand and were replaced by the voices of singers with negligible training but real personal presence. Their tones emerged as thin or throaty,[39] as shouts or uniformly calm renditions, as song-speech or as a pensive murmuring. Absent were the extended range, opulent intonations, and exploitation of open vowel sounds of the opera singer. Many could not read a note of music. Some of the most successful songsters had a compass of only a few notes—Fred Astaire was one. All sang trying to make the listener understand every word. The intent of popular vocalists was to make the music and the vernacular language of the lyrics sound clearly and convincingly and be perceived as central to people's concerns.

Like the education of songwriters, their best training was experience in the field and before audiences, not segregation in a European music conservatory. George Burns once stressed to Tony Bennett the importance of little clubs where performers had to stand and deliver, where they could have "the opportunity to get lousy before they got better, that it takes at least ten years to learn one's craft. . . . When you're starting out, you do a lot of things wrong, but that's how you learn."[40]

After a song left the desk of a songwriter, and very often before it got to a performer, it needed an arranger to add whatever was required in harmony or for enhancing singability and danceability. The arranger was also called upon to orchestrate the song in order to facilitate ensemble backup of the singer or to fit it to the needs of a particular dance band. As Bing Crosby said, "An arranger is the guiding spirit in making a successful record. He is the one who makes the voice sound good, or he can kill a good vocal or a good song if he's not skillful or not interested in the singer."[41] In order to get the most prominent bands and their vocalists to do a new number, individual arrangements were made. The adapter of songs had to work expertly, exploiting the modern instrumental combinations and tone productions of the post–World War I period—and the trendiest of all were the instrumentations and the distinctive timbres and pulsations of jazz.

The songs had to be not only published but carefully marketed. In the twenties, putting the song on records and plugging it over the radio were musts. In the thirties, many movies featured popular music. Two decades later it was television. One way or another, the public had to decide if it liked the piece and be able to get its hands on the music. During the twenties and thirties, a music publisher, normally located in New York City, tried to determine which of his songs might climb to the top of the heap. Market research thus had its beginning. Once the publisher made a decision, aggressive promoters hired by the firm branched out to clubs, dance halls, and broadcasting stations and visited band leaders and vocalists, pressing everyone and anyone to perform the selected songs. Free "professional" copies were handed out. Payola, a secret payment in return for the promotion of a song, became a fine art. The battle was more than half won if a radio network or a motion picture company shared in the ownership of a publishing house or record company and had a financial interest in pushing a song. All of this effort had as its final aim getting as many sponsored songs into the family circle as possible.

In the history of music, one of the most significant things about the 20th century was that compositions could be kept in existence as they originally sounded. This became possible with the invention of the phonograph record, then radio, and then film with a sound track. Thomas Edison originated the phonograph in 1877 and recorded sound on cylinders. Music really began to be recorded in 1901, and within five years all sorts of songs, dance pieces, and marches became available. At the same time the cylinder recording gave way completely to the flat disk (invented by Emile Berliner in 1887), which was capable of holding about four minutes of music. Shortly after World War I, millions of homes possessed phonographs and over 100 million records had been produced. This was the signal for a gradual changeover, from music actively played and sung from sheet music in many homes to music listened to on records in the home, despite the pianos in the parlors and the many guitars and ukuleles that continued to make the rounds.

In 1919, a recording of the song "Dardanella" sold almost a million copies. The next year "Whispering" sold over two million.[42] By the end of the twenties, records had taken the place of sheet music as the chief form of music making in the home. The first electrical recording of music took place in 1925, making home listening even more attractive. Around this time, the jukebox, a coin-operated phonograph housed in a flashy cabinet and having an assortment of records, came into existence. Push buttons allowed a selection to be made. Jukeboxes were soon manufactured by the thousands and found their way into restaurants, barrooms, social halls, and other public places where people gathered. In consequence, thousands of instrumentalists and singers were displaced, no longer needed for listeners' entertainment.

Another development that changed many people from recreational singers and instrumentalists to passive listeners was the radio. The start came in 1916, when David Sarnoff, of Marconi Wireless Telegraph, recommended to his boss the initiation of a plan to "make radio a household utility in the same sense as a piano or phonograph. The idea is to bring music into the house by wireless." Four years later, Frank Conrad, of Westinghouse, was playing records for listeners' entertainment with wireless equipment housed in a barn near Pittsburgh. The locals loved the experience. Encouraged by the response, Westinghouse, in November 1920, began the first commercial broadcasting of music over station KDKA, Pittsburgh. Within two years, some five hundred stations were operating; within seven years, around one thousand. The development of the microphone would also take place alongside that of radio.

The first national network, the National Broadcasting Company, was founded in 1926. Radio stations were now reaching the hitherto isolated rural areas of America. Although some broadcasts originated in cabarets, nightclubs, dance halls, and radio studios, most broadcasts featured recorded music—the products of Broadway and Tin Pan Alley for most, country music for a few stations, mostly in the South and West. This last was music deriving from or imitating the traditional styles of these areas, and currently being exploited commercially. Americans were delighted because they could enjoy music gratis snug in their homes, without having to buy a recording or a ticket to a performance.[43] After 1929, the Great Depression accelerated the move to radio. African-Americans had their own entertainers recorded on "race" records and available on a handful of radio stations.

Those people with a love for, or with commercial investments in, musicals radiating from Broadway were worried, and rightly so. They looked with consternation at the increase in sales of radio sets and feared that more and more prospective patrons were staying home. Certainly this was true for men and woman with more modest means, who left going out on the town to the more affluent. By 1924, Sol Bloom, congressman from New York and lover of the theater, foresaw the killing off of theaters in towns of 75,000 or less and a decrease of patrons in large cities, not excluding New York. In the same year, Jerome Kern was angered over the insufficient box-office take of his dying musical *Sitting Pretty* and claimed the public was being defrauded by radio (and recordings), because it gave them only imitations and pirated editions of the real thing, meaning live theater.[44]

However, the real killer of theater was motion pictures. With silent films, there was little threat. Ominous for the future, however, were the theme songs that were created to accompany the films. For example, in 1926, Lew Pollack wrote a lyric to Erno Rapee's song entitled "Charmaine," which was used to promote the film *What Price Glory*. Success came immediately to the song. "Ramona," lyric by L. Wolfe Gilbert, music by Mabel Wayne, was written, in 1927, to advance the silent film of the same name. Dolores Del Rio toured with the film, singing the song. A broadcast featuring her and the Whiteman orchestra on the song reached all corners of the United States. The next year, Gene Austin recorded "Ramona" and sold over two million copies.

In October 1927, Al Jolson starred in *The Jazz Singer*, which, though mostly silent, did utilize speech and music. Incorporated into the sound were three extant popular songs, "Blue Skies," "Mammy," and "Toot, Toot, Tootsie." Movie audiences went wild over them. The next year, Bud De Sylva and Lew Brown wrote a lachrymose lyric for Ray Henderson's music to "Sonny Boy," the first popular song written specifically to be featured in a film—for Al Jolson to sing in *The Singing Fool*. It was a hit. Movie moguls woke up to the realization that a great deal of money could be made from popular songs first heard and popularized in films. Finally, in 1929, came the first "talking picture" from beginning to end and with lots of music and dancing, *Broadway Melody*. It started a deluge of new movie musicals over the next few years. Some were adaptations of Broadway shows, but soon songwriters were being hired to write expressly for films.

As the Great Depression deepened, theatergoing dwindled to a trickle and the sheet-music trade did the same. At the same time, record sales dropped, from 104 million in 1927 to 6 million in 1932. Money to mount new shows was scant, and of the shows that were premiered, few continued. Yet, movies thrived, partly because ticket prices remained very low. It wasn't long before Hollywood was buying up the weakened music-publishing firms. Warner, in 1929, took over Remick. MGM bought Leo Feist in 1934, and Robbins the next year.[45] To eat, several prominent songwriters commenced working for Hollywood. This meant having no power over their songs. They might be used or rejected, kept as written or altered drastically, retained as a whole or truncated. Nonmusical, even unmusical, directors, producers, and actors judged the merits of the music. Havoc could ensue. When Cole Porter's *The Gay Divorce* was remade as Hollywood's *The Gay Divorcee*, all the Porter songs except "Night and Day" were thrown out, and the big hit of the film, "The Continental," came from Herb Magidson and Con Conrad, and not Porter. When Rodgers and Hart had Darryl Zanuck, a mogul of the movie industry, hear the lovely "Lover," Zanuck thought the song was poor stuff and told Rodgers to make it better. Later, Harold Arlen's extraordinary "Over the Rainbow" found itself in and out of *The Wizard of Oz* three times before the powers that be reluctantly allowed it a place in the film.[46]

A glum Harry Warren, a song composer for films par excellence, complained: "Most of my working life people weren't interested in who wrote the songs they heard and sung and whistled. Fact is, I think they believed the screen stars made them up in the studio. Well, I guess that's OK because, after all, we weren't meant to be seen and heard in those days."[47] He had contributed a long list of admired songs to films, including "Boulevard of Broken Dreams," "Forty-Second Street," "Lullaby of Broadway," and "Chattanooga Choo Choo," but scarcely anyone knew his name.

SONG IN THE PUBLIC CONSCIOUSNESS

At best the public recognized the names of only a handful of composers, like Berlin and Gershwin, and could remember scarcely any lyricist.

Americans might know Hoagy Carmichael as the composer of "Stardust," but unknown was its lyricist, Mitchell Parrish. An illuminating anecdote is told of Mrs. Jerome Kern and Mrs. Oscar Hammerstein arriving together at a party, and the hostess beginning to introduce them by announcing, "This is Mrs. Jerome Kern. Her husband wrote 'Ol' Man River.'" An annoyed Mrs. Hammerstein barged in, "Not true. Mrs. Kern's husband wrote *dum-dum-dee-dah, da dum-dum-dee-dah. My* husband wrote '*Ol' man river, dat ol' man river!*'"[48]

Yet the songs themselves did enter and influence the collective consciousness, even if the songwriters' names did not. Irving Berlin was by no means a famous name in 1911, even though he had recently completed "Alexander's Ragtime Band." The song, however, had become an immediate hit, on the tongues of all Americans. A fire broke out during a Philadelphia showing of a silent film, while the house pianist played "Hearts and Flowers." The audience panicked and stampeded for the exits. Only when the pianist resorted to the Berlin tune did the struggle to flee stop, order return, and calmer men and women file out whistling, humming, and singing "Alexander's Ragtime Band."[49]

Berlin demonstrated again and again his uncanny ability to penetrate into the consciousness of the United States when the time proved right for a song. "God Bless America," written, in 1918, for the show *Yip! Yip! Yaphank*, made no great impression until Kate Smith began to sing it in November 1938. The threat of war hung in the air. Tensions were growing. The public was ripe for something that would embody its love of country. That something was "God Bless America." Then World War II started. American soldiers, torn from home and loved ones, faced combat and possible death throughout the world. The film *Holiday Inn* came out in 1942, with Bing Crosby singing "White Christmas." It caught the mood of a nation and was sung on the home front and in military encampments in Africa, Europe, and Asia.

When Edna Ferber heard the just-completed Kern-Hammerstein "Ol' Man River," in 1927, she said, "The music mounted, mounted, and I give you my word my hair stood on end, the tears came to my eyes, and I breathed like a heroine in a melodrama. This was great music. It was music that would outlast Jerome Kern's day and mine." Her prediction proved correct. The song took root in America and spread to Europe. When the British were facing their severest testing in World War II, Winston Churchill recalled the song, saying that with the United States beside them, the progressive forward movement from one point to another on the way to completion of the war was "like the Mississippi, it just keeps rolling along. Let it roll."[50] There were Russian, German, French, and Italian interpretations of the song. International fame also came to the Harburg-Arlen "Over the Rainbow" after it was sung by Judy Garland in *The Wizard of Oz* (1939). It, too, traveled everywhere, even to China and India. Both songs have passed through the American consciousness and entered the international consciousness.

The incursion of American popular songs into transoceanic consciousnesses had already begun in the 19th century, when the songs of Dan Emmett, Stephen Foster, and George Root drifted around the world with American sailors and peripatetic professional American singers. With the post–World War I decades, European popular culture embraced America's popular songs wholesale, even as it gladly took up American films, dress, jazz, slang, and literature—much to the chagrin of Europe's cultural watchdogs. The process continued for the rest of the century. When the leading Latin American rock band, La Ley, from Chile, won a Grammy Award for the album *Uno*, their lead singer, Beto Cuevas, declared that in popular music and popular culture, America now "dictated to the world." All young people, in every country, he said, revered American rock music.[51]

NOTES

1. Respectively, George Root, *The Story of My Life* (Cincinnati, Ohio: John Church Co., 1891), 96; Alec Wilder, *American Popular Song* (New York: Oxford University Press, 1972), 92; Charles Schwartz, *Gershwin: His Life and Music* (Indianapolis: Bobbs-Merrill, 1973), 321; *The New Rolling Stone Encyclopedia of Rock & Roll*, revised and updated, edited by Patricia Romanowski and Holly George-Warren (New York: Fireside Books, 1995), s.v. "Pop."

2. Tony Bennett, with Will Friedwald, *The Good Life* (New York: Pocket Books, 1998), 36.

3. See Alex Ross, "Rock 101," *New Yorker*, 14 and 21 July 2003.

4. Respectively, Arnold Shaw, *The Jazz Age* (New York: Oxford University Press, 1987), 179; Edward Jablonski, *Irving Berlin* (New York: Holt, 1999), 199.

5. Nicholas E. Tawa, *Sweet Songs for Gentle Americans* (Bowling Green, Ohio: Bowling Green University Popular Press, 1980).

6. Russell Lynes, *The Lively Audience* (New York: Harper & Row, 1985), 147.

7. Stephen Holden, "Lingering on Delicious Byways," *New York Times*, 30 January 2002, www.nytimes.com.

8. Donald Clarke, *The Rise and Fall of Popular Music* (New York: St. Martin's Press, 1955), 102–3.

9. Charles Hamm, *Yesterdays* (New York: Norton, 1979); Nicholas Tawa, *A Sound of Strangers* (Metuchen, New Jersey: Scarecrow Press, 1982).

10. Walter LaFaber, Richard Polemberg, and Nancy Woloch, *The American Century*, 3rd edition (New York: Knopf, 1986), 38–47.

11. "Don't Be Cross with Me" (1908), lyric by Will Hough and Frank Adams, music by Joseph Howard.

12. Edward Marks, as told to Abbott J. Liebling, *They All Sang: From Tony Pastor to Rudy Vallee* (New York: Viking, 1935), 8.

13. David Ewen, *The Life and Death of Tin Pan Alley* (New York: Funk & Wagnells, 1964), 177.

14. Julie Malnig, *Dancing till Dawn* (New York: New York University Press, 1992), 1–51.

15. Richard M. Stephenson and Joseph Iacarino, *The Complete Book of Ballroom Dancing* (Garden City, New York: Doubleday, 1980), 34–35.

16. Stephenson and Iacarino, *Ballroom Dancing*, 11–12, 23–24.

17. David A. Jasen and Gene Jones, *Spreadin' Rhythm Around: Black Popular Songwriters, 1880–1930* (New York: Schirmer Books, 1998), 162.

18. Ewen, *Life and Death of Tin Pan Alley*, 182.

19. Jablonski, *Irving Berlin*, 43, 132.

20. Gary Giddins, *Bing Crosby: A Pocketful of Dreams, The Early Years 1903–1940*. (Boston: Little, Brown, 2001), 91.

21. W. C. Handy, *Father of the Blues*, ed. Arna Bontemps (New York: Macmillan, 1941), 27–28.

22. Edward Jablonski, preface to *Gershwin* (Boston: Northeastern University Press, 1990), x.

23. George Gershwin, introduction to Isaac Goldberg, *Tin Pan Alley* (New York: Ungar, 1961), viii; Oscar Hammerstein II, *Lyrics* (Milwaukee, Wisconsin: Hal Leonard Books, 1985), 11–12.

24. Hoagy Carmichael, *The Stardust Road* (Bloomington, Indiana: Indiana University Press, 1983), 128.

25. The Whiting information is found in Max Wilk, *They're Playing Our Song* (New York: Atheneum, 1973), 23, 140, respectively.

26. Laurence Bergreen, *As Thousands Cheer: The Life of Irving Berlin* (New York: Penguin, 1990), 76.

27. Goldberg, *Tin Pan Alley*, 100.

28. Wilder, *American Popular Song*, 67.

29. Ira Gershwin, *Lyrics on Several Occasions* (New York: Knopf, 1959), 109.

30. George Gershwin, preface to Goldberg, *Tin Pan Alley*, viii.

31. Ira Gershwin, *Lyrics on Several Occasions*, 362.

32. See, respectively, William G. Hyland, *The Song Is Ended* (New York: Oxford University Press, 1995), 42; Gene Lees, liner notes to *Eileen Farrell Sings Rodgers and Hart* (Reference Records, RR-32 CD); Hammerstein, *Lyrics*, 4.

33. Philip Furia, *The Poets of Tin Pan Alley* (New York: Oxford University Press, 1990), 7.

34. Hyland, *Song Is Ended*, 129; Wilk, *They're Playing Our Song*, 74.

35. Edward Jablonski, *Alan Jay Lerner* (New York: Holt, 1996), 179.

36. Philip Furia, *Ira Gershwin* (New York: Oxford University Press, 1996), 175.

37. Furia, *Ira Gershwin*, 263–64.

38. Ewen, *Life and Death of Tin Pan Alley*, 267–68.

39. It is interesting to note that "April in Paris" (1932) attracted little attention in the revue *Walk a Little Faster*; it became a hit when Marion Chase, her voice somewhat hoarsened by a sore throat, recorded it.

40. Bennett, *Good Life*, 40.

41. Bing Crosby, as told to Pete Martin, *Call Me Lucky* (New York: Simon & Schuster, 1953), 140.

42. Hamm, *Yesterdays*, 336–37.

43. Lynes, *Lively Audience*, 41–42.

44. Gerald Boardman, *Jerome Kern* (New York: Oxford University Press, 1980), 249–50, 259.

45. Jasen and Jones, *Spreadin' Rhythm Around*, 179–80.

46. Hyland, *Song Is Ended*, 197.

47. Ian Whittcomb, *Tin Pan Alley* (London: Paddington Press, 1975), 4.

48. Wilk, *They're Playing Our Song*, 36, 75.

49. Jablonski, *Irving Berlin*, 47.

50. David Ewen, editor, *American Popular Songs* (New York: Random House, 1966), s.v. "Ol' Man River."

51. Lydia Martin, "Chile's La Ley Carry Their Crossover Rock Tunes to the U.S. Market," *Boston Globe*, 13 July 2001, D6.

Chapter Two

A Closer Look at the Jazz Age

Our look is not necessarily a chronological one, but rather one in pursuit of the ideas and expressions favored by the music public and finding their way into the songs that animated the times. F. Scott Fitzgerald may have been the first person to use the term "Jazz Age," in order to explain the 1920s: the accelerated life rhythms, the growing awareness of popular culture, and aggressive endorsement of an emergent "modern" America. We ask what the music of the Jazz Age was like. Who were the singers? What realm did song inhabit? What were the themes of serious, novelty, and dance songs? What ended the Jazz Age?

World War I had continued its murderous course from 1914 to 1918, slaughtering people, destroying long-standing values, extinguishing human hope, and instilling disillusionment with religion, government, and society as it had existed. These were the antecedents to the Jazz Age, which lasted from around 1919 to 1930.

After the warfare ended, American authors would look with jaundiced eyes at what remained of civilization. They instituted novel approaches to writing that exposed the emptiness felt by many of them. Audacious intellectuals, devisers of innovative processes and techniques, venturesome artists and art composers, and insistent advocates of social reform struck out on fresh paths. John L. Lewis protested the treatment of laborers; Marcus Garvey and W. E. B. DuBois protested the treatment of black Americans; Margaret Sanger protested the hostility to birth control. The demand for women's rights was insistent. Ugly events occurred. The Ku Klux Klan rampaged against African-Americans; Attorney General A. Mitchell Palmer sanctioned raids against alleged communists; widespread discrimination fomented race riots; ignorant and uninformed people attacked scientific inquiry and the theory of evolution, which culminated in the Scopes trial; and the search for societal scapegoats resulted in the execution of the Italian immigrants Sacco and Vanzetti. Yet, none of these momentous events found their way into popular song.

Righteous prohibitionists killed "King Alcohol" with the Volstead Act, but gangsterdom still ministered to the thirsty, and illegal speakeasies proliferated. Otherwise law-abiding citizens took to illicitly fermenting and distilling alcohol at home and flavoring it with little vials labeled "Bourbon," "Scotch," "Rye," etc. The practice was rampant in the Boston where I grew up. The result was an increase in cynicism and lawlessness. Songs came out like "It's the Smart Little Feller Who Stocked up His Cellar," "What Are You Going to Do to Whet Your Whistle?" and "Everybody's Got a Key to My Cellar." Saluting the beginning of Prohibition, "Bimini Bay"[1] appeared in 1921, lyric by Gus Kahn and Ray Egan, music by Richard Whiting. This ode to drinking advised alcohol lovers to escape to a tropical paradise, where couples could spoon "'neath the julep tree, down old Bimini Bay. . . . Hear the cocktails a-calling . . . where they say absinthe will make ev'ry loving heart grow fonder" and "each night we'll sample our private stock." In 1925, Irving King published a song that made the rounds of America:

> Show me the way to go home,
> I'm tired and I want to go to bed.
> Oh, I had a little drink about an hour ago, and it's gone right to my head.
> Wherever I may roam, on land or sea or foam,
> You will always hear me singing this song,
> Show me the way to go home.[2]

A great many people were tired of war, crisis, and controversy. Some longed to bury, if not their heads, all their problems in the sand. They wanted to enjoy the pleasures of the moment without concern for the difficulties around them or those looming in the future. Carpe diem, not serious thinking, ruled the times. And the times were the Jazz Age, alias the Roaring Twenties. Escape entertainment was sought after as never before, and what better than songs to meet the demand? It helps us understand why popular music had to comply with this new condition and had to change more drastically than it ever had in the past.

Finally, it must be said that huge numbers of men and women continued to live ordinary lives, to work hard, and to ignore fast living. They hoped to earn enough to put a roof over their heads, clothing on their bodies, and food on the table. Indeed, huge numbers of farm laborers and unskilled workers never shared in the prosperity of the twenties. For the fortunate ones, technology and a growing abundance of material goods did make for more comfortable living conditions. Yet, they could not avoid the upheavals taking place in postwar society, if not economically, then socially and politically. Radio and recordings kept all of the Americans in touch with the world, as never before. Popular songs, in whatever ways they changed, were the staples filling their moments of leisure. Whether they wanted to or not, people had begun to live in a "modern," more liberated America, and this included the highly educated and gainfully employed and the less educated and impoverished.

Actually, the transformation had started during the war. Ordinary young men from every city and hamlet had gone soldiering in Europe and returned more knowledgeable about the world than heretofore. Whatever innocence they had possessed had been pounded out of them by bombs, shells, and bullets. They had wallowed in mud and choked on mustard gas. Yet, they also needed their diversions. During the war they sang about "Mademoiselle from Armentières" and tried to appear worldly-wise. On their return home, they weighed their recent experiences in their minds and zealously sang the Sam Lewis and Joe Young lyric to Walter Donaldson's song, "How 'Ya Gonna Keep 'Em Down on the Farm?" (1919). Would they stay put on the farm or leave it? Both songs were favorites of my father, a World War I veteran:

How 'ya gonna keep 'em down on the farm
After they've seen Paree?
How 'ya gonna keep 'em away from Broadway,
Jazzin' aroun' and paintin' the town?
How 'ya gonna keep 'em away from harm, that's a mystery.
They'll never want to see a rake or plow,
And who the deuce can parley vous a cow?
How 'ya gonna keep 'em down on the farm
After they've seen Paree?[3]

ZEROING IN ON THE 1920s

The war was over. What other transformations were taking place? In the decade following World War I, many Americans, including the artists, composers, and writers, took a fresh look at themselves. As usual after a major war, however, a sentimental yearning for the simplicities and securities of the "good old days" encouraged replicas of the sorts of songs in vogue in earlier times. Returning to what was well known was one way of getting relief from the confusions of the present. Many felt an exhaustion after war and conflict that left them lacking energy to tackle anything novel. For a while, overly romantic songs and operetta offerings came along to satisfy these needs. In this regard, "Alice Blue Gown" (1920),[4] lyric by Joseph McCarthy, music by Harry Tierney, is fascinating. The songwriters employ the gown as a symbol of all that was desirable in the past but is no longer retrievable. While the singer was wearing it, "the world seemed to smile all around." The gown was worn "till it wilted." Now it remains only in memory, "and I don't dare to hope there will be any more. But it's gone 'cause it just had to be"—a recognition of current conditions. Even the tune is in an old-fashioned though engaging waltz time, to be sung "slowly and tenderly." Most of the refrain goes at a smooth gait with nothing to jar the even pace—no syncopations, no ragging, no problems. The song appealed to the general mood and was constantly sung.

The real world after the time of the "Alice Blue Gown" was difficult to understand and if at all possible was looked at in oblique fashion. Economic recession had struck the United States soon after war's end. Contrarily, a song from 1921, lyric by Gus Kahn and Raymond Egan, music by Richard Whiting, proclaims "Ain't We Got Fun."[5] A newly married couple, "a happy girl and chappie," is penniless. He has no job. "The rent's unpaid, dear. We haven't a sou. . . . There's nothing in the larder." Living is hard "and getting harder." Ironically, the singer concludes with "There's nothing surer; the rich get rich and the poor get nothing. . . . Ain't we got fun." The refrain goes to a plain, unsyncopated tune. Mostly in quarter notes, the melody jogs along nondescriptly until it achieves its high point on "nothing surer; the rich get rich." The song's satirical and jaunty rejoinder to the dismal times, "ain't we got fun," chimed with the prevalent thinking.

Paradoxically, a desire for different, up-to-the-minute songs—music for contemporary modes of singing and dancing—also grew. Rag did capture the modern restlessness, but its unevenly ragged rhythms were often rough to move one's feet to. Something else was wanted and did come along.

Some new popular songs addressed a tangible theater audience in the cities. However they, along with those songs coming out of vaudeville, clubs, and ballrooms, were serenading a much larger audience that was out of sight—the homebodies who could not see the performers who sang to them. Radio and recordings, "the revolving biscuits," delivered music to them. Whether people stayed at home or went out in quest of entertainment, all were affected by modern attitudes that broke with traditional ideas and ways of expression, and that put a value upon trying something different, testing the rules of propriety, and partaking of the most up-to-date trends and fashions. It was left to a few active initiators and practitioners to define what was of the present time and what was "old hat." Eventually, the results had an effect on all strata of society.

At the outset of the twenties, many felt a combination of doubt and lack of purpose—effectively portrayed in Hemingway's novels. In addition, speakeasies and criminal activities were giving a boost to social disorder. The superficiality and false gaiety that the twenties promoted seeded F. Scott Fitzgerald's novels. On the other hand, as a portrayal of the twenties, this is an oversimplification. Women had entered the working force during the war, had enjoyed their independence and lack of restrictions. They now refused to return to their old submissiveness and insistently demanded the right to vote, which came to them in 1920. Their younger counterparts were behaving more outrageously than their mothers ever did. Freudian ideas had filtered through to the popular mind. Recognizing this, Rodgers and Hart issued "You Can't Fool Your Dreams," in 1920, with a Freudian touch: "You tell me what you're dreaming, I'll tell you whom you love."

Inhibitions were regarded as unconscionable restraints on the individual. Hence the popularity of the 1926 dance song "The Black Bottom,"[6] lyric by Bud De Sylva and Lew Brown, music by Ray Henderson. It was music that encouraged women to be themselves and express their uninhibited modern selves through dance:

Hop down front and then you doodle back,
Mooch to your left and then mooch to your right,
Hands on your hips and do the mess around.
Break a leg until you're near the ground,
Now that's the old Black Bottom dance.

Sexual morality had changed. Certainly "The Black Bottom" implied a shift in attitude and behavior. "Liberated" younger women appeared who cast off any check upon their natural instincts and active impulses, including the urge for sex. Bathing suits became skimpier and tighter. The wide availability of condoms and information about birth control encouraged a new attitude toward sexuality. Magazines like *Vanity Fair* catered to "the new woman." Margaret Sanger started the publication of her *Birth Control Review*, in

1917. Psychologists like Havelock Ellis, in *The Erotic Rights of Women* (1918) and *The Dance of Life* (1923), advanced the cause of "liberation." Mae West wrote and starred in an off-color revue, *Sex* (1928). Clara Bow and Louise Brooks, in recognition of their sex appeal, were called "It" girls.

"It" was a suggestive word, implying something risqué in the Jazz Age. As early as 1911, Berlin had offered the public a dance song, "Everybody's Doin' It," with the Turkey Trot dance in mind. As its popularity increased, state officials in New York and New Jersey took alarm and investigated the piece in order to determine whether it encouraged moral turpitude. By 1928, ways of thinking had loosened up considerably. Cole Porter in "Let's Do It"[7] had every insect and animal imaginable doing "it." Although the "it" referred to falling in love, the public understood the sly allusion to sex. His "Let's Misbehave" (1928) exposed the love activities of various creatures and suggested the same for humans.

> They say that spring
> Means just one thing
> To little love birds,
> We're not above birds,
> Let's misbehave![8]

One freethinking woman, Mabel Dodge Luhan, writes that around 1916, she and her friends became fascinated with Freud and Jung and their theories of psychoanalysis. She had sessions with a psychoanalyst and learned about the Electra complex, Oedipus complex, the libido, and the harmfulness of inhibitions. She cast aside her repressions, had an active sex life, and made herself over into a modern woman.[9] Thus was the "flapper" born; that is to say, the young woman who aggressively established her freedom from constraint and convention in her hairdo, clothing, and behavior. In 1925, Vincent Youmans's stage success *No, No, Nanette* had his chorus girls open the show singing:

> Flappers are we, flappers are we
> Flappers and fly and free.
> Never too slow, all on the go
> Petting parties with the smarties.
> Dizzy with dangerous glee.[10]

Irving Caesar and Otto Harbach wrote the lyric.

Four years later, the Billy Rose lyric to Vincent Rose's melody tried to reassure listeners, in "She's a New Kind of Old-Fashioned Girl."[11] Yes, she "dressed in flapper clothes," had "marcelled hair," and "liked to play around" and "cabaret around." However, "underneath the paint you will find a saint," and a woman "as good as her mother." To emphasize the conservative nature of the new kind of old-fashioned girl, the music is in a waltz time reminiscent of the 1890s dance.

Hoagy Carmichael says that sexual freedom had not really reached the town of Bloomington, Indiana, where he was brought up. However, even there the women "wore less and wore it in a slipping, careless way on the dance floors." The younger set put on silk stockings rolled beneath the knee, "so that every sitting-down showed the American female thigh, nude and lush, anywhere from kneecap to buttock." Lipstick was applied; hair was short and bobbed; the women poured perfume on without stinting. This was true not only of the factory girls and salesgirls, but also of the housewives and "society queens." Lots of them, he says, were flappers who smoked cigarettes and imbibed alcoholic drinks, at times to excess.[12]

A suspicion persisted that people should be getting more pleasure for themselves than they were. Their lives seemed meaningless, and anyway, nobody carried any weight with the powers that be. So why not divert yourself, engage mostly in superficial tittle-tattle, and delight in the shocking doings of the rich and famous? Why not search for the latest amusements, and cultivate what was chic. To get happy, one required the means. It followed that money mattered more than principles—so why not make money any which way you can?[13]

In 1923, "Any Place Where I Make Money (Is Home Sweet Home to Me),"[14] lyric by William Tracy and music by Dan Dougherty, captured this mandate and went on to become a nationwide winner. Jazzy syncopated rhythms pushed along a perky, high-spirited melody. Here was tuneful chicness, nothing old-fashioned. Ditto the sentiment "When you get a bank roll piled up on the shelf," you should "step right out and start in to enjoy yourself." Otherwise, "if you keep working 'till you've run, you die and then your relatives have all the fun."

The Jazz Age spawned not only the flappers and gangsters but also an unheard-of youth culture, a foretaste of the rock culture to come. Young people cultivated their own distinctive ways of dressing, talking, and acting. Flannels and crew cuts appeared everywhere, launching a new conventionalism. More adolescents were graduating from high schools and attending college. They were learning about the world beyond their own community and acquiring a freedom that their parents had never had in their youth. They engaged in their own activities, set up their own social establishments, and associated usually with others of like age, background, and social status. The social world of the better-off included varsity dances, fraternity and sorority pursuits, and sports-related activities. Cars gave them independence, particularly when Ford's Model A came along in 1927. A craze for cruising, partying, and dancing directed their activities. The hip flask filled with "hooch" turned into a sign of sophistication. Collegians loved to "go slumming," that is, to make excursions into the less savory parts of town, out of curiosity or for pleasure and excitement.[15] Interestingly, less affluent young men and women could easily be found who, although they could not afford college, tried to imitate the dress and manners of the college students.

Again turning to Hoagy Carmichael, he states that while he was a college student in Indiana, he and his friends loved cars because they provided liberation. They also "read about the wild Long Island girls with flailing arms, bobbed hair, and willing for anything. The golden flask, the contraceptive . . . the removable rear seat. . . . But Indiana U. and Purdue were both state schools, and had to split school funds voted by backcountry farmers who didn't hold with fancy living." So the students had to behave in a more circumspect manner than they did elsewhere. Collegian attitudes are colorfully delineated in an item J. D. Spalding submitted to *Kollege Kapers* while he was a student: "It's applesauce to say that football is the bee's knees this season. Every cake-eater knows that the way to land a flapper is to stroke the skins, badger the banjo, squeeze the sax, tease the trumpet. And if you're keen for a neck-session in a jalopy, whip out your uke!"[16]

Catering to youthful tastes in music and dancing were outfits like the Paul Whiteman Orchestra, Fred Waring and the Pennsylvanians, and Rudy Vallée and His Connecticut Yankees. They and other dance outfits led by leaders like Jean Goldkette, Hal Kemp, Ted Lewis, Isham Jones, and Ben Bernie were known as "society bands." Paul Whiteman acquired the title "the King of Jazz," although the soubriquet was more a tribute to his popularity, less to the pale facsimile of jazz music that he produced. Yet, in the 1920s, he was astute enough to hire musicians with unquestionable jazz credentials—Red Nichols, Tommy Dorsey, Frankie Trumbauer, Joe Venuti, Eddie Lang, and Bix Beiderbecke. The singer Bing Crosby would also start with him as one of the three Rhythm Boys.

Around 600 bands were operating in the middle of the decade. Trumpets, trombones, saxophones, clarinets, drums, a bass, piano, guitar or banjo but rarely violins were heard in these groups. They played the dances most in demand, whether Charleston, waltz, tango, or, most popular of all, the fox trot. Whether one wished to or not, in order to appear up-to-date, one had to conform to the dress code observed by the young crowd and to dance. Dancing now meant moving about, cheeks and bellies touching.

Zez Confrey's "Stumbling,"[17] a "unique fox trot song," published in 1922, tells of the hurdles confronting dance novices. The refrain goes to "a unique rhythm" that incorporates a melody often moving by threes against a solid two-beat-a-measure backing. (This is a treatment that would appear again, two years later, in Gershwin's "Fascinating Rhythm.") A young man takes his date to a dance hall and finds that "people rave and they crave just to do this [fox-trot] step." He and his girl decide to take a chance and try it. What was the result? "Stumbling all around so funny . . . I stepped on her toes." Then, "when she bumped my nose," he fell down. Feeling ashamed, he remarks, "That's the latest step, my honey, notice all the pep." She replies, "Stop mumbling, I like it just a little bit, quite a little bit."

Another song, "The Varsity Drag" (1927), lyric by Bud De Sylva and Lew Brown, music by Ray Henderson, was aimed directly at the college set. Donald Tomkins introduced the dance step in the 1927 musical *Good News*.

> Everybody down on your heels, up on your toes,
> Stay after school, learn how it goes!
> Everybody do the varsity drag.
> Rah, rah, sis, boom, bah!
> That's the dance they call the varsity drag![18]

Other songs enticed Americans onto the dance floor: A. J. Piron's "I Wish I Could Shimmy Like My Sister Kate" (1919); Charles Bayha and Maceo Pinkard's "Jazz Babies' Ball" (1920); and Cecil Mack and James Johnson's winner, "Charleston" (1923).

The place that jazzy young men and women dreamed most of visiting was New York City, the center of all that they prized. From this hub radiated the radio programs, the recordings, the best bands, the highest-quality singers, and all of the popular songs. They loved the ode to the city that Richard Rodgers and Lorenz Hart published in 1925, the song "Manhattan."[19] They sang, "The great big city's a wond'rous toy, just made for a girl and boy." The tune has its phrases start on an off-beat lurch and abrupt skip upward, a melodic-rhythmic scheme that hooks the listener, and has them end on long-drawn-out notes, which balance and effectively round off the opening.

A New York destination for the most daring of the collegians was the Cotton Club, which had opened, in 1923, in a run-down section of black Harlem. Sponsored by mobsters, the nightspot featured chiefly African-American entertainers catering to a mostly white clientele. The fine bands of Duke Ellington, Cab Calloway, and Jimmy Lunceford played here, and excellent vocalists like Adelaide Hall, Ethel Waters, and Aida Ward sang. The musical shows put on at the club were famous. Harold Arlen, a white songwriter who wrote music for the shows, said of their premieres, "Those opening nights were like no other nights in the theater, because even though it was a night club, you'd get everyone there from the mayor to anybody who was who. It was like a Broadway opening is today [1960]."[20] A similar situation existed in Chicago's Lincoln Garden, where King Oliver's band entertained Al Capone and his criminal acquaintances.

Contemporary writers liked to refer to the "Harlem Renaissance," a term embracing the black entertainers, popular composers of stature (like J. Rosamond Johnson, Eubie Blake, and Duke Ellington), and writers and artists (like James Weldon Johnson, Langston Hughes, Allen Locke, and Claude McKay). Two women stood out—Jessie Fauset and Zora Neale Hurston. However, the twenties were years when few African-Americans shared in the bounty whites were enjoying. The revitalization of the black community was superficial at best. And the onset of the Great Depression easily halted the apparent revival of black music, art, and literature.

SHOUTERS AND CROONERS

The singer supplied the actual one-on-one expressive connection between songs and music lovers, whether they were dancers, theater audiences, or invisible stay-at-homes spinning records and radio dials. A singer's ability to put across a song was affected not only by his or her natural talent and skill, but also by the excellence of the musical arrangement, the instrumental backing, the quality of the theater or hall's acoustics, and the ability of record and radio to capture the voice accurately. Vocal delivery could be almost anything—growls, moans, shouts, rasps, whines, murmurs, or throaty sounds. The test—did it entertain, did its expression reach the listener? One moment, the manner of singing was staccato and bouncing in an up-tempo number; another, smooth and silky in a slow love ballad; and still another, emotional and declamatory in musical complaints.

What was not usually desirable, although there were a few notable exceptions, were the vocal deliveries of trained operetta voices. The songwriter Alan Lerner said that as far as he was concerned, that sort of voice performed lyrics so that they were impossible to understand, because such singers "had been tutored in the art of singing in code." Lyric sopranos of high range were especially unfit for popular music, he thought: "Coloraturas speak no known language and sing so high anyhow that only the dogs in the audience can hear them."[21] One noted opera singer who succeeded nevertheless in crossing over was the basso Enzio Pinza, in Rodger and Hammerstein's *South Pacific* (1949). However, the setting was exotic; he played the part of a French planter, which covered his Italian accent; and the songs chosen for him contained elements of operetta style.

Before electrical amplification came along, all vocalists had to have carrying voices in order to fill a hall. Classic examples are provided by Sophie Tucker and Emma Carus, the vaudevillian who popularized Berlin's "Alexander's Ragtime Band" (1911). Al Jolson had a voice that filled a theater even to the second balcony, both when he vociferated "Swanee" and when he wailed about his Southland "Mammy." He needed an audience to sing to and disliked radio, microphones, and the whole idea of softly crooning à la Rudy Vallée. Crooners, he said, were "weak-voiced singers that would fall down if they didn't have a mike to hold on to."[22] Some, like Ethel Merman, continued to employ a stentorian singing style even after amplification had become available. Charles Schwartz writes of her appearance in Gershwin's *Girl Crazy* (1930), "More than anything else, it was her raucous, full-throated singing of 'I Got Rhythm,' which carried to every corner of the theater and the outside lobby as well, that made her a star overnight. When she belted out the tune and held a high C, she always brought the house down."[23]

In contrast, a new style of singing arose in the twenties, known as crooning. It would become the predominant way of singing popular songs, until rock 'n' roll came in. Crooning was a vocal treatment made possible by the microphone. This piece of equipment changed sound into electrical energy by way of a diaphragm that responded to the push-pull of sound waves. The carbon microphone was first developed around 1877, when Emile Berliner, David Hughes, and Thomas Edison were all working on the device. It later saw widespread use as a telephone transmitter. An important forward step in amplification took place with H. D. Arnold's development of the first practical electrical amplifier, in 1913. However, the ribbon or condenser microphone, which took hold after the midtwenties, provided the real breakthrough for singers. Edward Wente had originated it, in 1916, and soon singers realized that its flat frequency response was suitable for music. Because of its greater sensitivity and greatly improved accuracy in reproducing the voice, it quickly replaced carbon microphones for live performance, radio broadcasts, and recording sessions. For the first time, untrained voices lacking in strength could fill rooms with sound and at the same time communicate warmth and intimacy.

Crooning was thought by some, especially at first, to be vocalization lacking in manly strength as compared to Jolson's robust renditions. However, it soon was accepted by many as a nonthreatening, quiet vocalization utilizing a microphone. When done properly, the vocal sound impressed the ear as tender, personal, sincere, and moving. Indeed, so soothing and gentle was the impression left by crooning and so many women fell for the style adopted by male crooners that critics for a while accused crooners of effeminacy. Bing Crosby thought crooning meant someone "who sang with a band and crooned into a small megaphone or made mooing noises into a microphone," as once did Rudy Vallée. When he himself crooned, Crosby said, he tried to think of a song, not "in terms of notes," but in terms of what it "purports to say lyrically."[24]

Rudy Vallee, one of the first significant crooners, always claimed that he was a product of radio. After college, he gathered a band of seven instrumentalists and started playing at the Heigh Ho Club, New York City, in 1928. The next year, NBC wanted to assess radio's potential for putting songs across. It broadcast Vallee coast to coast and found that what he sang caught fire immediately. By the end of the experiment, radio had made him a nationally known figure. Vallee selected undemanding songs that suited his nasal delivery, often with the collegian in mind, and dropped the verse to sing only the refrain.[25] He and Will Osborne, another crooner, competed for radio dominance. Osborne claimed that he, not Vallee, had devised the art of crooning, overlooking the fact that Gene Austin, the Texas tenor, and Vaughn De Leath, "The Original Radio Girl," had arrived at crooning earlier in the twenties.[26]

Bing Crosby came along to eclipse Jolson and to supplant Vallee and Osborne in the early thirties. He was accomplished in exploiting a microphone to put across his relaxed, almost conversational sort of singing. He cultivated a likable, friendly image, like that of a trustworthy buddy. The taint of effeminacy was undetectable in him. Not for him the "heigh-ho" pitch elevation of Vallee. His phrasing was elegant and carefully shaded, and his tones came out with an ear-catching huskiness. He had an effortless and elastic sense of rhythm. His performances projected "a sense of comfort between audience, singer, and writer," claims David Brackett.[27] With Crosby's rise to popularity, popular singers studied his delivery and the way he sang "to you" rather than "at you."[28] For a while, he and the singer Russ Columbo competed for top place in people's affections. However, Columbo's accidental death, in 1934, cleared the way for Crosby's predominance among male crooners, until Frank Sinatra made his debut.

Female vocalists were said to damage the delicate vacuum tubes in transmitting stations during the first months of radio broadcasting. One woman, Vaughn De Leath, eliminated that problem by giving rise to a novel, quiet and soothing delivery, later called crooning, when she began with radio in 1920. She was immediately granted the sobriquet of the "First Lady of Radio" and soon after "The Original Radio Girl." The song with which she was widely identified was the Jimmy Kennedy–Will Grosz "Red Sails in the Sunset" (1935). Her manner of singing found favor with listeners and was quickly adopted by the young Rudy Vallee. It eventually led to the styles of Crosby and Sinatra. In the thirties, Kate Smith would try to supplant her over the air, by also calling herself the "First Lady of Radio." Sued by De Leath, Smith dropped the title.

Another radio crooner, Ruth Etting, had her start in Chicago's Marigold Gardens, where she met Moe "the Gimp" Snyder, a dubious character known for shady dealings with the underworld. Snyder, after she sought to divorce him, tried to murder Etting's new lover and future second husband, in 1937. The publicity did not hurt her career on the stage or over the radio. She sang with a husky moan in her voice that came to be known as torch singing. Famous for her rendition of Fred Ahlert and Roy Turk's "Mean to Me" (1929) and Lorenz Hart and Richard Rodgers's "Ten Cents a Dance" (1930), she was given the rubric "America's Radio Sweetheart."

A female crooner's interpretation could completely change a song's meaning. When the Gershwins issued "I've Got a Crush on You," in 1928, they put it out as a rapidly moving dance song meant to convey a light sarcasm. It failed to win a following. Some years later, Lee Wiley recorded it as a very slow number making a soft, amorous appeal from beginning to end and thus wiped out the sarcasm. This version of the song sold well, so of course the Gershwins were happy, despite the altered version.

Finally, vulnerability—rugged vulnerability for men, melting vulnerability for women—was the stock in trade of most crooners. To enhance their standing, they had to sing as if capable of being wounded and without defense against injury. The crooning tradition would continue into the rock-music era.

THE NATURAL WORLD OF POPULAR SONG

In an informative article on the great songwriters of the twenties, Edward Pessen writes that 75 percent of the lyricists and 50 percent of the composers responsible for the finest songs were Jewish. Of the five topmost songwriters, only Cole Porter was not Jewish. Almost all of these men and women were born in cities, in particular New York City. They had grown up in middle-class families (Irving Berlin a conspicuous exception) and had more than an elementary education.[29] Yet, hardly any discernible Jewish elements are found in their output. The world of popular song was supposed to have no set boundaries, address no particular ethnic group or social class, and try to remain open to all. Yet, it mirrored mostly the urban aspects of America—the cities and towns rather than the more rural areas.

Some songwriters liked to point out that their influences were not predominantly black American. Berlin was incensed when critics heard black styles running through his music. He stated that he and most of the other songwriters were of white birth and had felt the influence of various types of song, that is to say, "of Southern plantation, of European music from almost countless countries and of the syncopation that is found in the music of innumerable nationalities—found even in the music of the old master composers."[30] What Berlin omitted was the considerable influence of the American popular-song tradition and the styles that had surrounded him, including black American styles.

The best songs of the twenties encapsulate fresh ways to deliver the formulas for music and lyrics. Songs like Rodgers's "Manhattan" and Carmichael's "Star Dust" are fairly unique in the liberties they take. Other important songs, though they seem to be formulaic, are really different from each other in their rate of movement, rhythmic treatment, emotional qualities, and effect on listeners. One moment, a composer may write an old-fashioned ballad, at another, a tricky dance song, or a pseudospiritual, or a preposterous novelty number. Whatever the public seemed to call for was supplied. The United States during the Jazz Age was providing an environment favoring the rapid growth of popular music. Moreover, as the expansion took place, inventiveness and vigor were continually in evidence.

Rodgers and Hart said they never felt restricted by the formulas of verse and refrain construction. Instead, they took pleasure in the challenge of supplying something new within the approved conventions. Berlin insisted that whether one followed the formulas was not important, but keeping an eye on the public was—if it wearied of one musical direction, the songwriter had to switch to another. Since no one could tell what song would catch the public ear, said Cole Porter, he loaded his own shows with potential hits, which were given different treatments, and waited patiently until the public made up its mind: "It takes up to two months to discover whether a song is a real wow or just a flash in the pan. . . . It took all of three months to find out that [with] 'Night and Day' I had anything profitable." Sometimes the public immediately made up its mind, as when Rodgers watched Billy Gaxton sing the first presentation of "Thou Swell." Within eight bars, the song took off with the audience: "the audience reaction was so strong that it was like an actual blow. Though there were no audible sounds, I could feel the people loving Gaxton . . . and going wild over the song. The applause at the end of the number was deafening."[31]

A majority of Jazz Age songs made few allusions to devotion to country or God. People wanted romantic ballads, dance songs, and comic novelties. Warmly personal feelings, neat and simple designs, and multifaceted sentiments deriving from everyday personal experiences were in demand. Closely intimate confessions without relevance for other men and women were not. Berlin's "When I Lost You" was perhaps about the heartache he felt when Dorothy Goetz died five months after he married her, in 1912. However, the public had to see the song as making a universal statement about loss and grief for it to become a favorite. The Harry Smith–Francis Wheeler "Sheik of Araby" (1921) was inspired by Rudolph Valentino, in the silent film *The Sheik*, but it had to stand on its own merits when first introduced in the musical *Make It Snappy*. This languid, somewhat heat-drenched melody caused countless women to dream of the desert lover who demanded a woman's love and invaded her tent to requisition it. Rodgers and Hart's "Manhattan" (introduced in *The Garrick Gaieties*, 1925) achieved nationwide hit status beyond the Broadway revue through its seamless, unaffected rhyming, its laid-back, leisurely ambling tune, and its telling of the ordinary enjoyments available in an urban area. Over the next thirty years, several motion pictures featured it.

The nature of the popular song was achieving an unheard-of level of cosmopolitanism, ingeniousness, and sophistication during the twenties. Indeed, nothing could remain the same in a period affected by Prohibition, technical innovation, assaults on tradition, relaxed moral codes, intensely living young people, and ideas introduced from abroad that were being acclimatized to American conditions. The sound and subject matter of sentimental Paul Dresser and of the Yankee-Doodle-Dandy George M. Cohan no longer fitted contemporary conditions. Dresser's ballads seemed quaint and in fact so gushy as to appear comical to many in the 1920s. Cohan's crude swaggering in song belonged to a more juvenile America not yet feeling its cosmopolitan oats. The Americans of the 1920s wanted truer correspondences to their own lives and age.

Trite "love/dove and moon/June" rhyming was usually avoided or joked about. Note the fresh ingenuity of the rhymes in Rodgers and Hart's "Blue Room"[32] (which rescued the musical comedy *The Girl Friend*, 1926): "We'll have a blue room, a new room for two room. Ev'ry day's a holiday because you're married to me." This new mixture of rhyming and reiteration communicates the sentiment successfully. Later, the lyric has "ballroom," "small room," and "hall room." Then, instead of continuing with the expected repetition, Hart suddenly rhymes "trousseau" with "Robinson Crusoe." The effect is delicious, and the public thought so nationwide.

It was not part of the nature of the twenties to encourage the fake blackdialect coon and rag songs of the recent past. The musical recipes had changed. The public's palate now relished the suave lilting tunes of George, harnessed to the telling lyrics of Ira, Gershwin. It enjoyed the astute contemporaneity of Rodgers and Hart, the revitalized melodiousness of Jerome Kern and Irving Berlin, the blues-tinged sadness of Harold Arlen, and the surprising rhymes and witty sexual allusions of Cole Porter. American popular song impressed the world with its uncanny ability to take readings of contemporary living and express it with melodies, rhythms, and verse that captured the variegated moods of the time. Above all, the excellence of the tune, perhaps more than the lyric, established worthwhileness. No lyric came alive without its tune. Whatever virtues a song had were inexorably linked to its music. Regrettably, the sound of a song is not producible on these pages. The reader must turn to a live performance or a recording to appreciate its merits.

Howard Taubman concluded in 1949 that Cole Porter's music addressed a universal range of interests. He wrote that Porter sang not for "the smart set" but "for everyone. The sophistication in his lines represented a point of view many of us wished to achieve." His tunes had a common appeal. No one cared that "Night and Day" (which actually came out in 1932) has a 48-measure refrain instead of the customary sixteen. "The public is indifferent to

the musical ingredients that go into the fashioning of a tune. It recognizes—
through ear and heart—music with the ring of truth."[33]

What the American public also recognized was that the nature of the
music belonged first to the New and not the Old World. The twenties was
a dazzling decade in American music. Berlin espoused an individual
straightforwardness that went straight to the heart in "What'll I Do?"
(1926). Popular music influenced by jazz went to incisive rhythms in
Gershwin tunes like "I'll Build a Stairway to Paradise" (1922) and Harold
Arlen tunes like "Get Happy" (1929). Slower versions of popular
melodies expressed moods of longing or melancholy that were marked by
the occurrence of blue notes and minor intervals. Sadness could be invoked in a melody or harmony where a brighter sound would otherwise
have prevailed, as in Gershwin's "Somebody Loves Me" (1924) and Cole
Porter's "What Is This Thing Called Love?" (1929).

Recognition that America was producing something novel in popular
music, something characteristic of itself, had come well before the Jazz
Age. For example, Arnold Bennett wrote in the *London Times* (8 February
1913) some ambivalent remarks about the American public and its contemporary culture, especially as found in the music of Irving Berlin:
"There is not doubt that there is at present one class of creative and exec-
utive artists whom the public in the United States is disposed to idolize and
enrich—namely, the composers and singers of 'rag-time.' . . . It is the music of the hustler, of the feverishly active speculator; of the 'sky-scraper'
and the 'grain-elevator.' Nor can there be any doubt about its vigor—vigor
which is, perhaps, empty sometimes and meaningless, but, in the hands of
competent interpreters, brimming over with life."[34] Berlin, of course, cared
not a bit what Bennett wrote, since sale of his songs was brisk in England.

Even the fastidious, European-oriented music of Jerome Kern found itself changing. By 1914, in "You're Here and I'm Here," the music might
smack of the British theater song, but it also was taking on the inflections
of American dance. In the same year Kern's "They Didn't Believe Me"
gave off a guileless melancholy tied more to colloquial American than
transatlantic idioms. By "Can't Help Lovin' That Man" (1927), there could
be no doubt where he stood.

SONGS: EARNEST AND WITH FEELING

One of the most maudlin "sob" ballads of all time was "Sonny Boy." Its
authors expected it to go against the grain of the time. Instead it became a

hit, proving how capricious the public could be. One must conclude that the musical "weeper" never completely goes out of favor. The Jazz Age was supposed to be tough-minded, hard on sentimentality. But, as always, the weeper managed to survive. "Sonny Boy" was created in 1929 after Al Jolson telephoned the song team of lyricists Bud De Sylva and Lew Brown and composer Ray Henderson requesting a song. He peremptorily asked that it involve a child, in a situation that would encourage people to cry when they heard it in the film *The Singing Fool*. It was to be sent to him without delay. The team then joked about the request, believing it was out of step with the present age. As a gag, they put together the most mawkishly trite piece they knew how to concoct. In a merry mood, they telephoned Jolson, sang him the song, and to their amusement heard Jolson predict it would find immediate success. They laughed. It did.[35] The wailing quality of the tune suited Jolson's voice. Parents wanted a song that captured their love for their children and found it in "Sonny Boy."[36]

Climb up on my knee, sonny boy,
Though you're only three, sonny boy,
You've no way of knowing,
There's no way of showing,
What you mean to me, sonny boy.

Later Jolson added the lines:

And when the angels grew lonely,
Took you 'cause they're lonely,
Now I'm lonely too, sonny boy.

My own father got so wrapped up in the song, listening to it night after night, that my mother thought it would bring on bad luck. She smashed the recording and refused to allow him to replace it.

Contrast this with another composition whose earnestness was completely sincere and whose feeling ran deep, the famous "Ol' Man River" of *Show Boat* (1927), lyric by Oscar Hammerstein, music by Jerome Kern. Hammerstein described it as "a song of resignation with a protest implied, sung by a character who is a rugged and untutored philosopher."

Ol' man river.
That ol' man river.
He don't say nothin'
But he must know somethin'

Cause he just keeps rollin'
He keeps rollin' along.
Rollin' along.

The river does not plant potatoes or cotton, and those black people who
plant them are soon forgotten, as are those who

. . . sweat and strain.
Body all achin'
And wracked with pain.
pulling barges, lifting bales of cotton.

The vocalist ends by singing that he

. . . gets weary
Sick of tryin'
I'm tired of livin'
Feared of dyin'
But ol' man river
He's rollin' along.[37]

The clarity and power of the words and the eloquence of the melody have
helped the song to endure. It continues to today as a forceful hymn, on one
level protesting the existence of racial intolerance and discrimination, on
another level conveying the plight of all exploited laborers.

In 1927, two other songs, more superficially philosophical in nature,
came out. "Keep Sweeping the Cobwebs off the Moon,"[38] lyric by Sam
Lewis and Joe Young, music by Oscar Levant, advised, "No need wor-
ryin'; lose that frown; you'll soon be feelin' well. What good is your pin-
ing; find your silver lining; and keep sweeping the cobwebs off the moon."
The same tired advice is echoed in scores of other songs from before and
during the decade, drawing attention to a persistent human need for this
sort of assurance. "Back in Your Own Backyard,"[39] lyric and music by Al
Jolson, Billy Rose, and Dave Dreyer, airs another persistent but commonplace theme, "We leave home expecting to find a bluebird, hoping every
cloud will be silver lined. But we all return, as we live we learn, that we
left our happiness behind."

A different type of song that never ceased to leave an impression on the
public was the homesick ballad. Throughout the history of popular song,
it has been in demand. It, too, compromised the hardheaded image of the
Jazz Age, as it dreamt up a happy past that at no time existed. Laid bare

was a wistful yearning for a return to some romanticized age or unregainable condition or situation now long gone. "Nothing could be finer than to be in Carolina in the morning," murmurs the 1922 song,[40] lyric by Gus Kahn, music by Walter Donaldson. The singer dreams of meeting his "sweetie" where "the morning glories twine around the door" and "butterflies flutter up" as he goes "strolling with his girlie, where the dew is pearly early in the morning." If only he had Aladdin's lamp on which to wish. The tune moves in a light dancing motion, a series of eight long-short notes, culminating in the drawn-out vocalizing on "morning," for most phrases.

More baldly, "Dream Train"[41] (1928), lyric by Charles Newman, music by Billy Baskette, states, "Ev'ry night when I lie down and close my weary eyes, on my train of dreams I go to Paradise." In sleep the singer boards a "dream train" that carries him "back to the days that used to be." Tenderly, the refrain begins with prolonged tones on "Dream train." However, no airy lightness, as heard in "Carolina in the Morning," comes after. The melody proceeds with dignity, italicizing each phrase ending with syncopation. The fetching thing about the song is the atmosphere of pensive meditation it creates. As usual, the tune is the sugar coating that helps the sentiment go down.

We must believe that many in American society were overlaying themselves with only a thin hardboiled veneer that concealed a softer interior. How else does one explain the popularity of "My Blue Heaven"[42] (1927), lyric by George Whiting, music by Walter Donaldson? Every evening the protagonist hurries to "a little nest that's nestled where the roses bloom. Just Mollie and me, and baby makes three; we're happy in my blue heaven." No philandering, no wishing he were one of the boys, and no looking for a good time on the town. Harmonies are plain. The melody is completely diatonic, remaining in a standard major scale without chromatic digressions. Each music phrase makes a mild swing upward at its beginning then slowly descends to repose on a low note. The effect is restful. No syncopations ruffle the gentleness of the sound.

Quite a few songs of devotion follow suit. For example, the 1928 song "I'll Get By,"[43] lyric by Roy Turk, music by Fred Alhert, hews to a similar pattern, only this time the refrain tune moves soothingly up and down in sinuously winding fashion. We learn that whatever problems may arise, "I'll get by as long as I have you." Through the ages, this has been the unending declaration of lovers. Also ages old is the invitation of a lover to his beloved to "tip-toe thro' the tulips with me" in the evening, as in the 1929 song thus entitled, lyric by Al Dubin and music by Joe Burke. More will be said about love songs shortly.

Before we do so, we must remember, first, that popular songs were meant to please a host of people, not solely the cosmopolitan, fashionable crowd. All the songs just discussed existed in a fantasy land that men and women of the twenties knew did not exist. Nevertheless, they sang about their imaginative world and cherished its images because they wanted to. A fine melody elevated fantasy above everyday affairs. It enhanced the subject matter, made the words sound less mundane, and added crucially to the attractiveness of a song. For ordinary Americans, it was a matter of holding on to widely held benchmarks of excellence, however routine, and of retaining some hope that events are perhaps ordered for the best. People valued a pleasing tune, a rhythm that hooked them, a subject pertinent to their lives and experiences, and a fresh way of versifying. A successful song could be taken as a celebration in music and verse in which huge numbers of people might participate.

Love, as has always been true, was the principle raw material of popular song in the Jazz Age. By and large the lover-protagonist of a ballad revealed an attraction to and desire for a beloved who, as has been true in all of song's history, aroused delight, admiration, tenderness, or, if love was rejected and not requited, despair. It manifested itself in three basic ways: an avowal of love that is with any luck permanent, a plea for affection, or a distress call about a problem involving love. Essential for putting across a love song was a convincingly amorous melody, juicy but low-profile harmonies, and a repetitious oompah two-beat (in two-time) background rhythm. Because of the free-minded temperament of the "flapper" and the consort who subscribed to these songs, "two-time" took on the meaning, prevalent in the twenties, of deceiving a spouse or lover by secret love-making with someone else.

The listener is left in no doubt about the avowal of love expressed in Bud Green and Harry Warren's "I Love My Baby"[44] (1925), which begins, "Talk about your famous love affairs, Romeo and Juliet had theirs, I just found someone and someone found me." The refrain skips about on longer notes for "I love my baby" and then executes an abbreviated syncopated jiggle on "My baby loves me." This individual melodic treatment grabs listeners, holding fast to their attention until the refrain's end. Appropriate, too, is the contemporary slang that finds its way into the text: "We're hotsy-totsy, why shouldn't we be? She gives me kisses, each one is a smack; but you should hear 'em when I give 'em back." Another declaration of affection, Rodgers and Hart's "Thou Swell"[45] (1927), revels in a witty intermingling of Old English and modern slang: "Thou swell, thou witty, thou sweet, thou grand, wouldst kiss me pretty? Wouldst hold my hand? Both thine eyes are cute too, what they do to me. Hear me holler, I choose a sweet lollapalooza in thee." It addresses the tastes of contemporary sophisticates, as does the melody, which trips forward with light quick steps on a brief rhythmic pattern that repeats after each comma in the text.

Intriguing is the sense of excitement in Ira and George Gershwin's "'S Wonderful"[46] (1927). The exclamations in the refrain are almost delirious: "'S wonderful! 'S marvelous! You should care for me!" As if in a daze, the lover repeats the same three notes over and over again, at last breaking the spell on "You've made my life so glamorous." A glow of sophistication envelops the entire work. The same sense of sophisticated wonder holds true for Cole Porter's "You Do Something to Me"[47] (1929). The singer is mystified: "Tell me. Why should it be, you have the pow'r to hypnotize me? Let me live 'neath your spell. Do do that voodoo that you do so well." The tune swings up and down, slowly and expressively, until it reaches the last sentence quoted above. Suddenly the music wobbles about on triplets that enhance the tune, making it especially attractive and not one to be confused with any other.

Tuneful eloquence is also found in Rodgers and Hart's "With a Song in My Heart"[48] (1929), whose lyric verges on overstatement and the melody on operetta. The smoothly lulling tune nevertheless seems to rescue the text: "With a song in my heart, I behold your adorable face. Just a song at the start, but it soon is a hymn to your grace." A listener or two may feel that the protagonist "doth protest too much." The Gershwins' "Embraceable You"[49] (1930) resorts also to eloquence yet avoids the Rodgers and Hart artiness by injecting colloquialisms, like "Don't be a naughty baby, come to papa, come to papa, do!" and hiatuses in the tune—each phrase hesitating in its middle on a truncated note before dropping to a lower level. Devices like these plant the song firmly in American soil.

A love song can also be a plea for affection. Ira and George Gershwin's "Oh, Lady Be Good!"[50] (1924) is a clever and effective giving notice of discontent: "Listen to my tale of woe. It's terribly sad but true. All dressed up, no place to go, each ev'ning I'm awf'ly blue." The tone is light, debonair, and almost with tongue in cheek. Then the refrain begs, "Oh, sweet and lovely lady be good . . . to me!" to a lover who is "so awf'ly misunderstood" and "just a lonesome babe in the wood." As so often happens with a Gershwin song, the melody is magical but leaves the listener unable to explain why the enchantment. An indefinable "something" proves attractive. The enchantment may lie in the way melody, harmony, and rhythm seem to uniquely fit together or in the intelligent integration of music and verse. Always, a perception that important aspects of the song are newly and refreshingly made must prevail. The distinguishing features of such a Gershwin tune are all present—many repeated notes, a close linkage with the underlying harmony, and an unanticipated deflection that makes the tune exactly right—here, the octave plunge on "lady, be good!"

In Arthur Freed and Nacio Brown's "You Were Meant for Me"[51] (1929) the plea is more straightforward, the verse more routine. The lover stays awake all night bothered by unreturned affection: "If I but dared to think you cared, this is what I'd say to you." He goes on to declare in the refrain, "You were meant for me; I was meant for you. . . . The angels must have sent you and they meant you just for me." Longer notes in a standard major key compose the first eight measures of the refrain before the tune plunges into an orgy of descending chromatic semitones.

More telling and more individual is "Somebody Loves Me"[52] (1924), lyric by Ballard MacDonald and Bud De Sylva, music by George Gershwin. Now the plea for affection is to an unknown person. "When this world began, it was Heaven's plan," claims the vocalist, that "there should be a girl for ev'ry single man." He may be "clutching at straws," but he hopes he "may meet her yet." Then begins the refrain, "Somebody loves me, I wonder who she can be?" Gershwin displays his special genius for putting his finger on the effective detail when a blue note, a flatted third of the scale, gives a plaintive emphasis to the word "who."

THE TORCH SONG

A distress call about a problem involving love is the third category of love song stated earlier. Its principle purveyor was a female vocalist, usually working with a pianist, in a nightclub, hotel bar, or café. A scenario was set up that warmed people's sympathies and encouraged them to find the "sob song" irresistible. "Carrying a torch" meant being deeply in love without any return of affection. Torch songs were all about misery or failure in love. (Ira Gershwin had liked the term "ladies in lament.") They had been around from the beginning of the century, but their heyday was from around 1924 to 1934. Why did the rise in popularity take place? For one, the blues of black Americans and the country music of white Southerners were coming into the general consciousness of urbanites, and dominant in the two reper-toires were songs about despondency, mental depression, and being forever miserable. Second, it was a different fashion trend. If jazziness—lively, un-restrained, and flashy sociability—was the fashion, then the personal lament was the fashion to be out of fashion. Third, beneath all the superfi-cial, tawdry, and pretentious showiness that supposedly characterized the Jazz Age ran a postwar malaise, an unfocused feeling of mental disquiet, and moral ill-being that produced weariness and discomfort.

Later on, in 1933, Al Dubin would write a lyric for Harry Warren's "I've Got to Sing a Torch Song"[53] that was meant to go at a lugubrious pace: "I'd like to sing away my sorrow. . . . A lively jingle never cheers me." Arriv-ing at the refrain, we hear, "I've got to sing a torch song, for that's the way I feel. When I feel a thing, then I can sing. It must be real."

The proper rendition of torch songs necessitated a close personal rela-tionship between singer, often leaning against or sitting atop a piano, and her listeners. If in a revue or musical, she was often made to stand under a lamppost surrounded by darkness. She sang at a snail's pace, *molto do-loroso*, and with bent-note blues inflections. The vocalist had to seem to wear her heart on her sleeve and divulge her most personal feelings. The desired atmosphere of intimacy was facilitated through use of a micro-phone. Ruth Etting has already been mentioned as an outstanding practi-tioner. In 1929, she gave a sobbing interpretation to the Ahlert-Turk song "Mean to Me."[54]

> You're mean to me.
> Why must you be mean to me?
> Gee, honey, it seems to me
> You love to see me cryin'.

Her audiences treasured the rendition.

Fanny Brice was another who, like Etting, was married to a gangster, Nicky Arnstein. She became famous not only for singing lovelorn ballads like "My Man," but also for a hilarious parody of the genre in *The Ziegfeld Follies of 1936*, called "He Hasn't a Thing Except Me," words by Ira Gershwin, music by Vernon Duke. Brice started by singing, "I give you His Highness, a pain worse than sinus." Suddenly she ceased to sing. In-stead, she delivered a tirade against torch songs, informing the audience: "You know, I've been singing about this bum for twenty-five years. Some-times he's called 'Oh My Gawd, I Love Him So!' Or 'He's Just My Bill.' Or 'You Made Me What I Am Today.' Once he was even called 'The Curse of an Aching Heart.' But he's always the same low-life, always doing me dirt, and I must keep on loving him just the same. Can you imagine if I really ever *met* a guy like that, what I would do to him?"[55] It was a notice that the glory days of torch song were over.

In 1924, when torch songs were fresh on the public's mind, Ira and George Gershwin came out with "The Man I Love."[56] The piece was written for Adele Astaire to introduce at the start of the musical *Lady Be Good!* The singer aches for "the man I love," although she knows that "it is seldom that a dream comes true" and all she will ever do is wait for him. Down-turned pitches on some tones of the scale add melancholy to the yearning refrain, "Someday he'll come along, the man I love. And he'll be big and strong, the man I love. And when he comes my way, I'll do my best to make him stay." For some time the song failed to click until Helen Morgan gave it a weepy torch rendition while seated on a piano. In 1926, the Gershwins offered up "Someone to Watch over Me."[57] This forlorn and wearied-of-life piece was originally sung by Gertrude Lawrence, in the musical *Oh, Kay!* The music was soon making the rounds of all the cabarets. Sultry, whiskey-dampened voices sang, "I'm a little lamb who's lost in the wood. I know I could always be good to one who'll watch over me." The effect was enhanced when the back of the singer's throat injected a rough rasp into the sound. That was the way to intensify an emotional response.

The pain in "Love Me or Leave Me"[58] (1928), lyric by Gus Kahn, music by Walter Donaldson, is nearly palpable when translated by a fine torch singer: "Love me or leave me, and let me be lonely. You won't believe me, and I love you only; I'd rather be lonely than happy with somebody else." The refrain, its measures ceaselessly syncopated, takes an octave droop, from "love me" to "leave me," like a slump of the singer's spirit, before the tune resignedly labors upward on "let me be lonely." The directions are to sing "slowly (with feeling)." When interpolated into the musical *Whoopee*, it was boosted to fame by Ruth Etting.

Cole Porter's "What Is This Thing Called Love?"[59] (introduced in the musical *Wake Up and Dream*, 1929) is the quintessential torch song with its tale of desertion, "I felt the winter's chill, and now I sit and wonder night and day why I love you still," and the puzzled lament, "What is this thing called love? . . . Why should it make a fool of me? . . . You took my heart and threw it away." Theoretically in a major key, the tune introduces quantities of mournful bent tones and is to be sung "slow (in the manner of a 'Blues')." This impressive and fitting melody became one of the composer's most popular. Porter is thought to have drawn inspiration for this appeal to sentiment from hearing the indigenous music of Marrakech, Morocco.

Trending toward a more up-to-date and easy manner, "But Not for Me"[60] (premiered in *Girl Crazy*, 1930) of Ira and George Gershwin starts, "Old Man Sunshine listen you! Never tell me 'Dreams come true.' Just try it, and I'll start a riot." However, emotion is stripped naked at the refrain, "They're writing songs of love, but not for me." The enchanting tune and poignant lyric so persisted in people's affections that singer after singer took it up—first, Ginger Rogers, later Judy Garland, Connie Francis, and Ella Fitzgerald, among many.

Other classic torch songs include Berlin's "All Alone" (1924), Kahn and Moret's "Chloe" (1927), Wodehouse and Kern's "Bill" (1927), Rose, Eliscu, and Youmans's "More Than You Know" (1929), Mills, Bigard, and Ellington's "Mood Indigo" (1930), Razaf and Blake's "Memories of You" (1930), and Koehler and Arlen's "I Gotta Right to Sing the Blues" (1932). They are all appealing compositions worth a song lover's acquaintance. The melodies, not usually like those in other songs, occupy a niche of their own and a position appropriate for the Jazz Age and even beyond. All persevere in conveying a lamentation similar to that Oscar Hammerstein II wrote to Jerome Kern's tune for "Why Was I Born?" (1929).

> Why do I try to draw you near me?
> Why do I cry? You never hear me.
> I'm a poor fool, but what can I do?
> Why was I born to love you?[61]

NOVELTIES AND DANCE SONGS

Almost a century before the Jazz Age, absurd minstrel ditties had offset the serious sentimental songs; in the 1920s, novelty songs offset the intensely serious and lachrymose ballads. Nonsensical novelty songs, reproducing the irrational and meaningless side of the twenties, made frequent appearances. These were modest productions intended mainly as amusements for the moment and marked by simplistic tunes and unusual subject matter. They fitted well with a notion held by many that man's life was absurd and had no meaning outside one's own existence. Not surprisingly, as Americans occupied themselves with fads and pursued capricious whims, they also took up ridiculous ditties. The titles of some indicate the typical contents: "Come On, Spark Plug" (1923), "Keep Your Skirt Down, Mary Ann" (1925), "I'm Wild about Horns on Automobiles That Go Ta-Ta-Ta-Ta" (1928).

Toward the end of the decade, the public was singing about such silly issues as:

My father was a baker. . . .
That's how he made his dough. But often he would say to me,
"Here's what I'd like to know:
Where do the holes go in doughnuts when we eat the doughnuts up?"

and

Does the spearmint lose its flavor on the bedpost over night?
If you chew it in the morning will it be too hard to bite?
Can't you see I'm going crazy? Won't somebody put me right?
Does the spearmint lose its flavor on the bedpost over night?

A third song, out in 1928, begins:

Some kids say the world today is all upside-down.
Sometimes they're smiling; sometimes they frown.

and ends on an ominous note—shades of the Great Depression:

I went and bought my self a Rolls-Royce.
Oh gee, Oh joy,
While I was singing, the phone kept ringing
Then my broker said to me,
"That stock you bought at eighty-three is lower than the deep blue sea."
I faw down an go boom!

Certainly one of the most sung of silly tunes in the twenties was "Yes, We Have No Bananas"[62] (1923). Frank Silver and Irving Cohn, who concocted the piece, said their sudden inspiration to write it came after eavesdropping on a Greek produce huckster when he was enlightening a customer with the report, "Yes, we have no bananas." The song failed to click until Eddie Cantor put it into the revue *Make It Snappy* and created an uproar of laughter and applause. Within a few weeks, the piece was known throughout the country—the reason for its immense popularity remaining unfathomable. Perhaps it was the very ridiculousness of the song combined with the popularity, personality, and astute delivery of Cantor. The tune jogs along in a singsong manner; the message:

I sella you no banana.
Hey, Mary Anna, you gotta no banana?
Why this man, he no believe-a what I say?
You wanna buy twelve for a quarter? Yes, a quarter.
Well, just one look, I'm gonna call for my daughter.
Hey, Mary Anna, you gotta piana?
Yes, banana, no, no, yes, no bananas today.
We gotta no bananas. Yes, we gotta no bananas today.

In 1923, a popular comic-strip character was given song life in "Barney Google,"[63] lyric by Billy Rose, music by Con Conrad. It quickly became a hit after Olsen and Johnson used it in a funny vaudeville act. According to the song, "Barney Google, with the goo-goo-goo-ga-ly eyes" had a stupid horse, Spark Plug, who ran a race in the wrong direction. He also "had a wife three times his size. She stood Barney for divorce. Now he's living with his horse." When Barney died and tried to enter Paradise, "Saint Peter saw his face [and] said, 'Go to the other place.'"

Occasionally major songwriters tried something a bit out of the ordinary, something light but not silly, and gave it an unexpected flavor. Often the song testified to devoted affection but in a slightly singular fashion. Walter Donaldson's "Because My Baby Don't Mean 'Maybe' Now" (1928) contains not a suitor's declaration of love but an enthusiastic response to his girlfriend, who at last has made up her mind: "It means that I'll be happy; no more I'll have to guess. . . . When the preacher questions me, I'll say 'yes, sir, yessiree.'" The tune unfolds in an easy and sprightly manner and captures the sentiment exactly.

The De Sylva-Brown-Henderson song of 1929, "Button Up Your Overcoat," is not so much a song of ardent love as of amiable possession.

Keep away from bootleg hooch when you're on a spree,
Take good care of yourself, you belong to me!
Button up your overcoat when the wind is free,
Take good care of yourself, you belong to me!
Wear your flannel underwear, when you climb a tree,
Take good care of yourself, you belong to me![64]

Another example of an unusual treatment is Ira and George Gershwin's "Bidin' My Time"[65] (1930). The music has an informal country-music sound and is to be rendered in a lazy, unhurried style. Originally a "hill-billy" vocal quartet harmonized on it, in the musical *Girl Crazy*, and quar-tet harmonization continues to be the most effective way to present the mu-sic. The manner is relentlessly easygoing and free from strain. It must have been a welcome relief to a public that was anxious about the economic hard times that had arrived.

> I'm bidin' my time; 'cause that's the kind of guy I'm.
> While other folks grow dizzy I keep busy, bidin' my time.

Among the novelties of the twenties were tunes coming from Latin American countries. Three of the biggest hits were the Mexican "Cielito Linda" (1923), and Cuban "Malagueña" (1928) and "Siboney" (1929). Also very well received were Joseph LaCalle's "Amapola" (1924) and G. H. Matos Rodriguez's "La Cumparsita" (1926). Latin dances grew in popularity, especially the tango after it had been popularized by the Cas-tles. By the late 1920s bands consisting of Latin American musicians resident in the United States were making themselves known. The most famous of these was Xavier Cugat and His Gigolos, who played tangos, show tunes, and "dinner music." The rumba, which had come to the United States soon after the turn of the century, would not really catch on until the thirties. In 1930, Don Azpiazú and his Havana Casino Or-chestra arrived in New York City to play authentic Cuban music com-plete with maracas, claves, guiros, bongos, congas, and timbales. Azpi-azú would introduce the wildly popular "The Peanut Vendor" and "Mama Inez."[66]

Nevertheless, more representative of the Jazz Age were the dance songs born in the United States itself, with their syncopations, "bent" notes, dy-namic rhythms, and jazzy sound production. Preeminent was the "Charleston"[67] of James Johnson and Cecil Mack, which was made popu-lar in the 1923 black-American revue *Running Wild*. It so fitted the zeit-geist that it became the novelty dance craze of the twenties, spawning dance contest after dance contest. New York City hosted a Charleston marathon, in 1924, which lasted over twenty hours. Recognizing the dance's drawing power, *The George White Scandals of 1925* staged a mammoth theatrical representation of the Charleston put on by Tom Patri-cola and five dozen young women. It was:

> . . . a new tune, funny blue tune with a peculiar snap!
> You may not be able to buck or wing

Fox-trot, two-step, or even sing,
If you ain't got religion in your feet,
You can do this prance and do it neat.

Staged dancing became very vigorous with Josephine Baker, the African-American dancer. She visited Paris in 1928, and her *dance sauvage* provoked a passionately enthusiastic response. Parisians focused on her dance, hypnotized by her motions and the musical rhythms. The French, like the English, had already become addicted to American dance steps and rhythmic songs. They loved the uninhibited expression of the new music, jazz or just jazzy, from America. There were also vociferous critics in both countries denouncing the American corruption of their cultures, but unable to do anything about it.

New American tunes, blue novelty tunes with a peculiar snap, came out in droves during the Jazz Age. They often had a feverish quality to them—excited, restless, and even uncontrolled, as befitted these years of hyperactivity. George Gershwin was responsible for many of the most well-liked—"Swanee" (1919), "I'll Build a Stairway to Paradise" (1922), "Fascinating Rhythm" (1924), "Clap Yo' Hands" (1926), "Fidgety Feet" (1926), and "I Got Rhythm" (1930), to name six. Harold Arlen issued a stream of them, including "Jungaleena" (1928), and "Get Happy" (1930). Irving Berlin contributed "Shaking the Blues Away" (1927) and "Puttin' On the Ritz" (1929). Some other typical examples are Noble Sissle and Eubie Blake's "I'm Just Wild about Harry" (1921); Ray Henderson's "Five Foot Two, Eyes of Blue" (1925) and "Bye, Bye, Blackbird" (1926); Jimmy McHugh's "Diga Diga Doo" (1928); Wolfe Kahn and Joseph Meyer's "Crazy Rhythm" (1928); Harry Brooks's "Black and Blue" (1929); and Cole Porter's "Find Me a Primitive Man" (1929). Several of the songs already mentioned in this chapter can also be considered rhythmic compositions expressive of the decade.

Alec Wilder had reservations about some of these songs. While discussing Kern's "Can't Help Lovin' Dat Man" (from *Show Boat*, 1927), he commented, "I should make it clear that no one expects a rhythm song, as opposed to a ballad, to be melodically superior. . . . It doesn't have the turn of phrase or over-all quality of a relaxed rhythm ballad. There is a stiffness, a contrived quality throughout, as if it had been pieced together."[68] Wilder does not draw a clear distinction between a "rhythm song" and a "relaxed rhythm ballad." I suspect that among the former, he would include "Fascinating Rhythm" and "Charleston." He did express doubts about the melodic quality of most of Gershwin's output. Whether they sound rigid

and manufactured and melodically inferior are matters best left to individual music lovers. I for one find melodies so inextricably tied to rhythms
that they must be taken together. In varying degrees, this is true for all popular songs, whether stretched tight or easygoing. The relaxed ballad is a
slower, smoother, possibly more elegant species of melody, but not a format suited to all moods. The question of melodic superiority is difficult to
answer when it comes to popular songs. Some scholars try to explain it.
For most aficionados, the question is irrelevant. They respond subjectively
in response to their own moods, attitudes, and outlook.

DISASTER STRIKES

The immense economic and social disaster known as the Great Depression
began with the stock-market crash, in October 1929, and continued
through most of the 1930s, an unprecedented length of time. The crash was
brought on by lack of governmental oversight and regulation of business
and financial institutions. Living on borrowed money was a way of life.
The rampant speculation and easy credit in the stock market inflated prices
way beyond their true worth. An overproduction of goods failed to find a
ready market of consumers. The irregular sharing of the prosperity left
fewer skilled workers and farm laborers, unable to purchase and consume
what was produced. The country was financially overextended. The result
was "Black Tuesday."

Poverty and tragedy on a large scale was imposed on the American people. Businesses and banks closed their doors. Bankruptcies increased as in-
solvent debtors found themselves unable to satisfy the claims made upon
them. Unemployment soared. Breadlines lengthened. Hunger was a reality
for millions of citizens. The Bonus March of war veterans, in March 1932,
was answered by President Hoover's orders to the army to evict the veterans encamped before the White House—seen by many as a disgraceful
abuse of power. Labor unrest increased. The mood of the country turned
angry. The Jazz Age had received a fatal blow.

Consciously and unconsciously, songwriters, creatures of the times,
could not help but write some songs reflective of contemporary conditions.
Several of them so matched the mood of the American multitude that they
had wide currency. The frivolous, carefree Roaring Twenties were gone.
This did not mean that escapist songs would cease to be written. After all,
people did need relief from the daily struggle with reality and did want en-

tertainment that would afford painless pleasure and diversion. The next chapter will take up the escapist songs. Here, we are concerned with songs that were one way or another in direct response to the difficult living conditions imposed by the Great Depression and that indicated the closure of the happy-go-lucky era.

In the 1930 musical *Love for Sale*, Cole Porter came out with "Love for Sale,"[69] the biting keen of a penniless woman forced into prostitution for survival: "Love for sale. Appetizing young love for sale. . . . Love that's only slightly soiled. . . . Ev'ry love but true love." The melody emerges as a street vendor's call, as if physical love was a commodity like the apples that the unemployed sold on street corners. In the same year Lorenz Hart and Richard Rodgers wrote "Ten Cents a Dance" for Ruth Etting to sing in *Simple Simon*. Another penniless woman was trying to make ends meet any way she could.

> Ten cents a dance, that's what they pay me.
> Gosh, how they weigh me down.
> Ten cents a dance, pansies and rough guys,
> Tough guys who tear my gown. . . .
> Come on, big boy, ten cents a dance.[70]

The music and lyric are awash in bitterness.

Two years later, Harold Arlen's "The Wail of the Reefer Man"[71] was published with a text by Ted Koehler. A narcotics peddler offers "happiness for sale" to "a tired weary world." He claims, "When your woes surround you, don't let troubles hound you . . . joy is near" in the shape of a reefer. Again, as with Porter's song, the melody sounds akin to a street vendor's cry.

Neither of these two songs, however, became as admired as "Brother, Can You Spare a Dime?"[72] with words by E. Y. Harburg to music by Jay Gorney. Written in 1930, it was featured in the 1932 revue *Americana* and went on to become the musical complaint that characterized the Depression. Shortly after *Americana* opened, Bing Crosby recorded the song and within days it was the best-selling record in the land: "When there was earth to plow, or guns to bear, I was always right on the job. They used to tell me I was building a dream. . . . Why should I be standing in line, just waiting for bread? . . . Once I built a tower, now it's done. Brother, can you spare a dime?" The lyric and the tune, which unwinds lugubriously like a dismal chant, fed into the sullen anger that the jobless millions felt. The bare-bones melody is not so much sung as intoned. Each strain ends with a musical groan. In 1992, Tom Waits sang a current version of the song, which was chosen as the theme for the National Coalition of the Homeless.[73]

Harburg says that the early months of the Depression were a terrible period. He himself was flat broke and owed a lot of money to various people. One felt like crying, he said, when walking along the streets feeling fed up and seeing people who looked miserable as they stood in breadlines. He heard formerly wealthy men beg, "Can you spare a dime?" When Gorney played him the tune, Harburg remembered that phrase and went on from there. He wanted to write a commentary on the situation, not a begging piece, "about the fellow who works, the fellow who builds . . . and he's left empty-handed. . . . This is a man proud of what he's done, but bewildered that this country with its dream could do this to him."[74]

Before he was through with his career, Harburg would work with 48 composers on 376 published songs. Of the lyrics he wrote, 111 were to the tunes of Harold Arlen, a collaboration beginning in 1932. Asked about his work habits, he answered, "Being a very eclectic guy, I always like trying a new style, whether it was a sad social comment like the Dime song or something like 'Lydia, the Tattooed Lady' for a zany fellow like Groucho Marx. *I'm a chameleon.* I love putting myself into everyone else's shoes— and each composer lends me a pair."[75]

In 1933 came another classic of the Great Depression, "Stormy Weather,"[76] lyric by Ted Koehler, music by Harold Arlen. Ostensibly about the parting of lovers, it embodied the hopelessness of a nation: "Don't know why there's no sun up in the sky, stormy weather. . . . Life is bare, gloom and mis'ry ev'rywhere, stormy weather. . . . I'm weary all the time." The melody is distinguished by an unexpected "bent" note, especially when it calls attention and adds poignancy to the phrase "I'm weary all the time." In AABA form, the release's music sounds like an ominous drumbeat propelling us onward to a doleful termination on "Can't go on, ev'rything I had is gone, stormy weather."

Philip Furia admires Koehler's skill and acumen in writing the lyric: "While no one line is actually repeated, the omission of pronouns and connectives gives the lyric a nervous monotony (akin to Berlin's 'Supper Time,' also written in 1933). Koehler intensifies that relentless feel with *i*-rhymes that fall as incessantly as the rain; to keep them going he even opts for proper grammar ('my man and I' instead of the slangier 'my man and me') and splits 'time' over two notes to elongate the *i*."[77]

Ethel Waters, who introduced the song at the Cotton Club, did so as she took the typical torch singer's stance, under a lamppost, a bleak backdrop behind her, and a midnight-blue spotlight flickering on the scene. She said that singing it was a turning point in her life, at a time when her marriage was dissolving and she was working her "heart out and getting no happiness." She said, "'Stormy Weather' was the perfect expression of my mood, and I found release singing it each evening. When I got out there in the middle of the Cotton Club floor I was telling the things I couldn't frame in words. I was singing the story of my misery and confusion, of the misunderstandings in my life I couldn't straighten out, the story of the wrongs and outrages done to me by people I had loved and trusted." She stopped the show.[78]

Like children whistling in the dark, people sang Al Dubin and Harry Warren's "We're in the Money" (1933): "Old Man Depression you are through. . . . We never see a headline about breadlines today. . . . We're in the money . . . let's lend it, spend it, send it rolling along!"[79] Ginger Rogers presented it in the film *Gold Diggers of 1933*, and it took off from there.

The hard times that superseded the jazzy, roaring times thus had themselves pictured in their own characteristic songs.

NOTES

1. New York: Remick, c1921.
2. New York: King, c1925.
3. New York: Waterson, Berlin & Snyder, c1919.
4. New York: Leo Feist, c1920.
5. New York: Remick, c1921.
6. New York: Harms, c1926.
7. New York: Harms, c1928.
8. New York: Harms, c1928.
9. Mabel Dodge Luhan, *Movers and Shakers* (New York: Harcourt, Brace, 1936), 440.
10. New York: Remick, c1925.
11. New York: Berlin, c1929.
12. Hoagy Carmichael, with Stephen Longstreet, *Sometimes I Wonder* (New York: Farrar, Strauss & Giroux, 1965), 75.
13. See Frederick Lewis Allen, *Only Yesterday* (New York: Harper & Row, 1964), 64.
14. New York: Goodman & Rose, c1923.
15. Richard Crawford, *America's Musical Life* (New York: Norton, 2001), 717; Erica Hanson, *The 1920s* (San Diego, California: Lucent Books, 1999), 54–55, 69.
16. Carmichael, *Sometimes I Wonder*, 87–88; Ian Whittcomb, *Tin Pan Alley* (London: Paddington Press, 1975), 48, 50, respectively.

17. New York: Leo Feist, c1922.

18. New York: De Sylva, Brown & Henderson, c1927.

19. New York: Marks, c1925.

20. Mark White, *'You Must Remember This . . .': Popular Songwriters, 1900–1980*. (New York: Scribner's Sons, 1955), 22.

21. Alan Jay Lerner, *The Street Where I Live* (New York: Norton, 1978), 40.

22. Henry Pleasants, *The Great American Popular Singers* (New York: Simon & Schuster, 1974), 61.

23. Charles Schwartz, *Gershwin: His Life and Music* (Indianapolis: Bobbs-Merrill, 1973), 196.

24. Bing Crosby, as told to Pete Martin, *Call Me Lucky* (New York: Simon & Schuster, 1953), 148–49.

25. Rudy Vallee, *Let the Chips Fall* (Harrisburg, Pennsylvania: Stackpole Books, 1975), 105.

26. David Ewen, *All the Years of American Popular Music* (Englewood Cliffs, New Jersey: Prentice-Hall, 1977), 292.

27. David Brackett, *Interpreting Popular Music* (Berkeley, California: University of California Press, 2000), 40.

28. Henry Pleasants, *The Great American Popular Singers* (New York: Simon & Schuster, 1974), 142.

29. Edward Pessen, "The Great Songwriters of Tin Pan Alley's Golden Age," *American Music* 3 (1985): 184–85.

30. Laurence Bergreen, *As Thousands Cheer: The Life of Irving Berlin* (New York: Penguin, 1990), 121.

31. See, respectively, Richard Rodgers, *Musical Stages* (New York: Random House, 1975), 80; Bergreen, *As Thousands Cheer*, 45; William McBrien, *Cole Porter* (New York: Knopf, 1998), 223–24; Rodgers, *Musical Stages*, 109.

32. New York: Harms, c1926.

33. Howard Taubman, "Cole Porter Is 'the Top' Again," *New York Times,* 16 January 1949, www.nytimes.com.

34. Bergreen, *As Thousands Cheer*, 89.

35. White, *'You Must Remember This . . . ,'* 74.

36. New York: De Sylva, Brown & Henderson, c1929.

37. New York: Harms, c1927.

38. New York: Remick, c1927.

39. New York: Bourne, c1927.

40. New York: Remick, c1922.

41. Chicago: Forster Music, c1928.

42. New York: Leo Feist, c1927.

43. New York: Berlin, c1928.

44. New York: Shapiro, Bernstein, c1925.

45. New York: Harms, c1937.

46. New York: WB Music, c1927.

47. New York: Harms Music, c1929.

48. New York: Harms, c1929.

49. New York: WB Music, c1930.

50. New York: WB Music, c1924.

51. New York: Miller Music, c1929.

52. New York: Warner Bros., c1924.

53. New York: Witmark, c1933.

54. New York: Mills, c1929.

55. Philip Furia, *Ira Gershwin* (New York: Oxford University Press, 1996), 125–26.

56. New York: WB Music, c1924.

57. New York: WB Music, c1926.

58. Nashville, Tennessee: Donaldson Publishing Co., c/o Sussman & Associates, c1928.

59. New York: Harms Music, c1929.

60. New York: WB Music, c1930.

61. New York: Marks, c1929.

62. New York: Shapiro, Bernstein, c1923.

63. New York: Remick, c1923.

64. New York: De Sylva, Brown & Henderson, c1929.

65. New York: WB Music, c1930.

66. John Storm Roberts, *The Latin Tinge* (New York: Oxford University Press, 1979), 54–59, 76–77.

67. New York: Harms, c1923.

68. Alec Wilder, *American Popular Song* (New York: Oxford University Press, 1972), 57.

69. New York: Harms Music, c1930.

70. New York: Harms, c1930.

71. New York: Mills, c1929.

72. New York: Witmark, c1930.

73. Harold Meyerson and Ernie Harburg, with the assistance of Arthur Perlman, *Who Put the Rainbow in the Wizard of Oz?* (Ann Arbor: University of Michigan Press, 1993), 53.

74. Max Wilk, *They're Playing Our Song* (New York: Atheneum, 1973), 220–21.

75. Meyerson and Harburg, *Who Put the Rainbow in the Wizard of Oz?* 38.

76. New York: Mills Music, c1933.

77. Philip Furia, *The Poets of Tin Pan Alley* (New York: Oxford University Press, 1990), 248–49.

78. Ethel Waters, with Charles Samuels, *His Eye Is on the Sparrow* (Garden City, New York: Doubleday, 1952), 220.

79. New York: Remick, c1933.

Chapter Three

Swing Time

The Great Depression, which began in October 1929, persisted throughout the 1930s. Conditions improved at a snail's pace, leaving the nation's leaders perplexed about how to end the crisis and causing the people concern about how to keep roofs over their heads and food on the tables. The German Nazis, Italian Fascists, and Japanese militarists were becoming serious threats to international peace. Only the onset of World War II and the increase in defense spending would get the United States completely out of its economic slump. Entering the war on the side of Britain, France, and Russia addressed the problem of what to do about the dictatorships and military adventurism.

Franklin Delano Roosevelt was elected president of the United States by a landslide and took office in 1933, three and a half years after the crash. His first aim was to restore confidence. From 1933 to 1934, he tried to aid recovery and bring relief through business regulation, farm assistance, price stabilization, and public works. The National Recovery Act, the Public Works Administration, Agricultural Adjustment Administration, Civilian Conservation Corps, and Federal Deposit Insurance were the result. From 1935 to 1942, he sponsored legislation to assist working Americans. The Social Security Act was passed in 1935. In the same year the National Labor Relations Board was created. Later, the first minimum-wage law (75 cents an hour) took effect. The 8-hour day, factory safety regulations, and the protection of working women and children were advanced. The Federal Music Project came into being as a means for giving employment to musicians, including composers, and for offering free music education and performances to the public.

Promoting a faith in the dignity and strength of common men and women and an exploration of things American were parts of the Roosevelt agenda. Painters, sculptors, dancers, composers, actors, authors, and playwrights were called on to explore American history and folklore, depict the American people in American scenes, and capture the courage and worthiness of ordinary citizens on canvas and stage, and in music and literature. Everything was done to give hope and courage to those who were despondent and fearful. "Happy Days Are Here Again" became the campaign song of Roosevelt and the slogan for his administration. The lyricist was Jack Yellen and the composer, Milton Ager. A song plugger had convinced George Olsen and his band to introduce the song at the Pennsylvania Hotel on Black Thursday, at the start of the Great Depression. Olsen glanced at the title and with bitter sarcasm told his vocalist, "Sing it for the corpses." On hearing the music, the audience chimed in, singing in a manic and mordant manner. Cynically and otherwise, people everywhere took up the song. With Roosevelt it became the symbol for better things to come and the anthem of the Democratic Party.[1]

ENTERTAINMENT CIRCLES

Money had stopped its free flow by 1930. Ticket sales for Broadway musicals and vaudeville shows took a precipitous drop. Fewer productions were mounted and of these only one or two succeeded. Half-price tickets, giveaways, and all sorts of inducements brought only temporary benefits. People stayed home as never before and listened without cost to broadcasts over the air for their amusement. Radio, providing musical programs for the millions, was generating its own singing stars and making songs into hits. Spinning the dial, one came upon Rudy Vallée, Bing Crosby, the Mills Brothers, Kate Smith, and Eddie Cantor. The Chase and Sanborn Hour, Music by Gershwin, the Kraft Music Hall, and Your Hit Parade presented the finest vocalists and the latest songs every week to the unseen audience. Best of all, no admission charge prevented listening. "It was estimated that some thirty million people were glued to their chairs in front of the radio dial and speaker every evening of the week," writes David Ewen.[2] The most durable of the radio shows was Your Hit Parade, a weekly network program that began in 1935. In 1950, it moved to television and went on until 1959. The song bill included the most popular songs of the previous week as determined by an analysis of nationwide record and sheet-music sales. The guidelines behind this analysis were never made public. Whether on radio or television, the show was sponsored by the American Tobacco Company's Lucky Strike cigarettes.

Both George Gershwin and Irving Berlin were afraid that overplaying their songs on the radio made them short lived. "Unfortunately," said Gershwin, "most songs die at an early age and are soon completely forgotten by the selfsame public that once sang them with such gusto. The reason for this is that they are sung and played too much [over the radio] when they are alive, and cannot stand the strain of their popularity." Berlin complained, "We have become a world of listeners, rather than singers. Our songs don't live anymore. They fail to become a part of us. Radio has mechanized them all. . . . The radio runs them ragged for a couple of weeks—then they're dead."[3]

Paradoxically, radio was the vehicle for Berlin's comeback, in 1932. It was a period when he had an extremely unfavorable impression of himself as a songwriter, believing he was at the end of his career, an utter failure. He had written and discarded a song, "Say It Isn't So," that Max Winslow of Berlin's publishing firm thought had potential. Winslow convinced Vallée that he should sing it on his radio show, telling him that Berlin desperately needed something to cheer him up. Vallée, who was living through an agonizing divorce, sang the words with more than his usual feeling, made the song an instant hit, and reestablished Berlin's faith in his own creative abilities.[4]

Disc jockeys were coming to the fore. They handled radio broadcasts containing recorded music, casual conversation, and commercials. Around 1932, a disc jockey, Al Jarvis, put "The World's Largest Make-Believe Ballroom" on Los Angeles's station KJWB for one hour at noon. Listenership grew. Two years later, he had gone to three hours. In 1935, Martin Block came on New York's station WNEW and quickly had millions of listeners dialing in for his two-and-a-half-hour show, his own "Make Believe Ballroom."[5] Sponsors proliferated. The idea of spinning records along with commentary spread to additional stations. Between disc jockeys and jukeboxes, which numbered around 150,000 by 1937, the public could sample all sorts of musical fare without attending shows or purchasing records.[6]

Talking pictures were also taking over. Filmed musicals, in particular, became popular. A film could be duplicated many times and sent anywhere. Movie houses opened in every city and town and admission prices were kept low. Movies combined with radio were delivering lethal blows to live performances. Theater after theater was converted into a movie house. Filmgoers could buy cheap tickets, sit in the darkness walled off from the grim outside world, and lose themselves in fantasy. Bands, dancers, and singers gave them full value for the usual 10-cents entry fee. Unemployed songwriters began to look to Hollywood for work, and Hollywood soon found it needed in-house songwriters to insure a constant supply of new material for its singing stars. Even the most famous songwriters, now with fewer stage musicals to engage them, fled to Hollywood.

Working for the film industry, songwriters no longer had complete say over what they created. They wrote songs and sang them to a producer. However uninformed and incompetent to judge, the producer and whoever else he invited to sit in decided what to accept, reject, or demand to have modified. Jablonski writes, "The songwriters were then expected to go away; what happened then was decided by the studio's musical director, the arranger, the vocal arranger, the director, the star, the producer—possibly even the star's brother's uncle: everyone, that is, but the composer." Harold Arlen at one time made the mistake of questioning a producer's musical taste and qualifications and wanted to know how someone with so little knowledge could tell the composer what to do. He got the reply, "You're *standing* there, and I'm *sitting* here—that's why!"[7] At least, the paychecks came regularly. Top composers had to stay where they were, although with misgivings. To name seven and some of their films, there were Harold Arlen (*Let's Fall in Love*, 1934; *The Wizard of Oz*, 1939), Harold Warren (*42nd Street*, 1933; *Moulin Rouge*, 1934), Irving Berlin (*Top Hat*, 1935; *Follow the Fleet*, 1936), Richard Rodgers (*Love Me Tonight*, 1932; *Hallelujah! I'm a Bum*, 1933), Jerome Kern (*Roberta*, 1935; *Swing Time*, 1936), Cole Porter (*The Gay Divorcee*, 1932; *Rosalie*, 1937), and George Gershwin (*Shall We Dance* and *A Damsel in Distress*, both 1937; *The Goldwyn Follies*, 1938).

Film studios were aware that sheet-music sales had dropped and music publishers teetered on a financial tightrope. They began to buy up the weakened independent publishers. Warner Brothers took control of Witmark, De Sylva-Brown-Henderson, Harms, and Remick; MGM got Robbins; Fox Film, Red Star Publishing. Radio giant RCA acquired Leo Feist.[8]

THE SWING ERA BEGINS

Duke Ellington's "It Don't Mean a Thing (If It Ain't Got That Swing)" came out in 1932, with a lyric by Irving Mills.[9] Whether the music was sweet or hot, said the lyric, you had to "give that rhythm ev'rything you got" and start to swing. "Sweet" meant a relaxed suave rendition of a slower ballad, which was to be rendered with a warm, full tone; "hot" meant faster music that was more driving, emotionally intense, and marked by more aggressive attacks. In whatever version, swing music was intended for dancing. The beat was smoother and the phrasing more flowing than they were in the 1920s. Out of the "hot" style would evolve lively dancing described as jitterbugging. It required energetic and athletic activity consisting of some established steps enlarged with splits, whirls, somersaults, hurling bodies back and forth, and so forth. This swing dance was said to have started at the Savoy Ballroom, in Harlem, in 1926, and was then known as the Lindy Hop. The unique name "Jitterbug" was supposed to have been coined by Cab Calloway. However, it was really Harry White who actually invented the term. White was a trombonist, drummer, and arranger who had worked with Duke Ellington, and Elmer Snowden, before joining Cab Calloway. Calloway's trumpeter, Edwin Swayzee, overheard Mr. White using the term "Jitterbug" and then wrote a song entitled "The Jitterbug" for Calloway, after hearing White's use of the word. Calloway recorded the song in January 1934. It and the dance that it represented gained widespread recognition. The dance would remain especially popular until the middle of the forties.

In 1933, with the repeal of Prohibition and the pressures brought on by the Depression, speakeasies and cabarets that had been operating at the edge of the law closed their doors. Instrumentalists, including jazz musicians, were forced to seek new employment and found there was room for them in the dance scene, which was still very much alive. They were willing to play for low wages and this encouraged the growth of large bands catering to dancers and trying to fill huge halls with sound. This coincided with Decca lowering record prices to thirty-five cents, with more record companies soon following, so that sales went up from 10 million in 1933, to 33 million in 1938, to 127 million in 1941. Major entries in these recordings were vocalists singing popular songs backed by the "song-and-dance" ensembles that came to be known as swing bands.

Black bands, like those of Fletcher Henderson and Duke Ellington, had been developing the style that came to be known as swing during the late twenties and, by 1933, had given it a clearer definition. Henderson, aided importantly by Don Redman, made band arrangements that essentially defined the swing manner of playing. Ellington furthered the idea of a cooperative effort by all of his instrumentalists to flesh out a piece of music. Ellington would also premiere with his band and vocalists several of the outstanding songs of the era, some of them originally instrumental pieces—"Sophisticated Lady" (1933), "Solitude" (1934), "In a Sentimental Mood" (1935), "Caravan" (1937), "I Let a Song Go out of My Heart" (1938), "I Don't Get Around Much Anymore" (1942), and "Do Nothin' 'Till You Hear from Me" (1943).

It was not long before white bands, catering to young dancers, co-opted the style and sanitized it for white consumption. The previous choppy accent on every other beat, for a de facto 2/4 time, gave way to an even 4/4 time. Catchy rhythmic patterns were executed on a "ride" cymbal. Riffs, brief melodic phrases repeated in swinging fashion, were featured in the band arrangements. Also prominent were call-and-response passages where one section, say the brass, called out a phrase and another section, say the saxophones, responded. Openings were left for solo instruments to add brief jazzy licks (interpolated and usually unrehearsed phrases) to the music. The tuba and banjo went out of the instrumentation, and the string bass and guitar went in. Instrumentation now included saxophones in a reed section, trumpets and trombones in a brass section, and bass, piano, guitar, and percussion in a rhythm section. Clarinets were optional. If anything, melody grew richer, harmony more sophisticated. Each band, which numbered around 12 to 16 instrumentalists, also included one or two vocalists adept at singing to a swing beat.

Widespread recognition of the arrival of swing ensued when Benny Goodman and his band played the Palomar Ballroom, in Los Angeles, in 1935, using arrangements by Henderson and Don Redman. These arrangements were economical, clean, and subtle, with an easy and natural approach that left musicians comfortable and able to set off an infectious swing when playing them. In the thirties, quite a few swing bands came into prominence—those of Cab Calloway, Count Basie, Jimmy Lunceford, Jimmy and Tommy Dorsey, Bob Cosby, Artie Shaw, and Harry James. Adamantly "sweet" bands were also extremely popular—Guy Lombardo, Hal Kemp, Eddie Duchin, and Glenn Miller. So were novelty bands—Kay Kyser, Blue Barron, and Sammy Kaye. Each band tried to develop its own distinctive style, so that fans could readily recognize its identifying sound.

These bands allowed their fans, most of them young, to abandon the gloom surrounding them and imagine themselves happy, optimistic, and excited with life as they listened and danced. The music was democratic, often blurring the color line dividing black and white Americans, whether as instrumentalists, vocalists, composers, dancers, or listeners. Racial crossover, while not the norm, at least began to occur in the swing world. As befitted the changed democratic outlook, swing was seen to represent, not the elite and the "smart set," but the common people—the working class and the underdog.

Even more than in the 1920s, a great deal of the listening and dancing would take place, not on the dance floor to a live ensemble, but at home to music coming over the radio or from a recording. Swing bands and their vocalists were broadcast regularly from New York's dance palaces, and those in several other cities, including Hollywood's Palomar Ballroom, Atlantic City's Steel Pier, San Francisco's Mark Hopkins Hotel, New Orleans's Blue Room, and Boston's Raynor Ballroom. Whatever promised to be popular was immediately recorded and in this form sounded from the home phonograph, food joint's jukebox, and broadcasting studio's turntable.

Gershwin's rhythmically oriented songs proved sympathetic to swing-band delivery; Kern's romantically balladic songs fitted less comfortably— but all were used. Arrangers took whatever songs were the rage and recast them to match a band's manner of delivery and a vocalist's singing style. The greatest vocal drift away from a song's melody resulted from scat singing, an improvisation by a vocalist, using nonsense syllables instead of words. Not all songwriters were pleased. Richard Rodgers, for one, complained about not always recognizing the tunes because of the "musical distortions" encouraged by "the swing-band influence." He said he and the composers he knew had nothing against the bands and vocalists in themselves, "but as songwriters we felt it was tough enough for new numbers to catch on as written without being subjected to all kinds of interpretive man-handling that obscured their melodies and lyrics." However, after a song became well known, he saw "nothing wrong with taking certain liberties. A singer or an orchestra can add a distinctive personal touch that actually contributes to a song's longevity."[10]

THE TRANSFORMATION OF THE SINGER

After the initial years of the swing era, the younger fans of popular music experienced a gradual shift in interest away from swing bands and their leaders to singers. The changeover accelerated when the United States entered World War II, in December 1941, and James Petrillo and the Musician's Union declared a recording strike against the bands the next year.

Vocalists were not union members, so they were free to continue recording and win over greater and greater numbers of admirers. Young women with their boyfriends away in the armed forces and young soldiers and sailors distant from their sweethearts soon found that a crooning Frank Sinatra and a soft-voiced Peggy Lee, more than a loud band, gave vent to their loneliness and bridged the miles separating them.[11]

A different breed of vocalist came into importance, who represented more than just throbbing throats out of which music emerged. Whether male or female, singers became even more the absolutely indispensable links between every songwriter and musical organization and the public. Their performances, marked by easy yet pronounced rhythms and winning mannerisms, bonded them to their listeners. With the forties, singers would turn into persons revered as supremely great—stars wielding influence over the youth of America. Adolescent boys at home and young soldiers and sailors in the canteens and at open-air concerts found reasons to worship the female vocalist swaying in front of them, sometimes for virtues other than musical talent, among them physical. Adolescent girls and some young women in their early twenties took to screaming and swooning at a male vocalist even as he lovingly cradled his microphone and opened his mouth to sing. The "bobby-soxers," teenaged girls experiencing a youthful infatuation over a male crooner, became a symbol of the forties. In 1946, the winner of an essay contest on "Why I Like Frank Sinatra" wrote that the crooner made up for youthful feelings of being ignored: "We were the kids that never get much attention. But he's made us feel like we're something. . . . He gives us security in return for our faithfulness."[12]

A writer in *Newsweek* was puzzled over the hysteria that Sinatra triggered: "As a visible male object of adulation, Sinatra is baffling. He is undersized and looks underfed—but the slightest suggestion of his smile brings squeals of agonized rapture from his adolescent adorers." Paul Bowles, writing in the *New York Herald Tribune*, was disturbed and taken aback by the bobby-soxers: "The hysteria which accompanies Sinatra's presence in public is in no way an artistic manifestation." The display was offensive to him: "Witness the almost synchronized screams that come from his audience as he closes his eyes or moves his body slightly sideways." This "spontaneous reaction corresponds to no common understanding relating to tradition or technique of performance, nor yet to the meaning of the text."[13] At the end of a concert, bobby-soxers would stand by the hundreds at the stage door, yelling, letting out ear-piercing cries for their favorite crooner, while barely held back by the police barriers. This sort of behavior would carry over into the Elvis Presley era.

Rudy Vallée, Bing Crosby, and Kate Smith had started the parade of musical personalities in the early thirties. They were soon joined by younger additions to the singing set—among the men, Frank Sinatra, Perry Como, Vic Damone, Nat King Cole, Billy Eckstine, and Tony Bennett; among the women, Margaret Whiting, Ella Fitzgerald, Billie Holiday, Pearl Bailey, Sarah Vaughn, Patti Page, Jo Stafford, Dinah Shaw, Peggy Lee, and Doris Day. They all had familiarized themselves with swing bands and acquired experience performing with them. They learned to sense the beat instinctively and swing smoothly. Like the instrumentalists, they acquired knowledge of swing's subtler shadings and impromptu embellishments that went further than what was ordinarily asked of them as singers. Like the swing-band leaders, the singers also sought arrangers who knew how to adapt a song by rescoring it so that they would sound at their best when performing with a powerful band. Among the best known of these arrangers was Nelson Riddle.

When one of these vocalists sang a romantic song about love or a promise of marriage in a natural, informal yet feelingful manner, the crowds went into a frenzy. Even when not singing, Pearl Bailey commented, fans were very curious about celebrated performers. They wanted to know everything about them—how singers like her ate, slept, and so forth. Some young people thought singers were exalted beings whose lives had little connection with others. That was untrue, she said. Singers, like everyone else, felt a need of humanity. Below the surface, all humans had some problems in common, whether famous or unknown.[14]

It was not all fun and games for the singers. They did take their craft seriously. The vocalist Margaret Whiting says that her songwriter father advised her to sing ballads "with great affection and feeling," advice given to singers from the 19th-century beginning of American popular song. He insisted that she should believe in the words and "do them simply and honestly." Pearl Bailey writes that "to perform a song successfully, the singer must feel powerful emotions about the song, particularly its lyrics—and the audience must catch that feeling, too. . . . And so I sing, pouring forth my insides. Others who have lived fully will respond. If I help them to recall happier times, let them laugh. If they remember sad times, let them cry. If I sing of love, let that audience become aware of itself through my awareness of life." Finally, Tony Bennett said that he sang songs as if the words were about something he had experienced. He selected "songs that are full of powerful emotions, so that the public can 'dream along with me,' as Perry Como used to say. That's what I look for in a singer, too. Nat 'King' Cole, for example, just hypnotized me when he sang a song like 'I Realize Now,' because he revealed himself so honestly. That's the idea: to let the audience know how you feel."[15] These comments by singers are quite similar to those made by vocalists a hundred years before, thus indicating a universal approach to popular-song interpretation.

Some songwriters, like Gershwin and Arlen, more attuned to jazz than most of their colleagues, saw no reason why a vocalist could not give a special treatment to the music and add improvisations to their compositions. If the audience accepted what the vocalist was doing, they also accepted it. Some, like Kern and Rodgers, wanted scarcely any deviation from the music as they had written it. On the other hand, Bennett, who called himself "an interpretive performer," loved Arlen's tunes because they allowed him to treat the music in a variety of ways—dramatically or exactly as written. He said, "Harold's attitude was the opposite of Richard Rodgers's, who always insisted that his songs be performed exactly as he wrote them. He said, 'Hey, change it anyway you want, as long as it works.' Anything you did was okay with him as long as it pleased the audience. That was the most important thing to him."[16]

However, no matter who was writing the music, composers fashioned melodies with the singer in mind because they had had a great deal of practical experience with voices, knew where a singer might meet with difficulties, and wished to engage their audience as effectively as they could. During the Swing Era, they increasingly wrote keeping in mind the singer who would introduce their songs. His or her ability to deliver a piece and promote it to "hit" status had to be a consideration. When Porter knew that Fred Astaire would sing his song, he kept the range narrow, excluded long-held notes, and inserted many brief notes repeated rhythmically. When Ethel Merman complained that a song, "Blow, Gabriel, Blow," did not present her in the best light, he rewrote it. When Brash Caxton asked for a reworking of "Easy to Love," because he could not sing its high notes, Porter cast the song aside and substituted "All through the Night."

If writing for male singers like Sinatra, songwriters delivered compositions that exploited his style of comfortable intimacy—an intimacy that owed much to his Italian musical background[17] and his study of Crosby's crooning and of swing musicians from Billie Holiday to Tommy Dorsey.[18] For Perry Como, the songs had to adapt to his unhurried, easygoing approach. Tony Bennett preferred drama and emotion in his pieces. Vic Damone's voice had little weight and excelled in ballads of sentimental character or allowing a little buoyancy. All four had taken their cue from Crosby and mastered the use of a microphone to convey intimacy and the positions of the body appropriate to expressing a song's contents. For example, Sinatra had decided to be a singer and studied how to make the most of the microphone soon after he had dropped out of high school. His mother yielded to his demands for a microphone and bought him one wired to a sound system. He practiced at home and then entered amateur contests, made appearances in bars, and sang wherever and whenever the opportunity came up. He thus honed his microphone skills even as he gained singing experience. Sinatra commented, "I discovered very early that my instrument wasn't my voice. It was the microphone."[19]

A survey of male vocalists would be incomplete if I failed to cite important vocal groups, especially the Mills Brothers, an African-American quartet celebrated for its flawless harmonizing. Formed in 1931, the quartet quickly gained recording fame, starting with two early successes, "Tiger Rag" and "Nobody's Sweetheart," and continuing with songs like "I'll Be Around," "Till Then," and "You Always Hurt the One You Love." Their greatest triumph was their 1943 recording of "Paper Doll," with acoustic guitar, piano, and bass, which sold over six million copies. They were followed by a second successful African-American quartet, the Ink Spots, who achieved two important hits with "If I Didn't Care" (1939) and "To Each His Own" (1946).

On the female side, the Andrews Sisters, a lively, rhythmic trio together since 1932, achieved their first huge breakthrough with their recording of "Bei Mir Bist Du Schoen," Sholom Secunda's Yiddish tune given English words by Sammy Cahn and Saul Chaplin. They went on to become favorites with American servicemen during World War II, with their cheery, pleasurable, and optimistic renditions of compositions like "Boogie Woogie Bugle Boy," "Don't Sit under the Apple Tree," and "Rum and Coca Cola."

Female soloists, like their male counterparts, became experts in fronting a swing band and managing a microphone. They also contributed more than a little to the fame of the ensembles with which they appeared. Helen Ward joined Benny Goodman's band around 1934 and added her warm, natural voice and supple rhythms to the sound and her sexually suggestive microphone manner to the display. The male collegians and younger adolescents developed intense infatuations over her. She was followed by Helen Forrest in 1939. Forrest was noted for her pleasing, affectionate, rather soft and airy tones, and for her ability to swing freely with the band. In 1943, the renowned Peggy Lee took her place. She sang in a more flowing manner, revealing an easy dexterity, effortlessly controlled movement, and a matchless sense of rhythm. She was preeminent in slow ballads, especially those on hopeless love.

Billie Holiday, an outstanding black vocalist, was especially effective in the interpretation of ballads marked by pain and bitterness. Her grandfather had been a slave in Virginia; her mother was thirteen when Billie was born; her adolescent years were spent doing menial work in a Baltimore brothel. She loved the music making of Louis Armstrong and Bessie Smith and in spite of her harsh life began singing at 15 years of age. Her professional life had its start when she appeared as a vocalist and dancer in Harlem's night places. Later she toured with Count Basie and Artie Shaw. With Benny Goodman, she recorded about 200 songs from 1933 to 1944. Giving her distinction were her notable enunciation, matchless phrasing, and heightened dramatic delivery. These made her one of the most eminent jazz-swing song interpreters of her day. Even Gershwin's "Summertime" was marked by an astringency that the composer never intended when she sang it. She wrote out of her own experiences "God Bless the Child" and "Don't Explain," on monetary troubles and on a lover's unfaithfulness respectively, and gave them special meaning when she sang them. In "God Bless the Child" she sang of how the strong get stronger while the weak just fade away with their pockets empty and of how parents may have something, "but God bless the child that's got his own."[20]

Billie went through depression and mood changes. Her personal tribulations increased when she became addicted to drugs and alcohol. She died too soon, of a heroin overdose, in 1959.

Ella Fitzgerald, one of America's most loved black vocalists, began her career with Chick Webb's band, in 1934. She, like Billie Holiday, was regarded as an unusually talented female jazz-swing singer. Under the supervision of Norman Granz, she recorded several renowned *Songbooks*— a series of albums each devoted to the songs of a particular American composer: Duke Ellington, Cole Porter, Irving Berlin, Harold Arlen, Rodgers and Hart, George and Ira Gershwin, Jerome Kern and Johnny Mercer. She also collaborated with Count Basie and Duke Ellington, respectively, to put out the prodigious *On the Sunny Side of the Street* and *Ella at Duke's Place*. Endowed with a most attractive voice and an extensive vocal range, she sang so that one could always understand her words. Ella always sounded glad to be singing, executing even a pessimistic song such as "Love for Sale" so that it seemed blissful. Sammy Cahn speaks of "If You Ever Should Leave," which he wrote with Andy Kirk and gave to Ella to record. The lyric was heartbreaking, with phrases like "If you ever should leave, why would I want to live?" Yet, she stood before the microphone "in this dreary recording studio, singing as only Ella can, with a large hot dog with all the trimmings in one hand and a bottle of Coke in the other."[21] Possibly her stripping the song if its sentimentality helped put it across to the public.

A wonderful singer, Judy Garland was featured in the movie *Wizard of Oz*, released in 1939, in which she sang songs of Harold Arlen and E. Y. Harburg. Her tender, bittersweet, and yearning interpretation of "Over the Rainbow" would make it into one of the greatest hits on record. She had the knack of astounding the listener with her expertly swinging rhythms and her gift for putting feeling into her presentation that called to mind a consummate actress. The most well-known songs characteristic of Garland either reveal her loneliness and emotional defenselessness (like the above work and "The Man That Got Away") or relay a feverish trust in love ("The Trolley Song" and "Zing! Went the Strings of My Heart").

Sarah Vaughn came out of Newark, New Jersey, when she was 18 years old, to win an Amateur Hour contest at Harlem's Apollo Theater in 1942. By the next year she had started her singing career in earnest, appearing first with Earl Hines and Billy Eckstine. She received grounding in bop, the modern jazz developed in the forties, through an association with Dizzy Gillespie and Charlie Parker. By the late '40s and early '50s she was making well received recordings and appearing on television. In 1958–59 she succeeded in occupying the top of the pop charts with her rendition of "Broken Hearted Melody." Her contralto voice was quite flexible and commanded extensive range. She was noted for her scat singing, in which she substituted improvised nonsense syllables in place of a song's words and sounded as if she were a musical instrument. Vaughn was able to sound warm and rich on ballads like "Embraceable You," "I'm Glad There Is You," and "Nearness of You." Her interpretation of "Black Coffee" was like a torch song out of the blues tradition. Then there was the down-to-earth and effortlessly swinging treatment of "Lullaby of Birdland" and "You're Not the Kind," giving them the signature of a true jazz singer.

Finally, I cite Margaret Whiting because she provides an example of the varied contributions a few great vocalists out of the Swing Era made to American music. Daughter of an outstanding songwriter, Richard Whiting, she counseled him and other noted songwriters as they created new songs. She recorded more than five hundred works, at least twelve of them extraordinarily popular with the public. Among the first-rate songs that she introduced were "Come Rain or Come Shine," "A Tree in the Meadow," "Far Away Places," and one with which she was closely associated, "Moonlight in Vermont." She took part in major musical comedies and plays to the delight of audiences everywhere and also toured America concertizing extensively alongside three fine vocalists—Rosemary Clooney, Helen O'Connell, and Rose Marie. Further services involved acting on several boards and committees in show business, including the Songwriters' Hall of Fame, the Grammy Awards, and the Manhattan Association of Cabarets. Whenever she could, she lent a hand to young singers and songwriters. For a number of years, she conducted an admired master class for the Northwood University Musical Theatre Studio, in Texas.

SONGS FOR THE RECOVERY

As Americans in the thirties crawled slowly out of the economic pit, those who were able tried to hide private financial problems from sight, close their eyes to the absent economic activity and mass unemployment everywhere, and continue to live despite the problems surrounding them. Songs of social protest and socially aware musicals illustrating the plights of people left them unsatisfied. The Gershwins, hoping to experience another success with a sequel to *Of Thee I Sing* (1932), suffered a near flop instead when they mounted *Let 'Em Eat Cake* (1933). The audience had had enough of depression even when it was satirized. The songs from only two social-minded musicals made any impression after the early thirties, Marc Blitzstein's *The Cradle Will Rock* (with "The Nickel under My Foot") and Harold Rome's *Pins and Needles* (with "Sunday in the Park" and "Sing Me a Song of Social Significance"), both from 1937.

Men and women had an urgent need of more diversion for the mind. They desired lyric entertainment with more sweetness and light and less upset in order to enable them to get away from reality. To win over their audience and supply distraction, songwriters invoked a variety of styles—tangos, rumbas, beguines, marches, waltzes, polkas, blues, lullabies, sentimental ballads, love ballads, wisecracking songs, comic novelty pieces, and hot swinging numbers. They tested the water with Western, hillbilly, Latin, Hawaiian, and further nonstandard musical material. Rarely would they admit into a lyric the messages "We're broke; we're hungry; there's no tomorrow."

One song that was out of the ordinary, that made it despite all the odds, was Irving Berlin's antiracist "Supper Time." Given the unenthusiastic tolerance of blacks in the Northern states and the free hand granted the Ku Klux Klan in the South and Midwest, it should not have succeeded. Perhaps it was a more educated, more sophisticated, and more aware New York audience that found its message absorbing. In the 1933 revue *As Thousands Cheer*, Ethel Waters, who sang the song, portrayed a wife waiting for her husband to come home to supper, not knowing a mob has lynched him. As she tells of the experience:

> "Supper Time" was a dirge. It told the story of a colored woman preparing the evening meal for her husband who has been lynched. If one song can tell the whole tragic history of a race, "Supper Time" was that song. In singing it I was telling my comfortable, well-fed, well-dressed listeners about my people. I only had to think of the family of that boy down in Macon, Georgia, who had been lynched to give adequate expression to the horror and the defeat in "Supper Time." . . .
>
> After praying for help from Him I went on and sang "Supper Time." When I was through and that big, heavy curtain came down I was called back again and again. I had stopped the show with a type of song never heard before in a revue.[22]

Otherwise, songwriters avoided controversial and depressing offerings. They perceived themselves as writing for a mainly white audience that needed reassurance. "Berlin saw 'just around the corner . . . a rainbow in the sky,' and De Sylva, urging his listeners to 'rise 'n shine, don't be a mourner,' saw as did Berlin that 'things look fine around the corner.'" Al Dubin preached a cheerful brand of Keynesianism when, in the depths of the Depression, he sang: "We're in the money, come on my honey, let's spend it, send it, rolling along," writes Edward Pessen.[23] During the gloom of 1933, Berlin read the mood of Americans and supplied them with "Easter Parade," pure escapism packaged in holiday display. The next year, Porter acknowledged that times had changed and with perverse cheerfulness announced that now "Anything Goes"; furthermore, even if everyone had a story much too sad to be told, one could sing "I Get a Kick Out of You." If the Gershwins mirrored their own time in a lyric, it was in a roundabout way—triumphing over disappointment and disparagement in "They All Laughed," finding comfort in love when no work is to be found in "Nice Work If You Can Get It," and abandoning the look of sadness by seeking happiness on the dance floor in "Shall We Dance?" (all three from 1937). In 1938, "God's Country," lyric by E. Y. Harburg, music by Harold Arlen, claimed that Americans, despite everything, lived in God's country, where the grass was greener and troubles smaller.

NOVELTIES AND OTHER ONE-OF-A-KIND SONGS

Although in a majority of instances the composer wrote the music first and the lyricist wrote the words next, increasingly, after 1930, there was give and take between the two. The lyricist suggested changes in the music; the composer suggested changes in the words. On occasion, the lyric came first—as would be true for the songwriting team of Rodgers and Hammerstein. At all times, the lyricist listened carefully to the music, let it create a feeling or mood in him or her, then decided on the subject, and under the guidance of his feelings (and, of course, what would sell) wrote the text. If the tune seemed slow and brooding, the words followed suit. If the tune was fast and perky, the words would turn good humored or comic. When, for some reason, the tune struck the lyricist as perhaps idiosyncratic then the subject matter could be novel or atypical. The process of song creation was highly subjective, though guided by expertise and consciously or unconsciously sensitive to what was in vogue at the moment.

Ludicrous novelty songs representing the preposterous side of life continued to be popular and so were written in some quantity. Added to these were other pieces based on unusual subject matter. These compositions could not easily be grouped together with the more serious songs since they favored the lighter emotions, often interlaced with irony. At the same time, an underlying somber content was frequently implied. Apparently, the music public had become used to the older musical styles and topics and now wanted more variety, more out-of-the-way works, if only to hint at the new events that they were living through. Increasingly, songwriters realized that people would be attracted by fresh subjects and sounds, or by novel twists to old ones. An excellent illustration, "Lazybones" (1933),[24] lyric by Johnny Mercer, music by Hoagy Carmichael, is the celebration of a dropout who prefers sleeping and loafing all day rather than doing work or engaging in active play of any kind—not a standard theme. Contemporary listeners enjoyed it. They might have detected a light sarcasm in the words, which could indirectly be taken as a reaction to a period when no work was to be had and few felt much like playing anyway. The music shifts around torpidly as if in sympathy with the subject, remaining within a narrow range, winding unhurriedly up and down, and closing on sagging cadences. Rudy Vallée and Ben Bernie made the song popular on radio and in their club acts.

It would never be confused with another individual piece, Cole Porter's "Miss Otis Regrets" (1934),[25] which tells of a woman who shoots down a two-timing lover and then is lynched by a mob. No, "Miss Otis Regrets" is not tragic, like "Supper Time." It is ironic—a roundabout presentation of a contradiction between Miss Otis's apologizing for her inability to make a luncheon engagement and the circumstance of the execution, which necessitates calling off the appointment. Life and death by lynching are given an absurd interpretation. The listener is allowed to regard the incongruity of the situation with amusement and mild derision. All the while, Cole Porter remains detached from his subject and permits scarcely any emotion to intrude. The neutral tune evolves in a measured manner, evoking no sympathy for Miss Otis and no anguish over her execution. The composer improvised the song at a party given by Monty Wooley. Thereafter Wooley liked to make a first appearance at evening gatherings as a butler, with this song on his lips. One might consider the subject to be a sophisticated and stylish variant on the "Franky and Johnny" theme.

Neither of these two songs would be confounded with "On the Good Ship, Lollipop" (1934),[26] lyric by Sidney Clare and music by Richard Whiting. A very young and adorable Shirley Temple sang it originally in the film *Bright Eyes*. The ditty conveys a child's idyll, a charmingly simple and appealing fantasy of being surrounded by an abundance of sweet goodies, at a time when any overflowing quantity of affordable goods was bizarre even to think about. The melody sounds like a jingling play-song, a succession of likable up-and-down skips. Movie audiences, especially mothers of young children, exhibited an avid interest in singer and song. The melody comes out as an almost monotone recitation, with lots of repeated notes over fairly static harmonies. Shirley Temple's personality brings it alive. In contrast to "Lollipop," "Small Fry" (1938),[27] lyric by Frank Loesser, music by Hoagy Carmichael, allows no sweet child to emerge. The hateful boy is a "good for nothin' brat." The kid skips school and is seen strutting by a poolroom with a cigarette dangling from his lips—one won't but "could whip him with joy," which seems to be the moral behind the piece. A mock solemnity rules. The film *Sing, You Sin-*

ners, in which Bing Crosby sings it to 13-year old Donald O'Connor, quickly disseminated the music throughout the country. Then there is the 1935 musical balderdash about a trumpet or French horn, "The Music Goes 'Round and Around,"[28] lyric by "Red" Hodgson, music by Edward Farley and Michael Riley. Farley and Riley introduced the piece at New York's Onyx Club and it caught on. Jack Kapp, of Decca Records, who put out the piece, said: "At least everyone can sing Whoa-ho-ho-ho, and that is what made the song a hit."[29] Childish simplemindedness envelops the silly words that tell of music going round and round the brass tubing and coming out, "Whoa-ho-ho-ho. . . . Below, below, deedle-dee-ho-ho-ho." A rowdy heartiness envelops the equally inane tune. I remember how popular it was in a Cambridge sugar-cone bakery, where the workers standing in tubs of water and serving revolving baking machines sang it in demented fashion while the temperature hovered around 115° Fahrenheit. The circumstances seemed fitting for the song.

These five compositions clearly establish that no two novelty songs are alike. Each portrays an experience not resembling any of the remaining four. When a collection of novelty compositions are a bit arbitrarily grouped together as dance songs, they still differ greatly in sound and verbal focus. "Forty-Second Street,"[30] lyric by Al Dubin, music by Harry Warren, is an effective tap-dance number: "Forty-Second Street. Hear the beat of dancing feet." Indeed, it was written with dancers in mind, for the film *Forty-Second Street*, which came out in 1933. An intangible nonchalance invests the tune. A second number, "Stompin' at the Savoy"[31] (1936), lyric by Andy Razaf, music credited to Benny Goodman, Chick Webb, and Edgar Simpson, is a genuinely upbeat swing number and produces a very different effect on the listener. Almost every note is syncopated, and off-beat accents abound. It's a dizzying song that "gives happy feet a chance to dance," vigorously, too. Possibly something akin to the Lindy Hop was in the composer's mind. Both pieces help men and women to escape their troubles, of which the times supplied plenty, through some form of dance.

In no way do the two preceding dance numbers bear a resemblance to the Gershwins' triple-time "By Strauss" (1936),[32] a tasty waltz parody that gives "no quarter to Kern or Cole Porter" and complains that "Gershwin keeps pounding on tin." Gershwin's music is "drivel. It's only for night clubbing souses," writes the tongue-in-cheek Ira. His brother George provides the refrain with a fake-Strauss melody that is sent "lilting through the house." The next year, the Gershwins reversed direction and started swinging with "Slap That Bass."[33] The syncopations are fewer than in "Stompin'." Still, the exuberant spirit in the refrain's tune matches the words, singing of slapping that bass until it's dizzy and forcing feelings of misery to leave. The music sounds high spirited, outgoing, and joyously unrestrained. It assuages depression.

There were many strings in the Gershwin bow. In the same year, 1937, the Gershwins also wrote "Shall We Dance?" in order to feature Fred Astaire's singing and floating dance style. Instead of heavy stamping to a driving rhythm, the song repudiates aggressive sound, recognizes gracefulness, and invites the listener to "put on your dancing shoes . . . and walk on air." Later, among the manuscripts that George Gershwin left behind, Ira found a dance that he could put words to, "The Back Bay Polka," published in 1946.[34] It turns out to be a vivacious dance, corresponding to the Bohemian original, with a lively three-steps-and-a-hop pattern in duple time. I said earlier that, in order to find and please audiences, songwriters wrote in every imaginable style. The Gershwins certainly bear out this point.

That novelty songs were invested with a wide range of musical and verbal ideas is made evident by citing just the titles of six of the most popular— "Winter Wonderland" (1934), "Lullaby of Broadway" (1935), "We Saw the Sea" (1936), "A Couple of Swells" (1937), "Friendship" (1939), and "Chattanooga Choo Choo" (1941).

During World War II, one of the most outrageous and most popular novelty songs was "Der Fuehrer's Face" (1942),[35] which Oliver Wallace conjured up during a bike ride with his wife, and which Walt Disney featured in a cartoon film. Spike Jones and his City Slickers took up the ditty and presented it with plenty of crude raspberries: "Ven der Fuehrer says, 'Ve ist der master race,' ve HEIL! [razz] HEIL! [razz] right in der Fuehrer's face." Audiences could not keep themselves from laughing along with the song, vulgar as it was, whenever Spike Jones performed it. I saw boys marching up and down a Boston street, singing and razzing with such enthusiasm that a passerby laughed so hard that he lost his footing at the curb and fell down. Another singularly idiotic song came out the next year, "Mairzy Doats,"[36] lyric by Milton Drake and Al Hoffman, music by Jerry Livingston. The listener knew that the words were extremely foolish and the tune was a deliberately rhythmical triviality. Nevertheless, once heard, the enticingly catchy refrain could not be put out of one's mind: "Mairzy doats and dozy doats and liddle lamzy divey; a kiddley divey too, wouldn't you." Drake first conceived of the song as a takeoff on a nursery ditty and completed it in partnership with Hoffman and Livingston. At first neither publishers nor performers would take up the crackbrained composition. In 1943, Al Trace and his Silly Symphonists took a chance on it. The Merry Macs made a crispy recording of the piece. The song became a sudden phenomenon. "Rosie the Riveter" worked to its rhythms; soldiers marched to its beat. Its odd message apparently was able to give comfort and enjoyment to many during an anxious time in American history.[37]

In the forties and fifties came more novelties, like "The Surrey with the Fringe on Top" (1943), "I Cain't Say No" (1943), "Baby, It's Cold Outside" (1948), and "That's Entertainment" (1953).

Music from other countries was more often than not a novelty. A special sort of unusualness and fantasy infused those imported songs that, when fitted with an English lyric, caught on with the American public. They showed attractive quirks in melody and rhythm; made allusions to people, lands, and ideas other than American; and gave suggestions of the atmosphere belonging to another age or mode of existence. They invited people to slip away from the concerns of the moment.

Melodies originating in Europe had been a part of the American popular scene since the beginning of the 19th century. Later, American soldiers returning from overseas at the end of World War I had had a glimpse of cultures and learned songs other than their own. Songs originating elsewhere continued to appear in the American popular music of the early 20th century. In 1918, Chopin supplied the tune for the well-liked "I'm Always Chasing Rainbows." In 1921, *Blossom Time*, an operetta based on Franz Schubert's life and music, had proved to be a hit. However, in the 1930s, Americans had even greater knowledge of the world and its cultures than they had in the past, even if it was not a deep familiarity. Some of this awareness, it is true, instilled apprehension over the possibility of international conflict. The public viewed with alarm the increasing strength of the Nazis, Fascists, and Japanese warlords. At the same time, acquaintance with and curiosity about other manners of expression expanded. Newspapers, magazines, and newsreels brought intelligence of unfamiliar but fascinating ways of life. Immigrants from all over the world, not just from northwestern Europe, who spoke foreign languages, ate exotic foods, and listened to strange music, had domiciled themselves in the United States. It was to be expected that the diversity of the sources generating music capable of taking root in America would increase, though not overwhelmingly.

European art music continued to furnish tunes for American popular consumption. This was especially so from the late thirties on: for example,

Rimsky-Korsakov and "Song of India" (1937), Debussy and "My Reverie" (1938), Tchaikovsky and "Moon Love" and "Our Love" (both 1939) and "Tonight We Love" (1941), Ravel and "The Lamp Is Low" (1939), Rachmaninoff and "I Think of You" (1941) and "Full Moon and Empty Arms" (1946), Chopin and "Till the End of Time" (1945), Borodin and "Stranger in Paradise" (1953). The musical *Song of Norway*, based on Grieg's music, came out in 1944, and the musical *Kismet*, based on the music of Borodin, came out in 1953. So many borrowings were taking place that Les Brown and His Orchestra decided to respond with the song commentary "Everybody's Making Money but Tchaikovsky." Although the song subjects were mostly about love, their melodies and harmonies were entertaining novelties for most Americans.

More frequently encountered were popular-music imports. In 1934, Lew Brown added English lyrics to a Czech popular dance song, by Jaromir Vejvoda, which became the widely sung "Beer Barrel Polka."[38] It invited singers to "roll out the barrel," get "the blues on the run," and "have a barrel of fun." In the same year Wallace Beery was starring in the film *Viva Villa*, which introduced the Mexican folk song "La Cucaracha," about a cockroach that no longer wanted to walk ("la cucaracha, ya no quiere caminar") because it had no money to spend ("porque no tiene, porque le falta dinero para gastar"). More than one version of the Spanish words existed; more than one translation into English was published and sung. Both the Czech and Mexican compositions were rhythmically animated incitements to chase away gloom. The public welcomed them enthusiastically. Songs originating in Latin America continued to appear in some frequency; two of the most popular in 1939 were the Brazilian samba "Brazil," English lyric by Bob Russell and music by Ary Barroso, and "Frenesi," English lyric by Ray Charles and S. K. Russell, music by Albert Dominguez.

According to Sammy Cahn, he came upon two black entertainers singing Sholom Secunda's Yiddish song "Bei Mir Bist Do Schoen" in Harlem's Apollo Theater. The black audience did not understand the Yiddish words but appeared to love the music. Sensing the makings of a big hit, he told Tommy Dorsey about it, but the band leader only laughed at him. Americans in general, Dorsey replied, would never go for an idiom favored by eastern European Jews. He had made no allowances for the broadening of America's cultural horizons. Cahn went ahead anyway, writing an English lyric for the music, persuading a publisher to put out the song with his new words, and discovering that an Andrews Sisters recording parlayed the piece into big time, in 1937.[39] The lyricist's instincts were right. Jew and non-Jew were soon singing the bilingual wooing song, "Bei mir bist du schoen, please let me explain, bei mir bist du schoen means that you're grand."[40]

As the Andrews Sisters were capitalizing on the Yiddish song, Rudy Vallee was doing the same with Vincent Scotto's Corsican popular song "Vieni, Vieni." Vallee had introduced the song over the radio, in 1936, and then written a new English lyric for it, in 1937, which Witmark and Sons of New York published. It, too, is a bilingual wooing song: "Vieni, vieni . . . tusei bella . . . waiting for you . . . lonesome and blue." Both songs go at slightly brisker tempi and with more robust rhythmic pulsations than do standard love ballads. The next year the Latin song "Ti-Pi-Tin," music by Maria Grever, with an English lyric by Raymond Leveen, became well known.

So it went right into the rock era, when one of the biggest hits of all, "Volare," took center stage. It had won a prize at the San Remo Festival for its Italian composer, Domenico Modugno. First, a recording made by the composer and, next, a recording with Dean Martin singing new English lyrics by Mitchell Parish gave it hit status in the United States, in 1958. For months the music was heard nationwide on home phonographs, jukeboxes, and the radio, and as part of the repertoire of singers appearing in concerts and for social occasions. The public even enjoyed hearing the original Italian words, by Modugno and Migliacci, right after or before the English rendition: "Volare, oh, oh! Cantare, oh, oh, oh, oh!"[41] The song was an invitation to fly up into the clouds away from a world of uncertainty and disappointment. The text was backed by an irresistible tune that sounded briskly self-assured—as if the vocalist had cast off worries and was able to soar because free from care. I was living in Springfield, Massachusetts, at the time. An unemployed factory worker, who lived next to me, would come home day after day after futile job hunting and play the song through open windows at an aggressively high volume.

Also novelties were the admired cowboy songs romanticizing the lands west of the Mississippi, which singing cowboy-actors introduced in Westerns. The three most prominent vocalists in these films were Gene Autry, Roy Rogers, and Tex Ritter. Typical were Autry's "Tumbling Tumbleweed" (lyric and music by Bob Nolan, 1934), Roy Rogers's "I'm an Old Cowhand" (lyric and music by Johnny Mercer, 1936), and Ritter's "You Are My Sunshine" (lyric and music by Jimmie Davis and Charles Mitchell, 1940).

Rogers, regarded with the most favor of the three, specialized in music that helped Americans live through the realities of the time. Refusing to allow room for the disaster of the Dust Bowl and the need to vacate the waterless Great Plains, the tragic situation captured in John Steinbeck's *Grapes of Wrath*, Rogers wandered musically across the West, without a care in the world, with Cole Porter's stunning success, "Don't Fence Me In."[42]

An even better way to get away from the actual state of things was to escape to the never-never land painted in "Hawaiian" songs. The island setting was made still more dreamlike by plucked ukuleles and tremulously twanging steel guitars. Joseph Kekuku is credited with the idea of sliding a comb over the front of his guitar to produce the characteristic "Hawaiian" sound, in 1909. Five years later, a Pan-Pacific Exhibition took place in San Francisco, complete with hula girls, ukuleles, steel guitars, and ersatz songs like Charles King's "Song of the Islands." A new category of popular song was established thereby. In 1936, "Hawaiian" music started to achieve even greater prominence with "Hawaiian War Chant," the music adapted by Johnny Noble and Leileohako from the traditional Hawaiian chant "Tahu Wahu Wahi" and given English lyrics by Ralph Freed. Three years later it would be made especially the rage through Tommy Dorsey's high-speed swing-band arrangement featuring a driving beat propelled by tom-toms.

No slouch when it came to singing cowboy songs ("Empty Saddles," "Twilight on the Trail"), Bing Crosby served up counterfeit Hawaiian songs to adoring viewers of his 1937 film *Waikiki Wedding*. He brought into existence scenes without dust bowls, joblessness, needy Americans waiting in line for free food, and the overseas brandishing of German, Italian, and Japanese war weapons.[43] People longed to believe the words of Crosby's song "Blue Hawaii,"[44] words and music by Leo Robin and Ralph Rainer. Sung to a reassuring melody, it allowed listeners to feel safe and secure in a fantasyland where dreams come true and perhaps the singer's will also during a magical night with his sweetheart.

Lulling minds further with things men and women wanted to persuade themselves could happen was Crosby's singing of "Sweet Leilani,"[45] lyric and music by Harry Owens. It was a striking success. Not least in making it a winner was the tranquilizing tune that glided forth like the sliding tones of a steel guitar, as the singer dreamt of sweet Leilani, who was a "heavenly flower" dwelling in a "paradise for two."

Counterbalancing the songs that viewed Hawaii through rose-tinted glasses was the delicious parody of the genre, "Honolulu," in Blitzstein's biting *The Cradle Will Rock* (1937). Just before the song "Honolulu," the composer had also taken on crooners and the rhyming clichés of their songs, in "Croon Spoon."

SERIOUS SONGS

Songwriters continued to offer earnest, reflective compositions put forward as sincerely meant. During the difficult economic times, irony hid in many of them. One instance is "Let's Take a Walk around the Block" (1934), lyric by Ira Gershwin and E. Y. Harburg, music by Harold Arlen. A pseudo-frothy verbal veneer scarcely disguises a somber underlay. In the lyric, the protagonist is saving his nickels so that some day he'll "toddle off in swank," taking not "an ordinary Cook's tour" but "a 'cabin deluxe' tour." Meanwhile, until that illusory time arrives, "let's take a walk around the block." Arlen's tune proves effective though kept entirely simple and diatonic. The refrain is built on a straightforward and very brief rhythmic pattern repeated again and again.

Often the songs were not truly swing numbers. Indeed several of the most popular were contemplative or hymnlike creations designed to appeal to sentiment. In a second example, Gershwin eschews his usual bent for highly rhythmic music and provides a pensive lullaby in "Summertime,"[46] with words by DuBose Heyward, which opens his "folk" opera, *Porgy and Bess* (1935). Gravity prevails throughout. Stillness envelops the music as a mother sings to her baby with a melody that lingers on high notes and then dips gently from high to low three times before swaying back and achieving equilibrium in the middle of its range. At the same time, the accompaniment rocks back and forth between two slightly dissonant harmonies that add a frisson to the sound. Ironically, she sings, "Oh yo' daddy's rich an' yo' ma is good lookin'" and assures her little one that until it grows up, "there's nothin' can harm you, with Daddy an' Mammy standin' by." Note that as in the previous song, a misgiving about the future is suggested.

To expose further the wide variety of melody and subject matter in serious songs, we turn to one of the most loved compositions of all time, "Over the Rainbow,"[47] which Judy Garland introduced in the film *The Wizard of Oz* (1939). Strangely enough, MGM Studios thought the song of no account and at first wanted it eliminated from the movie. Fortunately, the producer Arthur Freed insisted on its inclusion. Arlen completed the music only after Ira Gershwin advised him to go easy on the harmonic texture and to quicken the tempo. It was E. Y. Harburg who invented title and words that were so exactly right for the music. Deep longing, accompanied by tenderness and sadness, was in Garland's voice when she sang the refrain melody's opening on an arresting wide upward leap, balanced by two smaller skips as the phrase winds downward until it ends on the low note with which it began—to the words, "Somewhere over the rainbow way up high, there's a land that I heard of once in a lullaby." Her singing of the song deeply affected the millions who saw the film.

A second song, which shares the topmost honors with "Over the Rainbow," is "White Christmas" (1942), words and music by Irving Berlin. Bing Crosby sang it in the film *Holiday Inn*, and it went on to become a classic of popular music, along with Berlin's "God Bless America," written in 1918 and achieving extraordinary popularity from 1939 on. The two Berlin songs got their first big boost owing to the dark wartime hours of the early forties, when people wanted to dream of a white Christmas exactly like the ones they remembered and prayed that God would stand beside them and the nation that they loved. Both, like "Over the Rainbow," have persisted in the memory of Americans owing to their messages and the distinguished, attractive, and singer-friendly tunes that put the words across.

Two uplifting compositions that won tremendous public approval came from the song team Rodgers and Hammerstein—"You'll Never Walk Alone,"[48] first heard in the musical *Carousel* (1945), and "Climb Ev'ry Mountain,"[49] first heard in *The Sound of Music* (1959). Both are solemn, sentimental, and hymnlike—fitting anthems for the countless school graduation ceremonies at which they were especially popular. Moving at a staid and dignified pace, the first song told the young who were facing the world for the first time: "Though your dreams be tossed and blown, walk on, walk on with hope in your heart, and you'll never walk alone." The second, coming three years after an earthy Elvis Presley proclaimed the reign of "Blue Suede Shoes," had a similar inspirational message about climbing every mountain and stream, following a rainbow until one's dream was found. That the admonition to chase after one's dream continued to have a huge number of subscribers, even later in the rock era, was evidenced in the acclaim given Johnny Mercer and Henry Mancini's "Moon River,"[50] of 1961, in which the Moon River is a dream maker and wherever it goes, the singer will go, too.

LIGHT LOVE SONGS

Cheerful, amusing, and readily swallowed songs that are more or less about love have always been around. However, they appeared with the greatest frequency during the Swing Era. They belied the seriousness of the times, provided some lightening of whatever oppressed, burdened, or distressed people, and bolstered those feelings of optimism that still survived. When Dick Powell and Louis Armstrong premiered "Jeepers Creepers"[51] in the movie *Going Places* (1938), they parlayed an unpretentious and laid-back piece into a hit. With words by Johnny Mercer and music by Harry Warren, the song breezily asked, "Jeepers creepers, where'd ya get those peepers?" and testified to their hypnotic effect. Articulated in short phrases confined to a narrow range, the melody was able to make a clear, distinct, and precise impression. Warren would do it again, in 1953, when he wrote the music, and Jack Brooks, the lyric, for "That's Amoré (That's Love),"[52] which Dean Martin sang in the movie *The Caddy* and then made into a best-selling recording. It announced that "when the moon hits your eye like a big pizza pie, that's amoré. . . . When the stars make you drool just like pasta fazool, that's amoré." The words appealed to one's sense of humor, and Martin's relaxed delivery of the melody and lyric helped the song find wide acceptance.

George Gershwin, with the help of his brother Ira's lyrics, was skilled in producing light love songs, in which the declaration of love seems incidental to the main thrust of the words. The music is always given an attention-holding rhythmic pattern; the lyric always makes an unusually idiosyncratic statement. Ira endeavors to speak suavely, sparklingly, and in a fresh manner about an irresistible "other." To give two examples, first, in "Let's Call the Whole Thing Off,"[53] romance has grown flat because the lovers can't agree about pronunciations ("You say eether and I say eyether, you say neether and I say nyther"). Yet, after all is said and done, they know they need each other, "so we better call the calling off off." Fred Astaire and Ginger Rogers first sang it in the film *Shall We Dance* (1937) and immediately followed the banter with a roller-skate dance. Men and women found enticing the amusing patter of the melody and the novelty of the visual and verbal wit. Second, in the same film, the dancing pair presented "They All Laughed," the title a parody of a persistent advertising catchphrase of the time, "They all laughed when I sat down to play the piano." Ira tells listeners that "they all laughed at Christopher Columbus," who claimed the world was round, at Edison, who captured sound on a disc, at Hershey, who came out with the chocolate bar, and so forth. Finally, the text concludes with "They all laughed at me wanting you . . . but you came through," so "Ho, Ho, Ho! Who's got the last laugh now?" George's refrain tune, starting on an offbeat, keeps the listener slightly off balance as it moves in short sudden motions to a teasing ending, whose harmonies move jokingly and abruptly into a distant key, as a last laugh, before landing safely but just as abruptly back on the home key.

Cole Porter was the absolute master of this sort of entertaining society verse and music, writing his own lyrics to his melodies. Like Ira Gershwin, he invented an endless number of witty reworkings of the love theme and managed to steer clear of the usual tired clichés. Like George Gershwin, he wanted his music never to sound trite or stereotyped. After Ethel Merman sang "I Get a Kick out of You"[54] enthusiastically in the musical *Anything Goes* (1934), there was no stopping the song. The vocalist gets no kick from champagne or cocaine but gets a kick "ev'ry time I see you're standing there before me," despite its being "clear to me you obviously don't adore me." The refrain melody has a penchant for switching again and again from four to three beats a measure, which imparts a special identity to the whole. Allowing love to have a more stimulating and intoxicating quality than alcohol and drugs and saying so in a slangy sophisticated way was curious to say the least. In the same musical, Porter unleashes another catalog of odd love comparisons, "You're the Top."[55] Now, the loved one is addressed with "You're the top! You're the Coliseum"; then comes comparison to the Louvre Museum, the Nile, the Tower of Pisa, and, even more bizarrely, to Mickey Mouse, a Waldorf salad, a Berlin ballad, and the feet of Fred Astaire. The lover is a failure and likens himself to a worthless check, but if he's at the bottom, "you're the top." The refrain melody abets the words as each of its two strains pauses after every three or four notes to generate a musical exclamation point and then rises stepwise from its lowest to its highest note for a climax. In the second strain, the music ascends to the highest level of all and remains there in order to conclude with a final "You're the top." A third song of the same type, "It's De-Lovely," appeared in the musical *Red, Hot, and Blue* (1936).

Porter's light touch can occasionally turn cynical. He is on the verge of doing so in "My Heart Belongs to Daddy"[56] (1938), whose off-color intimations Mary Martin sang while doing a modified striptease, in the musical *Leave It to Me*. The song tells us she has led a freewheeling life, but she no longer falls for "those boys who maul refined ladies." She tells them "to go to hell, I mean Hades," because "I've come to care for such a sweet millionaire," and she is not about to jeopardize a good thing. The songwriter crossed the border into real cynicism in "Always True to You in My Fashion"[57] (1948), where love is mocked. Lisa Kirk presented it in the musical *Kiss Me, Kate*. She claims love for her "fav'rite gent," who gives her joy "but not a cent." However, her object in life is not to pauperize herself in the name of love. So if any wealthy man, whether weird or normal, asks her out, she's for it. Yet, she explains to her lover, "I'm always true to you, darlin', in my fashion; yes, I'm always true to you, darlin', in my way." As one expects from Porter, the music sounds irresistible and just as flippant as the lyric.

Johnny Mercer sometimes mined a similar vein. In 1936, to music by Matty Malneck, he wrote "Goody, Goody,"[58] where a rejected lover gloats when his jilting girlfriend gets her just deserts: "You gave him your heart too, just as I gave mine to you, and he broke it in little pieces. . . . Goody goody for him, goody goody for me." Mercer was still mining this seam in 1963, with "Talk to Me, Baby," music by Robert Dolan. Here, a lover suggests that even if love cannot be returned, his opposite should continue to go through the motions and tell him lies.

The gibing but sophisticated love ditty continued in favor throughout the thirties and forties, various songwriters contributing to the genre. Even the usually sedate Jerome Kern got into the act with "I Won't Dance."[59] He had composed the song with an Oscar Hammerstein II lyric, originally for a London musical, *Three Sisters*. But when the song was interpolated into the film *Roberta*, in 1935, only the title was retained. Dorothy Fields aided by Jimmy McHugh substituted another set of words, as a vehicle for Fred Astaire. Kern's music was made to complement Astaire's dancing feet. At first Astaire informs Ginger Rogers, "I won't dance! Don't ask me," fearing that it will lead "the way to romance." She coaxes, "Think of what you're losing by constantly refusing to dance with me." She flatters him, saying he looks wonderful dancing the "Continental." Being Fred Astaire, of course he dances. Dorothy Fields did it again for Kern in "The Way You Look Tonight" (1936), in the film *Swing Time*, which is a love song Astaire sings to Rogers, who looks silly while shampooing her hair. Also in "You Couldn't Be Cuter"[60] (1938), where the vocalist sings, "You got me little fella, I'm sunk! I'm gone! I'm hooked!" As a final example, the best known light love song that Lorenz Hart wrote for Richard Rodgers was "My Funny Valentine"[61] (1937). Rodgers's insouciant melody, graceful and having a sophisticated charm, blunts the sting of the words about a beloved lacking in smarts, without a figure to speak of, and whose looks in general are "laughable, unphotographable." Nevertheless, against all odds, he loves her!

THE MORE SOBER LOVE SONGS

The bread-and-butter product of popular songwriters has always been the serious song that sings sincerely and, as far as possible, not routinely about love. A composer writes music with a love ballad in mind; a lyricist gives the music verbal meaning—via some special rendering of "I love you." Sentimentality was lessened by making melodies incisive to some degree, rhythms fairly driving, and harmonies rather astringent but tolerable. A trace of cynicism or mockery helped hold maudlin emotion at bay. So also could unexpected musical phrases and remarkable rhymes. Sarcasm is absent from the more romantic love ballads. By dealing with their subjects matter-of-factly and without maudlin garnish the songwriters keep ballads sounding genuine.

A great deal depended on the spark between the collaborators. For example, George and Ira Gershwin were an ideal team. George composed brilliantly proficient music to which Ira responded with brilliantly proficient lyrics. They warded off overemotionality. Pleasurable surprises were regularly incorporated into the music, rhymes, and subject matter. Turning to the lyricist Lorenz Hart, his penchant was clearly for writing pungent lyrics, which could be witty or filled out with black humor. They encouraged Richard Rodgers to write equally biting and sharply expressive music. Hart kept the composer rooted in a real world with songs like "My Funny Valentine," "The Lady Is a Tramp," "I Could Write a Book," and "Bewitched, Bothered, and Bewildered." Hart died in 1943. By then, Rodgers had already joined up with Oscar Hammerstein II—their *Oklahoma!* was staged in 1943. The new affiliation caused the composer to change into a writer of tender temperament; his music often turned sugary and sometimes a tad too dreamy. The former acerbic bite was almost gone. Gene Lees writes, "Hammerstein was an excellent lyricist. . . . But he was always advising us to whistle a happy tune and climb every mountain and assuring us that we'd never walk alone and preaching the virtues of happy talk. . . . He and Rodgers seemed to bring out the Pollyanna in each other, finally attaining their masterpiece of the cloying in *The Sound of Music*."[62] (Cloying to Lees; wonderfully expressive to the public.) Most fortunate were the songwriters who were responsible both for their music and lyrics—like Irving Berlin and Cole Porter. Berlin's unforced humanity and Porter's cosmopolitan urbanity allowed complete rapport between the sound and speech of their songs.

Ever since Americans began to express their feelings through music, the romantic ballad has taken precedence over all other secular songs. A recurrent theme in the history of song is the conceit that love is a dream. In 1933, Mack Gordon wrote the words and Harry Revel the music to "Did You Ever See a Dream Walking?"[63] The dream, described in rising musical phrases, is of a beloved walking, talking, dancing, and romancing. The music climaxes on "Did you ever find Heaven right in your arms, saying I love you, I do," just before concluding that the dream "was you." A second very popular love-dream song was "With My Eyes Wide Open," (1934), words and music by Mack Gordon and Harry Revel. Of the same order is "And the Angels Sing" (1939), lyric by Johnny Mercer, music by Ziggie Elman, where the lover hears angels singing when meeting the person adored. Especially attractive in this last song is the music of the release, starting on the words "suddenly the setting is strange." A tone that is unexpectedly lowered and rhythms that change with every measure make the listener sit up and heed the changed atmosphere.

Another recurrent theme is the idea that love promotes tunnel vision, as in "I Only Have Eyes for You"[64] (1934), lyric by Al Dubin, music by Harry Warren. "Are the stars out tonight?" asks the vocalist—is the moon shining, are we alone in a garden or on the street in a crowd? The singer doesn't know because "I only have eyes for you." As in two of the previous songs, the refrain's tune climaxes near the end.

Harold Allen writes a far more distinctive tune, and Ted Koehler a more individual lyric, than those of the previous three songs for "I've Got the World on a String"[65] (1932). A skip upward and a flick of an accent on a lowered note, followed quickly by a second skip up to a sustained tonic note (the keynote of the scale), sets the tone of the refrain melody. As in the other songs, the climax comes near the end. The lyric tells us that the whole world is in the singer's power and subject to his whim because he is in love. "I can make the rain go, anytime I move my finger; lucky me, can't you see, I'm in love."

A second important songwriter, Cole Porter, was responsible for the smoldering "So in Love"[66] (1948). To be completely and passionately in love, as here, is rare in a Porter lyric, although the singer cautions that the lover may be taunted, deceived, and deserted by the one loved. The melody is highly inventive. Structured conventionally, it unfolds with nothing repeated exactly as before. Chromatics, modification of the normal scale by the use of accidentals, alter crucial spots in the tune, when the words call for more intense or subtle projection—as in the feverish rise to a higher note and a small slide downward on "joy delirious," and the ending with a languishing downward list to signal the essential melancholy of being "so in love with you."

Passionate love ("Our young romance is so intense, we're close to imbecility") is also the subject of "Two Sleepy People"[67] (1938), lyric by Frank Loesser, music by Hoagy Carmichael. They are so in love they just sit late into the night holding hands and reluctant to say goodnight. Even marriage has not altered the situation; they still are the same two sleepy people, who in "dawn's early light" are "too much in love to say goodnight." Powerful emotion also invests "Come Rain or Come Shine"[68] (1946), lyric by Johnny Mercer, music by Harold Arlen. What is unusual is the pledge of eternal love and being true forever ("I'm gonna love you, like nobody's loved you, come rain or come shine"). Very few lyrics of the thirties and forties venture without hesitation to guarantee everlasting devotion.

More frequently encountered is the age-old complaint of a lover alone and missing a loved one, as in Mack Gordon and Harry Warren's "You'll Never Know" (1943)—a subject that had occurred again and again in 19th-century songs. And even more frequently encountered are the equally age-old songs about one-sided, unreciprocated love. Striking examples are Otto Harbach and Jerome Kern's "Smoke Gets in Your Eyes" (1933), Cole Porter's "I've Got You under My Skin" (1936), and Paul Webster and Duke Ellington's "I Got It Bad and That Ain't Good" (1941). In all of these songs, the melody assumes a position of greatest importance in qualifying the piece as a hit. Witness the report in the *New York Herald Tribune*, of 21 January 1934, when "Smoke Gets in Your Eyes" appeared in the musical *Roberta*, at the moment when the show was about to fail: "The latest and one of the best examples of a show profiting by a sudden outburst of public whistling, humming, and crooning of its score. It has swept the dance floors, radio studios and the clubs of the country." Countless arrangements of the music came out and were played on the radio, which the exceedingly particular Kern felt bitter about but could not financially afford to ban.[69]

Quite a few songs depart more completely from the tried-and-true formulas. In one or two extremely successful pieces, the refrain's music may be of unusual length and may break away from a standard formula, as in Porter's "Night and Day" (1932) and "Begin the Beguine" (1935), and Berlin's "Cheek to Cheek" (1935). In most divergent songs, while the general musical style may not deviate greatly from other serious-music approaches, the lyrics do. One slight departure from accepted writing methods pictures love as making the fictitious real, as in "It's Only a Paper Moon"[70] (1933), lyric by Billy Rose and E. Y. Harburg, music by Harold Arlen. The words state that paper moons, canvas skies, cardboard seas and trees, and other items of make-believe would become real "if you believed in me." The refrain melody begins on syncopation and continues to stress the normally unaccented beats, which generate a jaunty, off-kilter effect that lightens the sentiment. E. Y. Harburg explains, "The idea there was that the guy says to the girl the moon is made of paper, it's hanging over a cardboard tree, but there's a saving grace called love. Without it, life is all a honky-tonk parade. In other words, it's not make-believe as long as someone believes in it."[71] The musical in which the piece appeared, *The Great Magoo*, failed, but music lovers singled out the song and elevated it to a winning number. A second song of this type is "June in January" (1934), lyric and music by Leo Robin and Ralph Rainger, in which love changes cold winter into warm summer. The tune is smoothly agreeable, with plenty of notes in triplets, groups of three notes performed in the ordinary time of two notes, to add rhythmic variety.

Another small departure from the conventional is the song that describes the end of a love affair and a lover left all alone with his or her memories. "Thanks for the Memory"[72] (1937), lyric by Leo Robin, music by Ralph Rainger, is a remembrance of past happy days together and ends with, "Darling, how are you? And how are all the little dreams that never did come true?" The song became a Bob Hope sign-off. Another song, "They Can't Take That Away from Me" (1937), by the Gershwins, admits the loved one is gone, but the memory of the way she wears her hat, sips her tea, and gives out smiles haunt one's dreams. Fred Astaire, for whom the song was written, kept on performing it for years. A last example is Johnny Mercer and Harold Arlen's "One for My Baby, and One More for the Road" (1943), which Frank Sinatra sang to great effect, although Fred Astaire introduced it in the film *The Sky's the Limit*. The hint of flippancy in the previous two songs is absent. The vocalist is alone in a barroom very late at night and laments over the end of a brief but intense love affair. He listens to sad music from the jukebox and tells the bartender as he orders another drink, "Make it one for my baby and one more for the road."[73] He apologizes to the bartender for "bending his ear" and keeping him from closing and then cheerlessly departs into the night. The evocative music that went with the words was a favorite with the two singers and the composer. It appealed to the melancholic temperament of the war years and continued to have the power to stir the emotions in the postwar years. It has also found its way into the repertoire of other major singers, like Lena Horne and Tony Bennett.

Still another departure is the love song that turns into a troubling rumination. Walking along Al Dubin and Harry Warren's "Boulevard of Broken Dreams"[74] (1933), the vocalist contemplates a city shrouded in grief: "the street of sorrow," where "you laugh today and cry tomorrow" and "the joy that you find here you borrow" but can't keep long. In 1936 came the Berlin songs in the film *Follow the Fleet*, "including the haunting meditation disguised as a love song: 'Let's Face the Music and Dance.'"[75] The Gershwins released an especially poignant musical meditation in 1937, "A Foggy Day." Feeling blue, a stranger to London wanders through the foggy streets and finds nothing to cheer him in the gloom that permeates the town. The music suits the mood of the words, weaving an atmosphere of aloneness. Tacked on almost at the end of the song: "Suddenly, I saw you there" and it seemed that the sun was shining. Yet, the listener comes away from the song still sensing not so much the newly discovered loved one but the deep melancholy that won't let go, however much the sun is supposed to shine at the end.

A 20th-century concept, which rarely appeared in earlier song but did appear with some frequency from the thirties on, was the possibility of impermanent love. In the 19th century, up to the 1890s, love in songs was usually considered everlasting and remaining at an unshakably high pitch. Over the next four decades, the likelihood of love not being eternal was raised in song. The modern viewpoint of love perhaps being a now-and-again affair strengthened in the 1930s and generated "Let's Fall in Love"[76] (1933), lyric by Ted Koehler, music by Harold Arlen. The vocalist tells us to take a chance on love, at least try it; you might like it. There is the question, "We might have been meant for each other, to be or not to be." If not meant for each other, the lyric intimates, breaking up is in order. Much of the melody in "Let's Fall in Love" flows comfortably, swinging up and down without effort and with scarcely an accidental coloring the expression. Thus, the composer wins the listener over with the simplest of means. A second instance is Cole Porter's "In the Still of the Night"[77] (1937). The protagonist passionately demands to know: "Do you love me as I love you?" He fears his dream will fade away and his vision of love may not be reciprocated but die away "in the chill, still of the night." As often is the case with Porter, the melodic phrases never return unchanged, and the first two phrases lead upward to a vehemently emotional climax to the song before the closing melodic phrase.

Unbridled passion, with or without the notion of impermanence, steered many songs from the thirties on. On the one hand, love might be portrayed as a grand, intense, overwhelming attraction; on the other, it might be portrayed as akin to an obsessive irritation, psychotic or physical, that has an obdurate staying power. Rodgers and Hart's "I Didn't Know What Time It Was"[78] (1939) talks about love as a burning illumination. It allows the singer to feel "grand to be alive . . . to be mad, to be yours alone!" The same writing team came out with "Bewitched, Bothered, and Bewildered,"[79] in 1941. Now, a persistent, tormenting, and mystifying love gives the impression of witchcraft. The singer feels vexed, perplexed, and oversexed, therefore bewitched, bothered, and bewildered. In each song Hart's lyric was in response to Rodgers's eloquent music and helped interpret it for the public. That the public bought the interpretation was made obvious by the constant demand for both songs.

Witchcraft is made more explicit in the Mercer-Arlen "That Old Black Magic"[80] (1942). Black magic has imprisoned a lover who can't stay away from his object of desire. Just hearing her name enflames him with burning passion. He goes into a spin succumbing to "that old black magic" called love. Every melodic phrase consists mostly of repeated notes that call attention to the besetting nature of the lyric.

A large dollop of poetic license is found in "This Can't Be Love,"[81] lyric by Lorenz Hart, music by Richard Rodgers. The expected agonizing over affection is nowhere to be found. "This can't be love," sings the protagonist, "because I feel so well." The lover is happy and without the desire to sigh or sorrow, without the sensation of dizzy spells or a palpitating heart.

Finally, in the Bob Russell–Duke Ellington "Do Nothin' 'Till You Hear from Me"[82] (1943), the lover worries that word may have gotten to a partner that he or she is being betrayed by secret lovemaking with another. Indeed, unfaithfulness is taking place: "True, I've been seen with someone new, but does that mean that I'm untrue?" An explanation will be forthcoming. Although another's kisses and arms are proving exciting at the moment, "do nothin' 'till you hear it from me."

Contemporary love in its many facets was examined constantly in the Swing Era—whether romantic or commonplace, playful or serious, comic or sad, hopeful or cynical, ridiculous or sensible, and ephemeral or endur-ing. The language employed was of the time, seldom formal or artificial, more often casual and familiar, and frequently slangy. Whatever the com-munication, it was conveyed vividly and pithily in the songs that achieved the highest success. The music remained of equal, if not greater, impor-tance. It was designed for dancing and was almost constantly in a duple time that incorporated slow walking or quick running steps. Of paramount importance, as always, was ready singability. Melody put across the song. It had to grab people's ears swiftly, engage feelings, and linger agreeably in memory. This, the songwriters knew and the public expected. Composer and lyricist exercised their expertise as they created. Music lovers looked forward with justification to music they could enjoy. The best songs fully reflected the craftsman's know-how and the public's expectations.

NOTES

1. Arnold Shaw, *The Jazz Age* (New York: Oxford University Press, 1987), 227.
2. David Ewen, *All the Years of American Popular Music* (Englewood Cliffs, New Jersey: Prentice-Hall, 1977), 286.
3. Edward Jablonski, *Gershwin* (Boston: Northeastern University Press, 1990), 229–30; Laurence Bergreen, *As Thousands Cheer* (New York: Penguin, 1990), 328.
4. Bergreen, *As Thousands Cheer*, 305–6.
5. Steve Chapple and Reebee Garofalo, *Rock 'n' Roll Is Here to Pay* (Chicago: Nelson-Hall, 1977), 54.
6. Ewen, *All the Years*, 287; James Lincoln Collier, *Benny Goodman and the Swing Era* (New York: Oxford University Press, 1989), 304.
7. Edward Jablonski, *Harold Arlen* (New York: Da Capo, 1986), 87, 106.
8. Isaac Goldberg, *Tin Pan Alley* (New York: Ungar, 1961), 313–14.
9. New York: Mills, c1932.
10. Richard Rodgers, *Musical Stages* (New York: Random House, 1975), 193.
11. George T. Simon, *The Big Bands* (New York: Collier Books, 1974), 31–32.
12. Richard Crawford, *America's Musical Life* (New York: Norton, 2001), 717.
13. Reprinted in Arnold Shaw, *Sinatra: Twentieth-Century Romantic* (New York: Holt, Rinehart & Winston, 1968), 48–49.
14. Pearl Bailey, *Talking to Myself* (New York: Harcourt Brace Jovanovich, 1971), 143.
15. Respectively, Max Wilk, *They're Playing Our Song* (New York: Atheneum, 1973), 97; Bailey, *Talking to Myself*, 195; Tony Bennett with Will Friedwald, *The Good Life* (New York: Pocket Books, 1998), 85.
16. Bennett, *Good Life*, 159–60.
17. One of my students, a first cousin of Frank Sinatra, wrote me an extended paper on the Sinatra family and its intimate connection with music, both in Italy and the United States. This information was incorporated into my book *A Sound of Strangers*.

18. Henry Pleasants, *The Great American Popular Singers* (New York: Simon & Schuster, 1974), 189–92.

19. Pete Hamil, *Why Sinatra Matters* (Thorndike, Maine: Thorndike Press, 1998), 111, 118.

20. New York: Edward Marks, c1941.

21. Sammy Cahn, *I Should Care* (New York: Arbor House, 1974), 44–45.

22. Ethel Waters with Charles Samuels, *His Eye Is on the Sparrow* (Garden City, New York: Doubleday, 1952), 222.

23. Edward Pessen, "The Great Songwriters of Tin Pan Alley's Golden Age," *American Music* 3 (1985): 193.

24. New York: Southern Music Pub., c1933.

25. New York: Harms, c1934.

26. New York: Movietone Music, c1934.

27. New York: Famous Music Corp., c1938.

28. New York: Select Music Publications, c1935.

29. Gary Giddens, *Bing Crosby* (Boston: Little, Brown, 2001), 374.

30. New York: Witmark Sons, c1932.

31. New York: Robbins Music, c1936.

32. New York: Chappell, c1936.

33. New York: Gershwin Publishing Corp., c1937.

34. New York: Gershwin Publishing Corp., c1946.

35. New York: Southern Music Publishing Co., c1942.

36. New York: Miller Music, c1943.

37. Dennis Livingston, "The Ditty That Became a Hitty," *Remember*, October 1995, 7.

38. New York: Shapiro, Bernstein, c1934.

39. Cahn, *I Should Care*, 63–71.

40. New York: Harms, c1937.

41. New York: Robbins Music Corp., c1958, by Edizione Curci, Milan.

42. New York: Harms, c1944.

43. Giddens, *Bing Crosby*, 472, 481–82.

44. New York: Famous Music, c1937.

45. New York: Select Music Publications, c1937.

46. New York: Gershwin Publishing Corp., c1935.

47. New York: Leo Feist, c1939.

48. New York: Williamson Music, c1945.

49. New York: Williamson Music, c1959.

50. New York: Famous Music Corp., c1961.

51. New York: Witmark & Sons, c1938.

52. New York: Paramount Pictures, c1953.

53. New York: Gershwin Publishing Corp., c1937.

54. New York: Harms, c1934.

55. New York: Harms, c1934.

56. New York: Chappell, c1938.

57. New York: Buxton Hill Music, c1948.

58. New York: Crawford, c1936.

59. New York: Harms, 1935.

60. New York: Chapell, c1938.

61. New York: Chapell, c1937.

62. Gene Lees, liner notes to *Eileen Farrell Sings Rodgers & Hart*, Reverence Records RR-32CD.

63. New York: De Sylva, Brown & Henderson, c1933.

64. New York: Remick, c1934.

65. New York: Mills Music, c1932.

66. New York: Buxton Hill Music, c1948.

67. New York: Famous Music Corp., c1938.

68. New York: A-M Music, c1946.

69. Gerald Bordman, *Jerome Kern* (New York: Oxford University Press, 1980), 341–42. See also Dwight Blocker Bowers, *American Musical Theater* (Washington, D.C.: Smithsonian Collection of Records, 1989), 31.

70. New York: Harms, c1933.

71. Wilk, *They're Playing Our Song*, 222.

72. New York: Paramount Music, c1937.

73. New York: Harwin Music, c1943.

74. New York: Remick, c1933.

75. Bergreen, *As Thousands Cheer*, 356.

76. New York: Bourne, c1933.

77. New York: Chappell, c1937.

78. New York: Chappell, c1939.

79. New York: Chappell, c1941.

80. New York: Famous Music Corp., c1942.

81. New York: Chappell, c1938.

82. New York: Robbins Music, c1943.

Chapter Four

Change: Different Music Cultures Come to the Fore

The extolling of noble principles, warlike phrases and mottoes, and expressions of moral righteousness that had fired the patriotic songs of previous wars were difficult to come upon in the songs that were issued during World War II and, for that matter, during any of the more limited wars that came after.[1] War had become too cruel an affair and unacceptable a solution for problems to romanticize over. The innocence with which we had entered wars prior to World War II had faded away. Songwriters during World War II continued to plow mostly the fields already cultivated. They sensed that scarcely any new songs that pictured the war effort as a pursuit of noble principles and goals were making a strong impression on the public. "Praise the Lord and Pass the Ammunition!" (1942), by Frank Loesser, cannot stand comparison with Billings's "Chester," of the Revolutionary War, Francis Scott Key's "The Star-Spangled Banner," of the War of 1812, Julia Ward Howe's "The Battle Hymn of the Republic," of the American Civil War, or George M. Cohan's "Over There," of World War I. Attitudes were changing; a ceaseless and more widespread questioning of things as they were was becoming apparent. The conflict between nations prefigured the conflicts within America between cultures, races, ethnic groups, young and old, and social and economic classes. Popular song had to muddle its way through this dissension.

During the war, swing bands found their members drafted into the armed forces and their freedom to travel curtailed. Then, beginning in August 1942, a series of crippling strikes, called by James Petrillo and the American Federation of Musicians, prevented bands from making records and being heard over the radio, and, later, over television. In addition, the

American Society of Composers, Authors, and Publishers was putting ob-
stacles in the way of freely using songs from popular-music publishers and
from Broadway and Hollywood musicals. One consequential result would
be the shift of focus from ASCAP, which had ignored music styles that
seemed of lesser importance and status, to Broadcast Music, Inc. The latter signed up nonunion musicians—white country and western, black
rhythm and blues, and nouveau-folk—whose songs were published and
who were given airtime. Another result would be the rise of record companies outside of New York, especially in Chicago, Memphis, and
Nashville, that would record these singers and instrumentalists, and the increase in radio stations whose disc jockeys would publicize these recordings by giving them frequent performances. These radio stations could operate with a miniscule workforce and moderate expense. Each would
eventually focus on one or two facets of popular culture—black blues,
gospel, and rhythm and blues, or white folk, country and western, rockabilly, or old-time pop. When a listener tuned in on a station he pretty well
knew what he would find.[2]

Independent record companies increased their output of music that the
major labels had neglected, around 1947. Atlantic Records emerged under
the direction of Ahmet Ertegun, son of the former Turkish ambassador and
a lover of jazz and blues. Ertegun commenced signing up new performers,
most of them African-Americans, like the Drifters, the Coasters, Ray
Charles, Joe Turner, Laverne Baker, and Clyde McPhatter. The astute talent scout Jerry Wexler joined Ahmet Ertegun in 1953, along with Ahmet's
brother, Nesuhi, and also a noteworthy songwriting-production team, Jerry
Leiber and Mike Stoller. Atlantic was soon also distributing the Memphis
label Stax, which had recruited the black soul singer Otis Redding.
Leonard Chess's Chess Records was born in Chicago, in 1949, and promoted the blues performances of Muddy Waters, Howlin' Wolf, John Lee
Hooker, and others. Additional small record companies started to put out
doo-wop (VeeJay, Doone, and Cameo) and country and western (King).
Not least was Sam Phillips's highly influential Sun Records, of Memphis,
which had its inception in 1953 and was instrumental in bringing a host of
rockabilly stars to the public, Elvis Presley in particular.

As some of this fresh talent caught and held the attention of a sizable
segment of the public, the major record labels stepped in. First, they began
to produce tamer white "cover versions" for compositions introduced by
African-Americans and white Southerners that had established their popularity on a smaller label. As Tony Bennett explained: "What usually hap-

pened was that a smaller label would have a hit, like Francis Craig doing 'Near You,' with a little outfit called Bullet Records. When it started selling, RCA got into the act and 'covered' it with RCA's own instrumental version by staff arranger Larry Green. Sometimes white artists 'covered' black artists, or mainstream artists 'covered' country artists. Normally, the big label's profits would leave the independent label in the dust, so that majors were always on the lookout for successful independent tunes that one of their artists could cover."[3] First, the large record outfits "cleaned up" these songs for white consumption, with anything in the lyrics that might offend eliminated. Second, they elevated young, handsome white kids as pop idols. Third, they offered sizable amounts of money to buy the contracts and switch the most successful of the new stars to their labels.[4]

THE GENERATIONAL COLD WAR

World War II ended and the Cold War, a contest between the United States and the communist countries, started. The struggle stopped usually just short of violence but on two occasions erupted into war, in Korea and in Vietnam. The Korean War went on from 1950 to 1953 and fueled a blaze of superpatriotism and a refusal to tolerate criticism of government actions. In February 1950, McCarthyism was inflicted on the United States and with it the practice of making accusations of disloyalty, especially of pro-communist activity, which were usually unsupported by honest proof. It gave birth to suspicion, fear, and hatred of citizen against citizen. Conformity to a reactionary definition of America was exacted and the repression of liberal thought was sought. Although McCarthy would be censured in 1954, his activities would severely damage the political and social fabric of America, help seed the conflict between ultraconservatives and people with progressive principles, and highlight the differences between status-quo songs and emergent protest songs. In 1954, too, the Supreme Court ordered the desegregation of schools. Black marches and boycotts to desegregate schools, dining places, and public transportation were set in motion. Three years later, the Civil Rights Act came into force, and federal troops were sent to integrate the high school of Little Rock. Songs by African-Americans would soon highlight the transformations in mind-set that took place owing to these events. Sputnik was launched in 1957, inaugurating the space race and boosting the threat of nuclear war. Compositions by Bob Dylan and others would underscore the threat to humanity.

In short, the 1950s was a perpetually agitated decade that generated an unquiet mood in men and women and gradually produced music commensurate with the tribulations besetting society.

A younger generation was growing up with unrest surrounding it. Some seventy-six million "baby boomers" had arrived on the American scene by 1965. Finding no normalcy in these years of constant turmoil, they started to believe that adults had botched up their world thoroughly. They could not help but question the norms of behavior dictated by the same adults. It follows that among them were those who did not want to think, act, or behave like oldsters. Nor did they want the sort of song that pleased grownups.

Adults, in turn, were swamped with books of explanation and advice meant to ease the problems with children and modern living. All the books testified to the disturbances buried in people's minds. Dr. Benjamin Spock, in *Baby and Child Care* (1946), gave instructions on child rearing and put his accent on social adaptation. Perhaps naively, he trusted in the disapproval of youngsters of similar age to maintain discipline. (An unforeseen outcome was a possible abetting of adolescent rebellion in the future.) David Riesman's *The Lonely Crowd* (1950) spoke of adults shifting from inner- to other-directed society. To him, anxiety resulted from failure to fit in. (However, quite a few of those who did fit in still felt an emptiness for which they could not account.) David Potter, in *People of Plenty* (1954), spread some Pollyanna notions about ours being the land of plenty, where poverty had almost disappeared. (He somehow overlooked the millions living below the poverty level.) William Whyte's *The Organization Man* (1956) insisted that the individual needed to feel wanted by, or become an essential part of, a social group or a business. He understood adult conformity to be one end result. (But he dwelt less on the large psychological penalty attached to conformity.)[5] None of these books really helped adults and children identify with each other. Few adult publications captured and understood the discontent gathering force in youngsters.

After World War II, urban families had grown less stable. Businesses shifted employees from place to place without hesitation. The lot of numerous breadwinners was a constant moving about from state to state. Suburban society burgeoned as families sought "the good life." So also did the number of shopping centers and cars on the road. The values that had cemented traditional marriages of the past were having less sway. Divorces multiplied. Increasing numbers of marriages remained childless. Alfred Kinsey published *Sexual Behavior in the Human Male* in 1948 and *Sexual Behavior in the Human Female* in 1953. The books recognized a change in sexual mores and noted a profusion of out-of-wedlock sexual activity in postwar America. They defined sex as a biological need and suggested the necessity for a more progressive way of looking at sexuality. It was a way of looking that would find its way into adolescent behavior and into song lyrics.

Jacques Barzun, in *From Dawn to Decadence*, commented on the postwar period, saying that while the traditional family had not disappeared, numerous variations on it were becoming equally traditional—families where husband and wife both worked, families headed by a single parent, second marriages with a pooling of children from previous marriages, families where grandparents raised the children, unmarried relationships that produced children, and homosexual relationships with no or with adopted children. Children were farmed out to day-care centers and nannies hired by the day. Older latchkey youngsters went from school to empty homes. "Adapting schedules, abilities, and emotions to rearing children and furnishing the help requested by the school was a dismaying task, even when the hindrances of poverty and lack of literacy in the common tongue were not present. The upshot was that an increasing number of children found at home no encouragement to schooling, no instruction in simple manners, and no inkling of the moral sense. Some of the waifs bred in that way were those who took to drugs, became thieves before their teens and committed the conscienceless crimes falsely called mindless. They formed gangs, boys and girls together, with able leaders and strict rules."[6]

To more than a few young people, adults seemed overly preoccupied with the pursuit of material rather than spiritual things. Parents were accused of not pausing to try and understand their children. Often left to their own devices, boys and girls remained unencumbered with responsibilities. They found themselves at loose ends. If from the middle class, they received liberal allowances from their parents, but no guidelines on how to spend the money. Some of these adolescents felt out of harmony with their surroundings and a part of nothing. Before long, young people wanted to give their existence meaning. They looked for something that would fill the spiritual emptiness in their lives. Social causes, Asian gurus, and communal living would become three of those "somethings." So also would drugs, uninhibited sexual activity, and a passionate devotion to youthful singers. If from the lower economic class, they felt resentment because they did not share in the postwar affluence. If African-Americans, they felt roiling anger over discrimination, living conditions, and denial of economic opportunity.

Some novel messages, responding to the insalubrities of the times, were being sent to young people. They read about generational disagreement and the falsities of grownups in J. D. Salinger's *Catcher in the Rye* (1951). The *Mad* comics, of 1952, became *Mad* magazine, in 1955. In December of 1955 its cover sported the smirking face of "Alfred E. Newman," whose "What, me worry?" mocked America's leaders and became a slogan for youth. The pages of the magazine assaulted time-honored standards and suggested several forms of mayhem as replacements. The film *The Wild One* (1954) had Brando's motorcycle gang scorning the accepted wisdom about propriety and goodness. Another film, *Rebel without a Cause* (1956), made James Dean the butt of unfeeling parents, alias "the bad guys." Jack Kerouac's *On the Road* (1957) described the restlessness and bewilderment of young people. It also poured scorn on the usual modes of living and behaving. The conventional "square" was a creature for contempt. For some it was better to resemble the tramps, ruffians, drug addicts, and poor blacks. The 1950s were the beginning of a host of writings and filmings of what was depicted as the problems of society. They pointed out how muddled the human race was, and how suspicious were the motives that were behind human actions, however seemingly benevolent. Art and literature began celebrating the antihero, a nobody denied nobility of mind and spirit.

At the same time, recordings, radio, television, movies, and magazines were proposing alternatives to what adolescents had grown up with. One dominant idea was the adoption of the tastes and attitudes current among the poor and uneducated. "Lowbrow" dress, language, mannerisms, art, and music appeared to explore a new, more "honest" reality. Downward mobility could be a means of discovering life that was "genuine" and a way of smashing middle-class inflexibility and self-satisfaction.[7] Hence the increased valuation of folk song, country music, and African-American blues.

Without doubt conscientious parents concerned over the well-being of their children continued to head countless families. They tried to offer anchors to their young and prove a reliable source of support, stability, and security. By the same token, countless teenagers had a regard for their fathers and mothers and felt little desire to revolt or to discard handed-down beliefs. However, the discontented segments of youthful society would be painted large by the media, officialdom, and communal leaders. As a result, the nonconformists in the peer group would have a force greater than their actual numbers might have warranted. The young people on the sidelines could not help but take notice of and be influenced by the rebels.

For a while most youths remained conservative in their values and showed no interest in politics. At the same time, a distinct youth culture was emerging that diverged from that of adults. It was generating new idols, fads, and standards all over the country. Advertisers sensed money to be made from it, as did filmmakers and television programmers. They elevated new champions, celebrated new styles of dress, and aided in re-fashioning the new yardsticks for living. In order to enhance their influence, they also joined the progressive educators who considered teenagers a distinctive group deserving the liberty to realize their own characters and gifts. Boys and girls commenced trimming down what they habitually wore so as to appear disheveled, or carelessly dressed. Tattered, dirty, and uncoordinated clothing was meant to proclaim that the person's sympathy was with the great unwashed and that he or she took no pride in his or her appearance. Whether one went as a "beatnik" or an aggressive militant, differences in dress and hairstyle expressed his or her political feelings. Although some were sincere in what they were trying to express, others were only seeking light amusement. Some were outraged at the hypocrisy and narrow-mindedness they saw; many were possibly trying to get away from their isolated and tedious way of life by joining others in activities that afforded entertainment.

It was not long before all of these young Americans would be sponsoring a form of expression perfectly suited to their moods—rock 'n' roll music. It was rhythmic popular music distinguished by its prominent and relentless beat, atypical instrumentation, and greater variety in vocalization. It could sound tense or unworried, probing or happy-go-lucky. The Swing Era popular-music style now had to cope with an overwhelming infusion of African-American gospel and rhythm and blues, and of rural Southern white folk, gospel, and country and western music.

GETTING MUSIC TO YOUNG PEOPLE

Some things would not change until the midsixties. Among them were the contributions of songwriters not always involved with performance. Many of these writers worked in New York's Brill Building. The Brill Building, at 1619 Broadway, was at the center of New York's music quarter. It was once the location of the Brill Brothers clothing store, but in 1931, the Great Depression compelled the property owners to rent space to music publishers. Before long, Southern Music, Mills Music, and Famous Music

moved in. By the 1960s, the Brill Building was housing over 150 companies, including song-writing teams. Without leaving the building, one
could write a song and find a publisher to buy it. Also in the building were
music arrangers, recording studios with instrumentalists and singers ready
to record the piece, and hawkers available to promote the recording. The
Brill Building approach to writing songs, which involved the division between the songwriter and the performer, peaked in the sixties. Its songwriters supplied material to singers of country and western, rhythm and
blues, rock 'n' roll, and regular pop. The team of Jerry Lieber and Mike
Stoller wrote "Hound Dog" for Willie Mae "Big Mama" Thornton, in
1953. The Coasters made hits of Lieber and Stoller's "Searchin'" (1957),
"Yakety Yak" (1958), "Along Came Jones" (1959), and "Charley Brown"
(1959). These and other important songs, like "Spanish Harlem" (1960),
were recorded by over 125 singers, including Elvis Presley, Andrew
Williams, Aretha Franklin, and Sonny and Cher. An extraordinary success
came in 1966, when Peggy Lee recorded a widely praised performance of
the song "Is That All There Is?"[8] Quite a few of Lieber and Stoller's songs
effected a fusion of black rhythm-and-blues and country music, popularized through white entrepreneurial activity.

In the same building were Doc Primus and Mort Shuman. Primus had
sung the blues; Shuman was a lover of rhythm and blues. Presley recorded
more than twenty of their songs. The Drifters made a national impression
with their "Save the Last Dance for Me." The two men parted in 1965.
Shuman went to Paris, where he wrote, produced, and appeared in *Jacques
Brel Is Alive and Well and Living in Paris*. In the building, too, was Burt
Bachrach working with the lyricist Hal David and later with Carole Sager.
Bachrach would write for the Drifters, Dionne Warwick, Neil Diamond,
Patti Labelle, and several well-received films (*What's New, Pussycat*,
Casino Royal, and *Butch Cassidy and the Sundance Kid*). Warwick's
"That's What Friends Are For" was a well-received number. Many songs,
such as "Do You Know the Way to San Jose?" "Raindrops Keep Fallin' on
My Head," and "What the World Needs Now," have become part of the
American repertoire. Neil Sedaka and Howard Greenfield, Carole King
and Gerry Griffin, Jeff Barry and Ellie Greenwich, and Barry Mann and
Cynthia Wells were other highly thought-of creators of songs.

The Brill Building influence would die with the arrival of the British rock
groups and the increase in the number of singer–songwriters, "who would
put a premium on self-expression, making it unfashionable as well as un-
profitable to sing other people's songs."[9] A transitional figure in the change

was Paul Anka, a singer–songwriter who wrote many extremely successful songs for himself ("Diana," "You Are My Destiny," "Lonely Boy," and "Put Your Head on My Shoulder") and others ("It Doesn't Matter Anymore," sung by Buddy Holly, "Puppy Love," sung by Donny Osmond, "My Way," sung by Sinatra, and "She's a Lady," sung by Tom Jones).

Another sort of songwriter was attached to the smaller independent record companies. For example, Willie Dixon, born in Vicksburg, Mississippi, was an important factor in carrying blues forward to rock 'n' roll. He played the bass and worked at Chicago's Chess Records as songwriter, arranger, and producer adapting the country blues for rhythm and blues and for rock 'n' roll. (Country blues is a general designation meant to describe the widespread early appearance of guitar-powered blues. It was presented by black soloists, duos, and small string performers in a variety of regional styles.) Benefiting from his around 500 songs and guidance were Muddy Waters, Chuck Berry, Bo Diddley, and Little Walter. For Waters, he wrote "I'm Your Hoochie Coochie Man"; for Diddley, "Pretty Thing"; for Walter, "My Babe." All three pieces attained renown. In the sixties, his songs were covered by many rock groups, among them the Rolling Stones, the Doors, Cream, and Led Zeppelin.[10]

By the end of the 1960s, independent producers were producing most recordings for record companies. They sought to discover and develop music groups and oversee the entire production of records, technical and otherwise. Prominent among them were Norman Petty, a producer for Buddy Holly; Jerry Lieber and Mike Stoller, already cited as songwriters of hits like "Hound Dog," who worked with Elvis Presley, the Coasters, and the Dusters; and Phil Spector, also a songwriter and a developer of the "Wall of Sound" by means of overdubbing numerous instruments onto a basic singing track. Spector worked for a time with the Teddy Bears, Ike and Tina Turner, the Beatles, and the Ronettes, producing through them what he called "little symphonies for the kiddies."[11]

Technical innovation played an important part in the way music got to and was heard by the youthful public. The widespread use of electric guitars started in the late 1940s. Engineers had been experimenting with electric instruments in the 1800s, especially in music boxes and pianos. In the 1920s, electrical amplification advanced with the growth of radio. Lloyd Loar, at Gibson Guitar, developed a type of electric pickup for the soundboard of a viola and string bass, which sent the sound signals to an amplifier. However, the signals remained comparatively weak. Then around 1931, George Beauchamp, with Adolph Rickenbacker, originated an electromagnetic pickup, which picked up from the strings for the first commercially feasible product, called the Frying Pan. It was played flat on the lap. Rickenbacker would also come out with an Electro Spanish model. The Gibson company was promoting the electric guitar throughout the thirties and forties. Its Spanish-type electric instrument, the ES150, had a special pickup designed by Walt Fuller that was made well known through the playing of Charlie Christian, who would be a featured guitarist with the Benny Goodman band. Other early performers on the electric guitar were the country and western musicians Bob Dunn[12] and Merle Travis, and Eddie Durham of the Jimmie Lunceford band. The next important developments occurred in the late forties, when various designers (among them Paul Bigsby, Leo Fender, and George Fullerton) worked to develop a solid-body electric guitar.

An important step was taken when the guitarist Les Paul developed a pickup mounted on a solid body of wood; Gibson, in 1952, introduced its Les Paul model (Bruce Springsteen has played on one of these). In the 1950s, too, Leo Fender was offering a mass-produced solid-body electric guitar for sale, the Fender Broadcaster, renamed the Telecaster. Within a year Fender was also offering an electric "Precision Bass." The most successful guitar model came out in 1954, the Fender Stratocaster, which was played on by prominent musicians like Buddy Holly, Jimi Hendrix, Eric Clapton, and Bonnie Raitt.

The sound of drumming changed when, in 1957, Remo Belli began delivering plastic drum skins to drum makers. Rock bands would take to these innovations, their ensembles usually including an electric bassist, a completely outfitted percussionist, an optional keyboard player, and two electric guitarists—rhythm and lead. Added to these changes were the improvements in electronic equipment—tape machines, synthesizers, computers, digital sound, and large-capacity amplifiers and sound systems. It allowed rock musicians to produce recordings by multitracking (recording separate audio tracks for later mixing into a single audio track), overdubbing (transferring previously recorded sound onto a music track in order to produce a combined effect), manipulating and distorting sound at will, and creating a variety of novel soundscapes.

The medium used for delivering recorded music to the public also changed. For years record platters were limited to the 78-rpm format. The 10-inch disc, lasting about 3 minutes a side, was employed mostly for popular music, and the 12-inch disc, lasting around 5–6 minutes a side, for classical music. Then, in 1948, Columbia came out with the 12-inch 33⅓-

rpm LP, capable of playing around 25 minutes a side and with much greater fidelity than heretofore; and RCA, with the 7-inch 45-rpm disc with not nearly as much time on each side as the Columbia competitor. However, the latter became the favorite delivery vehicle for single popular songs. It, too, provided better sound than the previous 78s, as well as being smaller, lighter, and more durable. The reign of the 78-rpm disc was over. In the early 1980s, Phillips and Sony introduced the compact disc, whose fidelity surpassed by far that of the LP. It also could provide around 70 minutes of playing time. The LP, too, was soon a thing of the past. Becoming popular later would be the video cassette and DVD (digital versatile disc).

Improvements in playing equipment also continued, with less and less distortion in home amplifiers and speakers. By 1958, stereo recording and playback was offered. In 1962, the cassette tape was introduced and with it came the likelihood of home taping and the rise of musical piracy. Sony came out with the Walkman, in 1979, a light, compact battery-operated device for playing cassettes and listening to radio broadcasts by means of earphones, while walking or running. From then on, music could be listened to anywhere and at any time.

The movie musicals that were turned out from the fifties on featured the new music and brought it to an international audience. *Blackboard Jungle* (1955) made Bill Haley's band, the song "Rock around the Clock," and the new rock 'n' roll idiom celebrated. Elvis Presley's singing was featured in several movies. Bob Dylan's 1965 concert tour was released as a documentary, *Don't Look Back*, in 1967. Two famous documentaries, *Monterey Pop* and *Woodstock*, followed two years and three years later, respectively. The overwhelming popularity of *Saturday Night Fever*, with the disco music of the Bee Gees and the dancing of John Travolta, commenced in 1977. Country music held sway in *Coal Miner's Daughter* (1980), on the singer Loretta Lynn's life.

Of supreme importance to the new popular music was the advent of television, where the public could both hear and see the performers. The first experimental station, WGY of Schenectady, was born in 1928, but it was not until 1941 that the first commercial stations were licensed, WNBT of NBC and WCBW of CBS. Throughout the forties and fifties a steady growth in the number of television stations took place, so that by the first years of the seventies around 750 stations were broadcasting over the air and 70 million sets were located in American homes. The ascendance of television forced radio to abandon most programming and stay with news, talk shows, and recorded music presented by disc jockeys. Around the mid-1950s, Chuck Bore, working for Todd Storz and Gordon McLendon at different times, generated the "Top 40 Radio" format for their stations, and the concept would quickly spread. One unfortunate consequence would be a narrowing in the range of music offerings.[13] Variety shows and other theatrical entertainments featuring dancing and singing went to television stations. As a sign of the times, in 1950, *Your Hit Parade* abandoned radio for television. As for up-and-coming popular music, *Dick Clark's American Bandstand*, out of Philadelphia, could be viewed on almost 70 TV stations in 1957, with its teenagers dancing to records and the appearance of guest stars, among them James Brown, Bill Haley, Jerry Lee Lewis, and the Everly Brothers. Clark would also bring forward and make well known a number of young singers who were personable but, in some cases, not overly talented—three of them being Fabian, Frankie Avalon, and Bobby Rydell. Lip synchronization, the coordinating of a vocalist's lip movement with singing on a recorded song, came into use on the program. Two of the most popular variety-type shows with music that competed with each other for first place in the ratings, from 1956 to 1960, were the *Steve Allen Show* and the *Ed Sullivan Show*. Sullivan would continue on TV until 1971, presenting such luminaries as Elvis Presley and the Beatles.

AFRICAN-AMERICAN MUSIC

Racial discrimination was rampant throughout the first two-thirds of the century. One recalls how the Daughters of the American Revolution barred the great African-American contralto Marian Anderson from singing at their Constitution Hall, in Washington, in 1939, because of her race. She was vindicated when Eleanor Roosevelt sponsored Anderson's memorable performance on the steps of the Lincoln Memorial on Easter Sunday, before a vast gathering of 75,000 people. The greatest popular black stars who appeared before huge white audiences also met with humiliating treatment from a racist white society. Writing about Nat "King" Cole in the fifties and sixties, James Haskins says the public bought millions of recorded copies of his music and young women passed out when he sang, yet there was no certainty that he could find a night's lodging in a fine hotel. "They loved him in Vegas, on the stage, but they didn't like his musicians gambling in the casinos or his daughters eating in the dining room.

When he played in the South, he usually had to play before segregated audiences, and when he bowed to Southern customs, the National Association for the Advancement of Colored People (NAACP) called him an Uncle Tom. At the same time, fear of Southern opinion kept Madison Avenue advertisers from sponsoring a Nat King Cole television show."[14] It was a long uphill struggle for black popular musicians to gain acceptance as humans off the stage and for black popular music to be seen as worthy of attention in the white world. The way to this acceptance and attention was paved politically by the civil-rights movement and musically by the early inroads made by jazz and swing bands and by the gradual acceptance of gospel songs and rhythm and blues.

For a long while, white Americans who heard black song were disconcerted by its blast of emotion. They had trouble assimilating its rhythmic independence and high energy, and its reality-oriented lyrics. They expected something nice sounding and engaging; instead they got visceral emotion. The black audience did not concur with the white one. Bumps Blackwell, director of Specialty Records, said of black tastes in the fifties, "There was a definite trend toward a more basic and simple music in which feeling was the most important thing. A singer could make a hit recording if he sang with a lot of feeling, regardless of how imperfect everything else might be" and if he gave his music the "rhythm that the people loved and danced to and were buying. People were buying feel, and if you check every one of my hit records that's what they have."[15] It was not until the sixties that young whites in large numbers started to absorb the black point of view.

At the same time that rock music gained young adherents during the 1950s, the gospel songs and blues of African-Americans inched into the consciousness of white Americans and assumed noticeable positions in popular music, from which they have never retreated. An 18th-century thinker, Giambattista Vico, has identified three eternal and universal customs shared by all people, which involve elaborate ceremonies and solemnity—the rites of religion, marriage, and burial.[16] With all three, gospel songs (songs of celebration and commemoration) are involved. The music grew out of traditional spirituals and the practices of Southern church choirs. This music of the black Protestant churches (especially Pentecostal and Baptist) resonates with communicative power and a ringing quality within a declamatory or theatrical style. It is an emotional religious observance celebrated by soloist or chorus, or both. Melody is uncomplicated, often festooned with blue notes and portamento vocal glides, and may require an extensive vocal range. A pronounced rhythmic pulse is invariably present.

Gospel kept alive a spirit of community that resonates throughout much of the music of the rhythm-and-blues musicians. It testified to the mental and emotional disturbances that black Americans had experienced, conveying truths of deep meaning to them. Craig Werner states, "The gospel singer testifies to the burden and the power of the spirit in moans or screams or harmonies so sweet they can make you cry. The testimony touches what we share and what we deal with when we're on our own in that dark night of the soul." Evil invests the world and the Devil inspires much of it, whether it's sex, money, or hypocrisy, and the blues informs us of the evil. Gospel, says Werner, goes beyond that and stresses the reality of redemption. "If the blues give you the strength to face [another day] on your own, gospel promises or at least holds out the possibility that tomorrow may be different, better. With the help of the spirit and your people—in the church or on the dance floor you can get over"[17] what is troubling you.

Thomas A. Dorsey, songwriter, singer, and pianist, is known as the "Father of Gospel." His father was a revivalist preacher in Georgia. Young Thomas grew up with the sound of spirituals and blues in his ears and worked in the secular-music field during the 1920s. Beginning in 1929, he started to underpin religious lyrics with music influenced by spirituals, jazz, blues, and the popular music of the time, calling them "gospel songs." They quickly caught on in black church worship. "Precious Lord, Take My Hand" (1932) and "There'll Be Peace in the Valley for Me" (1939) are two of the best known of these Dorsey compositions. Both have been favorites in white country-music circles also. The latter work conveys the message of a person weary of life who must toil on until the Lord takes him away. In death he will leave behind grief, misery, and all of his troubles and find peace at last.[18]

The music, in triple time, moves sluggishly, as if indisposed to action. Harmony changes slowly, mostly once a measure, thus adding to the static quality. The melody remains within a comfortable singing range and balances every upward movement with a corresponding downward one. A quiet rapture envelops the opening of the refrain, on the words "There'll be Peace in the Valley for me some day," as the voice glides upward to its highest point. Otherwise, the song flows in tranquil channels.

Other black songwriters (Charles Tindley, Lucie Campbell, and W. Herbert Brewster) also mined the idiom. Outstanding singers like Mahalia Jackson, James Cleveland, and the Soul Stirrers championed gospel and made the world aware of it. Jackson's recording of Brewster's "Move On Up a Little Higher" sold over a million copies.

At first piano or percussion, or both, accompanied the singing. Electric guitars, string basses, and organs began appearing in the 1950s. Gradually, after World War II, gospel took on an increasingly overwrought, rough-textured, and ardent sound. At one moment the singer might wail; at another, hum, scream, roar, or slide into falsetto. Gospel singers, in addition to their church duties, began to appear in coffeehouses, festivals, night-clubs, theaters, and television shows and gained thousands of white devotees. In many instances these singers were trying to raise money for their church. Some, who may once have been church involved, branched out independently and turned commercial. Many a noted black pop singer had his or her start in gospel—three of them being among the first leaders of "soul" and "funk," Sam Cooke, James Brown, and Aretha Franklin. Gospel would have a significant input into the new popular styles that emerged in the fifties and sixties.

The secular counterpart of gospel in the early postwar years was rhythm and blues, which left a distinctive imprint on the history of black music from the end of the 1940s to around 1965. Because aimed at dancers, it laid emphasis on clearly accented beats and telling rhythms. Loud sound volumes prevailed. The intelligibility of the singer's words was frequently of lesser importance. Its duple-time songs grafted black-oriented lyrics and the blues structure onto the swinging beats of jazz and ornamentation similar to that of gospel song. Rhythm and blues could not help sometimes sounding similar to gospel since both shared parallel musical antecedents. It would also entertain influences from countries south of the United States—the samba of Brazil, the méringue (meringue) of Haiti and the Dominican Republic, the salsa of Puerto Rico, the mambo of Cuba, and the calypso style of Trinidad and Jamaica, which Harry Belafonte represented in lilting hits like the "Banana Boat Song" (1957). During the fifties rhythm and blues would bond with country and western music to produce rock 'n' roll. In the sixties, rhythm and blues would acquire an alternate name, soul.

However, at first there was just the blues, secular song popular with American blacks and first commercially recorded in the 1920s. Whether heard as a slow lament or a strident dance song it was meant to purge the singer of sadness. Country blues (Delta, Texas, and Piedmont) traveled with black migrants to cities like Chicago and Memphis and could not help but experience the influences of popular music and jazz. In the 1930s, accompaniment on guitar or piano alternated with that of small ensembles—guitar, piano, percussion, and sometimes harmonica. Influential practitioners like Big Bill Broonzy, Tampa Red, Memphis Minnie, and Little Brother Montgomery led the way.

After World War II, electrified instruments came into use, especially in Chicago, where Muddy Waters, B. B. King, T-Bone Walker, Howlin' Wolf, and Elmore James were active. Howlin' Wolf was one of the first Chicago bluesmen to employ instruments hitched to an amplifier and to develop a style that rhythm and blues ensembles would reproduce far and wide. About his influential colleague, Muddy Waters, the bass player, songwriter, and arranger Willie Dixon said, "There was quite a few people around singing all sad blues. Muddy [Waters] was giving his blues a little pep"—sounding like early representations of rhythm and blues.[19] Waters's impact would spread widely after he recorded for Chess Records such "race" hits as "I Can't Be Satisfied," "Feel Like Going Home," and "Rolling Stone." His was a rasping, citified, electric style deriving from Delta blues in pieces like "Got My Mojo Working," "I Just Wanna Make Love to You," and "Hoochie Coochie Man." Although Waters was a fine song creator in his own right, Willie Dixon had penned the last two songs. Waters and Dixon are credited with feeding many song hits to the Chicago bluesmen and with helping create a sound that gave a fresh, up-to-date twist to the blues. Sometimes this development allowed more than a little deviation from the blues, as in the last named song, recorded in 1952, which relies on a recurring three-chord foundation.

The Chicago blues of Waters, Wolf, and Dixon had a great deal of meaning for a younger generation of black urban Americans, capturing as it did the shrill feverish life of the city streets that they knew rather than the rural Delta from which the genre had originated. Besides, its eminently danceable beat pleased their black public mightily. White fans were also sampling this advanced blues sound, which was one reason why *Billboard* abandoned the "race" designation in its charts, substituting the label "rhythm and blues," in 1949. The citified blues would become, part and parcel, a component of rhythm and blues and early rock 'n' roll. Another highly talented bluesman, B. B. King, migrated to Los Angeles, where he recorded for Modern Records and racked up around twenty rhythm and blues hits in the fifties. He would later tour with an English rock group, the Rolling Stones.

When we listen to "Love Me Baby," which Big Bill Broonzy recorded in 1942, we can already hear the changeover from country blues—in the attention given to rhythm, the constantly recurring melodic fragment (known as a riff) coming from Broonzy's guitar, and in the addition of a fourth musical phrase to the traditional three of the blues.

Also important to the growth of rhythm and blues and rock 'n' roll were the "jump blues" performed by swing bands like those of Count Basie ("One O'clock Jump" and "Jumpin' at the Woodside"), Cab Calloway ("Jumpin' Jive"), Lionel Hampton ("Flying Home"), and others. The jump blues is a blues style typified by a swinging saxophone sound (or by other "horn" instruments), strong rhythms, and shouted vocals. Unusual for the blues, the jump blues does not give the guitar melodic prominence but consigns it to the rhythm section. Blues shouters delivered the vocals for these ensembles. The well-known "Mr. Five by Five," Jimmy Rushing, was the voice of Kansas City's Count Basie band from 1935 until 1950. His shouting vocal delivery had a harsh, grating sound that suited Basie's riffing "jump" style. When he sang a blues, like "I'm Gonna Move to the Outskirts of Town," Rushing elicited a typically seriocomic mood as he racketed away about a potentially unfaithful wife and moving out of the city to insure that their baby looked like him and not the milkman.[20]

However, the "jump" musician with the most direct connection with rhythm and blues and rock 'n' roll was Louis Jordan, who had around 50 rhythm and blues hits and twenty early rock 'n' roll hits—among them, "Caldonia," "Let the Good Times Roll," "Choo Choo Ch' Boogie," and "Saturday Night Fish Fry." Jordan's jumping music (its song structures and lyrics deriving from the blues) and his vocalizing bridged the gap between the swing band jump style, through rhythm and blues, to the rock 'n' roll of Chuck Berry and Little Richard. He and his band, the Tympany Five, advanced a shuffle beat (a rhythm where the main beat or a two-beat pattern divides into three smaller beats), the riff-filled arrangement, the unique electric-guitar playing of Carl Hagan, and the showy, uninhibited onstage personality of Jordan himself—all of which succeeded with black and white audiences. James Brown, the father of funk, when asked if Jordan was an influence, replied, "He was *everything*."[21] Jordan had colleagues who also were developing this distinct musical language—Big Joe Turner, Wynonie Harris, Floyd Dixon, Charles Brown, and Jimmy and Joe Liggins.

Feeding into the novel sound of the fifties was "doo-wop," music by mostly black male vocal groups harmonizing with a tenor lead on the song, and an accompaniment by three or four voices using nonsensical "doo-wop" syllables. Harmonies were close and sweet, and the bass was given more prominence than just as background. Characteristic of doo-wop, harmonies were produced by blowing air out of the mouth ("blow harmonies"). The major part of the repertoire was love ballads kept mostly clean of suggestive allusions. Doo-wop stemmed from a long tradition, going back to time-honored "barbershop" singing, and 1930s and 1940s black groups like the Mills Brothers, the Ink Spots, and the Orioles. Doo-wop had begun as an urban sound first fostered by moonstruck black teenagers on street corners of Northern cities. The sound caught on in the fifties. Several suave groups named after birds (Orioles, Larks, Penguins, etc.) won adherents to the idiom. Then came the popular Moonglows ("Sincerely"), Nutmegs ("Story Untold"), the Five Satins ("In the Still of the Night"), the Chords ("Sh-Boom"), and Frankie Lymon and the Teenagers ("Why Do Fools Fall in Love?"). White doo-wop singers would soon become visible (the Dions, the Belmonts, the Elegants, and the Four Seasons), often covering the songs of black doo-woppers.

One of the first doo-wop groups to earn an enormous reputation with white listeners was the Platters, led by Tony Williams. The Platters featured silky, urbane singing and outstanding voice blending. Their hits included "Only You," "The Great Pretender," and "The Magic Touch." They were also famous not only for their crossovers but for blending in standards, like "Smoke Gets in Your Eyes" and "Harbor Lights."

The term "rhythm and blues" was intended to represent a fusion of the several black trends mentioned above. Jerry Wexler thought up the expression "rhythm and blues" in 1947, when he was an editor at *Billboard* and found record companies marketing black popular music with degrading tags like Race, Sepia, and Harlem Hit Parade. He had the magazine list the chart name "rhythm and blues," in 1949, and under this designation include the various black styles. As the fifties went by, white youngsters began to catch the sound of black rhythm and blues over the radio, without always knowing whether the music was white or black, and found they liked it. They were captured by the pronounced dance beat and found excitement in the rough emotional voices. They were also entertained by the slyly sexual lyrics, as in Fats Domino's seemingly harmless but subtly spicy rendition of "Blueberry Hill," which he associates with encountering his sweetheart, who provides him with excitement and pleasure.[22] Big Joe Turner's "Flip, Flop, and Fly" tells of a Mississippi bullfrog that sits on a stump and has "so many women" he doesn't "know which way to jump."[23] Then there was Howlin' Wolf's bird, whose activities can be understood in two ways. By day he is a little red rooster too lazy to crow. At night his personality changes—dogs and cats turn cautious because the rooster is searching stealthily for prey.[24]

Interesting to note, when whites covered the rhythm and blues songs in the fifties, they usually altered the lyrics in order to make them more acceptable to their white mainstream audience. For example, the rhythm-and-blues number "Work With Me, Annie" (1954) had the words:

> Work with me, Annie,
> Let's get it while the getting is good.

The double meaning of "work" was too obvious, so the words were changed to:

> Dance with me, Henry
> Let's dance while the music rolls on.[25]

Another song, "Shake, Rattle, and Roll" (1954), featured the lines:

> Well, you wear low dresses.
> The sun comes shinin' through.
> And everything underneath shows.

Bill Haley changed the words for his performances to:

> You wear those dresses.
> Your hair done up so nice.

She may look warm, the singer comments, but her heart is ice cold. Haley explained, "We steer clear of anything suggestive! We take a lot of care with lyrics because we don't want to offend anybody. The music is the main thing, and it's just as easy to write acceptable words."[26]

After the fifties, white performers and audiences had fewer problems with accepting risqué verses, and by the midseventies the acceptance changed to no-holds-barred.

COUNTRY AND WESTERN

Country and western was a genre of American popular music having roots in traditional music of the Southeast and cowboy songs of the West. Its vocals were directed toward ordinary white Southerners and Midwesterners, and the music was generally kept uncomplicated in form and harmony. Typically, the vocalists sang romantic or melancholic ballads, accompanied by guitar. Often they were backed by a violinist, harmonica player, and sometimes a banjoist. Harlan Howard, composer of around 100 country hits, defined country music as "three chords and the truth." The "truth," as Loretta Lynn explains, often came from singers' experiences. She mentions songs that reflected her hardscrabble life in Butcher Hollow, Kentucky. Of her hit "Honky Tonk Girl," she says, "I got the idea for it from watching a woman I used to pick strawberries with cry in her beer over the father of her nine kids. He'd left her for another woman. She sat in the same booth every night in the bar I played, and drank her beer and cried."[27]

The subject matter more often than not made reference to personal problems or hardship—the wanderer longing for home, the lonely cattle herder, the farmer pushed off his land, the hopelessly inept person who could not deal with existence, the morally weak individual who escaped into liquor. The singer looked inward, pinpointed a condition, and dealt with it sometimes in romantic fashion, sometimes in a spiritual way. Normally, general economic conditions and social divisions were minor considerations. The conflicted protagonist was expected to find his own salvation, analogous to the path to salvation preached in the evangelical churches. However, the lugubrious, and often sentimental, songs of lost love, hard drinking, and hard times were relieved by other ditties whose high spirits and humor lightened considerably the weight of the serious ballads. Also popular were songs celebrating the liberated life of the open road. The lyrics, delivered in short, easy-to-grasp melodic phrases, had less irony, less whimsical exaggeration, less putting oneself down than in rhythm and blues. Sex was dealt with far more circumspectly. Serious songs remained adamantly serious; comic songs were completely unbuttoned.

The country vocalists sang with somewhat tight, nasal tones, sometimes introducing yodeling or "hiccup" effects. Yet, as country and western matured from the thirties through the fifties, the singing style of some vocalists started to approach that of pop singers, even of crooners. Their hope, of course, was to broaden the popular appeal and catch the attention of a crossover audience.

Commercial country music grew out of private music making, neighborhood barn dances, and gospel sings, writes Curtis Ellison. It came into being during a period of rapid modernization in the South. Commercial country music expanded quickly by way of the rustic radio programs of the mid-1920s, and through the promotion of recorded musicians to a national network of entertainers and their admirers. The participants continued to act like a huge "extended family at an endless church supper in a rural small town."[28] The principal centers were Louisville, Shreveport, Memphis, and Nashville.

"Country" music in the 20th century transcended its rural origins and as the years went by exchanged influences with black and white gospel, blues, and rhythm and blues. We find black artists like Howlin' Wolf, Ray Charles, Fats Domino, and the Supremes dipping into country and western and white artists like Bill Monroe, Hank Williams, and Jimmy Rodgers looking over blues and rhythm and blues. In addition, a few black country musicians appeared at the Grand Ole Opry, especially De Ford Bailey and Charlie Pride. For the same reason that "race" was dropped in favor of "rhythm and blues," so also was the more derogatory term "hillbilly" dropped in favor of "country." Many low-wattage small-town radio stations played it because their listeners requested the music. Atlanta's WSB was broadcasting "hillbilly" music in 1922. Five big shows featured country music: *The Barn Dance* of WLS Chicago, *Midwestern Hayride* of WLW Cincinnati, *Big D Jamboree* of KRLD Dallas, *Louisiana Hayride* of KWKH Shreveport, and *Grand Ole Opry* of WSM Nashville.[29] By the 1930s, Nashville had become the principal center for country and western, and *Grand Ole Opry* the principal dispenser of it.

The recording of "hillbilly" music had its beginning in 1923–1924, when "Fiddlin" John Cason recorded "Old Joe Clark" and Henry Dalhart recorded "The Wreck of the Old '97" and "The Lonesome Road Blues." However, country and western discs began to be issued in earnest in 1927–1928, when Ralph Peer signed up Jimmy Rodgers (who scored a big success with "Blue Yodel" and "Brakeman's Blues") and the Carter Family (who succeeded with "Wildwood Flower").[30] Rodgers was backed by a string band consisting of a guitarist, two banjoists, and a mandolin/banjo player.

The Carter Family was important in defining "country" song by the way they sang in harmony and synchronized the melody with the instrumental accompaniment. Their roots were in the Clinch Mountains of Virginia, where they heard and sang the Anglo-American folk songs, gospel songs, and *Sacred Harp* hymns of their rural community but at the same time knew many of the standard popular songs of the late 19th and early 20th century.[31] They were given to bringing back a melodic phrase more than once in their melodic strains. A regular pulse and the adherence to the basic chords of a tonality smoothed out the peculiarities frequently found in the traditional ballads and dance music. Their choice of subject matter and the great popularity of their songs further defined what country music was about. However, the Carter Family continued to be farmers essentially and, in a profound sense, amateurs. It was Jimmy Rodgers who saw himself as an entertainer and began to exploit the professional and commercial possibilities of country music. He elevated himself into some prominence as a singer, wrote songs, published them, promoted tours for himself and other country musicians, and made money. Through him, country borrowed from blues, jazz, and popular music. By 1928, Rodgers was introducing the Hawaiian steel guitar, in particular to accompany the more melancholic songs.[32]

As the thirties went by, musicians like Roy Acuff allowed some popular-music influences to color their "country" performances. Acuff took country and western music from an amateur to a professional level. His voice was like that of a genuine mountain boy. It went over well with audiences at the Grand Ole Opry. He backed himself with a combo (which included a Dobro)[33] that was named, at first, the Tennessee Crackerjacks, next, the Crazy Tennesseans, and later, the Smoky Mountain Boys. Acuff rose to stardom with his recording of "Great Speckled Bird" and "Wabash Cannonball." A. P. Carter, of the Carter Family, had published the last song in 1933 and it remains an example of the utter simplicity of early country music. Except for two brief spots where a chromatically lowered note occurs in the accompaniment, the song is completely in one key and so easy to sing it almost sings itself. The lyric is appropriate to a "road" song that celebrates train travel, as it describes a powerful locomotive that crosses the continent, undeterred by mountains.[34]

A large number of popular cowboy films appeared in movie theaters in the 1930s and '40s that featured the acting and singing of the greatly admired Gene Autry (first film in 1933), Tex Ritter (first film in 1936), and Roy Rogers (first film in 1938). Autry made "The Yellow Rose of Texas," "Tumbling Tumble Weeds," "Mexicali Rose," "Back in the Saddle Again," and "South of the Border" into hits between 1933 and 1940. Three of the favorite Ritter songs were "Boll Weevil," "You Are My Sunshine," and "High Noon." Rogers, who appeared with the Sons of Pioneers, did the same with "Whoppee Ti Yi Yo," "I'm an Old Cowhand (From the Rio Grande)," and "Cool Water." When they ended their careers, "western" was firmly attached to the "country" designation. One can get quite thirsty listening to a singer tell of facing a desolate wasteland under a burning sun with no water to be had anywhere. He and a companion, Old Dan, have scorched throats and bodies that cry out for fresh soothing water.[35] Not a single sharp or flat is inserted into the music. Harmony changes slowly, only once a measure. The melody is more declamatory than lyric, with a lingering on longer notes for the phrase "cool water." The downplay of variety in the music, skirting on the monotonous, brought home the words.

Country and western, in the thirties and forties, also came to include the dance songs popular in Texas and Oklahoma. They were performed by combos that included drums and the Hawaiian 6- to 8-string steel guitar.[36] Bob Wills, known as the "King of Western Swing," and his Texas Playboys conveyed effectively pieces like "San Antonio Rose," "Take Me Back to Tulsa," and "Faded Love." Wills's steel guitarist, Bob Dunn, was using an electrified instrument. In 1935, Wills was trying out the piano, saxophone, and drums. At times, the pieces Wills played were described as honky-tonk music. A "honky tonk" was a shoddy dance hall or gin mill, where heavy drinking was routine and country and western music was heard going full blast. Up-tempo songs about getting drunk, painting the town red, and getting into fights mixed with unhurried ballads about forlorn lovers and hardscrabble existence were heard nightly in these joints.

The celebrated Hank Williams and his Drifting Cowboys also wore the honky-tonk label, recording excellent country sellers like "I'm So Lonesome I Could Cry," "Jambalaya," "Cold, Cold Heart," "There's a Tear in My Beer," and "Your Cheatin' Heart." The tunes and lyrics were normally plain, down-to-earth, and built on standard country models: verse plus refrain, one repeated melody throughout, and harmonies mostly the three most basic chords. His songs began appealing to an audience broader than just the country one after Mitch Miller had Tony Bennett cover "Cold, Cold Heart," in 1951, and Rosemary Clooney cover his "Half as Much" and Jo Stafford cover "Jambalaya," in 1952. Williams's ability to tear away the barrier between pop and country and western made a tremendous impression on Tony Bennett, in 1951. At the time, the popular-music world and the country-and-western world rarely intermixed. Bennett says that at first he was reluctant to cover "Cold, Cold Heart," even though Mitch Miller pressed him to do so. He finally gave in and to his surprise "it kept climbing the charts until it was number one." He learned that Williams had been appearing at the Grand Ole Opry since 1949, was the most important figure in country music, and was racking up hit after hit in the Bible Belt and Midwest. Thanks to this song, Williams's music took hold with the rest of the country. "This was the first time a country song had crossed over to the top-forty mainstream chart—it even became an international hit. . . . We sold two million copies of 'Cold, Cold Heart,' and I'm sure he did quite well by it."

The song describes someone who has tried in every way to win over the woman he loves but finds that she can't forget a past grievance and persists in distrusting him. He is left wondering how he can get through to her in order to put to rest her suspicious mind and soften her cold heart.[37] The tune unfolds in easy, comfortable, clear-cut phrases. The musical complaint sounds tender and pleasing to the ear. The singer is not angry and accusatory but confused, mystified, and hurting. The subject was popular in country circles.

Another development within country and western was bluegrass music. Most country people trace bluegrass back to around 1939, when Bill Monroe put together his Bluegrass Boys and enlivened the old-style string-band music by adding a touch of blues and jazz. In 1945, Earl Scruggs joined Monroe's band. He picked his banjo in a three-finger style and added an energetic sound that was seen as essential to the "bluegrass" style. The bluegrass singing that was joined to the instrumental playing typically sounded at a high pitch. It was a combination of Monroe's lively speeds and high tenor voice together with Scruggs's distinctive playing that formed the foundation of the bluegrass sound. At first, bluegrass was simply a branch of country music in general. When rock 'n' roll came on the scene, in the mid-1950s, bluegrass's persistent use of banjo and fiddle caused it to be accepted as a separate country genre.

The influence of the early bluegrass groups has led to a practice that admits certain instruments into the usual band makeup: guitar, Dobro (a steel Hawaiian-style guitar), 5-string banjo, fiddle, mandolin, and string bass (electrified now and again). Instrumental breaks take place between a song's stanzas. The vocals may come from a tenor alone, a duo (lead and tenor), a trio (baritone added), or a quartet (bass added) normally to sing gospel. Both instrumentalists and singers are frequently expert musicians. The bluegrass public at first consisted of the rural mountain people of Appalachia who favored time-honored folk and old pop songs, or new pieces written in these styles. Later, bluegrass bands became favored also by the urban audience that was a part of the folk-revival movement.

One of the most important centers for country and western was Nashville, Tennessee, and the principal institutional force that pushed the music forward was Nashville's *Grand Ole Opry*, which made room for the various subgenres mentioned above.[38] George D. Hay had started *Grand*

Ole Opry as a business venture over a new Nashville radio station, WSM, in 1925.[39] He planned it to give a picture of an earlier age. The ambiance was that of a preindustrial, rural white existence that was created through old-time music and "hillbilly" characters. It proved appealing to a growing Southern and Western radio audience nostalgic for a simpler past free of the domination of mines, mills, and manufacturing towns. The music's drawing power would continue even when, by 1936, three-fifths of the people of Appalachia no longer farmed and one-half of them were on relief.[40] By 1941, the production had moved to the Ryman Auditorium. In that year, *Opry* heard Earnest Tubb on the electric guitar. In 1974, it moved again, to the Opry Land building.[41] Throughout these years it featured stars like Ernest Tubb, Hank Snow, Uncle Dave Macon, Eddy Arnold, Roy Acuff, Hank Williams, and Johnny Cash. Acuff started the Acuff-Rose music-publishing firm in Nashville, in 1943. Owen Bradbury set up a recording studio for local artists. Chet Atkins worked diligently to discover new talent for country and western music. Songwriters like Boudleaux and Felice Bryant arrived to supply "hit" material to singers who did not write their own songs, starting with "Country Boy," in 1948.

FOLKLIKE MUSIC

The term "folk music" has normally meant old music passed on orally from generation to generation, which has been given its shape by unnamed singers within rural communities. In the thirties, forties, and fifties, urban men and women acquired a fondness for folk music, especially that of the Appalachian tradition. This tradition encompassed ballads that had crossed the Atlantic with the earliest settlers from the British Isles and that had acquired, through the decades, realistic features redolent of the American soil. Their simple homespun character and unadorned melodies proved appealing. They breathed a naïveté that struck urban youths as honest and captivating. Some enterprisers soon turned to writing and singing songs that had the character of this anonymous tradition but whose lyrics had contemporary meaning.

Twentieth-century African-American blues and white country music both grew out of traditional antecedents. The folklike music that interests us here had a great deal of kinship with country music but usually existed as a parallel development. Its practitioners recognized that, although their music arose out of older traditions, they had to address today's audience and what it wanted, indeed needed, to hear. The audience comprised young zealots in pursuit of openness, authenticity, and new ideals and desiring music easy and enjoyable to play and sing.[42] They were attracted by the aliveness, stripped-down sound, and emotional straightforwardness of the music. Inevitably, styles changed as contemporary singers embraced musical influences outside of folk, especially with the 1960s. Some introduced rock-music elements into their songs and electrified their instruments; others changed into singer-songwriters who still employed acoustic instruments.

In the mid-20th century, the folk-music revival was intended to be a telling expression of the present time, not something resurrected from an ancient era. It owed a large debt to the Anglo-American musical traditions, to abolitionist sentiments of the past, to the settlement-house movements, says Robert Cantwell. Its proponents were concerned over the problems attending urbanization and industrialization. Young "folkies" united in a common cause against commercialism and commercialized music and for feminism, pacifism, and environmentalism.[43] For the contemporary "folk," the songs were the means for people to articulate their thinking, emotions, and concerns, even as the people of Appalachia had done in an earlier period.

During the 1940s, folk music started to become widely accepted. Folk festivals took place in several different parts of the country. They presented both professional and nonprofessional musicians to audiences numbering in the thousands. The word "hootenanny" was invented around 1941 to describe a folk jamboree of musicians performing for their own pleasure and for the enjoyment of enthusiastic devotees, most of them immersed in a kind of rustic romanticism. Its antecedents were the rural camp meetings, urban gospel sings, and musical conventions of the 19th century. Coffeehouses and college auditoriums gave forth the sound of folksingers to eager young listeners. *People's Song*, a magazine dedicated to the music, started up and was soon followed by People's Artists, an agency that found bookings for performers. The musical *Sing Out, Sweet Land*, utilizing only folk music, reached Broadway in 1944. Bona fide folksingers, like Leadbelly and Woodie Guthrie, and other performers, like John Jacob Niles, Tom Glazer, Burl Ives, Josh White, Oscar Brand, Susan Reed, and Pete Seeger, attracted a large number of ardent admirers.

Guthrie was born in Okemah, Oklahoma, and lived in California during the Depression. Among his musical influences were the country music of the Carter Family and Jimmy Rodgers, and several Tin Pan Alley songs that struck his fancy. He had also acquired a repertoire of traditional songs learned from his relatives and community. He himself created protest songs on current events, starting in the thirties, which spoke up for the manual laborers, those who were trampled upon and crying for justice, with songs like his *Dust Bowl Ballads*. When McCarthyism was rampant, the American liberal reformers and revolutionists out to transform society followed Guthrie's lead. He would become a celebrated figure to the folk crowds in the fifties and sixties. That songs of his crossed over into the urban sphere was to be expected given his musical flexibility. He said of himself that he was not a folklorist but a "poor folkist," with emphasis on the first word.

His two best-known songs are "So Long, It's Been Good to Know You" and "This Land Is Your Land." The latter song, a protest against the class inequality he saw during a cross-country trip, was written also in reaction to Berlin's "God Bless America" of 1940, which he found nonsensical and smug. To him, the Americans who sang it seemed too complacent and self-centered. He was also tired of hearing Kate Smith singing it repeatedly on the radio. Moses Asch recorded Guthrie's "This Land" in his new recording studio, in 1944, and six years later Howie Richmond was offering to publish all of Guthrie's songs. Young democratic spirits were lifted with a song that told them that the land from one coast to the other belonged to "you and me."[44] Among the vocalists who recorded it were Pete Seeger, Judy Collins, Bing Crosby, Harry Belafonte, and Fred Waring and the Limeliters.

Peter Seeger was a seminal figure in the folk-song revival. He was born into a musical family that advocated fundamental political, economic, and social reforms. His father, Charles Seeger, was a musicologist. His step-mother, Ruth Crawford Seeger, was an outstanding art composer. His half-brother Mike and his half-sister Peggy were singer–songwriters. Peter attended his first folk festival at the age of sixteen and then started to search out and sing folk and work songs to his own banjo accompaniment, often at informal folk sings. From Guthrie, he took the suggestion that folklike music was entirely appropriate for the radical communications that he and others like him desired to pass on to audiences. In 1940, he and Guthrie were members of a new ensemble, the Almanac Singers. "Sing the truth as simply as you can and repeat it as many times as it has to be repeated," was their guiding principal.[45] Seeger quickly graduated into combining his singing of folk songs with folklike compositions connected with working people, the promotion of unions, and the improvement of social conditions. He took to appearing at union halls, labor conferences, encampments of migrant workers, and public meetings where extreme right-wing activities were protested.

Robert Cantwell points to a major difference between Guthrie and other Almanac members like Seeger and Bess Lomax. "Whereas Seeger, Bess Lomax, and the other Almanacs may have enjoyed special access to the various reservoirs of folksong, in scholarly collections and the regional festivals, whereas they could appeal to communist ideology and to political situations as a context for new compositions, Guthrie was breathing in the cultural atmosphere in his music, first as a hillbilly and then as an Almanac, and continued to breathe it until he reached the physically negotiable limits of his disease, when as a skinny, tousled, unshaven bohemian in Washington Square, he became for a new generation the image that Jewish cowboys like Jack Elliot and Bob Dylan brought to perfection."[46]

It was to be expected that during the McCarthy era, the McCarthyites would attack Seeger and Guthrie as "Reds" and un-American. Seeger slowly established a repertoire including traditional ballads, children's play-ditties, black and white American worship songs, and labor-related broadsides. Yet, it was not until 1948, when he formed the Weavers, that he achieved celebrity status. Their recorded rendition of the traditional "On Top of Old Smokey," Guthrie's "So Long, It's Been Good to Know You," and the Weavers-Leadbetter "Kisses Sweeter Than Wine" and "Goodnight Irene" had strong sales. One foray into world music was extremely well received, the Haggiz-Modugno-Parrish "Tzena, Tzena, Tzena." However, blacklisting enforced by reactionary politicians and their ultraconservative followers hampered the Weavers' appearances. The group started to disintegrate in 1952 and was completely disbanded by 1955. Seeger continued to perform and record. He also helped the impressario George Wein launch the Newport Folk Festival, in 1959. Two of his own songs won widespread acclaim in the sixties—"Where Have All the Flowers Gone?" popularized by the Kingston Trio, and "If I Had a Hammer," which was written with Lee Hays and popularized by Peter, Paul, and Mary.[47]

By the end of the fifties, the folk revival had spread to all parts of the United States, its most loyal supporters being college students. In the early 1970s, writes Richard Crawford, Seeger gave three reasons for the strength of the revival. He said that young people wanted especially to be acquainted with American traditions and quickly perceived the excellence of folk songs. Furthermore, they endorsed and enjoyed the social commentaries set to folklike music. Finally, the music allowed not only for listening but also for playing and singing by utter amateurs.[48] "You were just to stand up straight and deliver your message. No frills. No fancy phony stuff," said singer Jean Ray.[49]

ROCKABILLY AND THE START OF ROCK 'N' ROLL

For better or worse, the popular-music culture of the United States, more than that of any European country, has remained relatively unconstrained by custom and emancipated from domination by elites—hence the enhanced possibility of innovation that allows its implementers to fall on their faces or rise to the skies. Rock music has been a singular development that in some manifestations has sounded completely and resoundingly ridiculous and in others, invigoratingly new and superbly cogent. A number of its musical examples are as fine as anything in the history of popular music. Essentially it was an amalgam of several black and white genres—the dominant guitar accompaniment of traditional black blues, the strong dance beat and plain melody of black rhythm and blues, the impassioned rhythmic gospel music of blacks and whites, the white string-accompanied country and western music from the Southeast and the cowboy West, and the urban popular music of Tin Pan Alley and Broadway. Rock would express itself in several distinctive modes loosely related to each other.

One of the crucial differences between rock and the popular music of the past was that it was far more about personality, performance, and presentation than it was about the music itself. Isolating a song from a particular singer and instrumental setting was not easily possible. For example, "Heartbreak Hotel," "Hound Dog," "Love Me Tender," and "Don't Be Cruel" remain closely associated with Elvis Presley and the ensembles with whom he recorded in the late sixties. Other performers have recorded them, but it is the early recordings by Presley that continue in the highest demand into the 21st century.

Coming forth into notice during the midfifties, this new sound was labeled "rock 'n' roll" music and, in the sixties, the designation was simplified to "rock" music. What emerged were not one but several kindred styles that in general reflected a certain attitude, a set of the mind. The novel music would go hand in hand with the relaxing of control over behavior by the constraints of morality and civility. The old sexual proscriptions would fly out the window.

Most of the white practitioners of rock grew up in a country-and-western atmosphere; most black practitioners became first known as rhythm-and-blues performers. It was at first music for working-class youth—a forceful clamor of drums, guitars, and bass that gave the impression of loud, crude vulgarity to oldsters. The clamor would increase when instruments were electrified and connected to more and more powerful amplifiers. Yet, amplification was not just for greater noisiness. The increase in intensity was sought to generate music with specific qualities found only in performances augmented by electronic means. Curiously, the louder the sound, the more some listeners could detach themselves from the rest of the audience and feel free to respond viscerally and emotionally and in complete accord with the performers. I have seen young people tightly packed together at concerts swaying to the music with eyes shut or staring at the stage and mesmerized by the sound. They were oblivious to the shoves and jabs coming at them from all directions and did not seem to take in what a person might say to them, assuming they could hear anything at all besides the roar of the music.

As never before in popular music, rock required the performer and audience to constantly act upon each other, whether live or through a recording. One could not discuss a composition merely on its own merits. The performer when completely immersed in the music was the cause for the song to be understood and received favorably; the audience listened, watched the performer's face, body, and gestures, and intuitively tried to grasp the meaning of an interpretation. If they grasped it, listeners screamed their approval and went forth to purchase the recording. The response to the singer's activities furnished evaluative information that shaped future performances. Only by means of this reciprocal influence did the music achieve consequence, one that impacted on musician and listener. Singer and guitarist had to realize that rock was as much about image as it was about sound, said the guitarist Roger Greenwalt. It was not enough just to sing or play. Along with the voice and guitar, a rock star had to perform with the whole body, with movement, keeping in mind that nothing existed outside the moment.[50]

An insistent money-making and profit-enhancing aspect was also present—as financial supporters, publicists, managers, and heads of record companies used performers and manipulated audiences for their own lucrative ends. This had taken place in the past, but never to the extent that came into place after the midfifties. These shadow figures knew that the larger the record sales, the greater the song's "artistic" achievement, as far as the rock culture was concerned. Rock music's continuance and potential for influencing people depended on its degree of approval. It became a dominant force in musical culture only by capturing the notice of huge numbers of people, who went out to buy recordings. For this reason the powers behind the scene insured, as never before, that the music they were sponsoring was heard at the same time in recorded form on radios, on public jukeboxes, at DJ'd dance halls, and on the home record player. Unheard and unsold records had no merit and were dead as far as the industry was concerned. *Billboard* and other music publications continuously ranked popular music as number one, two, and so on, according to sales figures. In short, as never before, the marketplace was the final determinant of a record's commercial and cultural worth.

Roy Brown, a blues shouter from New Orleans, wrote in 1946, and recorded in 1948, his important rhythm-and-blues number "Good Rocking Tonight," which was one of the earliest numbers to hint at the rock 'n' roll to come. In 1949 came two more protorock rhythm-and-blues numbers, the Ravens' "Rock All Night Long" and Goree Carter's "Rock Awhile." Even better, in 1951, Ike Turner and his Kings of Rhythm cut "Rocket 88" at Sun Records, rendering a gritty vocal about an automobile, with the singing backed by a blurred guitar and a tempestuous saxophone. Three years later Elvis Presley would enter the same studio to record a birthday gift to his mother.

One man instrumental in rock's emergence was Alan Freed, a Cleveland disc jockey who discovered, in 1951, that young white people were buying large amounts of rhythm-and-blues recordings. He began playing the music on his *Moondog* radio show, giving it the label of "rock 'n' roll" in order to attract more white listeners. The sound caught on so well that he opened a new show called *Moondog's Rock and Roll Party*. The music's pronounced rhythms and the lyric's lusty and straightforward comments on sex and various personal problems proved attractive to young people. They also enjoyed the spellbinding effect produced by the constantly recurring rhythmic patterns and music phrases. In 1953, Freed set up a "Rock and Roll" concert at the Cleveland Stadium. Thirty thousand boys and girls showed up for the ten thousand available seats. The turnout underlined the popularity of his venture. Freed left for New York City and station WINS, in 1954, and spread the rock 'n' roll gospel to hundreds of thousands of additional young people. Quickly, other disc jockeys started copying him. White musicians and composers took up the music. Inevitably, record companies stepped in. Freed's career would end with the payola scandal. He was indicted for accepting $2,500 as an undercover payment for insistently publicizing a list of songs, in 1960. His career lost its drive. In 1965, he drank himself to death.

Rock 'n' roll emerged more clearly as a white genre with the 1953 record "Crazy Man Crazy," sung by Bill Haley, formerly a white country vocalist man and conversant with rhythm and blues. Two years later Bill Haley and His Comets produced a bowdlerized version of Charles Calhoun's mindless "Shake, Rattle, and Roll." In 1955, the film *Blackboard Jungle* came out of Hollywood. It featured Haley and his group on "Rock around the Clock," a song written by Max Freedman and James Myers. The verbal balderdash, an invitation to enjoy the moment, went to a heavy, driving beat that generated tremendous excitement among the young, who were told to have fun and rock through the entire night.[51] Out of the blue it became *the* adolescent rock anthem, rising to the number-one position in the United States and the United Kingdom, where it stayed for eight weeks. It initiated the rock age. Haley never again equaled the success achieved by this song, and Elvis Presley swiftly eclipsed his renown.

The first white offerings of rock 'n' roll were given the designation "rockabilly," in order to indicate that its practitioners had cut their teeth on country and western and were fusing their idiom with that of rhythm and blues. Rockabilly ripened in Memphis, where Sam Phillips's Sun Records, a small regional outfit, nurtured it. One of the earliest appearances of the term was in *Billboard*, in a 1956 review of Ruckus Tyler's "Rock Town Rock." The rockabilly ensembles usually consisted of a prominent lead guitar, a persistent rhythm guitar, drums, and a slapped bass. A pronounced pulse was meant to supply an electric undercurrent to the vocal. A steady rhythm stressing the offbeats (called a backbeat) often came to the fore. Quite a few of the vocalists had attended evangelical church services while growing up and remembered their preacher's animated and theatrically eloquent sermonizing. They too wanted to communicate emotionally and spiritedly. Yaps, hollers, and hiccups helped communicate an essentially youthful message that often was silly or superficial, and made up of casually expressed lines about cars, clothing, dating girls, and resisting authority. In many rock offerings, the intent was earthy excitement, not engaging the mind. Among the most seminal musicians were Elvis Presley, Carl Perkins, Buddy Holly, Jerry Lee Lewis, and Roy Orbison. All were born to families that worked with their hands on farms or in mills, mines, and factories. A few, like Presley and Lewis, drew a great deal from rhythm and blues. Others, like Perkins and Holly, were less beholden to black styles.

All of them had performed in the country-and-western orbit and more than a few, particularly Perkins, Lewis, and Orbison, would return to their country roots later in their careers.[52]

Orbison, a singer–songwriter, was more a country than rock musician. His big operatic voice presented painstakingly created lyrics on lonesomeness and emotional grief. When, first, Sun Records took an interest in him, he was too shy to become a rockabilly star. Orbison moved on to Nashville and lived as a songwriter for other musicians, with songs like "Claudette," named after his wife, for the Everly Brothers. A series of haunting ballads came from him beginning in 1960—"Only the Lonely" (1960), "Crying" (1961), "Dream Baby" (1962), "It's Over" (1964), and "Oh, Pretty Woman" (1964). When a motorcycle accident killed his wife in 1962, and a fire killed two of his children in 1968, he withdrew from the world. He later tried making a return to his former popularity, but the results were uneven. He died while at last he was staging a major comeback, in 1988. Orbison would be a major influence on Bruce Springsteen.

Presley had grown up in East Tupelo, Mississippi, and Memphis, Tennessee, with the sound in his ears of country (Hank Williams, Roy Acuff, Eddy Arnold), blues ("Big Bill" Broonzy, "Big Boy" Crudup), Memphis blues singers (Howlin' Wolf, B. B. King), black popular singers (Billy Eckstine, Ink Spots), and mainstream popular singers (Bing Crosby, Perry Como, Eddie Fisher).[53] He had also participated in the singing at Pentecostal church services, which he had attended with his parents. His musical experiences laid the groundwork for his ability to cross the line at will between black and white modes of singing. In 1954, Sam Phillips recorded Presley in "That's All Right," by the bluesman Arthur "Big Boy" Crudup, and "Blue Moon of Kentucky," a waltz by the bluegrass musician Bill Monroe. Joined by the country electric guitarist Scotty Moore, bassist Bill Black, and drummer D. J. Fontana, Presley toured the South, impressing the young with his good looks, forceful personality, jerky and twisting torso motions, exuberant quasi-erotic gestures, and persuasive singing. In 1956, Colonel Tom Parker took over his management, transferred him to RCA, and advanced him to international stardom. He successfully marketed Presley as a combined country-and-western, rhythm-and-blues, and popular singer. Over the next two years, a string of number-one recorded hits dominated the charts and went a long way toward defining the rockabilly style: "Heartbreak Hotel," "I Want You, I Need You, I Love You," "Don't Be Cruel," "Hound Dog," "Love Me Tender," "Too Much," "All Shook Up," "(Let Me Be Your) Teddy Bear," "Jailhouse Rock," and "Treat

Me Nice." "Heartbreak Hotel" prospered because it was an exceptionally potent ballad about the pain and despair that accompanied disappointment in love. Presley managed a dramatic presentation that conveyed convincingly the ballad's poignant despondency. He followed it with his passionate second number-one song, "I Want You, I Need You." His third contribution, "Don't Be Cruel," amounted to pure pop music as Presley crooned in touching fashion. "Hound Dog" was a hard-driving interpretation of a Jerry Leiber and Mike Stoller rhythm-and-blues piece. The next ballad, "Love Me Tender," was a contemporary rendition to new lyrics of the 1861 sentimental ballad "Aura Lee," music by George Poulton. It became the theme song for Presley's first movie, a Western centered on the Civil War period. This was the first of a series of films that featured his singing.

Presley succeeded in winning over black and white American youths and European adolescents yearning for someone to capture what they felt. After he appeared on television's *Milton Berle Show*, in 1956, dismay filled the New York critics. "Mr. Presley has no discernible singing ability," declared Jack Gould, in the *New York Times*. Jack O'Brian criticized the singer, in the *New York Journal-American*, for "caterwauling his unintelligible lyrics in an inadequate voice, during a display of primitive physical movement." The *Daily News* reported Ben Gross as saying that popular music had "reached its lowest depths in the 'grunt and groin' antics of one Elvis Presley." Religious publications condemned him right and left.[54] The censures only put the imprimatur of adolescent approval on the Presley antics. His three appearances on the *Ed Sullivan Show* (September 9 and October 28, 1956, and January 1, 1957) set a record for television viewership.

In 1958, three more number-one hits were recorded: "Don't," "I Beg You," and "Hard Headed Woman." Theodore Gracyk maintains that the Beatles, Bruce Springsteen, and countless other rock musicians regarded the Presley performances through 1958 as defining rock 'n' roll and demonstrating that it was a manner of performance, not a compositional style. Presley's repertoire consisted of songs adapted from country and western, rhythm and blues, 19th-century sentimental ballads, and Tin Pan Alley.[55]

He entered the U.S. Army in 1958 and served to 1960. After 1958, several more huge sellers were recorded, but they did not seem to have the same vitality of his earlier songs. Nevertheless, the publicity engineered by RCA and Hollywood increased his fame, for which he suffered the consequences. Wherever he went, teenage girls hounded him and attacked his person. This had been true even at the very beginning of his career. He was nineteen years of age when he appeared at Kilgore, Texas. An eyewitness said:

> The cat came out in red pants and a green coat and a pink shirt and socks, and he had this sneer on his face and he stood behind the mike for five minutes, I'll bet, before he made a move. Then he hit his guitar a lick, and he broke two strings. So there he was, these two strings dangling, and he hadn't done anything yet, and these high school girls were screaming and fainting and running up to the stage, and then he started to move his hips real slow like he had a thing for his guitar. . . . He made chills run up my back.[56]

After his discharge from the army, matters grew worse. A series of successful films featuring Presley heightened the attention given him. On tour, he feared leaving his hotel room and, except when concertizing, waited until after midnight to venture outside. He had grown to be the most significant force in the history of popular music. When he reached twenty-three years of age, his best performances were a thing of the past. By 1968, he was complaining, "I'm so tired of being Elvis—I don't know what to do. I just wish I could do something else." Isolated because of his success, he was lonely, moody, and occasionally violent. Ironically, his first enormous hit, "Heartbreak Hotel," forecast the loneliness to come. He laments abandonment by the woman he loves and goes down to the end of a desolate street to live at Heartbreak Hotel. He feels so lonely he could die.[57]

Presley turned more and more to drugs and was dead by 1977.[58] The stress engendered by touring, fans' smothering adulation, and drugs were phenomena that would afflict one rock musician after another, resulting in more than a few premature deaths.

Out of Tennessee to Memphis and Sun Records, in 1954, came the rockabilly artist Carl Perkins, a fine singer, and guitarist. Unlike Presley, he was also an exceptional songwriter. It was hearing the Presley recording of "Blue Moon of Kentucky" that brought Perkins to Sam Phillips and started him toward prominence. Beginning in 1955, some of the music that came from Perkins sounded with an originality that augmented his sizable influence on the rockabilly world. Much of what he wrote, it is true, belonged to country and western. However, one number in particular made him famous well beyond the country-and-western boundaries, especially when Presley took it up: "Blue Suede Shoes," written in 1955 and published in 1956. Perkins said that the song came along at the right time: "Teenagers wanted their own identity. They wanted to wear their leather coats and their ducktails. Up to that point, if their dad wore a crew cut, they did. With that song they could step up in their daddy's face and say, 'Hey man, don't step on my shoes.'"[59]

He would write additional songs that, like "Blue Suede Shoes," major rock musicians would cover, among them "Boppin' the Blues" and "Your True Love." Early on tragedy struck. He was involved in a car crash that killed his brother and drove him to drink. He continued to write, perform, and record until his death, in 1998, but could achieve only minor rockabilly hits after the accident.

Another great singer, guitarist, and songwriter, Buddy Holly, had a Texan country-and-western background but added the weighty backbeat of rhythm and blues to his blend of country and popular styles. However, his singing never assumed the black rhythm-and-blues colorations that the young Presley frequently used. His manner strikes the ear as good-natured and engaged in a kind of cultivated artlessness, with portamento effects between a normal and falsetto voice occasionally thrown in. However, like Presley's, his performances put on view an effortless swinging sense of rhythm that easily won over listeners. With his accompanying ensemble, the Crickets, Holly reinforced the typical instrumentation for rock bands—lead and rhythm guitars, bass, and drums. Although Norman Petty supervised the earliest recordings of the group, Holly himself assumed a major role in the arranging and record production of his music. Petty showed him how to produce records through layering one taped track over another (called overdubbing) and simultaneously utilizing two parallel taped tracks (called doubletracking). Holly experimented with vocal-group backing and an orchestra, which helped initiate a new kind of popular song that observed the rock conventions.[60] It should be added that Petty and Holly broke up their connection in October 1958, four months before Holly's death.

With Jerry Allison, he wrote his first acclaimed crossover hit, "That'll Be the Day," in 1957. He is certain his girl won't leave him nor make him cry. Her threats to leave are lies and she will remain with him until he dies.[61]

He quickly came through with another winning composition, "Peggy Sue," a girl he declares that he desires, loves, and needs.[62]

Other songs that became standards and continued to be performed long after the rockabilly era had faded away were "Words of Love," "Rave On," "Maybe Baby," "Not Fade Away," "Everyday," and "Oh, Baby." Holly's life ended with a plane crash, in February 1959. However, his idea that he and the Crickets should compose and perform their own original songs in

arrangements adapted especially to their strengths was an important anticipation of the way many rock bands of later times would operate. In a brief
three years, he shaped a number of pieces that had an effect on almost
every important musician of the rock age, including Bob Dylan, the Beatles, the Rolling Stones, Elton John, and Linda Ronstadt.

The uninhibited Jerry Lee Lewis, second only to Little Richard in his
lack of restraint during performance, grew up in Louisiana. Curiously, his
first influences were country music and the gospel songs heard in the Assembly of God church close to his home. He took up the piano and was ex-
pelled from Bible schools for playing "music of the Devil," namely rockabilly. He went to Memphis and Sam Phillips at Sun Records, who advised
him to pattern his style after Presley's and to get more experience. His
emerging from the throng of secondary musicians came in 1957, with the
recording of his "Whole Lotta Shakin' Going On." When he appeared on
the *Steve Allen Show*, in the same year, Lewis battered the piano keys without reserve, lashed out at the piano stool, sending it into the audience, and
shook his hair all over his face so that he looked demented. It would become his modus operandi. The boys and girls occupying the seats loved his
exuberance, while the adults viewed his antics with astonishment.[63] Over
six million copies of "Whole Lotta Shakin' Going On" were sold after the
television appearance. "Great Balls of Fire," "Breathless," and "High
School Confidential" were three more successes. Then, in December 1957,
he married a thirteen-year-old cousin (his third wife). When this became
common knowledge, his rockabilly career came to a standstill. He reverted
to country-and-western performance, in 1968, writing several winning
songs in the idiom. This endeavor also began to fail in the late seventies,
when he grew more and more unstable and pointed guns at people. His career came to a halt at the beginning of the eighties after a suspicious
drowning took the life of his estranged fourth wife and his fifth wife died
suddenly under questionable circumstances.

Central contributors to rockabilly, the Everly Brothers, from Kentucky,
grew up with country-singing parents. The two brothers, Don and Phil,
were soon going beyond Nashville in their singing but retained a folksy
country style, especially in their bluegrass vocal close-blending harmonization. They kept steady aim at the teenage market when they performed.
The brothers added electric to their acoustic guitars and a strong beat to
songs written by Boudleaux and Felice Bryant. Their renditions proved irresistible to adolescents. The Everlys scored their first major hit in 1957
with "Bye, Bye Blues." This was followed by other successes: "Bird Dog,"

"Devoted to You," "('Til) I Kissed You," "Wake Up, Little Susie," and "All I Have to Do Is Dream." The Everly Brothers had a wide influence—on British rock bands like the Beatles, on folk songwriters like Simon and Garfunkel, and on country singers like Gram Parsons, Emmylou Harris, and Linda Ronstadt.

Three more white musicians who to some extent belonged in the rockabilly category were the strutting, leather-clothed Gene Vincent, the robustly voiced Brenda Lee, and the agreeably mild Rick Nelson. Far more significant than these three were three contemporaneous black musicians whose influence on the direction that rock 'n' roll would take was extraordinarily great—Chuck Berry, Fats Domino, and Little Richard.

Chuck Berry, born in 1926, grew up in St. Louis and cut his teeth on gospel, rhythm and blues, and country music. He would write most of the songs that he sang, introducing country elements into his rhythm and blues sound. Berry formed a trio, with a drummer, pianist, and himself on guitar. In 1955, he met and impressed Muddy Waters, who recommended him to Leonard Chess, of Chess Records. Berry showed Chess his song "Ida Red." Chess reacted favorably but recommended changes in the music. The name also changed to the more elegant "Maybellene," and the music was given a countrylike sound over a boogie-woogie pulse. Berry played guitar passages that were somewhat close to what was heard at Nashville. These he tailored to a bluesy execution. The insistently hard rhythms of Johnny Johnson's piano, Jerome Green's maracas, Jasper Thomas's drums, and Willie Dixon's blues-rooted bass added excitement to the sturdily pulsating backbeat. After the song was sent to Alan Freed for airing, it became a front-runner. Helping advance the piece among young listeners was its droll, impudent adolescent viewpoint. After his success, Berry devoted himself to writing mainly brief musical sketches of adolescent living. In addition, Berry's dazzling stock of guitar riffs soon were seen as the embodiment of rock 'n' roll. At the same time, Berry got a swift introduction to sharp business schemes when he learned that the professed sponsors, Freed and his colleague Russ Fratto, had claimed the song's authorship and thus its profits. The lyric told the story of Berry's driving a Ford and catching up with his disloyal girlfriend, Maybellene, riding in a Cadillac, and the drag race that ensued.[64]

A raw, boldly stated beat propelled the rhythms. He enunciated his words clearly and sang with a commonplace nasal voice somewhat after the country fashion. He could have been mistaken for a white singer, thus facilitating crossover to the white market, which was his objective. This song, like several other of his favored songs, caught the uneasy moods and unsettled minds of white youths of the time, however simplistic the message.

"Roll Over Beethoven," another triumph, expressed his annoyance at his sister never giving up the piano as she practiced classical piano pieces. Other successes followed in the fifties, like "Johnny B. Goode," and "Sweet Little Sixteen." His lyrics remained rather juvenile because aimed at the huge immature adolescent market. When he wrote songs that were more in the rhythm-and-blues frame and addressed grownups, he did less well.

Berry was arrested on a morals charge and served a two-year prison term. After his release, in 1964, he found that white British and American musicians were covering his pieces. More songs were written and sung by him and taken over by others. Only one more composition came in for widespread notice later, "My Ding-a-Ling" (1972), although it had taken shape before his imprisonment.

Fats Domino was two years younger than Berry but achieved his first rhythm-and-blues hit in 1950, with "The Fat Man" ("They call me the fat man/Because I weigh 200 pounds"). His New Orleans background made him familiar with blues, jazz (including boogie-woogie and stride piano), pop, and Latin and Cajun dance. These were blended into his style. At first he remained contentedly with rhythm and blues. However, by 1955, rock 'n' roll fever was growing and, like Berry, he tried for the adolescent market. "Ain't That a Shame," "Bo Weevil," "I'm in Love Again," "Blueberry Hill," "Blue Monday," "I'm Walkin'," and "Whole Lotta Loving," compositions written with assistance from trumpeter Dave Bartholomew, went over in a big way with white youngsters. Strong feelings and extravagant assertions were not part of his vocabulary. He was never one to exploit sexual matters. He saw no profit in protesting the existing power structure in society. Instead, he won over a large following with his deft piano playing, warm, elegant melody, lyrics that demonstrated his keen perception of his audience, and skill at giving his songs a cleverly apt expression.

Even if he never had the magnetic personality of a superstar like Elvis Presley, Fats Domino wrote music that did not seem to become dated. His best efforts continued to communicate immediately and naturally in a way that retained their freshness. Vocalists enjoyed singing his numbers and audiences continued to prove receptive to them.

Little Richard, born Richard Wayne Penniman in 1935, came out of Macon, Georgia, after constant exposure to the gospel song of the Pentecostal church and the rhythm and blues heard in dives, roadhouses, and medicine shows. Twenty years later, in New Orleans, he broke through with the frenetic "Tutti Frutti," about a girlfriend who is close to driving him crazy. Yet she knows how to love him to distraction.[65]

It was a cleaned-up version of the salacious original,[66] which invites youngsters to throw off restraints and act as they wish. This loud singer-pianist wrote several successful songs in the late fifties that aided in delineating early rock 'n' roll—seven of them, "Long Tall Sally," "Slippin' and Slidin'," "Ready Teddy," "Rip It Up," "Jenny, Jenny," "Lucille," and "Good Golly, Miss Molly." He pounded the piano; he yowled, crooned, and shrieked his juvenile and sexually suggestive lyrics to receptive audiences. Frequently, his performances seemed a triumph of performance manner over solid quality in music and text. He appeared in three rock-'n'-roll films, where he sported his six-inch pompadour and mounted energetic interpretations of his music. Young people loved him; their elders thought he was demented.

Little Richard's bisexual disposition clashed with his strongly held religious beliefs. For two-and-a-half years, beginning in 1957, he forsook rock 'n' roll to become an evangelical preacher but eventually returned to rock. In the late 1970s, he again abandoned rock for religion, after he found himself falling deeper and deeper into drugs and bizarre sex. He said: "My true belief about Rock 'n' Roll . . . is this: I believe this kind of music is demonic. I have seen the rock groups and the punk-rock people in this country. And some of their lyrics is demonic. They talk against God. A lot of the beats in music today are taken from voodoo, from the voodoo drums."[67]

He not only broke new ground in rock music but also pioneered the rock-'n'-roll lifestyle, according to Robert Palmer. From him, rockers learned to inflate, not subdue, their unconventional behavior. His and his combo's (the Upsetters) gender-ambiguous appearances opened the way to the Rolling Stones, Alice Cooper, David Bowie, Prince, Boy George, and the cross-dressing Kurt Cobain and James Moreland.[68]

The violent reaction that early rock 'n' roll gave rise to was vehemently expressed for several years. A backlash of angry feeling among Southern whites was caused by a fear of black–white integration, sexual relations, intermarriage, and what they saw as the introduction of African savagery into white music. Classical musicians like Pablo Casals and Howard Hanson warned of atrocities against the ear and contamination of the airwaves. ASCAP songwriters and singers of established popular music, whose ability to attract large audiences decreased, attacked what they interpreted as unmusical and uncouth alternatives to what had proved worthy and desirable in popular music. One of them was Alan Lerner. He wrote, in 1955:

> There is a wider difference today between popular and show music than at any time that I can remember. So much popular music today turns its back on melody and resorts to gimmicks, freak arrangements, trick voices, contests to see who can make the weirdest cacophony. The taste in popular music has deteriorated to the point of cannibalism; mere gutter sounds.[69]

Another critic, Sinatra, bitterly complained, in 1957: "Rock 'n' roll smells phony and false. It is sung, played, and written for the most part by cretinous goons and by means of its almost imbecilic reiteration. . . . It manages to be the martial music of every sideburned delinquent on the face of the earth."[70] Priests and preachers denounced the corruption of youth. Rock shocked; lyrics seemed worthless; rock life led to irresponsibility, delinquency, drugs, and a libidinous existence.

Seeing money to be made and critics to appease, white musicians began to cover black songs, often gentling the music and bowdlerizing the lyrics to promote acceptance. Pat Boone sang watered-down versions of songs Fats Domino, Little Richard, the Flamingos, and Etta James had originally aired. He changed James's "Roll with me, Henry" to "Dance with me, Henry." About "Tutti Frutti," Boone said: "I had to change some words because they seemed too raw for me. I wrote, 'Pretty little Susie is the girl for me' instead of 'Boys, you don't know what she do to me.'" Black musicians never profited from the white covers. Bo Diddley, who started with rhythm and blues and then had difficulties achieving a success in rock, grumbled: "With me there had to be a copy. They wouldn't buy me, but they would buy a white copy of me. Elvis got me. I don't even like to talk about it. . . . I went through things like, 'Oh, you got a hit record but we need to break into the white market. We need to get some guy to cover it.' And I would say, 'What do you mean?' They would never tell me it was a racial problem."[71]

What became established without question was that rock music was here to stay, criticism notwithstanding. The important leaders of the music business could not afford to stay on the sidelines if the possibility of gaining huge profits existed. They and many young musicians saw that the future was with this new popular music. The "new" was evident in the melody, rhythm, instrumentation, and percussive sounds. The message of the lyric would wait until the sixties to take on an outright rebellious, if not belligerent, tone.

NOTES

1. Alec Wilder, *American Popular Song* (New York: Oxford University Press, 1972), 502.

2. David Manning White, introduction to *Pop Culture in America*, ed. David Manning White (Chicago: Quadrangle Books, 1970), 12–14.

3. Tony Bennett with Will Friedwald, *The Good Life* (New York: Pocket Books, 1998), 108.

4. For a discussion of the major and small, independent record labels of the 1950s, see Brock Helander, *The Rockin' '50s* (New York: Schirmer Books, 1998), 33–37.

5. Walter La Faber, Richard Polemberg, and Nancy Woloch, *The American Century*, 3rd ed. (New York: Knopf, 1986), 387, 390.

6. Jacques Barzun, *From Dawn to Decadence* (New York: Harper Collins, 2000), 793–94.

7. Richard Crawford, *America's Musical Life* (New York: Norton, 2001), 718.

8. Mark White, *'You Must Remember This . . .': Popular Songwriters 1900–1980* (New York: Scribner's Sons, 1985), 129–33.

9. Ken Emerson, "When the Epicenter of Pop Had a Broadway Address," *New York Times*, 26 August 2001, www.nytimes.com.

10. Helander, *Rockin' '50s*, 82–83.

11. See Steve Chapple and Reebee Garofalo, *Rock 'n' Roll Is Here to Pay* (Chicago: Nelson-Hall, 1977), 78.

12. Gunther Schuller, in *The Swing Era* (New York: Oxford University Press, 1989), p. 564, n. 33, writes that Bob Dunn apparently was "the first to apply a homemade pick-up and amplifier to the guitar, in January 1935." Schuller adds, "Eddie Durham's resonator-amplified solo on Lunceford's *Hittin' the Bottle* was recorded eight months later and issued in early 1936."

13. Schuller, *Swing Era*, 60.

14. James Haskins with Kathleen Benson, *Nat King Cole* (New York: Stein & Day, 1984), 9.

15. Charles White, *The Life and Times of Little Richard* (New York: Harmony Books, 1984), 45.

16. Giambattista Vico, *The New Science of Giambattista Vico*, 3rd ed. (1974), translated by Thomas Goddard Bergin and Max Harold Fisch (Ithaca, New York: Cornell University Press, 1984), 97.

17. Craig Werner, *A Change Is Gonna Come* (New York: Plume, 1999), 28–31.

18. New York: Hill & Range Songs, c1939.

19. David P. Szatmary, *Rockin' in Time*, 2nd ed. (Englewood Cliffs, New Jersey: Prentice Hall, 1991), 4.

20. He maintained his shouting style away from Basie, as when I heard him with a local jazz combo behind him, at Lennie's on the Turnpike, north of Boston.

21. John Chilton, *Let the Good Times Roll* (Ann Arbor, Michigan: University of Michigan Press, 1994), 107, 123, 126.

22. Al Lewis, Larry Stock, and Vincent Rose, "Blueberry Hill" (New York: Sovereign Music, 1940).

23. Joe Turner and Charles Calhoun, "Flip, Flop, and Fly" (New York: BMI Unichappell Music, 1955).

24. Willie Dixon, "Little Red Rooster" (Chicago: Hoochie Coochie Music, 1953).

25. Charlie Gillett, *The Sound of the City: The Rise of Rock and Roll*, 2nd ed., 1983 (reprint, New York: Da Capo Press, 1996), 19.

26. Gillett, *Sound of the City*, 20–21.

27. Loretta Lynn with Patsi Bale Cox, *Still Woman Enough* (Waterville, Maine: Thorndike Press, 2002), 120.

28. This and the previous paragraph owe thanks to Curtis W. Ellison, *Country Music Culture* (Jackson, Mississippi: University of Mississippi Press, 1995), xvi–xvii.

29. Gillett, *Sound of the City*, 9.

30. David Ewen, *All the Years of American Popular Music* (Englewood Cliffs, New Jersey: Prentice-Hall, 1977), 306–7; Arnold Shaw, *The Jazz Age* (New York: Oxford University Press, 1987), 135–36, 197, 203.

31. Bill C. Malone, *Country Music, U.S.A.* (Austin, Texas: University of Texas Press, 1985), 65.

32. Ellison, *Country Music Culture*, 29, 32, 35, 28–39.

33. The Dobro is an acoustic guitar usually played on the lap. It produces a trembling, moaning sound.

34. New York: Peer International, c1933.

35. Bob Nolan, "Cool Water" (Nashville, Tennessee: Valley Publishers, c1936).

36. The steel guitar produced a whining, glissando sound obtained by sliding a small metal bar across the raised strings.

37. Nashville, Tennessee: Acuff-Rose, c1951.

38. I began listening to country-and-western music while teaching at Hobart College, in Geneva, New York, in 1947. A financially strapped student from Tennessee, to whom we had sublet a bedroom, used our radio night after night to tune in country stations. He graduated to become a noted director of documentary films.

39. At first the program was called *Barn Dance*. The name change to *Grand Ole Opry* took place in 1927.

40. Ellison, *Country Music Culture*, 9, 11–12.

41. Helander, *Rockin' '50s*, 5–9.

42. Fred Goodman, *The Mansion on the Hill* (New York: Vintage Books, 1998), 4–5.

43. Robert Cantwell, *When We Were Good: The Folk Revival* (Cambridge, Massachusetts: Harvard University Press, 1996), 356.

44. New York: TRO-Ludlow, c1956.

45. Simon Frith, *Sound Effects* (New York: Pantheon, 1981), 28.

46. Cantwell, *When We Were Good*, 135.

47. A good introduction to the early years of the folk movement will be found in Ewen, *All the Years of American Popular Music*, 481–85.

48. Crawford, *America's Musical Life*, 745.

49. Frith, *Sound Effects*, 29.

50. John Seabrook, *Nobrow* (New York: Knopf, 2000), 126.

51. Philadelphia: Myers Music, c1953.

52. *The New Rolling Stone Encyclopedia of Rock & Roll*, revised and updated, edited by Patricia Romanowski and Holly George-Warren (New York: Fireside, 1995), s.v. "Rockabilly"; Charles Gower Price, "Sources of American Styles in the Music of the Beatles" *American Music* 15 (1997): 211.

53. Charles Hamm, *Yesterdays* (New York: Norton, 1979), 401; Crawford, *America's Musical Life*, 227–28.

54. Peter Guralnick, *Last Train to Memphis* (Boston: Little, Brown, 1994), 285.

55. Theodore Gracyk, *Rhythm and Noise: An Aesthetic of Rock* (Durham, North Carolina: Duke University Press, 1996), 6.

56. Szatmary, *Rockin' in Time*, 37–38.

57. "Heartbreak Hotel," words and music by Mae Boren Axton, Tommy Durden, and Elvis Presley (New York: Tree Publishing Co., c1956).

58. Szatmary, *Rockin' in Time*, 55–56.

59. Bill Flanagan, *Written in My Soul* (Chicago: Contemporary Books, 1986), 20.

60. Helander, *Rockin' '50s*, 100–101.

61. New York: Melody Lane Publications, c1957.

62. New York: Peer-Southern, c1957.

63. Szatmary, *Rockin' in Time*, 39–40.

64. New York: Arc Music, c1955.

65. Nashville: ATV Venice, c1955.

66. White, *Life and Times of Little Richard*, 50.

67. White, *Life and Times of Little Richard*, 197.

68. Robert Palmer, *Rock & Roll: An Unruly History* (New York: Harmony Books, 1995), 141.

69. Edward Jablonski, *Alan Jay Lerner* (New York: Holt, 1996), 249–50.

70. Jablonski, *Alan Jay Lerner*, 134–35.

71. Szatmary, *Rockin' in Time*, 27–29.

Chapter Five

White-American and British Songs in a Decade of Turmoil

In the fifties the controversies over racial discrimination, dress and behavior codes, birth-control pills, legalized abortion, women's liberation, and America's involvement in Vietnam had not yet torn the country apart—although the McCarthy witch hunt almost succeeded in doing so. They loomed large in the next decade. Whatever feelings of happiness and confidence in the future had existed in the fifties, they faded away in the passionate sixties. Broken promises and untrustworthy pronouncements corrupted society. Yet, matters did not look so bad in 1961. John F. Kennedy became president and promised a New Frontier that would abolish poverty, promote harmony among all Americans, and boost the arts and the quality of life. Norman Rockwell, America's favorite artist, painted "The Golden Rule" for *Look* magazine, depicting babies, children, and adults of different races. Above was the pious caption "Do unto Others as You Would Have Them Do unto You." After Kennedy's murder, in 1963, Lyndon Baines Johnson promised to continue and complete what his predecessor had proposed. Rockwell continued to contribute his share in the effort, in 1967, with "New Kids in the Neighborhood," for *Look*, showing a black family peacefully moving into a white neighborhood and the values young and old had in common. By that time, Rockwell was striking many, especially black Americans, as living in a false never-never land. The African-American singer Pearl Bailey took a view opposite that of Rockwell:

> America has grown old too fast. Our people ask questions we cannot answer anymore, because we have started to lie. We have lied and lied and lied to

ourselves and to one another. Now it seems that we don't know right from wrong. We cannot free ourselves.

We cannot lie any longer by telling ourselves that we are free and democratic people. We cannot send men to fight just wars when they are at war with each other at home. We cannot tell ourselves that our children play happily when they spit on their fingers and rub each other to see if skin color will come off. We cannot tell ourselves we have a civilized nation when we cannot accept civilization as a whole with all its people. . . . We must look at our society as it is.[1]

In 1960, black students staged a "sit-in" protest at a lunch counter in Greensboro, North Carolina. The birth control pill was approved for sale. The next year, shortly after Kennedy's inauguration, "Freedom Fighters" against racial segregation were being waylaid and assaulted. Thousands of troops were being sent to Vietnam. In the fall, a black James Meredith, protected by 3,000 troops, forced white Mississippians to allow his enrollment at the University of Mississippi. In 1962 came the Cuban missile crisis. Betty Frieden's *The Feminine Mystique* was published in 1963, kindling the feminist movement. Then there came the march on Washington and Martin Luther King's speech, "I Have a Dream." By year's end, Kennedy had been assassinated and President Johnson had assumed the presidency. The Voting Rights Act was passed in 1965. Over the next four years, several civil rights activists and Malcolm X were murdered. Violent riots occurred in Watts and Detroit. The National Organization for Women (NOW) was established. Military action in Vietnam increased, as did the people killed—American soldiers and Vietnamese civilians. The year 1968 saw the horrifying My Lai Massacre, the killing of Martin Luther King and Robert F. Kennedy, and the Chicago police battering young people at the Democratic National Convention. Nixon was elected president in 1969. Hundreds of thousands of antiwar demonstrators marched on Washington. In 1970, the Kent State University massacre of antiwar protesters took place, and ten days later black students died at Jackson State College. Four hundred universities closed early when their students proved uncontrollable. By the end of the turbulent sixties and the beginning of the seventies, a large number of young people held distinctly different attitudes from those that youngsters had held ten years before. They subscribed to the idea that "the times they are a-changin'." This was the social and political context especially for folk music, folk rock, and rhythm and blues.

On the other hand, millions of people were annoyed at the disruptions on the domestic front. Especially in nonurban areas, they tended to be conservative in principles, action, habit, and thought. Some just wanted to be left alone to pursue their own private interests. Others were alarmed by and disgusted with the revolting young people. A few intolerant whites hated African-Americans and those they saw as educated young white extremists. They wanted these people suppressed. Superpatriots with a "my-country-right-or-wrong" mind-set wanted them jailed or shipped off to the Soviet Union. Others feared chaos and felt that activists were pushing matters too fast and attacking anyone who stood in their way. More sophisticated critics saw the impatient youths who advocated radical change as naive, acting prematurely, and refusing to see what was good about their country. Liberal leaders promoted discussion of societal problems, careful study before proposing solutions, and gradualism in achieving reform. Sincerely concerned Americans questioned the growing absence of self-restraint and the disrespect for the social and moral laws that held society together. In short, a strong opposition to what the revolutionists were advocating and to the tactics used to achieve their goals was also present during the sixties. A large part of the opposition would comprise "the silent majority" that the Republican Party would work hard to win over. This was sometimes the social context for much traditional popular music and even more country and western.

TRADITIONAL POPULAR MUSIC

Rarely did the traditional popular music of the sixties and after reflect the decade's social and political turbulence. Traditional here refers to the long-established urban song styles that had been in place since the beginning of the century and practiced by songwriters like Berlin, Gershwin, and Porter. The prevalence of this sort of music became greatly diminished, but the musical forms that had grown out of Tin Pan Alley and Broadway never disappeared during the second half of the century. They continued to find support among adult Americans who prized what impressed them as a more urbane, civilized, mature, and easy-on-the-ear sound. These adults saw the mutinying young people as having forced their views on others and repudiating in unthinking fashion everything from the past while examining nothing for its continuing value to human living. Even if told that rock music had absorbed many elements of traditional pop, lovers of the older styles wanted their own songs served to them unadulterated or only circumspectly amended. Traditional pop therefore would retain its imaginative and emotional appeal for this older generation. Its importance grew mostly out of the way it enter-tained the individual, not out of the way it benefited society as a whole, as some youthful agitators were proposing. Additionally, its importance grew out of the romantic sentiments expressed, which abjured raw sexuality and what seemed to be childish petulance. Finally, the music could stand secure on its own merits. It had solid melody, smooth harmonies, and a supportive but not obtrusive beat. It did not need to acquire meaning as an appendage to a particular performance or performer, as much as did rock. Rightly or wrongly, these were assertions frequently made, especially in the sixties.

In many ways, the most strident critics of rock music were as intolerant as their militant opposites who wanted all music of the past to be wiped out. Fortunately, as time went by, the ranks of the oppositionists thinned. Gradually, boys and girls grew into adults, and songs in older and newer styles more easily crossed over the gap between them, occasionally shar-ing attributes and therefore appealing to a broader audience. In addition, music lovers did exist in every decade who had an appreciation both of tra-ditional pop and some forms of the newer music.

Unfortunately for the older music, with the sixties, the means of com-munication (radio, television, newspapers, and magazines) that reached and influenced a majority of the people ceased giving traditional pop the attention and news coverage of before. The medias saw their future with the younger set. At the same time the music business shrank its recorded and sheet-music offerings of traditional pop. It thought to maximize its profits by concentrating more on rock.[2] Max Wilk lamented at the end of the sixties:

> I stepped inside a record shop. Outside the store window featured the latest hits on LPs and cassettes. Down the street, the film version of *Fiddler on the Roof* was playing, but this store was featuring the latest recordings of Cat Stevens, Chicago Sly and the Family Stone, Joe Crocker, Frank Zappa, and the Mothers of Invention. The "groups," the purveyors of "youth-oriented" music were all over the place.
>
> Show tunes? In a small bin, about eighteen inches deep.
>
> Jazz? In the same segregated area.
>
> Pop singers *á la* Sinatra, Dean Martin, Ella Fitzgerald, Barbra Streisand, and Steve and Eydie? Also tucked away in a small pocket of their own.
>
> Sheet music? Forget it.[3]

If people don't hear, get no information about, and can purchase no record-ings of a style, then it does not exist for them. This seemed about to happen to traditional songs. Writers committed to rock began to describe them as romantic "treacle" or "somnolent and squeaky clean," or weak, "watered-down pop." They said Perry Como was a mossback who "crooned for suburban snoozers," while Frankie Laine ridiculously "whinnied 'I must go where the wild goose goes,'" and Patti Page in silly fashion "warbled 'How much is that doggie in the window?'"[4] The writers of course prejudiced the outcome with the examples they chose to tear apart. For example, a respected singer, Rosemary Clooney, may have gained recognition singing the "Come-On-a-My-House" trifle, but her repertoire was built on songs like Lawrence and Gross's "Tenderly" and Adler and Ross's "Hey There," which her fans found highly meaningful and beautifully interpreted.

One saving grace was the cabarets, where people could go for drinks, entertainment, and perhaps food. In the sixties, these places were usually denominated "clubs." They were mostly of modest size. Wedged around small tables would be fifty to a hundred people. The clientele was mostly adult and cosmopolitan in its tastes. The performers, many of them relatively unknown, presented songs after the style of Broadway and Tin Pan Alley. Singers appeared on an undersized stage with a piano present and coped the best they could. New York's Bon Soir put on the still unrecognized Barbra Streisand near the beginning of the 1960s. Some excellent vocalists made first appearances at New York's matching clubs Upstairs at the Downstairs and Downstairs at the Upstairs.

The seventies saw cabarets opening to entertain the gay community. One of these, The Tubs, sent Bette Midler on to fame. This entertainment movement will be taken up in a later chapter.

As a final comment, traditional popular-music styles and ways of singing would also make their way into genres not usually associated with the likes of Kern, Berlin, Rodgers, and Porter. Whether in country music, rockabilly, folk-rock, Motown, sweet soul, and the offerings of American and British singer–songwriters, the shift toward traditional (also called classical) pop did occur both in the songs written and the crooners singing them.

VARIETIES OF COUNTRY MUSIC

Like traditional popular music, the country music of the sixties hardly ever gave any sign of the decade's turbulence. In the sixties, regional country music metamorphosed into a form of music aimed at a nationwide public.

No longer were rural areas of the South as culturally isolated as they had been. National television programming and movies were bringing them a perspective that the past had denied them. Musicians like Johnny Cash and the sadly short-lived Patsy Cline were able to travel the road toward classical pop and also toward rock even while retaining their country audience.

It was a decade when country singer and country listener seemed part of a family, and a concert was seen as a gathering of relatives and friends. The music was heard not only in public entertainment halls, nightspots, and summer festivals, but also in all sorts of celebratory gatherings, such as those in rural parks like New River Ranch, in Maryland, and Sunset Park, in Pennsylvania.[5] Mingling with their secular tunes were Christian religious songs delivered by singers like Jake Hess ("Mr. Gospel Music"), J. D. Sumner, Bill and Gloria Gaither, and Janet Paschal.

The Mecca for country-music lovers continued to be Nashville, Tennessee, and its Grand Ole Opry. Young and old still came here to clap, whistle, and shout their approval of favorite performers and pieces. The songwriters and vocalists kept the lyrics personal, centered on an individual's lifestyle, shortcomings, and emotional life. The public savored and sorrowed over serious narrations about suffering and heartache; they laughed hugely at comic numbers; and they sang lustily during informal sing-alongs. The spectators wore casual clothing and countenanced only cheerful dispositions. No suits; no ties; no formal gowns. During concerts, people could be seen strolling back and forth to the refreshment booths surrounding the auditorium in order to purchase food and drink.[6] The importance of the Opry among country-music people is exemplified in Iris DeMent's lyric to the 1992 song "Mama's Opry." The lyric tells of her mother's rural community and of neighbors gathering for hoedowns. Her mother enjoys the songs of the Carters and Jimmy Rogers. Every Saturday, the lyric continues, she would faithfully turn on the radio and sing along with the performers and dream of singing at the Grand Ole Opry.[7]

Most country singers felt that their real climb onto the higher rungs of the country ladder came when they first appeared at the Opry. This, Loretta Lynn admitted concerning herself. When she first arrived at the Opry, in 1960, she said that she and others like her were called "hillbilly singers" and got little respect. "We lived in old cars and dirty hotels, and we ate what we could." By the mid-1970s, country singers had gained greater status, were heard on radio all over the United States. At the same time, she added, the Grand Ole Opry and its country offerings had become "big business" and was paying better.[8] Some country singers thought the Opry had grown old and calcified and had become too much "big business." Merle Haggard, for one, said that he had a high respect for Nashville and the Grand Ole Opry, on whose stage had appeared all of the greatest country musicians, but he had become angry at "the 'system'" that had assumed possession of its management. By the end of the seventies it was passing over some really talented though less popular people for the sake of enhancing its profits, musicians like Grady Martin and Johnny Gimble. Haggard commented that "country music is feelin' and *heart*, not a bunch of stuff some asshole says the public wants because he's made 'an extensive study of the market.'"[9]

Women vocalists, among them Tammy Wynette, Loretta Lynn, and Dolly Parton, were coming to the fore who publicly cultivated their deliberately artless mountain-lass images but were sharp careerists and masterful singers, usually in rapport with their audiences but sometimes presenting themselves as contrarians. Country fans were mostly God-fearing social and political conservatives, and so the performers had to appear likewise in most of their songs. When Lynn produced "Dear Uncle Sam," about the Vietnam War, in 1965, it was not a war-protest song but an expression of love "for our land" and personal empathy with women whose men had died in Asia.[10]

Yet, Lynn had also felt the ferment over feminism gripping the nation. She did not always avoid lyrics likely to promote dissent, as proved by "The Pill," in 1975. Country radio stations and their conservative Christian listenership condemned her song for advocating birth control. She rebutted, stating that she was writing and singing about matters that were a daily concern for women. As for birth-control pills, she said that everyone took them except her "and I have the kids to prove it." She loved her children but was "too busy trying to feed 'em and put clothes on 'em" to enjoy them. "That's why I was so proud of my song, 'The Pill,' that was my biggest selling record early in 1975. I really believe in those words. It's all about how the man keeps the woman barefoot and pregnant over the years. I think it's great that women have a way of protecting themselves now, without worrying about the man."[11] Performing "The Pill" in her customary lively and effectively forceful manner, she sang about throwing away her old maternity dress, wearing miniskirts and hot pants, and compensating for the years she was socially out of circulation, because now she was taking birth-control pills.[12]

Parton bowed to country ways with her 1974 hit, "I Will Always Love You." However, she also sang her own ode to women's rights, in "To

Daddy," in 1978. It was about a wife and mother whose husband takes her for granted, denies her affection, and uses her like chattel, so she leaves home to gain her freedom. This song also did not sit well in some country circles. However, on balance most songs done by these two women and other performers remained personal statements about a person's inner feelings and relation to loved ones and to his or her immediate environment, with little attempt to promote political causes or debate social issues.

Tammy Wynette made conventional noises in "Stand by Your Man," which she and Billy Sherrill wrote. She sings that however mean and unfaithful he may be, a woman should be there for her man when he needs her—offering a warm presence when he feels cold and forlorn.[13] It was a sentiment endorsed by most of the country-music public.

However, she also made a contrary commentary in songs like "I Don't Wanna Play House," written by Billy Sherrill and Glenn Sutton. The song states that after watching her parents constantly at odds, her mother crying, and then her father saying goodbye, she knew that marriage was unpleasant and not for her.[14] This sort of domestic situation was familiar to country audiences. Although the individuals involved might prefer to keep it private, its projection in a personal, emotional ballad to the sound of an ingratiating melody was apparently acceptable, since it tugged at the heartstrings.

Wynette divorced her husband, George Jones, in 1975, which drove him to seek solace in drugs and alcohol. Two years after the divorce, he wrote "He Stopped Lovin' Her Today," about his love that would not end until his death. He sang it with "raw intensity at a time of deepest anguish" in a recording that skyrocketed on the country chart in 1980–81, to be named by fans as the number one country song of all time.[15] It, too, was a personal and emotional ballad of the sort that has continuously appealed to country-music fans.

One significant alteration in country music that took place in the late fifties and sixties, to which these three women contributed, was something known as the Nashville Sound. It was mainly the sound of country, with the introduction of elements from pop. Steel guitars, drums, discreet synthesizer modifications, and augmented instrumental ensembles contributed to a change in tone quality. Singers modified their "cracker" accents. Melodies bowed more to the popular music made in the North. An early initiator of the style, Eddy Arnold, was a country crooner from Tennessee with a suave marketable voice and an admiration for Gene Autry. He helped popularize country music among city dwellers with a glossy sound that blended his voice with tender steel guitars and, on occasion, opulent orchestral harmonies. As his popularity grew, the Grand Ole Opry invited him to sing there. In 1944, he recorded for RCA "I'll Hold You in My Heart," which sold more than a million records and made him a star. This triumph continued with later Arnold recordings, including "Bouquet of Roses," and "Anytime." Arnold's records sold not only to country fans but also to people who as a rule bought only pop. Owing to his general celebrity, he was featured in many television appearances. Arnold eventually had his own TV series, *Eddy Arnold Time*. In the sixties his singing style became even less entrenched in country and smoother sounding. It led to a new string of successes, beginning in 1965. One of these was "Make the World Go Away," by Hank Cochran.

A second blender of pop with country was Patsy Cline, from Virginia. She achieved her breakthrough in 1957, when she called national notice to herself in an Arthur Godfrey Talent Scout Show, singing "Walking after Midnight." Her participation in country's flirtation with pop found approval with her growing following. In order to explain Cline's popularity, Loretta Lynn said, "She was really like Hank Williams, the way she got this throb in her voice and really touched people's emotions."[16] She went on to record one of her most successful songs, "I Fall to Pieces," by Harlan Howard and Hank Cochran, in 1961. The lyric is about a neglected lover who has been relegated to a "just your friend" status. (The frustrated, abandoned, and unfairly treated lover, of course, was grist for the country mill.) She wails about coming apart whenever she sees him, and although he acts as if they had never met, she cannot forget him.[17]

Although, as befits a country song, the sheet music shows the harmony remaining diatonic, constantly in a standard scale, and without complexity, the tune leans strongly toward traditional pop sounds. The opening phrase, for example, with its wide jump upward, and its winding down to a rest stop, could fit easily into a classical pop tune from the thirties. Cline sings with a sizable, open country voice, but the backing of "crying" strings and soft steel guitar, to which the producer, Owen Bradley, has added a bit of an echo, also points to pop influences.[18] From "Crazy" to "Release Me" and "Leavin' on Your Mind," she recorded hit after hit. Regrettably, record companies rarely gave her and other country singers the opportunity to record the gospel songs they had grown up with and loved—a state of affairs that would change only slowly as the century wore on.[19] Her life was cut off early, in a 1963 plane crash. Nevertheless, Cline's influence would continue in the singing of Loretta Lynn and Reba McEntire.

A third architect of the country-pop sound was the mellow-voiced Jim Reeves from Texas, who got more than his 15 minutes of fame as a country-pop singer of ballads. RCA gave him a contract in 1955, and around the same time he began appearing at the Grand Ole Opry. His greatest recorded success was a song that would influence subsequent country musicians, the 1959 "He'll Have to Go," written by Joe and Audrey Allison. A sweet, simple waltz-time tune went to a lyric about a lover's telephone call, during which he tries to win his girl back from another man, who now has attracted her. The song itself was not so different from the hundreds of honky-tonk numbers that had preceded it. What was unfamiliar, but welcomed by the country audience, was Reeves's caressing, dark-shaded, and deeply felt musical expression as his voice progressed smoothly over a subdued accompaniment. After scoring with several more hits, he died in a plane crash, as had Cline, in 1964.

One of the most important country-pop singers, John Denver, was also a songwriter of some distinction. His "Leaving on a Jet Plane" (1969) proved to be a success, coming from the throats of Peter, Paul and Mary. His own recording of it drew attention to his arrival as a singer. "Take Me Home, Country Roads" (1971), a track on the album *Poems, Prayers, and Promises*, was his introduction to singing stardom. Two years later, Olivia Newton-John made it into a hit in Britain. The tune moves along in easy syncopations. The rhythm has a pleasantly rambling sound. The harmonies are given a plein-air sonority that adds considerably to the music's attractiveness. As for the words, the blissful Blue Ridge Mountains, the home to which he wants to return, is an imaginative construct for the New Mexico–born Denver. The place seems almost like heaven with its old country roads and traditions. It is where he belongs.[20]

Nostalgic songs about a home one wants to return to, make-believe or real, are at least as old as "Home, Sweet Home," by Howard Payne and Henry Bishop, which came out in 1823 and has retained its favor among Americans to today.

Truer to Denver's life was "Rocky Mountain High," published in 1972, about the time he moved to Aspen, Colorado. Although the song also sold well, the melody is not as attractive; dwelling in near-irritating fashion mostly on one tone. In addition, the harmony is more static. Yet, the song exposed the easy-listening style he would pursue in the future. The words did fit his situation, since he loved the Rockies intensely. The lyric tells of his 27th year of age and arriving at a new place where it seemed like he had arrived "home" at last.[21]

Other well-received songs of the '70s followed, among them "I'd Rather Be a Cowboy," "Sunshine on My Shoulders," "Annie's Song," and "I'm Sorry." John Denver's popularity began to sag in the eighties. His death came in the crash of a plane he was piloting, in 1997.

THE COUNTERCULTURE

What of the music and attitudes of the young people who rejected or opposed the dominant values and conduct of society? For them, traditional pop and country and western were irrelevant to contemporary conditions and tastes. Indeed, Morris Dickstein wrote, in *Gates of Eden*, "For the culture of the sixties the watchword was liberation. The shackles of tradition and circumstance were to be thrown off; society was to be molded to the shape of human possibility."[22] He was of course referring to the cultural liberation and lifestyles of the young, most of them from the middle class, who had discarded the principles and behavior of mainstream society. These were years when alienation was the order of the day.

A segment of the young exhibited naïve idealism in its belief that through one's actions and manner of living it could encourage the "Age of Aquarius" to begin, an era when reconciliation, awareness, and honesty between people, and thus peace for all, would triumph. They were romantics, à la Rousseau, who believed that babies were born with natural understanding and wholesomeness, unchanged yet by society's edicts, which squashed the natural life force. Therefore, humans had to be free to experiment, expand their potentials, and find where their talents lay. The American tribal love-rock musical *Hair* advanced this view, especially in the song "Aquarius," written by James Rado and Gerome Ragni, with music by Galt MacDermot. It announced the age of Aquarius, where there was harmony, understanding, sympathy, and trust; an age without falsehood and division.[23]

This Arcadian vision seemed credible for a short time to the "flower children," notwithstanding their uncertainties as to how the individual should be set free. ("Flower children" denoted the young, mostly middle-class subculture that promoted universal love and peace and that was usually characterized by communal living, long hair, and soft drugs.) They wanted to escape from the lies, evasions, dishonest declarations, and needless warfare that had degraded American society and imprisoned its spirit. Liberation came through shared living, unconventional dress, exchanging sexual partners, and euphoric mental states brought on by drugs—whose use seemed to them free of adverse consequences. Amiability, good-natured ineptness, and uncontrolled vivacity affected many of these unconventional youngsters (as they would remember to their discomfiture when they were much older).[24] Innocence would soon prove an awkward instrument for arriving at utopia. Marijuana and LSD intensified colors and musical sounds, distorted the sense of time, produced passivity, and generated introspection. At the same time, thinking became clouded, judgment unreliable, and performance below average. LSD brought on partial psychotic and hallucinatory states, occasionally pleasurable, on more than a few occasions frightening. It would eventually lead to a psychedelic music reproducing sounds sympathetic to the LSD-induced mood and disposition.

In contrast to the flower children were the student militants of the New Left. Little agreement existed at first between the two camps, though a major center for both was Berkeley and Haight-Ashbury, in California. "Make love, not war" changed to the imperatives to carry out "democracy in the streets" and "trust no one over thirty." The radicals believed in actively fighting institutional authority (the social, economic, and political leaders who presided over the nation) and the culture associated with it. Corruption existed not only in the present but also in the past. History was bunk. Even Abraham Lincoln, Shakespeare, and Beethoven were fraudulent figures. Antidraft protests, the forced closing of colleges, and public rioting were their weapons of choice. Radical feminist libertarians formed NOW and attacked men who made women into an oppressed class and laws that denied women control over their bodies and destinies. However, as the Vietnam War raged and antiblack assaults continued, some young people felt these protests were not enough. They wanted to bring down "The System" through acts of violence. Calling themselves Students for a Democratic Society, the Weathermen Underground, and the Black Panthers, they robbed banks, planted bombs in mail-collection boxes and public buildings, and in a few instances murdered people.

Like most flower children, most revolutionaries eventually turned into more responsible adults. In 1970, young Bill Ayers, who rejected his privileged upbringing to become a member of the often violent Weathermen, decreed, "Kill all the rich people. Break up their cars and apartments. Bring the revolution home; kill your parents; that is where it's really at." He would later become a professor at the University of Illinois and claim that what he had said was intended as a joke.[25]

Most young men and women dedicated to a transformed mode of living used music to connect with each other and festival gatherings as communal rituals via music. The most famous of these gatherings were the Monterey Pop Festival, of 16–18 June 1967, and the culminating Woodstock Festival of 15–17 August 1969. Other important festivals took place in Atlanta and Seattle. Monterey had 200,000 people in attendance. They came to hear performers like Jimi Hendrix, the Mamas and the Papas, the Who, and Janis Joplin. Hendrix during performance acted as if gripped by a fanatical frenzy and seemed to make physical love to his guitar, which he then burned. Joplin's performance was not precisely singing. She wailed her pain, oftentimes screeched like a terror-stricken creature, behaved as if in a crazed state, and was totally naked in exposing her feelings. Both Hendrix and Joplin were constantly under the influence of drugs and would prematurely end their lives with overdoses. James Miller writes, "It was largely thanks to Joplin that amateurish shouting became a valued emblem of heart and soul vocalists, including, later, Johnny Rotten of the Sex Pistols and (an even finer Janis Joplin disciple) Kurt Cobain of Nirvana."[26] In the same year as the Monterey festival, the *Rolling Stone* magazine, which was completely devoted to the popular music of the young, brought out its first issue and cataloged each permutation in rock, from rockabilly to rap.

Woodstock had 400,000 in attendance. Added to Hendrix, Joplin, and the Who were other music celebrities like the psychedelic Grateful Dead and Jefferson Airplane, Country Joe and the Fish, and Arlo Guthrie, son of Woody Guthrie. The feeling of communality lasted only four months. It took a tragic blow at the Altamont Festival, December 1969, where the Rolling Stones performed, large numbers of the audience overdosed on drugs, and members of the Hell's Angels motorcycle gang, hired to guard the stage, stabbed a youth to death. Then, on 4 May 1970, came the Kent State Massacre. After anti–Vietnam War student demonstrations, some of them violent, Ohio National Guardsmen turned on the boys and girls and shot four of them dead. The entire country was horrified. It was a mortal wound inflicted on the activist-youth era. Swiftly, Neil Young wrote and Crosby, Stills, and Nash recorded "Ohio," which quickly became a top-selling hit and was sung by hundreds of thousands. It warned that President Nixon's "tin soldiers" were coming, four people were dead in Ohio, and now everyone was on their own without protection from the law.[27]

Real-life events were finally affecting young minds. Hope had died little by little with the deaths of President Kennedy, Pope John XXIII, Martin

Luther King, Robert Kennedy, Malcolm X, and Medgar Evans. White back-lash, the George Wallace run for the presidency in 1968, and the sneers of Vice President Spiro Agnew encompassed a darker United States. At the be-ginning of the seventies, youth had lost any hope that because Americans landed on the moon, America could conquer its myriad social problems. The widowed Jacqueline Kennedy, who had seemed to symbolize the dreams of President Kennedy, showed feet of clay when she married Aris-totle Onassis. No longer was any aspect of America seen as redeemable as it had been before. Optimism was gone.[28]

FOLK TO FOLK-ROCK

The Newport Folk Festival of 1963 was the high point for the neo-folk movement, especially when Pete Seeger, Bob Dylan, Joan Baez, Peter, Paul, and Mary, and the Freedom Singers appeared arm in arm to chant "We Shall Overcome," Dylan's "Blowin' in the Wind," and traditional hymns. The singers were dedicated to the audience's "dream of freedom, brotherhood, and peace."[29] Not surprisingly, joining the audience were many flower children. However, the bulk of the folk following came from the burgeoning college-student population.

Songs written after folk models were the ideal vehicles for the youthful believers of the early sixties. They advocated integration, worked for in-terracial solidarity, and solidly endorsed King's "I Have a Dream" speech and the freedom fighters' "We Shall Overcome" hymn. They distinguished themselves from the majority of young people by repudiating commer-cialized popular culture and reshaping folk music to speak to their own in-terests and principles. For example, in song aimed at a mass commercial market, love almost always meant an ardent desire, usually physical, for someone of the opposite sex. For the folk people, love frequently took on an ideal form and embraced all of humanity. They refused to focus on petty, inconsequential personal matters but concentrated on opposing wrongs of consequence to large numbers of people. Thus was the protest song shaped, a musical gesture of extreme disapproval of things as they stood. Its outspoken lyrics and tales were set to folk-flavored tunes that at-tracted listeners of all ages, but especially the young whose minds were not already channeled.

Such songs were as old as mankind and, more recently, had taken on contemporary meanings with the offerings of Woody Guthrie and Pete

Seeger. Back in 1940, Guthrie said of his songs, like "This Land Is Your Land," that:

> I don't sing any songs about the nine divorces of some millionaire playgal or the ten wives of some screwball. I've just not got the time to sing those kinds of songs, and I wouldn't sing them if they paid me ten thousand dollars a week. I sing the songs of the people that do all of the little jobs and the mean and dirty hard work in the world, and of their wants and their hopes and their plans for a decent life.[30]

While the Vietnam War raged with unabated violence, in 1965, nineteen-year-old P. F. Sloan wrote and Barry McGuire recorded "Eve of Destruction." The song was unusual for detailing the horrors of warfare and America's double standards about who was drafted and who exempted. Its subject was the "grunts" who did "the mean and dirty hard work" and the deceivers busily speaking out of both sides of their mouths. Within a few months it gained a huge following not only among college students but also among noncollege young people. It serves as an example of how effective protest songs could be in the sixties. Supporters of the war tried to squash the song, but it had taken on a life of its own and resisted suppression. The music was nondescript; the verse was clumsy; yet the song hit home. This was no feel-good piece. Angrily, the song informed young men that they were licensed to kill but not to vote and even though they hated war they had to shoulder a rifle. It warned that marching by itself could not bring integration about. It exposed American hypocrisy—saying we condemned Red China but accepted what had taken place in Selma, Alabama; we prayed piously but hated our next-door neighbor—and warned that America was on the eve of self-destruction.[31]

Unfortunately, musical griping left many believing that they had acted for their cause. Clearly, if not treated circumspectly, protest songs encouraged a false sense of doing something about evil and could insulate singer and listener from the unjust and immoral parts of real-life society. Nevertheless, genuine folk-protesters did put their bodies on the line to promote racial integration in the South, did promote social-welfare legislation, and did help bring about the end of the Vietnam War. And feeding the movement songs that excoriated present-day conditions were singer–songwriters with strong convictions and talent, like Phil Ochs and Tom Paxton.

Around the midsixties, musicians cultivating the folk field were thriving commercially. Outfits like the Kingston Trio and Peter, Paul and Mary were bringing folklike sounds into the core of popular music. Whether protest or otherwise, the folk stress on truthfulness, social engagement, and, above all, authenticity was gradually taken up by thousands of performers. Authenticity meant appearing sincerely and honestly genuine, and not false to yourself or your listeners, in the songs you sang.

The college students Bob Shane, Nick Reynolds, and Dave Guard, who formed the Kingston Trio in San Francisco, in 1957, learned the folk songs that would compose their repertoire from radio broadcasts and recordings. They sharpened their skills by singing to acoustic guitars for college audiences and passing a basket around for contributions. They graduated to singing in coffeehouses and college auditoriums. The three young men produced their first big impression on more general audiences in the early fifties, with their wholesome looks and dress, downplay of subjects that were overly controversial, and successful combination of folk with commercial pop sound. The Kingston Trio stimulated audiences into singing and clapping as they sang in lively rhythmic tempi and with a brisk white gospel tang. They did away with the excessively scrupulous renditions of folk revivalists bent on strict adherence to the musical and performance styles of the original singers. They never forgot they were entertainers first—not preachers or musical archivists. Their topmost hit was the traditional murder ballad "Tom Dooley," recorded in 1958 and selling millions of discs.

> Hang down your head, Tom Dooley,
> Hang down your head and cry.
> Hang down your head, Tom Dooley,
> Poor boy, you're bound to die.
> I met her on the mountain; there I took her life;
> Met her on the mountain, stabbed her with my knife.

A folk ballad like this took youngsters out of themselves and allowed them to linger in a fantasy world that seemed more genuine and honest than was offered by their reality. The Kingston Trio motivated thousands of middle-class youngsters to play folk instruments, especially acoustic guitars, and to study and sing traditional ballads. At the same time, they helped solidify a good-sized audience for the folk musicians to come.[32] However, popularity for the Kingston Trio itself decreased in the sixties, the decade of dissent and anti-Vietnam activity. To some extent, they shored up their protest credentials by recording Pete Seeger's "Where Have All the Flowers Gone?" and making it into a hit in 1962. Its evocatively simple tune, only 18 measures long, and its gentle lyric fashioned after a folk lament were rendered in a straightforward, unassuming manner. Hearing it again in 2003, while our sad adventure in Iraq continued, I still felt the song's impact:

Where have all the flowers gone? . . .
Where have all the young men gone? They're all in uniform.
Oh, when will they ever learn?[33]

However, the year 1962 brought a fresh musical group to the fore, which had a stronger identification with the protest movement. Urban-folk fans began to switch to this new ensemble, and the Kingston Trio could not maintain its high position. The three musicians split up in 1967.

The new trio known as Peter, Paul, and Mary was launched in Greenwich Village, when Peter Yarrow, from Cornell, met up with Noel Paul Stookey, from Michigan State University, and Mary Travers, a singer traveling the urban-folk circuit. They began singing in New York and, in 1962, made their recorded debut with *Peter, Paul and Mary*, an album containing a song of the same title that had a New Testament orientation. The album swiftly attracted a huge American music public. In it, the trio's version of "If I Had a Hammer," lyric by Lee Hays and music by Pete Seeger, was not only an admired song, but also an anthem of the civil rights movement. The hammer is the symbol of hammering out danger and words of warning and of achieving justice, freedom, and brotherly love everywhere.[34]

They solidified their success during the next year with Yarrow and Lipton's "Puff, the Magic Dragon" and Bob Dylan's "Blowin' in the Wind." Their recording of "Blowin' in the Wind" helped bring Dylan into the spotlight. The melody is limited in range and unremarkable in itself, except perhaps for the effortless three-note syncopation repeated in most measures. Probably it was the lyric that ignited the imagination and triggered the fervor of a generation aiming at social change.

Yes, 'n' how many ears must one man have before he can hear people cry?
Yes, 'n' how many deaths will it take till he knows that too many people have
    died?
The answer, my friend, is blowin' in the wind.[35]

In 1963, they appeared in Selma and Washington with Dr. Martin Luther King, Jr. In addition, they labored hard in the antiwar cause, performing at protest rallies and "teach-ins." In 1969, they assisted in spurring the civil-rights march on Washington and sang before the hundreds of thousands who gathered for that momentous occasion. By 1970, Peter, Paul, and Mary had recorded thirteen albums that reached the top of the popularity charts. However, 1970 was the year they decided to disband and go their individual ways, in part owing to their exhausting schedule of almost nonstop touring. They came together again as a trio, in 1978, agreeing not to let performances dominate their lives. With the Vietnam War over, they turned to other causes, which they advanced in song—against the nuclear bomb, publicizing the misery of Central America's poor, upholding the rights of blacks in South Africa, and making Americans aware of the homeless people in their midst. A large portion of their earnings over the next twenty years went to alleviate the suffering they sang about.

While this trio was having its heyday, a convincing urban-folk singer named Joan Baez was establishing a reputation for honesty and an unswerving devotion to human causes. What is more, she had a thrilling voice and a warmly intense delivery. From the first she displayed a fondness for the chanteys and ballads of Appalachia and the American frontier. She started off as a Boston University student doing traditional folk songs in the coffeehouses of Greater Boston during the midfifties.[36] She flunked out of college. An appearance at the Newport Folk Festival of 1959, which George Wein and Albert Grossman started, established her reputation. From then on listeners credited her delivery with a folk purity and her performances with a genuineness untainted by pandering to commercialism. Her long straight black hair, absence of makeup, and plain sandals encouraged newspaper and magazine writers to set her up as a folk "Goddess," "Madonna," or "Virgin Mary," as she was sometimes labeled. Her pristine soprano sound and sincere expression was coupled with an unfussy presentation and a relaxed way with music and words. Admirers thought her singing was the epitome of the urban-ballad style.[37]

Soon after the festival, Baez joined the protest movement and won wide approval for singing compositions associated with liberal causes, like "We Shall Overcome." After the midsixties, she was even more deeply involved with opposition to the Vietnam War and fighting politics-as-usual. By 1965, too, Joan Baez had begun to sing less the old traditional folk songs and more the compositions of a group of contemporary songwriters: Bob Dylan, Leonard Cohen, Phil Ochs, Tim Hardin, Pete Seeger, Malvina Reynolds, Richard Fariña, and others. Her sponsorship of this music led to the addition of fresh urban folklike songs and present-day viewpoints to musical exchanges previously confined to the old ballads of rural America.

Baez's finest early work included many Dylan songs, like "Don't Think Twice," "Gates of Eden," "Farewell Angelina," and "Love Is Just a Four-Letter Word." Her account of Phil Ochs's "There but for Fortune" is an extraordinary rendition, a political declaration that can powerfully affect some listeners. In 1965, Baez was instrumental in establishing the Institute of Nonviolence, in Carmel, California. She was most popular with urban-folk aficionados, and here her audience was sizable. However, she never won over the millions outside of that circle. After the Kent State Massacre, youthful contentiousness died down, as did the sale of her recordings and attendance at her performances. She wanted to retain some sort of audience and knew her preaching was hurting her career. Becoming more personal in the lyrics and more contemporary in the music seemed the solution. She said, "I was fading into oblivion. . . . I realized . . . music was a very big part of my life. It really mattered to me. I didn't want it to end."[38]

Like other singers, Baez had sensed the transformations being made in popular music owing to the Beatles' popularity and the folk-rock innovations of Bob Dylan. She had already started to fill out her acoustic-guitar accompaniment with other instruments, in *Farewell Angelina* (1965), *Noel* (1966), and *Joan* (1967), in which a large instrumental ensemble had backed her singing. She tried adding country musicians for an album of Dylan songs. In 1972, with *Come from the Shadows*, she veered more definitely in a pop direction. Baez was also trying to write her own songs, as in *Gulf Winds* (1976). On occasion her turn toward the personal became autobiographical. She had helped Bob Dylan, when he was still little known, by singing his songs and having him perform beside her. A liaison between the two ensued. However, after the self-centered Dylan became widely recognized, he abandoned her and apparently was not above mocking her person and belittling her talents. She answered him, in 1975, with an accusatory love ballad "Diamonds and Rust," which took his behavior to task. She recorded her composition with an electric band and dubbed strings. Her lover, she sings, had wandered into her arms and stayed for a while because he felt confused and distraught. He had soon deserted her. She once loved him dearly, had paid for it with suffering, and was not about to excuse him for her pain.[39]

All this said, she never compromised her principles by becoming too commercially oriented and throughout her career always stood up for one cause or another, in speech, action, and music. Her influence on other songwriters was demonstrated in the 1997 album *Gone from Danger*, where she presented new compositions by young songwriters who had followed her lead. Folk-rocker Sinead Lohan furnished the fine-sounding "No Mermaid" and "Who Do You Think I Am." Baez interpreted three of Richard Shindell's pieces, one of them "Reunion Hill." We find songs by Dar Williams ("February," and "If I Wrote You") and Betty Elders ("Crack in the Mirror"). Baez includes one of her own pieces, "Lily." The compositions and performance pleased her followers exceedingly.

Bob Dylan, who broke with Baez after she helped him get started, was born Robert Allen Zimmerman. He would have a tremendous influence on urban-folk history and songwriters. He was a mediocre singer and compromise was more in his nature than it was in Baez's. Yet, songs that he wrote set examples for singer–songwriters, folk-rockers, and country-rockers. His greatest fame came in the sixties.

While attending the University of Minnesota, he tried singing folk songs at coffeehouses, using the name Bob Dylan (after Dylan Thomas). Early influences were Hank Williams, Woody Guthrie, and the bluesman Jesse Fuller. He left for New York City, in 1961, visited the hospitalized Woody Guthrie, and joined the Greenwich Village folk scene. Robert Shelton's favorable review in the *New York Times* got him noticed by John Hammond of Columbia Records, who produced *Bob Dylan*, Dylan's first album, containing mostly folk and blues numbers, in 1962.

Dylan busied himself writing music, the result being the 1963 *Freewheelin' Bob Dylan*. It took the urban-folk world by storm. He learned that the less he unswervingly copied Woody Guthrie and his disciples, the more he improved as a songwriter. Harnessed to a harmonica and acoustic guitar in hand, he added a thin, whiny, and raw vocal delivery that put off critics who attended his performances. Yet, admirers spoke of his fervor and integrity, and the validity of his messages. The album contained original songs showing his political and social awareness. "A Hard Rain's A-Gonna Fall" warned about the tragedy that the Cuban missile crisis and nuclear threat foretold. "Oxford Town" was in response to James Meredith's registering at Mississippi State. Dylan's more personal side was captured in "Don't Think Twice, It's Alright." In song after song, he demonstrated his acute perception of what the urban-folk protesters sought to articulate and then articulated it more clearly and distinctly than they had dared hope. Young people were soon accepting him as the leader of the protest-folk fellowship. Joan Baez, struck by his talent, supported him and recorded his songs, and Peter, Paul, and Mary's cover of his "Blowin' in the Wind" pushed it to top-pop status. With the 1964 album *The Times They Are A-Changin'*, Dylan continued his production of protest ballads. The titular number sings of the growing breach between parents and their young, in a format deriving from the "Come all ye" folk-ballad type. It begins with "Come gather 'round people wherever you roam," after the time-honored folk fashion. The words are set to an unexciting, waltzlike, declamatory tune, with plenty of repeated notes and remains within a limited vocal range. The monotone voice sounds morose and severe. None of this deterred the Dylan fans. As in the lyric, they declared that the time was one of change. They felt free of their parents' criticism—theirs was the new road; their parents' the old road.[40]

However, within a few months *Another Side of Bob Dylan* showed increased blues influences and a downplaying of political commentary. Possibly he was responding to the mounting criticism that accused him of leaning toward smug social moralizing. More probably, he sensed that audiences were beginning to get tired of protest music. He now sang of personal problems and unsatisfactory love relationships. A sign of his leaving folk-protest behind was the breaking off of his relationship with Baez. Dylan's own comment was "Those [protest] records I already made I'll stand behind them, but some of that was just jumping on the scene to be heard and a lot of it was because I didn't see anybody else doing that kind of thing. Now [fall 1964] a lot of people are doing finger-pointing songs. . . . Me, I don't want to write for people anymore. You know—be a spokesman."[41]

One song that definitely signaled this turning away from urban-folk circles and their advocacy of acoustic instruments was his sanctioning of the Byrds' electric rendition of his "Mr. Tambourine Man," a song that refers to the effect of drugs on the senses. Drugs take you on a magic trip with your senses stripped away and your hands left without feeling.[42]

In the fall of 1963, Nat Hentoff had interviewed Dylan for *Playboy* and reported him as commenting:

> I wouldn't advise anybody to use drugs. Certainly not the hard drugs; drugs are medicine. But opium and hash and pot—now, those things aren't drugs; they just bend your mind a little. I think *everybody's* mind should be bent once in a whole.[43]

The same year saw the coming out of his album *Bringing It All Back Home*, using electric instruments and drums on a number of songs. Dylan also appeared at the Newport Folk Festival as a rock devotee, supported by

the Paul Butterfield Blues Band. It shocked Pete Seeger and produced boo-
ing from the folk purists. This was also the year he attracted the general
pop audience with "Like a Rolling Stone." In the usual Dylan style, the
music to the verse consists mainly of repeated notes and the song's
melodic range remains narrow. The subject involves the punishment of the
once privileged, who are now penniless and homeless. It was, for critics, a
study in juvenile ill feeling, plus a sense of hurt and disenchantment with
the world.

Adding to his series of successful albums, he released *Blonde on
Blonde*, in 1966, which quickly won adherents to its sharply defined rock
sound. It went from the rowdily entertaining "Rainy Day Woman," to the
extensive fantasizing "Stuck inside of Mobile with the Memphis Blues
Again," and to the tugging at emotional strings in "Visions of Johanna"
and "Sad Eyed Lady of the Lowlands." Accompanied by his own instrumental group, the Band, he toured the United States and the United Kingdom, meanwhile issuing more songs and discovering that scores of other
singers were using his material. At the same time, his drug habit was growing out of control.

Owing to a motorcycle accident, on 29 July 1966, he withdrew from the
public eye for a while but continued to write—his new music mingling
country with folk influences. *John Wesley Harding* (1967) and *Nashville
Skyline* (1969) resulted. Noticeable in the former is its pastoral quietness
and minimalist use of notes. It presents Dylan in a subdued, nonaggressive
frame of mind. He appeared to be surveying an earlier time and style. In
the latter album, he traveled an informal country-music route, even singing
a duet with Johnny Cash in "Girl from the North Country." Unhappiness
in love occurs in songs without the sarcasm and sullenness of 1964–1965.
He was followed to some degree in this country direction by the Byrds and
the Flying Burrito Brothers, who also were admirers of Gram Parsons, a
trailblazer in the country-rock genre. Social-minded critics reprimanded
Dylan for elevating the music of narrow-minded Southerners. A number of
supporters who had heretofore adjusted to his changes in style repudiated
the musical transformations of the late sixties.

After these recordings, the new songs took on an uneven quality and
Dylan came in for a great deal more criticism. In 1975, he sought a recovery of his former popularity with *Blood on the Tracks*, which tried to return to the forcibleness of ten years before. However, at the end of 1978,
he declared himself a born-again Christian and hastily issued some religious albums, which bewildered and displeased even his most loyal fans.

Over the next several years he was constantly reinventing himself and went from one style to another, never settling anywhere. At last, in 1997, with *Time out of Mind*, an album consisting entirely of new songs, he managed to please again the popular audience. They accepted its communications, including some on personal isolation and living with private pain. In 2001, he issued a new album, *Love and Theft*, that contained songs of little weight that introduced waggish humor and lighthearted expression into the lyrics. The accompanying music was a pastiche of various pop-song styles going back to the beginning of the 20th century.

Over the years, Dylan has unquestionably been a leading pop figure and created many admired songs. He explored a wide range of emotions and united lyrics to melodies that fitted together exceptionally well. His most moving messages have been on occasion gentle, or wistful, or spiritual. Now and then, he seems overly odd, resentful, clever, or illusionary. We are not sure how to take him in his risqué and childish moments. He does not act as expected. When Dylan was inducted into the Rock and Roll Hall of Fame, in 1988, the singer–songwriter Bruce Springsteen said:

> Bob freed the mind the way Elvis freed the body. He showed us that just because the music was innately physical did not mean that it was anti-intellectual. He had the vision and the talent to make a pop song that contained the whole world. He invented a new way a pop singer could sound, broke through the limitations of what a recording artist could achieve, and changed the face of rock and roll forever.[44]

Dylan was never as "authentic" as the urban-folks wanted to believe. He enjoyed being unpredictable. This was underlined, on 3 August 2002, when he appeared (no longer a traitor to the cause) at the Newport Folk Festival wearing a bogus beard, a shaggy wig, and a cowboy hat. His continuous standing as a supreme representative of American pop culture is a result of his astonishing aptitude for sensing the changes in the direction of pop fashion and constantly adjusting his music to suit. Consciously or sometimes accidentally, he has skipped from position to position and altered his musical expression with perceptive astuteness to accommodate the changing times. In short, he has been both a successful opportunist and a brilliant artist able to encapsulate the needs and passions of the post–World War II generations in his compositions.

Some other important urban-folk singers would also abandon the folk purists. Judy Collins, for example, started off as a traditionalist and then went in for protest singing and political activism, like Baez. Then, like Dylan, she turned to personal songs when protest faded in the late sixties. In the albums *My Life* (1967), and *Wildflowers* and *Who Knows Where the Time Goes?* (1968), she revealed an introspective side in compositions by Leonard Cohen, Joni Mitchell, and herself. She later sang folk, pop (a light restrained version of folk-rock), and show tunes in orchestra arrangements and toured with Richie Havens, Janis Ian, and Roger McGuinn. However, as she entered the new century she conceded that singers like her, from the old urban-folk circle, had "no future in the increasingly youth-obsessed major-label world" and founded her own label. Major record companies, she said, just were not interested in any singer who "doesn't go platinum."[45] Collins was one of several dedicated singers who were trying to keep the urban-folk movement alive, nourished by comparatively modest audiences and small independent record labels; among the others were Mary Chapin Carpenter, Kris Delmhorst, Dave Carter, and Tracy Grammer. An astute Joni Mitchell once tried to explain the reasons for Collins's and her own difficulties with attracting a mass audience:

> I have, on occasion, sacrificed myself and my own emotional makeup, singing "I'm selfish and I'm sad," for instance. These are not attractive things in the context of rock and roll. It's the antithesis of rock and roll—which is "Honey, I'm a lover and I'm *bad*!" You don't go saying these other things in pop circles because they're liable to bring terrible results: unpopularity, which is what you don't want.[46]

Janis Ian, mentioned above, had achieved her first big hit in 1966, when 15 years of age. "Society's Child" invited controversy with its theme about interracial love ("Walk me down to school baby / Ev'ry body's acting deaf and blind / Until they turn and say 'Why don't you stick to your own kind'"),[47] which was set to an attractive melody. Over the next few years, she grew bolder and soon was to be counted among the folk-rock group. By the album *Present Company* (1971), she was recording with excellent sessions players and showing an ability to deal not only with urban-folk commentary, but also blues and rock. Two more much-admired songs followed, "Jesse" (1973) and the poignant "At Seventeen" (1976), where she wakes up to the truth that love is for beauty queens and girls with clear skin but not for her.[48] She continued performing and producing albums that sold well, but no subsequent song reached the popularity heights of these three.

Paul Simon and Art Garfunkel, like Collins and Ian, tried to beat the odds against folksingers after the sixties. Both had come from Newark, New Jersey, and tried the musical waters in 1955 with their first song, "The Girl for Me." Although they had some success in 1957 with "Hey Schoolgirl," nothing was really grabbing listeners. Finally, in 1966, Tom Wilson, a producer for Columbia Records, took the liberty of replacing the folk-faithful acoustic accompaniment to "Sound of Silence," written by Simon and recorded by the duo in 1963. Wilson threw out the acoustic-guitar sound and replaced it with electric guitar, bass, and drums, thus creating a fresh, decisive rhythmic track. The song, now in folk-rock clothing, went on to head the *Billboard* charts.[49] (The composition had originally been inspired by the March 1964 murder of Kitty Genovese in a Queens apartment, where at least 38 people were on the scene, looked on, but didn't lift a finger to stop the killer.) Its ingratiating melody is skillfully crafted, with short rising phrases that reach a climax on a high note. Then the melody curves lower and lower to rest on its opening low note. Meanwhile, the harmony remains ambiguous. Ostensibly the song, in the minor mode, remains in one key, but constant references to another key and lack of strong progressions in the home key add a background of some uncertainty to the proceedings. This musical ambiguity can be taken as a counterpart to the people who see evil and remain silent and uninvolved. The lyric ends with a description of a light shining on thousands of people who talk without speaking, hear without listening, and write songs that singers fail to communicate to each other—all because no one has the courage to intrude on the sound of silence.[50]

Simon's poetry reveals imagination, acuteness of mind, and emotional involvement. It has a fineness of feeling and grasp of underlying truth that would have been unacceptable six years before to urban-folk listeners, not to mention the nonacoustic instrumental sounds.

The next out-and-out hit was Simon's "Mrs. Robinson," a sharp-pointed, sardonic statement about American society, which was introduced into the film *The Graduate*, of 1966. A third extraordinary hit was the 1970 "Bridge over Troubled Water," a simple elegy. Simon assigned it a tune of touching loveliness suspended over far richer and varied harmonic progressions than those of "Sound of Silence." Simon, according to the directions on the published music, wished it sung "moderately, not too fast (like a spiritual)." The moving lyric begins by assuring the listener that if he feels tired and a nonentity there will be someone to sustain him. Tears will be dried. A friend will be there if times are rough. "Like a bridge over troubled water, I will lay me down."[51]

Yet, whatever we say about the lyric, we should remember Simon's comment: "When people write about songwriting they tend to write about lyric writing. It's very hard to write about music. What do you say about it? Music is a nonverbal experience. It's easier to address words. There are very few songs that are popular because their lyrics are good. There's quite a lot of songs whose lyrics are meaningless that are big hits and people love them. The music part of songwriting is much more potent and powerful than the lyric part."[52]

In 1971, Simon and Garfunkel went their separate ways. The next year, Simon started a solo career as a singer–songwriter. Some of the new songs were excellent. None achieved anywhere near the acclaim of the songs he had written, and he and Garfunkel had recorded, in the sixties.

The change from urban-folk into folk-rock that had already found an early exponent in Dylan and that others soon adopted would go down quite well with young men and women after the sixties. The switchover included use of electric instruments and drums, accepting some of the standards of music making employed to reach huge general audiences, and submitting to a system of making records that was dominated by producers and heads of record companies. Oftentimes, folk-rock and country-rock could not be clearly differentiated—as with Seals and Crofts, the Lovin' Spoonful, the Youngbloods, Buffalo Springfield, and the Butterfield Blues Band. After all, both had grown out of the Southern folk tradition. Folk-rockers continue to obtain nourishment from their roots. For example, the blunt, droll, and rocking Dan Bern, Iowa-born performer and songwriter, has always been open to the music of the older and dependable folksinger, and writer of folklike ditties, Greg Brown, who is also from Iowa.

After giving impetus to folk-rock, certain performers living in California, among them the Mamas and the Papas and the Byrds, would venture into psychedelic rock, which attempted to simulate the effect of psychedelic drugs like LSD on the senses.

CALIFORNIA DREAMING

California in the sixties was seen as a fortunate state enriched by defense contracts, a burgeoning electronics business, and financial well-being. In the south, a mild climate and stress-free living promoted a condition of contented pleasure seeking. Young lotus-eaters, given to indolence and ease in living, abounded in this part of California. They were soon es-

pousing a "surf music" that would advance the vision of a Californian Ar-
cadia with sunny beaches, stunning girls in scanty swimsuits, muscular
surfers riding the swells, and carefree drivers of showy cars. Surfing was
a Hawaiian sport imported to California and taking hold in the sixties.
Films like *Gidget* (1959), *Barefoot Adventure* (1962), *Beach Party* (1963),
and *Bikini Beach* (1964) helped popularize the activity. By 1965, California had over 100,000 surfers.

Dick Dale, Lebanese-born but brought up in Southern California, attempting to exploit the sound of the electric Fender guitar, put together an
amplifier-reverberation unit, and continued on to give "surf music" its
characteristically "fuzzy" resonance. He loved surfing. With a band called
the Deltones, he played at Balboa's Rendezvous Ballroom, where surfers
gathered. He introduced his new sound in 1961. In that same year, songwriter Brian Wilson, his brothers Carl and Dennis, cousin Mike Love, and
friend Al Jardine formed the Beach Boys, after the example of Dale and
the Deltones. They polished Dale's sound, nurtured a lively compelling
rock beat, and added elegant harmonies and succeeded in generating some
alluring, airy, and energetic songs. Their rise in popularity came in 1963
with *Surfin' U.S.A.* Appealing music advanced lyrics that abetted adolescent fantasies and wish fulfillment. Typical of their songs, Brian Wilson's
"Surfer Girl" (1963) sweetly serenades a girlfriend with a wistful tune and
a plea for love to a little surfer girl.[53]

In the same year came Wilson's "Your Summer Dream," about driving
with one's female companion to a beach, and walking along the shore with
her, hand in hand.[54] The next year, Wilson's gusty "I Get Around," about
boys driving along the streets looking for girls, took a more masculine
turn. The song portrays a "cool guy" with money to spend and a car to
drive. He and his buddies have acquired such a reputation for toughness
that the bad guys leave them alone.[55]

The popularity of the Beach Boys was a reminder that however large
the number of liberated, free-thinking, serious-minded young people, an
even larger number preferred not to engage with the world's problems,
which they thought were better left to the adult years, if they were taken
up at all. They liked better their own immature dreams of going out on
dates, driving at high speeds, and carefree living. When the Beatles appeared in the United States, the Beach Boys were one of the few American bands to give them real competition. Wilson's songs presented engaging visions of happy teenage years, the fresh pleasures of surfing,
fleeting calf love, and the joy of having an automobile and going on a

date. The Beach Boys visited Europe in 1964, and won over a host of British fans. Biographer Steven Gaines writes, "Their music, perceived as the encapsulation of the American dream, was in some ways more popular in England than in the United States."[56]

Wilson's masterpiece with the Beach Boys was the 1966 album *Pet Sounds*, although it sold slowly when it first was issued. Thirty-five years later a VH1[57] poll would judge it one of the three best albums in rock history.[58] With this album, Brian Wilson and the Beach Boys veered away from the happy sounds and jubilant lyrics contained in their previous songs. It was natural that fun-loving kids refused to go along. No longer did the music present happy teenagers captured in short, enticing, and unchallenging songs. Instead, the lyrics turned inward, finding both optimism and doubt in oneself. Melody, harmony, rhythm, and lyric work perfectly together in song after song—for example, the throbbing rhythms go well with the lyrics of "Don't Talk (Put Your Head on My Shoulder)," and the quality of the harmonies enhances "God Only Knows." In "Wouldn't It Be Nice" the vocalist wishes longingly for something that may not happen— wishing and hoping and praying for marriage and the happiness it may bring.[59]

However, the song "God Only Knows" acknowledges that lovers can part and life will go on, however unsatisfactory it may be.[60] The final song in the album, "Caroline, No," is about heartbreak over the transience of love and life. The long-haired girl he has once known is gone, along with her glow of happiness. His heart breaks and he wants to cry as he watches his sweet Caroline on the road to death.[61]

It was an influential collection of songs that affected the development of future musical events and artists. It spurred the Beatles into recording their *Sgt. Pepper* album. Elton John said it "blew my mind." Punk and country interpretations of its songs came out later.[62] One more song released in 1966 had a wide sale, "Good Vibrations." After that year, drugs and personality conflicts pulled the band apart. The Beach Boys lost much of their clout.

The Byrds (Jim McGuinn, Gene Clark, David Crosby, Chris Hillman, and Michael Clarke), organized in Los Angeles, were another Southern California band of the sixties. They started by dispensing folk-rock in 1964–65—Dylan's "Mr. Tambourine Man" and Seeger's "Turn! Turn! Turn!" Indian raga and jazz were added to their style, and in 1966 the remarkable "Eight Miles High" and "Fifth Dimension" further pushed up their standing. At the same time, critics condemned them for singing about or under the influence of drugs. The songs proved to be a knowledgeable mix of assertive psychedelically shaded rhythms and words with full folk-rock harmonizations. Clark, McGuinn, and Crosby's drug-infused "Eight Miles High," for example, speaks about being "eight miles high" and touching down onto a street whose signs are meaningless.[63] McGuinn's be-numbed "Fifth Dimension" begins by wondering how he is still on his feet even though the world seemed to have fallen to pieces and he thought he was dead.[64]

One of their best albums, *Younger Than Yesterday*, was issued in 1967. It went from hints at Hindu melody in "Mind Gardens," through a variety of styles, to a song having roots in the country music of the Southeast, "Time Between."[65] Dissension among members caused the band to founder and by the midseventies their glory days had passed.

The Mamas and the Papas, formed by John Phillips in 1965, was another Los Angeles group that had a folk base. They sang of the more favorable side of life though shaded with some of life's darker moments, clothed in highly pleasing harmonizations, starting with their "California Dreamin'" of 1966. That and their other hit, "Monday, Monday," were from Phillips's pen. Dressing like hippies, they quickly attracted a following from San Francisco's Haight-Ashbury residents, especially after their praise of the hippy lifestyle in "San Francisco (Be Sure to Wear Some Flowers in Your Hair)." The Monterey Festival of 1967 was directed by Phillips. Shortly after, the group gave a concert in London, recorded an album, and dissolved.

The younger Eagles were also formed in Los Angeles. They fostered a country-rock sound and achieved five extraordinary hits, "Best of My Love" (1975), "One of These Nights" (1975), "New Kid in Town" (1977), "Hotel California" (1977), and "Heartache Tonight" (1979). Although most of their songs follow the confident line of the Beach Boys, "Hotel California," by band members Don Felder, Don Henley, and Glenn Frey, is unusual in that it reveals the grubby underbelly of Southern California life.[66] A man stops at night at the hotel symbolizing California. A pretty woman welcomes him at the door and he is told it's a lovely place that goes with the lovely face he has just seen. He soon learns that "her mind is Tiffany-twisted," she drives a Mercedes Benz, and knows "a lot of pretty, pretty boys" but little else. She admits, "We are all just prisoners here, of our own device." After witnessing a surrealistic feast, he takes fright and runs for the door. However, the night man turns him back, saying he may think he is checking out but he can never leave.[67]

Yet, the California dream of endless summer has persisted into the 21st century. Sheryl Crow, touting her new album *C'mon, C'mon* in 2002, said, "I'm communication central, and I'm sick of the minutiae that fill my day. In the song ["Soak up the Sun"] I wanted to get back to the feeling that bands like the Eagles gave us. They were the sounds of summer, of wanting to get in your car and be free and to turn the radio up really loud and have experiences. We forget."[68]

Looking northward, to San Francisco, we find that Jack Kerouac arrived there in 1951 and published *On the Road* six years later. Allen Ginsberg came in 1953, and two years later gave the public his notoriously heathen poem *Howl*. By then the Northern California community of beatniks, or Beats, was in full swing—people who loved eccentric acts and garb. Beats often revealed an obsession with exotic and imprecise chatter about life and with expressing one's own persona whether in talk, behavior, adorning oneself and habitation, or through music, art, and poetry. In 1965, their name changed from Beats to hippies, when they began to come together for "trips," gatherings where under the influence of a hallucinogenic drug, like LSD, they were put into a condition of euphoric dreaming and turned to expressing themselves through weird clothing, improvised dancing, and floating around in a state of ecstasy.

Two psychedelic-rock halls opened in San Francisco, in 1965, the Avalon of Chet Helms and the Fillmore Auditorium of Bill Graham. Two years later, Graham would open Fillmore East in New York. When a band played in such a hall, it was accompanied with strobe lights, flashing colors, films flickering on the walls, and LSD-spiked beverages. To accommodate the West Coast music crowds, *Rolling Stone* magazine was started. By 1967, some 50,000 hippies were living around Haight-Ashbury and were attracting college students there, with the promise of mind expansion through drugs, and sexual freedom via the birth-control pill. Into the picture entered Timothy Leary, advocating the use of LSD, a powerful psychedelic drug, for mind release. Alongside him, Ken Kesey promoted hallucinatory visions in his Acid Test Festivals.

California dreaming now meant constant fantasizing in a drug haze and no longer the more innocent dreaming of the early Beach Boys. Psychedelic bands offered music experiences, through "acid-rock" that simulated the intensified sensory perceptions brought on by LSD (lysergic acid)—so said Paul Kantnor of Jefferson Airplane. Phil Lesh, of the Grateful Dead, insisted that psychedelic music expanded awareness and consciousness. The liner notes to *The Psychedelic Sounds of the 13th Floor Elevators*

(1966) state, "Recently, it has become possible for man to chemically alter his mental state and thus alter his point of view. . . . He then can restructure his thinking and change his language so that his thoughts bear more relation to his life and his problems, therefore approaching them more sanely. It is this quest for pure sanity that forms the basis of the songs in this album."[69] Outfits like the Grateful Dead built on an eclectic mix of influences and introduced long, unpredictable improvisations. Their music offered hallucinatory-like musical experiences. "As the hippie movement faded," Graeme Boone writes, "the Dead provided the impetus to a vast culture of followers known as Deadheads, whose musical and social ideals" stemmed "directly from those of the hippies, with elements of pacifism, openmindedness, hedonism, and the usual psychedelic drugs." The Dead continued to perform to huge crowds until the death of Jerry Garcia in 1995.[70]

The performances of these bands were oftentimes associated with an audience experiencing severe sensory distortions and deliriums or extreme sensations of either happiness or depression. The musicians borrowed whatever they needed from traditional pop, rhythm and blues, folk, country, classical music, and traditional Indian music. (Ravi Shankar was appearing then to play classical Indian music on the sitar.) The most noted groups were Quicksilver Messenger Service, the Grateful Dead, Moby Grape, the Jefferson Airplane, Sly and the Family Stone, Country Joe and the Fish, 13th Floor Elevators, and Big Brother and the Holding Company. In Los Angeles arose their counterparts—Love, the Doors, Clear Light, and Kaleidoscope. In New York there was the Velvet Underground. In London there was Pink Floyd. Most such groups stayed together about two years before disintegrating. Their sound could be torpid and without edges. Or it could be aggressively loud, and bludgeon the senses (in this regard, it was a precursor of punk). Jim Morrison, with the Doors, went into violent demonstrations of sullen cruelty and sexual gratification on stage, screaming with lewd gestures the words to songs like the sexual invitation of "Light My Fire," or like the thought of murdering his father and having sex with his mother in "The End." By itself, a Morrison lyric seems to be juvenile bluster. However, with "the sexually charged delivery, Ray Manzarek's dry organ, and Robert Krieger's jazzy guitar," the words became "eerie, powerful, almost shamanistic invocations that hinted at a familiarity with darker forces and, in Morrison's case, an obsession with excess and death."[71] On the other hand, Grace Slick and the Jefferson Airplane provided a more memorable psychedelic classic, "White Rabbit," in their album *Surrealistic Pillow*. In this surrealistic song, the band tries to persuade listeners into experimenting with drugs, and makes reference to Lewis Carroll's "white rabbit," in *Alice's Adventures in Wonderland*, to underline the idea. The music starts softly and grows to a climax, at which point the singer Grace Slick urges a listener to "feed your head." As with Alice, a pill can make you large while another can make you small. If chasing rabbits and you are about to fall, say that a caterpillar smoking a hookah has called you.[72]

Janis Joplin joined Big Brother and the Holding Company in 1966 and gripped fans at the Monterey Festival with her blues-streaked screams, groans, and howls, and the rough sounds of rage, horror, and torment. Drinking, exchanges with her audience, and lengthy incoherent soliloquies filled out the interludes between songs. She delivered with searing conviction music numbers like Willie Mae "Big Mama" Thornton's Delta blues piece, "Ball and Chain," that describes love as a painful ball and chain from which she wants rescue.[73]

Joplin wore herself down on alcohol, drugs, and sex. She would die of a drug overdose in 1970. Jimi Hendrix, the passionate guitar burner, who also appeared at the Monterey Festival, was also dead of a drug overdose in 1970. By the seventies, the peak of psychedelic music had been reached. Crime, disease, and death spread through Haight-Ashbury and its like communities. Band members started to undergo conversion. Even the Grateful Dead decided to let go of their devotion to LSD; they turned to country-rock. However, it was tragic that once introduced, drugs would never leave the rock-music world. Whether as "potheads" or "dopeheads," young people got addicted. Again and again rock musicians and fans would lead ruined lives or overdose and die.

Another development in the West and Mideast was adolescent garage-rock. It was revealed in the crude muscle of amateur bands whose white suburban members were rebelling against the professionalism, in particular the display of extreme competence blemished by absence of freshness, which had begun to pervade performing groups. The usual place for practicing was the garage, hence the name. Most of them never went beyond local recognition and bore names like the Makers, the Murder City Devils, Shadows of Knight, the Count Five, the Standells, the Seeds, the Mysterians, and the Gentrys. They prided themselves on their musical ignorance, though inevitably the more they performed the better they became. Stevie Nicks, formerly with Fleetwood Mac, came close to the garage-band mentality when she admitted in April 2001 to her lack of musical training: "I never took a music class or music reading class. So I never learned a bunch of chords. I know your basic chords on the guitar, but I don't know minor 7ths. . . . It's like all the time I would say to people, 'I'm going to take guitar lessons' or 'I'd love to take piano lessons.' But they would say to me, '*Don't!*' They would add, 'If you go and get trained, you won't write the same songs anymore.' "[74]

The garage rockers started by plucking clumsily on their guitars. They used mostly three basic chords and simple, thudding rhythms. The music was heavily distorted with unpleasant snarls from the guitars, belligerent growls from the vocalists, and distorted feedback from the electronic amplifying systems. Overpowering screeches and sneers competed with deafening fuzz-toned guitars. (Electronic devices distorted the sound to give it a fuzzy quality.) It was a method of performance that punk rockers like the Sex Pistols would emulate later. Indeed, the guitarist Lenny Kaye compiled a *Nugget* album, in 1972, which featured several garage bands, and in the liner notes invented the term "punk-rock" in reference to their music making.

The final garage group, Iggy Pop and the Stooges, came to life in Michigan, in 1967, after the musicians attended a concert by the Doors. From the beginning of their performances, Iggy Pop (James Osterberg) was deliberately offensive with his odd ill-mannered behavior, like that of a juvenile delinquent, and the noisy, unyieldingly hard rock beat that accompanied him. A cultivated incompetence and nihilism was part of their act. After making a couple of albums, the group had to cope with Iggy's heroin addiction and found itself foundering. Later, Iggy joined David Bowie, who helped him return to normality, record some fine-selling music, and gain a little monetary stability. During the sixties and beyond, performers who were the complete opposites of Iggy Pop and the Stooges thrived by catering to the youngest adolescents. Motown's Jackson 5 was one such group. On the white side were the Osmonds. In 1962, brothers Alan, Jay, Merrill, and Wayne were taken on by Disney and won over the very young, more owing to their looks than to their playing ability. They quickly began music lessons to catch up, which they did. Then Marie and Donny came on the pop scene. Fourteen-year-old Donny went on to "bubblegum" fame with the 1971 release of "Sweet and Innocent." (Bubblegum refers to an inconsequential sort of music characterized usually by feeble lyrics and repetitive phrasing that was aimed at age levels as low as ten or nine.) Singer and song were adored by swoony girls who had not yet entered their teens.

The Monkees embarked on a different tangent after they were manufactured in 1965, in Los Angeles. Several hundred youths were auditioned by television producers Bob Rafelson and Bert Schneider, intent on launching a photogenic band that could compete with the Beatles. Four were selected to do the vocals and counterfeit the playing of instruments, which parts were added by capable but uncredited studio musicians. Excellent songwriters created their material—Neil Diamond, Carole King, Neil Sedaka, and the Monkee member Michael Nesmith, among them. A TV series was created for NBC and the prefabricated Monkees acted their way to stardom. Screaming teenage mobs attended their shows, millions bought their records, and Monkee merchandise sold well nationwide. Especially well received were Diamond's song "I'm a Believer" and Tommy Boyce and Bobby Hart's "Last Train to Clarksville" (both 1966). In 1967, a fed-up Nesmith confessed the truth to the New York newspapers, but the band continued to have hits until the end of the decade.

In further explanation of the term "bubblegum," it was first coined to cover the sort of music making in which the Monkees engaged. However, its principal application began when Buddah Records was formed, around 1967, in order to put out shamelessly money-making pieces for 9-year-olds. The songs were kept short, pleasant, undemanding, insubstantial, and ear-catching. This "manufactured" music was produced by record makers who frequently employed studio musicians to play and sing at a recording session. Often a false band name appeared on the record label in order to encourage youngsters to believe an actual outfit had performed the music. Titles like "Yummy, Yummy, Yummy," "Sugar, Sugar," and "Goody Goody Gumdrops" attracted the preteen listener. It was all a concocted innocence. Writing in *Mojo* magazine, Dawn Eden said, "From the get-go, bubblegum was a purely commercial genre. Producers like Buddah Records' Jerry Kosenetz and Jeff Katz had no higher aspiration than to make a quick buck and get out. Yet, with the help of talents like Joey Levine, they propagated a musical form that continues to influence acts the world over. . . . Power pop aims for your heart and feet. Bubblegum aims for any part of your body it can get as long as you *buy* the damn record."[75]

In most instances no musical talent was evident; the greatest talent went into lip-synchronization. A few artificial bands were called the 1910 Fruitgum Company, Tommy James and the Shondelles, the Lemon Pipers, the Archies, the Partridge Family, and the Ohio Express. All of them, with the help of studio musicians, succeeded with danceable, bubbly, throwaway music. Once a fan had purchased and heard one piece, advertisements urged the preteen-aged boy or girl to purchase another single or album from the music factory. By the early seventies, the original bubblegum furor was over. However, the bubblegum concept has continued into the 21st century with groups like Milli Vanilli, the Spice Girls, 'NSync, Backstreet Boys, and Britney Spears. They are given exaggerated publicity, presented as a staged spectacle, and sold to the unwary and unsophisticated. Johnny Podell, who represented Britney Spears and other bubblegummers, commented in the fall of 2002 that when most of his clients grew up their careers were over: "The teen pop thing is mostly synthetic. The majority don't get to the next level."[76]

THE BRITISH INVASION

The first thing that must be kept in mind is that the British popular music of the last half of the 20th century, as was true of the first half, borrowed heavily from American popular music, whether from Tin Pan Alley and Broadway shows or from country and western, folk-rock, rhythm and blues, and rock 'n' roll. The famous British rock bands that started to come over in the sixties built themselves on American foundations—starting with the Beatles, Rolling Stones, and the Who. They built so well that soon they were threatening to rise higher in people's affections than any of their white American competitors.

The four Beatles (George Harrison, Ringo Starr [added in 1962], John Lennon, and Paul McCartney) grew up as children of working-class people in Liverpool. They were not excited about attending school but did become enthusiastic about the American music they were hearing in local clubs and dance halls, and on radio and recordings—country and western, rhythm and blues, rockabilly, and some of the prevalent pop. Presley, Chuck Berry, Carl Perkins, and the Everly Brothers were more immediate influences. When they made their first appearances as a performing group their repertoire was selected from the different American sources just named. They had a professional engagement in Hamburg, Germany, where Brian Epstein heard them in 1961 and noted the enthusiasm of the young German crowds.

Epstein became their manager, and landed them interviews with the Decca and Parlophone record companies. He taught them how to dress and behave so that the public might accept them as neat and wholesome boys. He suggested songs that they could be comfortable with. They learned to do as they were told because they felt this would lead to fame and fortune. Signing on Parlophone, the Beatles made their first sizable impression in

Europe with "Love Me Do" and "P.S. I Love You," in 1962. The next year, the album *Please, Please Me* came out and met with wider appreciation. At last, in 1963, Capitol Records released the single "I Want to Hold Your Hand" and the album *Meet the Beatles* in the United States. American enthusiasm for the Beatles commenced to grow. Up to this point in time British popular musicians had made scarcely a dent in the American market. An astute investment of $50,000 to promote the Beatles resulted in success. Publicists whipped up anticipation of their impending arrival in the United States. Swiftly, the excited public interest in the Beatles reached amazing heights. On 7 February 1964, the four teenage Beatles flew in to New York City to be greeted by a hysterical and riotous throng of youngsters, mostly adolescent girls. Some critics claimed that Brian Epstein had paid a claque to lay siege to the young men, brandishing signs and creating a photogenic uproar.[77] On 9 and 16 February they appeared on the *Ed Sullivan Show*. Girls shrieked and hurled themselves at the stage or fainted and fell to the floor. "Beatlemania" had begun. Young Americans were completely sold on them. In some ways the entrance of the Beatles into New York was a repeat of the Jenny Lind (the "Swedish nightingale") arrival in the city on September 11, 1950, with ballyhoo carefully engineered by P. T. Barnum, and of the "Lindomania" that ensued.

The Beatles were wunderkinder—adorable foreigners with lots of energy, adorable accents and fringed haircuts, and delectable ditties about and for girls. If you were under 20 and female, you might easily come under their spell. They could even reach the preteen set with their brief two- or three-minute demands on attention, simplistic lyrics, and inoffensive and melodious rock sound that went at an unhurried speed. To this, the Beatles added an unfussy background accompaniment, uncomplicated rhythmic patterns over plain bass lines, and a lead singer or the group singing in unison. For example, "I Want to Hold Your Hand," written by Lennon and McCartney, has a likable, pleasantly singable tune cast in a Tin Pan Alley structure. From beginning to end, the melody divides into brief, clear-cut phrases. The only surprises are the unexpected wide upward leap of the voice on the first occurrence of the word "hand," and the surprising chord changes in the harmony. These supply some electrical current to the music. The artless lyric captured a prevalent teenage sentiment when it tells of how a young person will understand that all one wants is to "hold your hand."[78]

From the 1940s and Sinatra onward, a new popular-music obsession had caused adolescents to behave as if demented every few years. This had been especially true of girls from 9 years of age on up, whose frenzied response to a band or individual musician looked a great deal like a reversion to primitive times. (It is not coincidental that the tongue-in-cheek film *What a Way to Go!* featuring Shirley Maclaine, was released in 1964, in which a pop-music star is torn apart by his frenzied fans.) David Dempsey referred to "the Orpheus effect" of the Beatles, whom girls worshipped but were ready to tear apart if given the chance. The teenage culture had a religion, he writes, the cult of popular personalities of their own age.[79] At a later date Bob Sheffield summed up the effect of the Beatles' early songs on him when he was an adolescent, writing, "Every time I hear 'I Feel Fine' or 'Eight Days a Week,' that's me in the back row screaming and pulling my hair out. Just check out 'I Want to Hold Your Hand,' which explodes out of the speakers with the finest singing, drumming, guitars, lyrics and girl-crazy howls ever recorded."[80]

As they became more confident in themselves and their ability to sustain their popularity, the Beatles changed their style. After 1965, the lyrics grew more intricate and symbolic. Interestingly, the year before, they had met Bob Dylan, who introduced them to the pleasures of smoking marijuana, the charms of folk-rock, and the virtues of meaningful verse. They had also witnessed the California psychedelic bands and learned about impressionistic, stream-of-consciousness texts, disguised references to drugs, and the exploitation of unusual electronic sounds. Their ambition now was to reach an older group and not worry about pleasing the preteens. They made their first two films, *A Hard Day's Night* and *Help!* Critics and the public applauded both, finding them clever, funny, and imaginative.

The first album indicating the new Beatles perspective was *Rubber Soul*, released at the end of 1965. It was a diverse compilation, stretching from the pensive "In My Life," to the sharp satire in "Nowhere Man" and the sitar-colored atmospherics of "Norwegian Wood." In their songs, the "I" viewpoint gave way to something more generalized. The music exhibited more thought and original expression than before. The approach somewhat resembled the style of the American folk-rockers, and had the guitar brought forward and the percussion pushed back. The pathetic "Eleanor Rigby," written by Lennon and McCartney, and included in the 1966 album *Revolver*, exemplifies the change. (The album would also include Lennon-McCartney's achingly despairing "For No One," Harrison's caustic "Taxman," and Lennon's LSD-laced "Tomorrow Never Knows.") The sound of the song's introduction is based on an ancient mode, rather than the major or minor scale, and much of the principal melody is in still another ancient mode, which contributes to a folk flavor. Melodic phrases vary in length. Yet the tune itself swings along gracefully and sounds unforced. It had the power to catch the interest of the more mature listener. The emotionally evocative lyric begins high up in the musical range as twice we hear the voice wail, "Ah, look at all the lonely people!" Then the main text begins, telling of a forlorn Eleanor Rigby who gazes longingly out of her window waiting and longing for a wedding that will never take place.[81] The songs pushed the right expressive and psychological buttons. The Beatles' followers took to the changes— so much so that the *London Evening Standard*, for 4 March 1966, reported John Lennon as boasting, "We're more popular than Jesus now. I don't know which will go first—rock 'n' roll or Christianity."

Soon after *Revolver*, the Beatles grew weary of constant travel and appearing before screeching adolescents. Harrison, for example, said the young audiences made so much noise at concerts, they drowned out the music. All they wanted the Beatles to sing were just "the same 10 dopey tunes," nothing new.[82] They abandoned public performance in favor of working in the studio and tried to explore a larger realm of ideas. In 1967 they released the circuslike *Sgt. Pepper's Lonely Hearts Club Band*. It became not just a music album but a cultural representation of current youthful thinking involving drugs, facile mysticism, worldwide fellowship, and liberation from family ties. Into the experimental electronic pot went white rock 'n' roll, black rhythm and blues, English music-hall songs, and classical music. Out came the exuberant title song, the vaudevillian dance song "When I'm Sixty-Four," and the surrealistic "Lucy in the Sky with Diamonds."

When John Lennon took up with Yoko Ono and divorced his wife, Paul McCartney composed a little song to comfort Lennon's son Julian, in 1968. Lennon said that he took the song very personally and helped rewrite it. In due course "Hey Julian" changed into "Hey Jules" and finally became the single "Hey Jude." In addition to the four Beatles on guitars and drums, a 36-piece orchestra contributed richness to the recording. Within half a year, over 2 million copies were sold. Up until this time, it was one of the lengthiest popular songs ever circulated as a single, lasting 7 minutes and 11 seconds. A consoling lyric was attached to a rambling yet pleasing melody. Like "Eleanor Rugby," the tune at first gives off decided country-folk overtones. Unlike the earlier song, a major key prevails, rather than an antique mode, and the harmonies soothe rather than sadden. And there were a lot of young people who wanted comforting musically and verbally, however vicarious the experience. McCartney sings the vocal, and soon Lennon enters in harmony. The words advise a young boy to make a sad song better by letting "her" into his heart.[83]

Their last recorded album, *Abbey Road*, was made in 1969. After this, the Beatles broke up, each going his own way. In 1980, John Lennon was murdered by a Beatles fan and the myth about the Beatles suffered a major blow. Nevertheless, what would stand was their key contributions to rock—their international popularization of the music, their plaiting the several disparate strands of rock, folk, traditional pop, rhythm and blues, and country and western together to form a resilient whole, and above all, the long list of original songs, qualitatively admirable and providing enchantment to a vast adoring audience. Individual Beatles continued to put out songs. In 1971, for instance, Lennon published "Imagine," which conceived the world living as one and at peace, and Harrison published "My Sweet Lord," which made public his yearning for "my lord (hare Krishna)." Both, particularly the latter, made an impression on their fans. However, things were not the same and the Beatles could never be put together again.

On the heels of the Beatles came a second British band, whose effect was vastly different from that of the Beatles. The Rolling Stones (Mick Jagger, Keith Richards, Brian Jones, Bill Wyman, and Charlie Watts) were formed in 1962 and signed on Andrew Oldham as their manager in the next year. They relished playing rhythm and blues and rockabilly (after Muddy Waters, Chuck Berry, Buddy Holly, and Elvis Presley), had no wish to perform endearing tunes, and tended to shout their lyrics. Theirs was a hard-rocking music marked by a heavy aggressive beat, high amplification, and unusually energetic performances, which gave them an angry sound, even when love was the subject. Like black musicians, they cultivated an earthy image. Performances were filled out with sexual innuendos and unmannerly body language. American teenagers loved the performances. The Rolling Stones were rebellion personified. As Jagger cynically put it in 1975, "That's what we wanted you Americans to think, that we were dirty and raunchy. That was our image over there. If those dumb American birds dig that kind of shit, why shouldn't we do it?"[84] They deliberately made the most of the moral decay surrounding them and took caustic delight in exposing society's pretensions and hypocrisy. At the same time, they redoubled the general public's censorious mind-set toward rock.

By 1965 they were presenting their own material, as in the bluesy, riff-emphasizing "(I Can't Get No) Satisfaction," of Mick Jagger and Keith

Richards, in which the central idea is to convey the pointlessness of doing anything in a chaotic world. No matter how much one tries, he accomplishes nothing.[85] The next year they were deeply into Eastern mysteries, destructive behavior, taking drugs, and psychedelic-leaning music. With *Aftermath* (1966), they crossed the threshold into a macabre, alarming place—hallucinatory, drug-drenched, and packed full of sex, struggle, suffering, and death omens. Morris Dickstein, with this album in mind, wrote: "One of the virtues of rock songs is their frank sexuality, with lyrics and performance that complement the physicality and energy that's there in the music. Even when the sex verges on the sophomoric, as it does on 'Going Home,' it's far more honest than the disembodied romantic clichés of the fifties. . . . But the rock scene gave rise to its own sexual distortions, especially in the way sex gets expressed so heavily in terms of power games."[86]

The 1967 album *At Their Satanic Majesties Request* and the 1968 *Beggar's Banquet* demonstrated the darker side of the Rolling Stones. The latter album contained the bizarre "Sympathy for the Devil." Mick Jagger wrote it without his usual help from Keith Richards. However, Richards suggested changes in the rhythm, which Jagger heeded. The music when finished sounded like a samba, a bit mesmerizing and a bit weird. Jagger, an avid bookworm, pointed to Baudelaire's influence on "Sympathy." Yet, he was then also fascinated by Mikhail Bulgakov's allegorical novel of good and evil, *The Master and Margarita*. The verse turns conventional morality on its head, telling us that all police officers are lawbreakers, transgressors are people consecrated to virtue, and the Devil reigns unrestrained.[87] This was the time of the Watts riots, the My Lai Massacre, and the assassinations of Martin Luther King and Robert Kennedy. Society seemed sinking more into chaos than ever. Nothing made sense. The Rolling Stones and their American listeners found morality defunct and incapable of holding back the evil that needed "some restraint." The song also foretold the preoccupation with evil of heavy-metal bands like Black Sabbath, Van Halen, and Metallica. Two important albums came next, *Let It Bleed* (1969) and *Exile on Main Street* (1972). After these albums came out, although the Rolling Stones continued to create hits, their influence subsided.

Another British phenomenon of the sixties was the antisocial Who, led by guitarist and songwriter Peter Townshend. Technically the Who were part of the British teenage movement that started in the 1960s, whose members were called mods (British teenagers who tried to appear sophisticated and wore fancy clothing, often inspired by Edwardian dress). The Who made singular and grotesque music, different from anything being done by anyone else at the time. They devoted themselves to what seemed senseless and outrageous (living as they believed in a senseless and outrageous world) and played and behaved in a way that anticipated punk rock. For example, they moved their feet alternately as in marching, but without advancing, leaping about insanely, spinning mikes around for no reason, increasing feedback from their amplifiers, and occasionally demolishing their instruments. Like the Rolling Stones they attracted a large circle of fans.

Especially when they began, they played in the unusual, lawless fashion just described. With *My Generation* (1965), *I Can't Explain* (1965), and *The Who Sell Out* (1967), they appeared to be a disturbing but at the same time powerful force. An appearance at the Monterey Festival, in 1967, enhanced their reputation in the United States. A couple of years later, they came out with *Tommy*, a 90-minute rock musical about a boy who goes deaf and dumb after he witnesses his father's murder, becomes a pinball wizard, attracts a following, and then self-destructs. It put the Who in good standing with critics. Made into a movie in 1975, it featured fine musicians like Ann-Margaret, Elton John, Eric Clapton, and Tina Turner.

In 1978, their madcap drummer Keith Moon died, and the death seemed to drain some of the character from the group. They continued playing but not with their former swaggering spirit. Peter Townshend also went off on his own as a singer–songwriter. In 1985, he would give advice on how to construct a song so as to catch the attention of listeners:

First the rhythm. You have to be able to dance to it, drive to it, or smooch to it. It's almost like journalism. State your case in the first few bars, tell people what this is going to be about, use a catch phrase. Get them in the first few seconds. . . . Then you have a verse to create an atmosphere. . . . But then don't abuse these people! They want entertainment! . . . Give them the catch again, keep them interested. Then go and write another bit, amplify it a bit more. This time you can write pretty heavy stuff because you've got them. Then it's time to . . . give them a break; go off and give them a guitar solo or write something we call a middle eight. Maybe even change the subject. . . . Then close your argument; . . . wrap it up in the last verse. And finally . . . give them the catch again. . . . That's the frame. You can bend it around a little bit, but the definitive rock songs have been written against that very powerful, simple set of limitations.[88]

NOTES

1. Pearl Bailey, *Talking to Myself* (New York: Harcourt Brace Jovanovich, 1971), 15.

2. See Deborah Grace Winer, *The Night and The Music* (New York: Schirmer, 1996), 70.

3. Max Wilk, *They're Playing Our Song* (New York: Atheneum, 1973), 8.

4. Robert Palmer, *Rock & Roll: An Unruly History* (New York: Harmony Books, 1995), 16.

5. Stephen Braun, "A Pack Rat's Legacy of Live Country Music," *Boston Globe*, 23 September 2001, A26.

6. Curtis W. Ellison, *Country Music Culture* (Jackson, Mississippi: University Press of Mississippi, 1995), 5–6.

7. Nashville: Songs of Iris/Forerunner Music, c1992.

8. Loretta Lynn with George Vecsey, *Coal Miner's Daughter* (Chicago: Regency, 1976), x.

9. Merle Haggard with Peggy Russell, *Sing Me Back Home* (New York: Times Books, 1981), 242–43.

10. Nashville: Sure-Fire Music, c1965.

11. Lynn with Vecsey, *Coal Miner's Daughter*, 62.

12. Nashville: Coal Miners Music, c1975.

13. Beverly Hills, California: Al Gallico Music Corp., c1968.

14. Beverly Hills, California: Al Gallico Music Corp., c1967.

15. Ellison, *Country Music Culture*, 139–40.

16. Lynn with Vecsey, *Coal Miner's Daughter*, 101.

17. Nashville: Tree Publishing Co., c1960.

18. David Marsh, *The Heart of Rock and Roll* (New York: New American Library, 1989), 265. He calls it a cosmopolitan piece, of a genre that would rule Nashville for a decade or so.

19. Loretta Lynn with Peter Bale Cox, *Still Woman Enough* (Waterville, Maine: Thorndike Press, 2002), 167.

20. New York: Cherry Lane Music, c1971.

21. New York: Cherry Lane Music, c1972.

22. Morris Dickstein, *Gates of Eden* (New York: Basic Books, 1977), ix.

23. New York: United Artists Music, c1966.

24. Ben Brantley, "'Hair': When Love Was In and Youthful Confidence High," *New York Times*, 5 May 2001, www.nytimes.com.

25. Dinitia Smith, "Life with the Weathermen: No Regrets for a Love of Explosives," *New York Times*, 11 September 2001, www.nytimes.com.

26. James Miller, *Flowers in the Dustbin* (New York: Simon & Schuster, 1999), 266.

27. Beverly Hills, California: Broken Arrow Music, c1970.

28. See Tom Wicker, introduction to *The New York Times Great Songs of the Sixties*, ed. Milton Okun (New York: Quadrangle Books, 1970), 15; Bruce J. Schulman, *The Seventies* (New York: Free Press, 2001), 2–3.

29. Robert Cantwell, *When We Were Good: The Folk Revival* (Cambridge: Harvard University Press, 1996), 351.

30. David P. Szatmary, *Rockin' in Time*, 2nd ed. (Englewood Cliffs, New Jersey: Prentice-Hall, 1991), 86–87.

31. Los Angeles, California: Universal Duchess Music, c1965.

32. Cantwell, *When We Were Good*, 2, 316–17.

33. New York: Fall River Music, c1961.

34. New York: Ludlow Music, c1962.

35. New York: Witmark & Sons, c1962.

36. I was listening to her and Buffy Saint-Marie in coffeehouses during these early years and can testify to the voice and delivery.

37. Cantwell, *When We Were Good*, 338, 340.

38. David Ewen, *All the Years of American Popular Music* (Englewood Cliffs, New Jersey: Prentice-Hall, 1977), 645.

39. Santa Monica, California: Chandos Music, c1975.

40. New York: Witmark & Sons, c1963.

41. Szatmary, *Rockin' in Time*, 99.

42. New York: Witmark & Sons, c1964.

43. Bob Spitz, *Dylan* (New York: Norton, 1989), 328.

44. "Bob Dylan," *Mr. Showbiz Celebrities*, on the web, entered on 10 September 2002.

45. Scott Alarik, "An Energized Judy Collins Takes Charge," *Boston Globe*, 3 August 2001, D13, 15.

46. Timothy White, *Rock Lives* (New York: Holt, 1990), 333.

47. Nashville: Dialogue Music, c1966.

48. Hollywood, California: Rude Girl, c1976.

49. Fred Bronson, *The Billboard Book of Number One Hits*, 4th ed. (New York: Billboard Books, 1997), 190.

50. New York: Paul Simon Music, c1964.

51. New York: Paul Simon Music, c1970.

52. Bill Flanagan, foreword to *Written in My Soul* (Chicago: Contemporary Books, 1986), xi.

53. Hollywood, California: Guild Music Company, c1963.

54. New York: Screen Gems, c1963.

55. Los Angeles: Irving Music, c1964.

56. Steven Gaines, *Heroes and Villains: The True Story of the Beach Boys* (New York: New American Library, 1986), 117.

57. VH1 is a cable-TV network featuring popular music.

58. David Bauder, "Musical Artistry of Brian Wilson Finally Recognized," *MSNBC.com*, 30 March 2001.

59. Los Angeles: Irving Music, c1966.

60. Los Angeles: Irving Music, c1966.

61. Los Angeles: Irving Music, c1966.

62. Steve Morse, "All-Star Tribute to Brian Wilson," *Boston Globe*, 3 July 2001, F8.

63. Nashville: Sixteen Stars Music, c1966.

64. Nashville: Sixteen Stars Music, c1966.

65. *The Billboard Illustrated Encyclopedia of Rock*, edited by Lucinda Hawksley (New York: Billboard Books, 1998), s.v. "Byrds."

66. The Eagles supposedly had in mind a Hotel California located in Todos Santos, Baja California Sur, Mexico. At the time it was a shabby lodging place frequented by hippies. Local people claim that the Eagles drummer, Don Henley, who cowrote the track, had stayed in the hotel.

67. Los Angeles: Red Cloud Music, c1977.

68. Joan Anderson, "California Here We Come," *Boston Globe*, 14 June 2002, C14.

69. Palmer, *Rock & Roll*, 157.

70. Graeme M. Boone, "Tonal and Expressive Ambiguity in 'Dark Star,'" in John Covach and Graeme M. Boone, editors, *Understanding Rock* (New York: Oxford University Press, 1997), 171.

71. *The Rolling Stone Encyclopedia of Rock & Roll*, edited by Holly George-Warren and Patricia Romanoski, with consulting editor Jon Pareles (New York: Rolling Stone Press, 2001), s.v. "The Doors."

72. Los Angeles: Irving Music, c1967.

73. New York: Bro N Sis Music, c/o Carlin America, c1965.

74. Steve Morse, "Stevie Nicks Goes It Alone, for Now," *Boston Globe*, 29 April 2001, M12.

75. Carl Cafarelli, "An Informal History of Bubblegum Music," home.att.net/~bubble gumusic, c2000.

76. Laura M. Holson and Alex Kuczynski, "Britney Spears Aims for a Second Act, as an Adult," *New York Times*, 6 October 2002, www.nytimes.com..

77. James Miller, *Flowers in the Dustbin* (New York: Simon & Schuster, 1999), 214.

78. Los Angeles: Universal Duchess Music Corp., c1963.

79. David Dempsey, "Why the Girls Scream, Weep, Flip," reprinted from *New York Times Magazine*, 23 February 1964, in David Manning White, editor, *Pop Culture in America* (Chicago: Quadrangle Book, 1970), 222–26.

80. Bob Sheffield, "Beatles Save the World for Second Time," *Rolling Stone*, 15 February 2001, 28.

81. London: Northern Songs Ltd., c1966.

82. Allan Kozinn, "George Harrison, 'Quiet Beatle' and Lead Guitarist, Dies at 58," *New York Times*, 1 December 2001, www.nytimes.com.

83. London: Northern Songs Ltd., c1968.

84. Szagmary, *Rockin' in Time*, 130.

85. New York: ABKCO Music, c1965.

86. Morris Dickstein, *Gates of Eden* (New York: Basic Books, 1977), 207.

87. New York: ABKCO Music, c1968.

88. Bill Flanagan, *Written in My Soul* (Chicago: Contemporary Books, 1986), 163–64.

Chapter Six

Black-American Music Comes to the Fore in the 1960s

Singing, dancing, playing instruments, and enthusiastic listening to music typified black Americans from their earliest days in the New World. No less was this true of the sixties—whether they were rural or urban dwellers, poor or well off. The constant sound of straight blues, rhythm and blues, gospel, and jazz regularly supplied social events with a festive quality that often could become quite noisy. To cite one example, one summer in the late 1960s, my wife and I attended a wedding-anniversary celebration in Boston's black Roxbury district. As we mounted the stairs to the second floor apartment, deafening dance rhythms pounded into our ears. Two couples, climbing the stairs before us, entered the open door-way dancing vigorously. After we ourselves entered, we pushed through the dancers (some were no more than six or seven years old and two or three looked at least eighty) looking for the host and hostess. Everyone was having a thoroughly good time. Against the opposite wall was our hostess and a long table loaded with food and drink. After greeting her, we remarked on the enthusiastic gyrations of one couple. She pondered a moment, then said, "Their feet are just helping them handle their harass-ments." Whether she meant just the couple or all the guests was not made clear. Later we heard the recorded vocalizations of singers like Ray Charles and Sam Cooke, alongside exclamations of approval. Around eleven o'clock, I took a break with three other men to go for an hour or so to a jazz club on Washington Street, in the South End, where we caught Andy McGhee playing sax.[1] When we returned to the party an older man had sat down with an acoustic guitar to give out blues numbers. He had recently come up from the South. Just before departure, everyone remained standing and sang two gospel songs.

Music was indeed an aid in handling one's "harassments." The aggravations assuaged by music have had a long history. I am certain they remained burned in the memory of more black people than the couple that the hostess mentioned. Furthermore, the sixties were a decade when, in the face of racial discrimination and belittling of black culture, African-Americans were looking more than ever at themselves and their antecedents. They knew that the intolerance inflicted upon them was unfair and to be fought and the belittling was untrue and to be negated. The situation had grown intolerable and they rose up to do something about it. Marches, sit-ins, complaints over subpar schools, and demands for work and wage equality grew out of the discrimination. Music gave an expressive form to their grievances and, more importantly, their cultural world.

Increased enrollment in colleges and universities and the insistence on meaningful positions in the workforce permitted a few black Americans to demonstrate the capabilities they had rarely been allowed to exercise. A new look at black people's origins, their characteristic organizations, typical upbringing, and identifying culture increased awareness of what their contributions had been to American society. Two of their most outstanding cultural contributions were in music and dance. Since colonial times, white Americans had helped themselves to songs, dances, dance steps, and instruments belonging to the black community, like the bones and banjo. Ragtime, jazz, blues, spirituals, and gospel songs from African-Americans had added substance to America's music and given it uniqueness, too often without acknowledgment. The time had arrived for blacks to insist on coming out of the cultural shadows and taking their place in the sun. Rhythm and blues took on three aspects—the capture of the emotional context of the African-American experience, called "soul"; the assertive affirmation of black just claims to respect, called "funk"; and the outreach to convince white society of the special musical abilities of blacks, which was "Motown."

Before the sixties, a handful of black entertainers had earned wide popularity in American society by singing in popular idioms familiar to white Americans. This continued in the sixties—for example, with the picture-perfect Dionne Warwick singing from the Burt Bachrach songbook; a decade later she would sing with her cousin, Whitney Houston, who delivered a velvety voice, stunning looks, and silky, tuneful ballads. Houston's first album, *Whitney Houston* (1985), immediately shot up to number one on the pop and rhythm-and-blues charts.

Immense as talents like Warwick's and Houston's were, however greatly the singers pleased the general public, and though rhythm-and-blues numbers were included in their repertoire, only a restricted area of the black experience was explored. Many African-Americans wanted more than this. They wanted a popular music that would fully represent them as African-Americans and that would capture the strength in black living and feeling. They wanted black singers to devote themselves to singing songs of black songwriters that would aim to satisfy black audiences without compromising to white tastes. The groundwork had already been laid, in the music of country blues, gospel song, and rhythm and blues. What was wanted was a music that would carry on where these three had left off—not necessarily something absolutely new; rather, lyrics and tunes more completely responsive to the needs and desires of black men and women in the changing world after 1960.

A highly original black musician and virtuosic guitarist, Jimi Hendrix, had come along in the sixties with his eccentric musical language and noise, which were on exhibit in hard-rock pieces like "Purple Haze" and "Foxy Lady." He was responsible for some singular blues in "Red House" and "Voodoo Chile." He had supplied music lovers with warm ballads like "The Wind Cries Mary" and "Little Wing." However, in black circles he was known as a rock musician who sought to gain attention by ostentatious display, like making erotic love to and then burning his guitar before thousands of spectators at the Monterey Festival. Born in 1941, he abused his body and died in 1970. There existed a credibility gap between him "and the majority of those black people who listen to music," wrote his biographers, Shapiro and Glebbeek. This gap, he was never able to cross, "much as Jimi wanted to and much as he paid due homage to his musical roots in country blues and jazz." Quoting black music critic and author Nelson George, Shapiro and Glebbeek write, "the problem with Jimi's music for a black audience was 'You just couldn't dance to it. . . . To the audience of Stax and Motown and James Brown, "Purple Haze" and "Hey Joe" just didn't do the do. . . .' Like [Chuck] Berry, his success with guitar-based music made him an outcast on Black Main Street."[2]

SOUL MUSIC

Soul describes the black popular music that emerged in the late fifties and the sixties. Writers are found who claim "soul" is another term for rhythm and blues and in many respects they are correct. The term "rhythm and blues" applied to black music has never gone away and continues to today. They argue that the word "soul" gained prominence when *Billboard* decided to drop the term "rhythm and blues" and replace it with "soul," in 1964. One reason for doing so was to account for the gospel and blues shouting style that was making a more pronounced appearance in black music, but which was as old as Bessie Smith.[3] About this time, gospel choirs were making concert appearances in coffeehouses, and I heard several of them in a Springfield, Massachusetts, below-street-level coffeehouse. They came out swinging as they moved onto a small platform and loudly and energetically sang of their love for Jesus and hope at arriving in the "promised land." More of the same followed. After a brief intermission, they began performing again, this time singing secular songs on impassioned love just as ardently as they had the gospel compositions. Without the aid of the lyrics, a listener could scarcely have distinguished between what music was spiritual and what was worldly.

About the time of the appearance of this gospel group, or perhaps a few years before, a new generation of performers was digging deeper into black music in order to bring fresh meaning out of the sounds of rhythm and blues—the result was "soul music." Among the first to try were Sam Cooke, Ray Charles, Aretha Franklin, and Otis Redding. Despite attempts to do so, no precise definition of soul music is possible and no one definition can cover the different faces of soul. It is too personal an idea ever to be objectively defined—it reflects pride in blackness, getting in emotional touch with one's inner self, and linkage to their community, whose vagueness allows all black people to identify with each other. Asked to explain the term, Otis Redding explained with a trace of evasiveness that soul was "something that you really have to bring up from the heart."[4]

Soul music has customarily been linked to the singing in the black church, and can be taken as a fusion of gospel and rhythm and blues and as a vehicle for expressing the growing feeling of black pride. At first, it would catch the attention mostly of working-class people but soon it would also capture the fancy of middle-class blacks and eventually prove attractive to white ears. Soul advanced the cause for social and political change by establishing a potent cultural link between black and white Americans. Paradoxically, there was a risk that soul also could aid in buttressing white typecasting of blacks and encourage continued resistance to integration. In addition, white people might come to the concerts in order to find entertainment, but leave with their racial prejudices still intact.

As heard in its lyrics, soul comes more out of the real world and less out of the realm of romanticism. It dwells in a place where one lives poor and where work is dull, draining, and constant. It is also a place of passion, cruelty, and drugs. Sex is depicted as part of real life and available to rich and poor. Soul speaks of it openly. Sensuality is to be enjoyed to the limit, even when promiscuity or adultery is involved. Real life calls forth disillusionment and resentment over slow desegregation, over the lack of means for enjoying advertised products, and over the second-class citizenship that is the African-American's constant lot. Hence, black writer Claude Brown's assertion: "Soul is sass. Soul is arrogance. . . . Soul is walkin' down the street in a way that says, 'this is me, muh-fuh!' Soul is that nigger whore comin' along . . . ja . . . ja . . . ja, and walkin' like she's sayin', 'Here it is, baby. Come an' git it.' Soul is being true to yourself, to what is *you*. . . . Soul is that uninhibited, no, *extremely* uninhibited self-expression that goes into practically every Negro endeavor. . . . And there's swagger in it, man. It's exhibitionism, and it's effortless."[5]

The genuine singer of soul is assumed to have endured poverty and troubles related to his or her race, to have suffered the everyday tribulations that came with blackness, and to introduce into song the values that allow black listeners to have a rapport with the vocalist. The singer Tina Turner, for example, who became a superb communicator with black audiences, had led a hard life and would only sing songs she could relate to. She, like other talented black singers, made important contributions to songs, even though she did not author them. About one, the successful "I Might Have Been Queen," Jennette Obstoj, the songwriting colleague of Rupert Hines, said that she wrote it particularly for Tina. Obstoj first met with her, listened to the story of Turner's personal life, and used it as a starting point for the lyrics. On another occasion, Tina was handed the song "What's Love Got to Do with It?" by Terry Britten and Graham Lyle. She was unhappy with the "pop" sound of the piece, feeling it was not "rough enough" and reflected neither her nor her black audience. She modified the song's sugariness by making the instrumentation less refined and more rugged, and added nonpop turns. It became a hit. Tina commented, "I have input, not just in song selection but in treatment, too."[6]

The vocalist, like the music, is not far removed from the church and gospel song—indeed, most soul performers got their first musical experiences singing gospel in a black church. Consequently, a great deal of soul music, alongside its more bitter messages, admits the gospel sounds of joyousness and certainty, and the expectations of a better future. Screams, shrieks, shouts, and moans are a part of the exuberant vocabulary of many soul singers; they signify emotion given its free vent. Oftentimes, singers become so unrestrained, so extremely high-spirited, that they project sheer emotion through the way they sing only, with word meaning secondary. Like gospel, soul is also a rhythmic music, one that never drags, that instigates movement in feet and body, that invites dancing. The beat is weighty, insistent, and demands that a person get up and move. Above all, soul is an assertion of collective black identity. It is black self-esteem and expression, whether found in soul music or in soul food or in soul brothers, rather than just in the cheeky impudence that Claude Brown underlines.[7]

"Hot soul" and "sweet soul" as represented by Ray Charles and Sam Cooke are two faces of the popular music developed in the late 1950s and 1960s by black Americans. The hot side is a fervent music distinctive for its earthy expressiveness, its sometimes raucous vocals, its insistent self-assertion, and its passionate sensuality. The sweet side is no less expressive, but tends toward quieter vocals, more reflective or plaintive declarations, and touches of a quietly ardent spirit. Blind pianist and singer Ray Charles, competent in pop, jazz, gospel, country and western, and rock 'n' roll, brought the fervor of gospel into rhythm and blues and became known as the father of soul. He had grown up in utmost poverty. "You hear folks talking about being poor," Charles once said. "Even compared to other blacks . . . we were on the bottom of the ladder looking up at everyone else. Nothing below us except the ground." The path to prominence that he traveled was not an enjoyable or easy experience. For a long while, he literally went hungry as he picked up short engagements when he could. It was not until the beginning of the 1960s that he would achieve real fame.

He introduced a call-and-response method of performance, gospel shouts, howls, and moans, and lyrics deriving from the blues that together indicated a new type of popular music. Charles departed pop and his previous imitation of Nat King Cole to make this fresh start in 1952 with "It Should Have Been Me." Starting in 1955, he traveled with his own 7-piece band and the Raelettes, a gospel-style female supporting vocal group, and achieved a coast-to-coast hit with "I've Got a Woman." His voice took on a grating, excited quality and his pianism, an evangelical-like urgency. He came through with hit after hit, like the 1959 "What'd I Say?" which some radio stations banned as being too sexually suggestive. His black audience treasured his personal involvement with his songs and his stress on the problems of adult living and loving in his lyrics. Nelson George writes, "Charles made pleasure (physical satisfaction) and joy (divine enlightenment) seem the same thing. By doing so he brought the realities of the Saturday-night sinner and Sunday-morning worshipper—so often one and the same—into a raucous harmony."[8]

Charles said of himself, "If any description of me comes close, it's the tag 'rhythm and blues.' I've fooled around in the same way that blacks have been doing for years—playing the blues to different rhythms. That style is pure heart singing. Later they'd call it soul music. But the name doesn't matter. It's the same mixture of gospel and blues with maybe a sweet melody thrown in for good measure. It's the sort of music where you can't fake the feeling."[9]

Charles's versatility was proved when he boosted Hoagy Carmichael's "Georgia on My Mind" (1960) to the head of the *Billboard* charts, giving it a sorrowful, gospel-derived interpretation. The next year he scored again with Percy Mayfield's novelty number "Hit the Road Jack," which he found open to call-and-response treatment. When, in 1962, he recorded Don Gibson's country-and-western song "I Can't Stop Loving You," Charles said, "I'm not singing it *country-western*. I'm singing it like *me*."[10] After 1962, he reduced his emphasis on gospel and soul, substituting songs out of jazz, pop, and Broadway shows. His singing continued to retain a special quality that was constantly attracting people, black and white.

Over the next three decades, he took on almost every type of popular music and sent it into new territory. Through his efforts, rhythm and blues became highly regarded generally, jazz increased its mainstream audience, and country and western music was put on the path to broad acceptance. At the same time, Ray Charles was involved in the early definition of rock 'n' roll.

Like Charles, songwriter and performer Sam Cooke fused gospel music devices and worldly subject matter into a viable combination that spoke deeply to black listeners, crossed over to attract white listeners, and greatly influenced some of the most prominent black and white performers to come. He would become one of the most popular and influential black singers to emerge in the late fifties and early sixties. Cooke successfully integrated a mix of gospel music and secular themes and, like Charles, contributed to the early foundation of soul music. Cooke's pure, clear vocals were widely imitated, and his suave, sophisticated image set the style of soul crooners for the next decade.

Turning away from the multifaceted approach to singing of Charles and calling attention mostly to the sensuous, if not sensual, quality of his transparent tenor delivery, Cooke won a devoted following and, along with

Charles, smoothed the progress of soul music. When he appeared with the Soul Stirrers, a fifties gospel group, his lightly tripping voice roused black church attendees who listened appreciatively to gospel hits like "Nearer to Thee" (1955), "Touch the Hem of His Garment" (1956), and "Jesus, Wash Away My Troubles" (1956). In 1957 he went from "gospel-stirrer" to "soul-stirrer" with "You Send Me," composed by his brother Charles "L. C." Cooke. He delivered his secular pieces with the same conviction and fervor as his gospel songs.

Cooke's repertoire included compositions that he had composed, some of them warmly felt love ballads like "You Were Made for Me" and "Cupid," and subtle dance songs like "Twistin' the Night Away" and "Having a Party." He would have a strong influence on Motown singers, all of whom admired the soft, rich tones that so won over the public and the expression of emotion beyond words that he pioneered. His tragic end came in 1964, when he was shot to death under mysterious circumstances. His biographers said of him: "What Cooke had that the dominant culture valued—on top of good looks and a beguiling voice—was the ability to bring a crowd to climax and hold them there. . . . Sam Cooke lived his life at the center of cultural change. He was there when gospel music's coded message of hope and rebellion bloomed into the civil rights movement. And his sound—soul music—helped spread that message out into the mainstream culture."[11]

Like quite a few African-American musicians, Sam Cooke was realistic and never counted on the permanence of any success based on the continuing friendliness of white Americans. He always maintained his association with his black audience. This explains "the reason why, in the last years of his life, Cooke developed close friendships with Malcolm X and Muhammad Ali, the two black men who accounted for many of white America's worst nightmares," claims Craig Werner.[12] Music lovers are more familiar with Cooke's impressive singing than they are with the role he played in advancing African-American civil rights. He refused to sing to segregated audiences. In addition, he eventually refused to groom himself in white fashion. For example, he was soon letting his hair grow normally instead of smoothing it down to look as if it were "white." Cooke was one of the first black singers to obtain complete rights to his own recordings. Moreover, he started to help young unknown African-American musicians to get footholds in the music business.

Aretha Franklin, as much as Charles and Cooke, set forth the meaning of soul music in the sixties and seventies. She is a giant in American pop and projected soul as an intense gospel-like experience. She was also one of the major figures in popular music as a whole. Franklin earned the so-briquets "Lady Soul" and "Queen of Soul" because her singing was the embodiment of soul fraught with emotion that owed so much to gospel. Her amazing number of successful songs with Atlantic Records, among them "I Never Loved a Man," "Chain of Fools," "Baby I Love You," "I Say a Little Prayer," "Think," "The House That Jack Built," and particularly "Respect," reveals how intensely Franklin relied on her gospel inheritance and made it the foundation for her soul singing. Otis Redding wrote and first recorded his song "Respect" in 1965, but it made only a decent showing. Franklin's 1967 recording of it shot to the top of the *Billboard* charts and caused Redding to exclaim, "I just lost my song. The girl took it away from me!"[13] The underlying harmonies are only the three most basic ones. Melody, which for the most part adheres to a standard scale, commands attention when it suddenly zooms up to a blued interval on the word "respect." In her interpretation she included her own powerful feelings plus a visceral excitement that reached her audience. The control over her melodic rhythm as she weaved her tones around the beat is fascinating. Her singing is a feminist declaration and, by no difficult stretch of the imagination, a black demand for social and political recognition. Whatever her man wants and needs, she says, "you know I got it!" What she is asking for is some respect when he comes home.[14]

The year that she recorded "Respect" Franklin spoke of her attitude toward her music: "If a song's about something I've experienced or that could've happened to me, it's good. But if it's alien to me, I couldn't lend anything to it. I look for a good lyric, a good melody, the changes. I look for something meaningful. When I go into the studio, I put everything into it. Even the kitchen sink. I *love* to record. I love music."[15] The statement is similar to declarations that other fine singers have made, whether black or white.

Growing up in Detroit in the fifties, Franklin could point to a gospel-singing mother who encouraged her daughter's singing. Aretha, still a young girl, sang at the church where her father was the minister. Her first recording, *The Gospel Sound of Aretha Franklin*, was made when she was fourteen years of age. At 18 years of age, Franklin left for New York City and tried her hand at secular music. She recorded for Columbia in the first half of the sixties, but never achieved celebrity status. It was not until Franklin exchanged Columbia for Atlantic, polished her technique through studying Ray Charles, and worked with producer Jerry Wexler that her emotionally meaningful and sizzling persona really appeared. Teamed with the Muscle Shoals Sound Rhythm Section, she recorded her first Atlantic single, "I Never Loved a Man (The Way I Love You)." It was a sharp, affecting, and blues-tinged rendition of the piece.

As she went from hit to hit, Franklin became a symbol for the mounting self-confidence and pride that African-Americans felt as they struggled for their rights. She would later continue to maintain her hold on an immense public, not only owing to her secular soul songs but also to her selection of other music that would complement her singing style—some her own creation, and compositions out of gospel, pop, and rock, including songs of the Beatles and of Simon and Garfunkel.

When Aretha Franklin recorded *Aretha Live at Fillmore West*, in 1971, she added interpretations of popular songs to the album. Stephen Stills's "Love the One You're With" was refashioned into something personal to her. Bread's oversentimental "Make It with You" had a hearty and rather jaunty sensuality injected into it. She brought her gospel-soul background to bear with her lively, pulsating usage of the Beatles' "Eleanor Rigby" and the exultant "Don't Play That Song." For most of the remaining songs she sounded as if conducting a revival meeting, achieving a burning climax in the album when Ray Charles joined her in the memorable "Spirit in the Dark" and the inspirational "Reach Out and Touch (Somebody's Hand)." She had written "Spirit in the Dark" in 1970. Since then, it has become a gospel and soul standard. The spirit can be taken as consecrated or corporeal, gospel or soul—she never explained. It starts with a soft gospel cry but speedily turns into a solid rhythm-and-blues beat as she asks her audience how it is feeling. The song inquires whether people are "grooving" on the spirit of the dark. It becomes more urgent with a plea to arise and start dancing with eyes covered and hand on hip "that is as much a call to political action as Martha Reeves and the Vandella's 'Dancing in the Street,'" says Craig Werner.[16] The viewpoint shifts from motivator to recipient who now feels "the motivation." In response to her plea, "the rock groove joyously explodes with a sanctified energy."[17]

During the late sixties and early seventies, she was unbeatable in the way she connected with concert audiences. She liked to move to the edge of the stage in order to be close to her listeners. She sang about what mattered to her and to them, expecting them to be "realists . . . who accept it like it is. I express problems. There are tears when it's sad, and smiles when it's happy." Without hesitation, her followers behaved as if they were her personal friends.[18]

Franklin continued to be successful through the early seventies with "Spanish Harlem," "Bridge over Troubled Water," and "Day Dreaming." In addition, she recorded several gospel pieces with James Cleveland and the Southern California Community Choir. All songs found tremendous favor in both black and white communities. In later years, she managed hits while collaborating with Luther Vandross. However, most critics agreed that the recordings made after the early seventies were not as important as her earlier ones, when she reigned as "Lady Soul." She occupied the popular-music heights until 1975, at which time Natalie Cole supplanted her as "soul queen" and the media anointed Cole to be the new Aretha Franklin. The younger singer had attracted people because of her youthful and robust singing manner and because her father was the much-loved Nat King Cole. In 1976, Cole singing "This Will Be" won the female Grammy Award, thus toppling Franklin from her perch. The media pursued Franklin and invented a rivalry between the two women that caused Franklin to dislike Cole. Natalie Cole, who looked up to Franklin, felt hurt and humiliated.[19]

Stax/Volt Records of Memphis, an affiliate of Atlantic Records, was responsible for encouraging the "Memphis Soul" style, which tended toward the earthy and strident. The company was the creation of brother and sister, Jim Stewart and Estelle Axton. In the spring of 1959 Stax recorded its first black group, the Veltones doing "Fool in Love" and "Someday." Their studio was soon backing its singers with the exceptional instrumentalists Booker T. and the MGs. Stax created a big soul hit, in 1961, with Carla Thomas, daughter of the recently deceased great rhythm-and-blues singer Rufus Thomas, singing "Gee Whiz." Jerry Wexler came up next with Sam and Dave, who put across two soul standards, "Hold On, I'm Comin'" and "Soul Man." Then there was Wilson Pickett, who coauthored a highly respected soul piece, "In the Midnight Hour," with Steve Cropper. The reliable singer–songwriter of soul, Otis Redding, appeared at Stax in 1962, and issued his first big album, *Pain in My Heart*, in 1964. He swiftly became a leader in the soul field. He alternated between an attitude of persuasive defenselessness in love ballads and a boldly assertive manner, with some improvisation introduced, in his up-tempo songs. Besides "Respect," he created choice songs like "I've Been Loving You Too Long (to Stop Now)" and "Satisfaction" (1965 and 1966 respectively). Oftentimes, when in a soul mood, he could become completely rapturous and sing like one possessed. On 10 December 1967, he died when his plane crashed into Lake Monona, in Wisconsin. Ironically, the pensive "(Sittin' on) The Dock of the Bay," recorded three days before, became his only record to sell in the millions.

Curtis Mayfield was another dynamic authority in black music, acting as a singer–songwriter and producer especially in the sixties and seventies. He wrote many soul–love ballads and smart dance songs. Of the former, "Woman's Got Soul" and "The Making of You," and of the latter, "Move On Up" and "Get Down," immediately come to mind. He also contributed potent and sincerely felt pieces on the fight for black civil rights. In 1964 Mayfield marked the advances African-Americans had achieved and advised them to "Keep on pushing / We can't stop now," on a sumptuously harmonized hit record that featured his voice and guitar, and the backing of the Impressions. Whether personal or civil rights messages, his songs, making the most of his eloquent falsetto, were welcomed by thousands in the black community—among the songs, "I'm So Proud" and "Amen" (1964), "People Get Ready" (1965), and "We're a Winner" (1968). By 1968, he had turned to using a deep, hefty, and somewhat muffled funk-bass sound. He was in complete sympathy with James Brown when Brown sang the even funkier "Say It Loud, I'm Black and I'm Proud," in 1968, and with Marvin Gaye when he sang the 1971 hit "What's Going On." Mayfield's 1972 sound track to the film *Superfly* produced four Grammy nominations. The dance songs from it later became favorites for "sampling" by the young hip-hop crowd.

Soon after, in the seventies, he worked with soul divas Gladys Knight and Aretha Franklin, but he won less and less admiration in the eighties. At his death, in 1999, his friend and partner Marv Heiman said Mayfield had tried to improve the world he lived in through his songs. "He wanted people to think about themselves and the world around them, making this a better place for everyone to live," Heiman said.

The late sixties, too, saw the rise of Ron Townson and the Fifth Dimension. Typical of the soul singers, Townson started in a gospel choir. Untypically, he took voice lessons, earned a college degree, and appeared in Broadway productions. During their heyday, Townson and the Fifth Dimension were fed songs by outstanding songwriters Jimmy Webb, Laura Nyro, Marc Gordon, and John Phillips. In 1968, two conspicuously successful songs were written by Nyro: "Stoned Soul Picnic" and "Sweet Blindness." The next year, their popularity grew with Nyro's "Wedding Bell Blues" and the medley "Aquarius / Let the Sun In," by Rado, Ragni, and MacDermot, from the musical *Hair*. Their last hit was "Your Love," in 1977.

In the eighties Luther Vandross broke away from his supporting singing roles to achieve prominence in his own right as a soul singer. He bucked the contemporary trend, seen particularly in rap, of singing about naked and willing women, violent behavior, shoot-outs, and the vileness of his enemies. He was an unabashed soul singer hymning on the vulnerability of adult lovers and the differences between short-lived and everlasting love. He made his solo entrance in 1981 with "Never Too Much" and went on to record soul-baring favorites like "Forever, For Always, For Love," "Any Love," and "The Night I Fell in Love." In 2001, he tried to explain the "soul" in soul music in an interview. He said rap and rap-cum-rhythm and blues would not replace soul:

> Soul music is still a pure form. It's what I sing and what Aretha Franklin sings and what Gladys Knight sings and what Patti LaBelle sings. That's soul music. A lot of R&B has now become a technique that a lot of different demographics can do, or can emulate, or can assimilate. But soul music is a whole life's experience. . . . It's not just some singing technique where you riff with 50 notes in your verse, and therefore, 'Voila, I'm a soul singer now!' "[20]

His point was that soul resided in the person and in the authentic capture of black feeling—the singer's and the audience's. It grew out of the encounters in life and not skill in performance.

White performers were soon thrusting themselves forward into the "soul business." They both liked the sound and sensed that money could be made of it for themselves—Mitch Ryder and the Detroit Wheels, the Righteous Brothers, and Hall & Oates, to name three. However, most of the "blue-eyed soul" musicians had little staying power and soon disappeared from sight, while the black performers continued to thrive.

FUNK

After the middle of the fifties, another black musical expression came into use to describe a parallel movement to soul music—funky music. The word "funky" no longer had its old meaning of an unpleasant smell or an allusion to sex. It now referred to an earthy musical style and feeling, one distinguished by a heavy, skillfully executed beat that was clearly contemporary and by an overpowering sound. Funk stemmed from soul, but also owed a debt to African rhythms, blues, jazz, and rock 'n' roll. No specific chord changes characterized it. In fact chord changes were not needed, and a piece could remain on one harmony from beginning to end. It was primarily the overriding syncopated rhythm, solid bass line, sometimes complex texture, and yelled vocals that defined funk musically. In many instances, the same musical passage might recur over and over again. Also characteristic of funk were the short riffs (brief melodic figures, usually repeated) that the supporting instruments inserted. Tunes, at best, were rudimentary and sometimes nonexistent. The singer rarely crooned; his words needed not to be understood so long as the voice, gestures, and body language seemed to embody raw, urgent energy and, as often, sexuality. Quite a few numbers evolved during dance-jam sessions. Funk eventually would lead to disco and hip-hop. Its adherents were in total sympathy with the black power trend toward greater militancy and the aggressive demands for black recognition. They were as approving of Malcolm X and the Black Panthers as they were of Martin Luther King and the NAACP.

Funk's leader appeared in James Brown and his 1963 funky declaration "Out of Sight." In 1965, "Papa's Got a New Bag" had the instrumentalists riffing in mesmerizing fashion over one harmony. In the same year, "I Got You (I Feel Good)" opened with an unconstrained shriek. Afterward, the listener heard a deafening mix of highly energetic instrumental riffs, drum eruptions like machine-gun fire, rapid running guitar patterns, and singer Brown's voice drenched with sexual excitement.[21] The "Cold Sweat," of 1967, found him lustier, bolder, and sexier. He clinched his claim to funk leadership, in 1968, with "Say It Loud—I'm Black and I'm Proud." His harsh shouts, screams, and groans were outward-directed and unqualified expressions of liberation. Not for him soul's quietude and inward gaze into the most closely personal areas of the mind. He wanted to stir up a rowdy frenzied release of the self, and to capture rhythmic energies corresponding to the rough vehemence of his politicized soul mates.

"Say It Loud" has no tune to speak of. Brown yells his words rhythmically. He calls on his listeners to "Say it loud, I'm black and I'm proud," and they respond "I'm black and I'm proud." Brown continues by reciting the wrongs inflicted on blacks, saying they have experienced constant censure and bad treatment, yet are criticized for being pushy and nasty. However, they have launched a movement for equality and will not quit until they get their rightful share of America.[22]

With this song, Brown became a cultural hero, frequently referred to as "Soul Brother Number One," someone the frustrated and aggravated black community could look up to. Eventually he possessed wealth and independence, and became a symbol of an African-American free to live as one chooses and unchained from racism. It was a burden of obligation that he took seriously, seeing to it that his songs conveyed frank social meanings. He backed programs to assist black boys and girls in the urban slums, talked to them at their schools, and put his money into new black enterprises. For a while he also performed for the troops in Vietnam. After the assassination of Martin Luther King, Brown publicly begged black Americans to remain calm.

James Brown went on to presage disco in 1971 with his song "Sex Machine." Its pulsations belonged completely to the dance floor; its declarations akin to male bluster. He was capitalizing on the fact that teenagers loved to dance and to ruminate on sex. Robert Palmer informs us that young people, white as well as black, craved the sound that Brown and others like him were producing, with its "no-holds-barred Dionysian frenzy."[23] His records sold; his concert appearances multiplied. He held on to his position as a key player in black music for more than a decade. After the mideighties, substance abuse, beating his wife, general weird behavior, and threatening a crowd with a shotgun drained away his reputation and he would no longer occupy a position of high cultural authority.[24] Despite that, he would be a seminal figure in the development of disco and rap.

No one person, however much a leader he may seem to be, can really give complete definition to a style. Performers other than Brown were also developing their own version of the funk sound, among them Sly and the Family Stone, Booker T. and the MGs, George Clinton and the Parliament-Funkadelics, the Commodores, the Ohio Players, and Kool and the Gang. A typical progression through several styles favored by African-Americans is provided by the Isley Brothers. They started as gospel-singing brothers in Cincinnati. Three of them left home for New York City in 1957 and recorded their first winner, "Shout"—an ardent, occasionally strident call-and-response presentation, but with a sense of dignity rooted in "gospel testifying." For a brief time, they recorded with Motown and sang the sweet soul classic written by Motown's Holland-Dozier-Holland team, "This Old Heart of Mine." For a while after this they only maintained but did not further their status. At last, in 1969, they shuffled the family members in their group, adding three more, and achieved their biggest success with "It's Your Thing." For the next few years the Isley Brothers experienced repeated successes with songs that were very much in the disco-dance style and that surged forward with a driving beat, rough twists in the phrasing from the guitar, and varied combinations of the voices. Some winning numbers that came with a heavy rock beat were "Summer Breeze," by Seals and Crofts, and "Love the One You're With," by Stephen Stills. Decidedly delving into funk rock were the Isley Brothers' original songs, "Fight the Power," "The Pride," and "Take Me to the Next Phase," which also signaled the advent of hip-hop and rap. "Don't Say Good Night (It's Time for Love)" and "Between the Sheets" offered enticingly sex-laden soul. With additional family members the Isley Brothers forged on to the end of the century. At the beginning of the 21st century, two brothers were left—Ronald exploiting his falsetto voice and Ernest playing the guitar and writing songs whose main subject was getting close to a woman.[25]

Rhythm and blues, whether defined as soul or funk, continued as a viable music medium into the 21st century. By then, it had also found its way to Africa and bonded with African singing and rhythms to form a new genre named Afrobeat. When new black musical movements have arisen in America, like disco and hip-hop's rap, rhythm-and-blues musicians have not hesitated to incorporate some of the up-to-the-minute techniques into their own style, in effect freshening it up. On the other hand, when disco has threatened to become too mechanical and rap too misogynic and abrasive, they have acted to counter the aberrations. Young female soul songwriters and singers have especially come to the fore around the year 2000—Alicia Keys and India.Arie especially, but also Erykah Badu, Jill Scott, Lauryn Hill, Sunshine Anderson, Syleena Johnson, and Angie Stone. They are not afraid to relieve tough, unsentimental messages with humorous ones and obdurate rhythms with melody. Jon Pareles cites them all in a *New York Times* article, saying, "These women make music that maps a way out of pop's current dead ends: thuggishness, saccharine romance, self-loathing and whiny hostility. Their songs are realistic yet doggedly optimistic, political as well as personal and willing to be both sensual and spiritual."[26] These women look back as far as the sixties and seventies—to soul, funk, Motown, the Beatles—in order to gain insight into the present. They have lots of street smarts and won't allow themselves to be bullied or put down. India.Arie, in "Video," from the album *Acoustic Soul* (2001),[27] sings with a refreshing honesty, saying she's no supermodel but she's learned to love herself without reservations because she sees herself as a queen. In "Brown Skin," from the same album, she sings with assurance about her love for her and her lover's brown skin when they embrace, fusing their color.

MOTOWN

Motown, in Detroit, was the creation of Berry Gordy, in 1959. The term "Motown" is a contraction of Motor Town, the nickname given to Detroit as the auto capital of the United States. From the beginning Gordy was openly and energetically seeking to increase his profits as much as possible through his musical ventures. Black owned and run, and featuring black artists mostly from Detroit, Motown went on to become one of the dominant forces in American popular music during the sixties and the biggest business belonging entirely to blacks in the United States. It was the first all-black music establishment to astutely and profitably prepare, combine, and promote black singers and persuade the white American majority to listen to and buy the music of black artists in wholesale quantities.[28] Gordy knew what would sell and took pains to achieve a constant crossover into the white market while retaining his hold on the black population (more in urban and Northern rather than rural and Southern areas). He redefined soul music by making it sound melodious, suave, and sophisticated to white ears.

Gordy's first triumph came with "Shop Around" (1961), sung by Smokey Robinson and the Miracles, all young men from Detroit, with Gordy at the piano. He lucked out again, in the same year, with "Please Mr. Postman," sung by the Marvelettes, four young women also from Detroit. Between 1959 and 1970, of the almost 550 songs recorded by Motown, two-thirds of them were major successes, an extraordinary feat when the average for the better-known record companies was 10 percent.[29] Gordy had a worthy songwriter/producer in William "Smokey" Robinson, who achieved major breakthroughs for Motown with the songs he wrote for the Marvelettes, the Temptations, and Marvin Gaye. Gordy later put together one of the most notable writer/producer teams in the music business with Lamont Dozier and the brothers Brian and Eddie Holland. He also had one of the finest groups of sessions instrumentalists in popular music, the fabled Funk Brothers. They included the terrific James Jamerson, an imaginative bass and Fender guitar player, and Johnny Griffith, an outstanding keyboardist. The Funk Brothers provided the impetus for achieving the greatest Motown hits from 1959 to 1972. Maxine Powell, manager of a modeling school, came in to instruct the singers in posture, speech, and clothes selection. Maurice King and Cholly Atkins taught and rehearsed them in putting on stage acts and choreographed dancing for them, rather than having them just stand and sing.

Gordy unearthed and brought out the capabilities of several outstanding musical groups—Smokey Robinson and the Miracles (1958); the Sanitones and the Marvelettes (1960); Diana Ross and the Supremes, Marvin Gaye, the Temptations, and the Contours (1961); Martha and the Vandellas (1962); and the Spinners and the Four Tops (1963). Others associated with Motown, sometimes briefly, were Ike and Tina Turner, Little Stevie Wonder, Gladys Knight and the Pips, Michael Jackson with the Jackson 5, and the Fifth Dimension.

A special Motown sound was developed, far less hard edged than that of Stax Records and Memphis. Rhythm was not pounded out in choppy chunks, but kept more filled out, smoother, and with a straightforward, contagious, danceable pulse called the "Motown backbeat." The sound was fairly even and transparent in quality, although overdubbing (the insertion of recorded music into a recording that contains music recorded earlier to generate a combined sound) and a careful selection of harmonies produced a great deal of richness. The words sung by the lead singer were easily understandable, and the lyrics and melodies owed as much to white pop as to black blues. Romanticized love constituted much of the subject matter.

Gordy adamantly demanded the highest degree of technical excellence from musicians and recording engineers. At the same time, Motown gained a name for music that sounded fine over car radios and small portable cassette or radio players. He tried out different instrumental and vocal combinations, fiddling with sound quality and producing several interpretations before choosing one. He more often than not knew a marketable product when he listened to a song, and he had a talent for identifying whatever the problem was in a performance, then correcting it so that when finally released a composition would sell. After they recorded an album, performers went on tour to publicize it. Berry was out to make hits. If not a hit, a song or album was a waste of time.

Many of his singers had had rough lives before Gordy discovered them. He made certain that they were taught how to sing, dance, speak properly, present themselves on stage, and conduct themselves socially.[30] Handling knife and fork was almost as important as handling a stage mike. White Americans found not only that the Motown idiom provided pleasure, but also that the singers were alluring and the presentation was attractive. They bought in large numbers the offerings of Motown.

Gordy relied a great deal on the Holland-Dozier-Holland songwriting team. Brian and Eddie Holland joined Lamont Dozier to create songs that were major Motown achievements. They produced swiftly and routinely an enormous body of compositions for Motown performers and were dubbed the creators of the "Sound of Young America." The music of the three men stood for the Motown sound. Attributed to them was Motown's flowing, effervescent style that combined likable lyrics with the ardor of gospel, the practices of rhythm and blues, and the smoothness of pop. Holland-Dozier-Holland composed over 200 songs, among them some of the biggest hits of the 1960s. Their employment by Gordy helped fashion Motown Records into a dominant musical powerhouse.

Diana Ross and the Supremes were one of Gordy's most successful creations. The young women who made up the group had grown up in Detroit's Brewster housing project. He saw them as uncut gems ready to shape and polish. They were provided with the training and sparkle that would facilitate their ready acceptance by audiences. Gordy, who had taken them on in 1961, immediately sensed that it would profit him greatly to forward Ross's career. She had a confident manner and a magnetic personality that caused her to be noticed. Her voice showed individuality, excellent quality, and a wide compass. It could touch gently on a lyric or assert itself over whatever the accompaniment, and communicate each line persuasively. Her pronunciation was without fault and easily understood; her singing beguiled the ear. J. Randy Taraborrelli, Ross's biographer, writes that "Where Did Our Love Go," "Baby Love," and "Come See about Me," all written by the Holland-Dozier-Holland team, were momentous hallmarks for the Supremes and Motown, when they came out in 1964. The three songs were given light instrumental backing, made obeisance both to Tin Pan Alley and rhythm and blues, and were supplied with appealing texts. The combination of writing team and musicians proved its worth when the records they made impressed the listener as sounding warm, valid, and authentic. Brian Holland commented, "Berry said that if the kids believed this material that belief would be translated into sales, which it did." These songs became the decisive factor for what came to be known as "the Motown Sound."[31]

Why their immense popularity in the sixties? For one, their romantic warbling about affairs of the heart attracted a significant number of white youngsters who were put off by the protest songs of the time; secondly, many black youngsters still wanted a reliable source for danceable melodious music rather than the harsher summons of funk; and lastly, adults could enjoy nonthreatening, nonstrident music with connections to the more harmonious and sweet-sounding songs of the past. To listen to "I

Hear a Symphony" (1965), "You Can't Hurry Love" (1966), and "Reflections" (1967) meant feeling vitally young again, fantasizing with one's emotions in full play, and enjoying to the full the boy-girl-love connection. For example, the first song declares a fresh love that is inviting, exciting, and real. "I thank you love," the singers exclaim for a lover in whose embrace one hears symphonies and alluring melodies.[32] As is true for many performances, the combination of the visual attractiveness of the vocalists, the sensuous singing, and the genuinely appealing tune set to a suave rhythm won over scores of fans.

Reflecting on their appeal, Maxine Powell remarked, "They were taught how to handle an audience. And Diana, specifically, was taught not to 'soul,' as they used to call it. In other words, she would not bend all over and act like she was going to swallow the mike while making ugly faces. I told her that in a first class place like the Copa, no one's gonna pay good money to watch someone make faces. I wanted her to get rid of the eye-popping routine, and she did."[33] Ross departed the Supremes in 1969 to pursue a solo career. In 1972, she appeared as Billie Holiday and sang with assurance from Holiday's book, in the film *The Lady Sings the Blues* (1972).

The male counterpart to Ross was Marvin Gaye, who was a doo-wop singer when Gordy discovered him. Gaye was an able songwriter and singer with a three-octave range. His early enthusiasms included Frank Sinatra, Perry Como, and Billie Holiday. His honeyed tenor voice dispensed romance in crossover success after success in the sixties and seventies, beginning with "Stubborn Kind of Fellow," in 1962. Then came hits like "Pride and Joy" (1963), "Try It Baby" (1964), "How Sweet It Is to Be Loved by You" (1965), and "Your Precious Love" (1967). Several numbers paid homage to his wife, Anna, daughter of Gordy. Young white people championed his music and danced to its rhythms. As an example of the way Gordy worked over a song, "How Sweet It Is" was first a Jackie Gleason phrase that he sensed had possibilities and had the Holland-Dozier-Holland songwriters make into a song. He then had the song given a jazz arrangement and had a jazz band do the instrumentals. Gaye's singing, recorded separately, was then overdubbed onto the track. It revealed Gaye in an animated, lighthearted mood, possibly stimulated by Anna. It quickly won an international following.[34]

Gaye differentiated himself from soul singers by saying he was going after the general popular market: "Pop means selling whites, and R&B or soul meant selling the sisters and brothers back in the neighborhood.

Everyone wanted to sell whites 'cause whites got the most money." He admitted, "Secretly, I yearned to sing for rich Republicans in tuxes and tails at the Copacabana. No matter, I listened to Smokey Robinson, a very smart cat, when he told me, 'Treat your fans right. Respect them and they'll respect you.'" He did foster a close relationship with his fans. Especially, he cultivated female fans by acting as if he had "a relationship with a woman. They feel like they know you, and they do. You've exposed your deepest emotions to them. . . . They've stuck with me 'cause they feel my sincerity."[35]

Yet, at the end of the sixties, Gaye had become upset over the murder of Malcolm X and King, the Watts riots, and the violence and pain being experienced by black men and women. He was also tired of Gordy's insistence on thinking of music as entertainment with no recognition of the tensions besetting society, especially African-American society. He insisted on complete artistic control over his music, got it, and put out the 1971 album *What's Going On*, which contained perceptive, passionate assessments of Vietnam, social and political freedom, and global conditions. Three of the pieces rose to the top of the Billboard charts. Some later releases were frankly sexual. In 1982, he left Motown; in 1989 he was dead.

The Jackson 5, including 11-year-old Michael, was one of the last groups to profit from Motown's large-scale scheme of upgrading performance ability. Signing on in 1968, the Jackson boys lived with Ross or Gordy and trained under Suzanne de Passe in Los Angeles, where Gordy had relocated Motown. Michael, more than his brothers, deeply felt the influence of Gaye, Ross, and Smokey Robinson. From Gaye and Ross he found out how to put across a song and cultivate an attractive stage presence. From Robinson he learned about the importance of selecting the right ingredients for a song to become accepted. Gordy's example taught him to be "purely commercial in his thinking—how many records are being bought by his fans, how long does it take to get to number one, how many tickets are sold."[36] The group struck it rich with the 1969 recording of "I Want You Back." They would go on to create twelve other enormous Motown hits by 1975 and receive a commendation from Congress for their "contributions to American youth." Much of their repertoire consisted of light bubblegum, but decidedly attractive, rock music. It boasted simple and repetitious music attached to one-dimensional lyrics—all aimed at very young boys and girls. Most of the songs were composed by Motown's "Corporation" team—Freddie Perren, Fonce Mizell, Deke Richards, and Gordy. In 1975, the Jackson 5 left Gordy and Motown in order to assume control of their own professional lives. After departure, they turned more to the sound of funk, but little by little Michael detached himself from the group to proceed independently. His sister Janet broke through to the public with her 1986 album *Control* and has continued to record hits. However, her vocal talents seem to be more limited than those of her brother Michael.

Gordy and Motown's hegemony over American popular music lasted until 1970. The Holland-Dozier-Holland writing team resigned in 1969. Gordy's move to Los Angeles, in 1970, because he wanted Motown to be closer to the movie and television industry, caused his label to become less focused. Some of his most important protégés tired of his total control over their lives and struck out on their own, weakening the Motown roster. The firm would continue to register successes but rarely as before.

A popular latecomer to Motown was the group Boyz II Men, who concocted a smooth pop, doo-wop, rhythm and blues, and hip-hop fusion that made people want to dance. Their debut album *Cooleyhighharmony* (1991), with especially admired "Motownphilly" and "It's So Hard to Say Goodbye to Yesterday," made it to the top again for Motown. In 1992, Eddie Murphy's film *Boomerang* featured them. Two years later, the album *Boyz II Men II* boosted Motown even further. One of the most popular songs of the 1990s was "One Sweet Day," which they recorded with Mariah Carey. After they made *NathanMichaelShawnWanya*, in 2000, Wanya said, "We make music and there's soul that just influences all the music we do." Shawn added, "We just wanted to get back to the basics. Get back to the fundamentals."[37]

NOTES

1. Andy and I quickly became good friends. He and Alan Dawson would become members of a jazz quintet in residence at the University of Massachusetts at Boston that I would put together. Mae Arnett was the vocalist.

2. Harry Shapiro and Caesar Glebbeek, *Jimi Hendrix, Electric Gypsy* (New York: St. Martin's Press, 1990), 503.

3. Charles T. Brown, *The Art of Rock and Roll*, 2nd ed. (Englewood Cliffs, New Jersey: Prentice-Hall, 1987), 108.

4. David Ewen, *All the Years of Popular Music* (Englewood Cliffs, New Jersey: Prentice-Hall, 1977), 677.

5. Arnold Shaw, *The Rock Revolution* (Toronto, Ontario: Crowell-Collier Press, 1969), 114.

6. Lisa A. Lewis, *Gender Politics and MTV* (Philadelphia: Temple University Press, 1990), 78–79.

7. Arnold Shaw, as quoted in David P. Szatmary, *Rockin' in Time* (Englewood Cliffs, New Jersey: Prentice-Hall, 1991), 172.

8. Nelson George, *The Death of Rhythm & Blues* (New York: Pantheon Books, 1988), 70.

9. Ray Charles and David Ritz, *Brother Ray* (New York: Dial, 1978), 177–78.

10. Fred Bronson, *The Billboard Book of Number One Hits*, 4th ed. (New York: Billboard Books, 1997), 111.

11. Daniel Wolff with S. R. Crain, Clifton White, and G. David Tenenbaum, *You Send Me* (New York: Morrow, 1995), 354.

12. Craig Werner, *A Change Is Gonna Come* (New York: Plume, 1999), 40.

13. Mark Bego, *Aretha Franklin* (New York: St. Martin's Press, 1989), 96.

14. Los Angeles: Irving Music (East Memphis Music), c1965.

15. Bego, *Aretha Franklin*, 97.

16. Werner, *Change Is Gonna Come*, 124.

17. Werner, *Change Is Gonna Come*, 124.

18. Bego, *Aretha Franklin*, 106.

19. Bego, *Aretha Franklin*, 166–68.

20. Steve Morse, "Luther Vandross Is Still Doing Justice by His Brand of Soul," *Boston Globe*, 21 October 2001, C6. See also Renée Graham, "Vandross Stays True to Himself," *Boston Globe*, 3 July 2001, E1, 6.

21. David Marsh, *The Heart of Rock and Roll* (New York: New American Library, 1989), 155–56.

22. Los Angeles: Warner-Tamerlane Publishing Co., c1968.

23. Robert Palmer, *Rock & Roll: An Unruly History* (New York: Harmony Books, 1995), 242.

24. *The New Rolling Stone Encyclopedia of Rock & Roll*, revised and updated, edited by Patricia Romanowski and Holly George-Warren (New York: Fireside, 1995), s.v. "James Brown."

25. Jon Pareles, "Two Brothers Who Are Carrying on the Family Act," *New York Times*, 1 January 2002, www.nytimes.com.

26. Jon Pareles, "'All Id' and Proud of It, Mary Gray Sings On," *New York Times*, 9 September 2001, www.nytimes.com. See also Nikole Killion, "Alicia Keys Unlocks Doors to Success," *MSNBC.com*, 29 June 2001, and Jon Pareles, "Wresting Control of Cupid's Arrows," *New York Times*, 21 August 2001, www.nytimes.com.

27. Los Angeles: WB Music Corp., c2001.

28. Don Waller, *The Motown Story* (New York: Scribner's Sons, 1985), 11.

29. Brown, *Art of Rock and Roll*, 113.

30. Brown, *Art of Rock and Roll*, 114–16.

31. J. Randy Taraborrelli, *Call Her Miss Ross* (New York: Carol Publishing Group, 1989), 99.

32. New York: Stone Agate Music, c1965.

33. Taraborrelli, *Call Her Miss Ross*, 121.

34. David Ritz, *Divided Soul: The Life of Marvin Gaye* (New York: McGraw-Hill, 1985), 93.

35. Ritz, *Divided Soul*, 73, 79.

36. J. Randy Taraborrelli, *Michael Jackson* (New York: Birch Lane Press, 1991), 453.

37. "Boyz II Men," *BoyzIIMen* on the web, n.d.

Chapter Seven

Out of the Seventies

Richard Nixon was elected president in 1969, after his diligent cultivation of the "moral majority" and his "Southern" strategy resulted in attracting a greater part of the votes. The seventies began with the massacre of four students at Kent State, 4 May 1970. The Ohio National Guard had directed deadly fire at anti-Vietnam war protesters. Eleven days later, Mississippi police killed black protesters at Jackson State. A mother's cry went out, "They are killing our babies in Vietnam and in our own backyard." When the film *The Godfather* appeared, in 1972, a feeling grew that the mayhem and murder on the screen was getting to be normal behavior for the United States. George McGovern ran against Nixon in 1972 and lost. All sorts of popular musicians—like Barbra Streisand, Simon and Garfunkel, Peter, Paul, and Mary, Carly Simon, Dionne Warwick, and James Taylor—had urged young people to turn out and vote. Ironically, half of the college students and most other young people who did vote went for Nixon. Curiously enough, Nixon was seen as more honest, decisive, and trustworthy than McGovern. It all proved that "the greening of America" was not taking place.[1]

After the murder of the protesters and the signing of a peace treaty on 27 January 1973, anxiety and withdrawal from any participation in public life replaced student dissent and confrontation. The national mood subsided into a sullen silence. Democracy had taken a severe blow. More was to come. In 1973 the oil embargo started as did the Watergate investigation. Vice President Agnew resigned in October for accepting bribes from building contractors. Nixon resigned the presidency after the Watergate scandal, on 8 August 1974. The FBI and CIA were exposed for illegally spying on American citizens, and engaging in wiretapping, break-ins, and secretly opening private mail. Some people asked rhetorically, "Wasn't it the CIA that had introduced LSD to students?" The loss of trust in government and politics was now extreme and would last into the next century. Materialism and personal gain replaced idealism and doing for others. President Gerald Ford, from 1974 to 1977, tried to restore normalcy but his administration's conduct of government was largely ineffectual. Jimmy Carter succeeded him and, though he was a morally admirable person and meant well, he also mostly failed as president, especially after the Iranian-hostage crisis of late 1979. At the same time, oil prices kept on climbing upward, putting a constraint on industrial expansion. As a people, Americans at best were marking time economically, socially, and spiritually.

It was the decade of hot pants, platform shoes, string bikinis, pet rocks, and streaking. The practice of exchanging sexual partners, including husbands and wives, grew. Swinging sex clubs multiplied as did divorce. Escape through visceral entertainment was desired and came to the fore with disco in 1975. Two years later, the film *Star Wars* reached the height of popularity, and *Saturday Night Fever* fed the craze for disco dancing. Young men and women wildly gyrated on dance floors doing various "hustles" and nonsensical numbers like "YMCA" and the "Bus Stop." The rage for this new dancing was even greater than it was for the Twist of the sixties. The avoidance of reality by occupying one's mind with illusory situations and frenzied dance-floor activities had taken over millions of people. Seemingly a corrective to the constant pleasure seeking was the religious revival, complete with the rise of Christian contemporary music (or CCM) like "Spirit in the Skies" and "Everything Is Beautiful." However, this could also be taken as a form of escape. A reborn Christian might be a person leaving all his thinking and worries to God. Carter grew quite concerned with the nation's unease, hedonism, and turn to escapism. He warned of the malaise overcoming the citizenry and asked people to take responsibility for each other. No one thanked him for his comments. Even the radicals of the sixties were turning into the yuppies (young and well-educated urbanites who had well-paying positions and affluent lifestyles) of the seventies. Tom Wolfe was calling them members of the "Me" generation. The pursuit of personal interests was making more and more sense, particularly to men and women who felt they existed in a meaningless and irrational world. George Packer said that in the seventies people developed a taste for the absurd:

Children of the 1970s, having inherited a reflexive cynicism toward authority without a cause greater than recycling or a sacrifice more painful than gas
lines, learned early on to feel envy, shame, and resentment. The last thing
anyone growing up in the '70s imagined was that a great historical transformation was occurring.[2]

Everything would come to a head in 1980, with the election of that
supreme conservative and nonintellectual, Ronald Reagan, and his assur-
ances that America was great, the American people were great, and life
was about as well as one could wish.

To some critics, the seventies were the all-time low of popular music, a
decade that favored "power ballads," which were usually love songs with
heavy percussive sounds and driving guitars, and arena rock—trivial pop
in a glossy, extravagant setting. To other critics, the decade favored entertaining musical sedatives that sidetracked serious thought. Yet out of the
body of power ballads and ostentatious glitter would emerge some impressive popular musicians and enduring compositions.

While the principal driving force behind this music was still the adolescent, there was now a 30-plus generation that had grown up with rockabilly and the like. John Orman writes that supporters of rock did not really
want to think about large-scale problems: "Rock music allows the fan to
escape, to relax, and to dream. It helps conjure images of a continuous
state of adolescent life. It allows thirty and even forty-year olds to sing the
praise of the teenage existential condition."[3]

What cannot be denied is the mass manufacture of musical Pablum, controlled and parlayed into hits by the recording industry of the East Coast,
to which the center had shifted from California. International conglomerates were buying up and dictating to the musicians. By decade's end, they
were promoting a small selection of leading names with arena tours, satu-
ration advertising, and gaudy stage productions. In 1995, Sony put out
three CDs labeled "Greatest Hits of the Seventies" (A26219-21). If one is
patient enough to listen to all 40 tracks, the handful of worthy numbers is
buried under the weight of the musical dross—at least, so it seemed to me.
Nelson George, in *Billboard*, opined that the "age of corporations" had arrived in music. Bruce Schulman agreed:

The release of *Frampton Comes Alive* in 1976 marked the signal event in the
emergence of corporate rock. A&M Records discovered a mediocre, undistinguished British rocker named Peter Frampton and packaged him as something for everyone—part guitar hero, part punk, part heavy metal, part Dead-

head, part bluesman. *Frampton Comes Alive*, like most other Seventies corporate rock, offered music with no soul, no message, no recognizable quality. . . . Yet, it became the biggest-selling album of all time—the first multiplatinum record.[4]

During the seventies, too, a new kind of performer came to view—the chameleon, always ready to adapt his or her public personality and tailor a singing style to suit the prevalent fashion. Some people of this type had a modicum of inborn talent. They were created almost out of whole cloth by the music industry, and were completely remakeable by their handlers. A few did have talent but were steered hither and yon, striving to remain up to date in their repertoire and vocal delivery. A case in point was Cher, who gave careful consideration to advancing her career. She was a high-school dropout married to Sonny Bono and then to Gregg Allman for a while. In order to prove irresistible to her audiences, she had her nose and teeth straightened, her teeth capped, her breasts firmed up, and her body reshaped. She courted the attention of newspapers and magazines. Cher was determined to be a number-one singer and actress, and she achieved both. Her usual singing voice was bold, deep, and with a spacious vibrato. She started as a '60s folk-rocker, went over to pop-rock, wailed power ballads and disco numbers in the '70s, converted to a New Wave glitter-rock queen in the early '80s, turned to punk, became an exponent of arena-rock, and in a later reincarnation tried hip hop. Hers was a huge, as if neon-lit personality that filled every stage she sang upon. Her followers were legion.

To be sure, it was the sensationalists, the few Americans bent on showing off, who were the darlings of the media and got the most attention. The countless others who led decent, quiet lives were not as newsworthy. The same went for music. Not all of it was a qualitative bust. The seventies did give rise to a number of exciting developments whose influence continues to today.

TRADITIONAL POPULAR MUSIC IN THE SEVENTIES AND BEYOND

"Old-fashioned" music lingered on in spite of everything. Still around for the older adults who enjoyed it was traditional popular music that paid allegiance to the styles of the jazz and swing periods. It goes without saying that the over-forty crowd would continue to go with the music of their youth. They and a lesser number of younger Americans liked a solid time-honored sort of tune. Some longed to slip away into song and get away from the major contemporary problems that eluded solution. Critics called it escapism; a few sympathizers called it therapy or, simply, recreation. At any rate, the music existed in a plane parallel to but not of the contemporary world of Nixon, Ford, and Carter.

The film *Cabaret*, with its songs and setting early in the century, was a huge success in 1972. Not surprisingly, a large number of clubs featuring music in styles like those in the film changed their designations to "cabaret." They carefully cultivated intimate settings with an ambiance of unfussy refinement, so that the blue-jean set and dressed-up couples could feel equally relaxed and comfortable. The Hotel Carlyle's elegant Carlyle Room, the Algonquin Hotel's Oak Room, and the Rainbow & Stars of the Rainbow Room, the Ballroom in Chelsea, the St. Regis Roof, and Freddy's were noted New York cabarets. Local musicians like Andrea Marcovicci, Marcia Lewis, Julie Wilson, and Diana Krall and famous ones like Eartha Kitt, Barbara Cook, Connie Francis, Rosemary Clooney, Nat "King" Cole, and Tony Bennett found employment at the nightclubs. The cabaret musical came into being toward the close of the eighties—*Nunsense* and *Forbidden Broadway* among them.

The cabaret movement remained vital into the next century, with club rooms thriving in several cities outside of New York. Traditional pop kept on winning new audiences even as the older one died off. The nurturing of mainline singers, songwriters, and songs continued. Their appeal to adult musical taste and their support of established and carefully wrought forms of song persisted. When Barbara Cook appeared at New York's Café Carlyle, in 1993, she was 66 years old but still retained her beautifully sonorous voice. She sang Kahn and Donaldson's "Carolina in the Morning" (1922) in a revival-meeting interpretation that left the audience frenzied with excitement. Next, without a microphone, she quietly sang Berlin's "What'll I Do?" (1924). Cook conveyed the uncomplicated waltz tune with its moving lyric about loneliness in a voice naked in its emotion. A hushed audience listened in close rapport with the singer.[5] This was the sort of experience that kept audiences returning. Cook, by the nineties, had already won many accolades beginning in the midfifties for her acting abilities and the richness of her tone. She had appeared on Broadway in Rodgers and Hammerstein's *Oklahoma!* and *Carousel*, Bernstein's *Candide*, and Willson's *The Music Man*. She decided to apply her talents less to musicals and more to cabaret appearances beginning in the seventies.

Musical theater companies throughout the country continued to successfully revive older musicals by Rodgers and Hammerstein, the Gershwins, Cole Porter, and others. New American ones with new hit songs also appeared that competed with the never-ending stream of Andrew Lloyd Webber's staged British musicals with their mechanical devices and sentimental appeal—Stephen Sondheim's *Company*, *Sweeny Todd*, and *Sunday in the Park with George*; Charnin and Strouse's *Annie*; Hamlish and Kleban's *Chorus Line*; Darion and Leigh's *Man of La Mancha*; and Ahrens and Flaherty's *Ragtime*. As with Sondheim, a tricky matter was that the more one integrated a song into the story, the more difficult its existence apart from the musical and thus its ability to achieve wide recognition. As a consequence few Sondheim songs have achieved any height of popularity on their own—one exception being, possibly, "Send in the Clowns." Musicals whose songs spring out of traditional pop continue to appear. In 2001, Mel Brooks produced the musical version of his *The Producers*. It was an immense Broadway success. Reviewers and audiences praised it for its top-notch entertainment and satisfying songs. At the turn of the century, several musicals were drawing in the crowds: *Thoroughly Modern Millie*, *I Love You, You're Perfect, Now Change*, *Contact*, *Cabaret*, *My Favorite Year*, *Chicago*, and *Sideshow* were seven of them.

Every decade found new musicians successfully cultivating the traditional-song field. In the late fifties and the sixties there were Bobby Darin, Frankie Avalon, Johnny Mathis, and Paul Anka (composer of "Diana," "My Way," and "Lonely Boy"). Neil Sedaka won approval to a marked degree with "Breaking Up Is Hard to Do," in 1962. Dean Martin had a winner in "Everybody Loves Somebody," in 1964, although the Taylor-Lane song had been around since 1950. Later came Barry Manilow, Michael Feinstein, and Harry Connick, Jr. (actor, singer, and songwriter). All three seemed natural offshoots of the Swing Era. Manilow reached the top with his own "Mandy" (1974), and with Bruce Johnston's "I Write the Songs" (1976), and the Kerr-Jennings "Looks Like We Made It" (1977). Connick's background was in the jazz of his native New Orleans and in the singing of Sinatra. His first album for Columbia came out in 1987 and two years later he was achieving hits on the sound track to the film *When Harry Met Sally*. He wrote his own songs for the successful album *We Are in Love* (1990) and the immensely popular *To See You* (1997). In 1999 he capitalized on the growing nostalgia trend in America by recording *Come by Me*, which included a lot of older classics. Dark timbered and sultry sounding Susannah McCorkle, who committed suicide in 2001, sang like a passionate disciple of Billie Holiday. Three great ladies of song were Audra McDonald, Liza Minnelli, and Barbra Streisand. Tony Bennett was ubiquitous, whether the year was 1952 or 2002. All of them consistently drew large crowds. After a concert in New York, in November 2002, where she sang numbers composed between the two world wars, McDonald explained the continuing popularity of the classic songs as attributable not only to the attractive melodies and appealingly sophisticated lyrics but also to the basic atmosphere of even the melancholic music, which was optimistic.[6]

Barbra Streisand, an admirer of Judy Garland, was a top-selling singer and admired film star. She displayed elegance and vocal expertise and at the same time offered superb entertainment. Films like *Funny Girl* and *Hello, Dolly!* and recorded hits like Hamlisch-Bergman's "The Way We Were" (1974), Diamond-Bergman's "You Don't Bring Me Flowers" (1978), and the Gibbs' "Woman in Love" (1980) show her at the top of her form. Linda Ronstadt, singing Nelson Riddle's arrangements, made three albums that sold very well—*What's New* (1983), *For Sentimental Reasons* (1984), and *Lush Life* (1986). She was an all-around artist, competent in folk, country, rock, traditional pop, and operetta. In 1980 she proved her versatility by appearing in Gilbert and Sullivan's *Pirates of Penzance*.

Bennett has not been as adaptable as Ronstadt. Although he has examined the Hank Williams and Ray Charles repertoires, he has shown little enthusiasm for increasing his inventory with songs by the younger songwriters. Since 1950, when Bob Hope took him under his wing and had him change his name from Joe Bari to Tony Bennett, he has stayed mainly with the songs of the Jazz and Swing Eras, and his knowledge of these is immense. Singing them, he has made a name for himself as an urbane and flexible artist with a husky lyricism that has characterized his singing over several decades. Over the years, he has also retained an aptitude for altering his timing and phrasing with a swing vocalist's feeling of spontaneity. This has enabled him to introduce the music and words of the songs effectively. "I Left My Heart in San Francisco" was his signature song. It won a Grammy Award for "Record of the Year" in 1962 and helped Bennett win another Grammy Award for "Best Solo Vocal Performance, Male," that same year. In 1970, he did release an album entitled *Tony Sings the Great Hits of Today* (a collection of contemporary cover tunes), which he sang and recorded after much nagging from his producer, Clive Davis. Bennett says: "I started planning the record by listening to as many current hits as I could stand. I mean some of these songs made me physically nauseous. Even Clive Davis says in his book that I became so nauseous before the first recording session that I literally threw up."[7] He refused to do a follow-up album. Since the beginning of the eighties, Bennett has experienced a sustained revival, attracting many new, as well as holding on to his old, fans.

At the turn of the century the active and talented vocalists included Diana Krall, Mary Cleere Haran, Karen Akers, Andrea Marcovicci, and Ann Hampton Callaway (also composer of "The Nanny Named Fran" and "At the Same Time"). To the older songwriters like Henry Mancini ("Moon River," 1961; "Days of Wine and Roses," 1962), Stephen Sondheim ("Send in the Clowns," 1973), and Burt Bachrach ("Magic Moments," 1957; "What's New, Pussycat," 1965) should be added younger ones still making their mark—like Dave Frishberg, Adam Guettel, Ricky Ian Gordon, and Jason Robert Brown.

However diminished its role in the music world, traditional popular music remained very much on the scene at the beginning of the 21st century. In Boston alone, during one week in July 2002, music lovers gathered to catch Hershey Felder performing his *Gershwin Alone* show, Natalie Cole singing songs popularized by her father, among them "Let's Face the Music and Dance," "Unforgettable," and "What Difference a Day Makes," and Dianne Reeves doing pieces like "Fascinating Rhythm" and "Love for Sale." Felder, who had limited talent, nevertheless had people insistently singing along with him, then leaving the theater with "their arms around one another" and walking "down the street singing 'Our Love Is Here to Stay,' 'Someone to Watch over Me,' or any of the other great tunes." Singing to 3,500 fans, Natalie Cole had couples sitting arm in arm, or hugging each other, or executing impromptu dance steps. Dianne Reeves, revealing "a jazz sensibility," delivered "music for the soul."[8]

COUNTRY AND WESTERN IN THE SEVENTIES

Conventional country-pop prevailed for a few years among country-music fans, but it was apparent that upcoming performers like Charley Pride and Conway Twitty were refusing to conform entirely. By the seventies, a different country trend emerged, known as Outlaw Country. The Outlaws were intensely independent singer-songwriters who rebelled against Nashville's dictatorial power structure. They refused to be governed by the established rules or practices prevalent in country music. Perhaps inspired by the counterculture of the time and with Waylon Jennings and Willie Nelson at their head, the Outlaws set in motion a defiance of the Nashville system and a venturing forth as free spirits. Nelson recorded his bellwether album *The Red Headed Stranger* in his home state, Texas. Jennings disavowed his old recording contract and took control of his career—taking charge of what he would sing and record. After liberation from Nashville, the Outlaws won a huge following. *Wanted! The Outlaws* (1976), bringing forward Waylon Jennings, Willie Nelson, Tompall Glaser, and Jessi Coulter, became the first country album to sell over one million copies. The fugitive activities of Nixon and Watergate and of the FBI and CIA's unlawful spying were in the distant background, perhaps, but assuredly they had encouraged a general mood for some manner of revolt.

Although it was a turning away from the carefully manipulated, pop-compromised Nashville sound, Outlaw did not return to the usual practices of country music. It showed itself as a trenchant type of country, which nevertheless took some inspiration from the blues and rock 'n' roll. Whether Waylon Jennings, Willie Nelson, Billy Joe Shaver, Merle Haggard, Johnny Cash, or Kris Kristofferson, they were fresh musical leaders who demonstrated a unique, defiant way of performing. Before discussing this and other trends in country music, I cannot emphasize enough that scarcely a performer ever remained devoted to one approach. A country singer at one moment could be completely traditional and sing to acoustic guitar and a modest string-band accompaniment, at another lean strongly toward classical pop and use an augmented ensemble of varied instrumentation, or go over to country-rock and wed a countrified vocal to the strong rhythmic beat of a lean rock band. Some of the country performers might even at one time have deserted country altogether and taken up classical pop or rock. Why the changes? Not to be discounted was the need for musicians to go where employment was offered them. Second, they grew restive staying with one manner and wanted variety. Third, some sought to attract a larger or more diverse audience. Last, there was the commercial temptation, to go in a direction where they could more easily promote hits.

For example, Jennings was from Texas and early on came under the care of rockabilly singer Buddy Holly, in whose band Jennings played bass. Only after this did he go on to advance himself in country circles. Yet, he carried with him fresh ideas generated by his work with Holly. Soon he was fighting for his independence from a Nashville structure where producers increasingly gave the orders and imposed their concepts and their set ways for selecting and recording a piece on their performers. His was an affecting yet rugged vocal style that won support from a broad spectrum of people. His performances often had constant, actively moving bass rhythms supporting his melodies. Songs like "Amanda," "Lonesome, Ornery and Mean," and "Mental Revenge" laid bare Jennings's strong emotions and his dogged independence. Thoughtfully and untiringly, Jennings helped delineate the tormented cowboy essence of archetypal country. Jennings also honored his swinging western antecedents in songs like "Are You Sure Hank Done It This Way" and "Bob Wills Is Still the King." During the eighties, he attracted additional mainstream attention as "the balladeer" of the television show *The Dukes of Hazard*.

Willie Nelson was born in Texas and, while a young man, made a living giving radio shows and playing in honky-tonks, which usually were inexpensive, noisy, and crudely colorful dance halls. At the same time, he busied himself writing songs. He was a capable guitarist, but when he arrived in Nashville, Nelson took a job as bassist with the Ray Price band. Price adopted Nelson's "Night Life" as his theme song, and its widespread acceptance won fame for the songwriter and enabled him to venture forth with his own band. By featuring black Charley Pride, even in tours of the South, Nelson defied the racism that prevailed. Nelson's music making during the sixties helped ignite the move to Outlaw, although his greatest success as a songwriter would not occur until the seventies. Through his singing and songs, he balanced up-to-date and narrowly rural musical concerns. By so doing he initiated a renewed awareness of country music. Nelson joined Jennings, in 1976, to achieve country heights with "Good Hearted Woman" and the album *Wanted! The Outlaws*. By the 1980s, the Urban Cowboy movement was supplanting Outlaw and Nelson in the affections of the public. However, he would persist in influencing a younger crop of country songwriters, from the urban-cowboy eighties to the present.

Curiously, Nelson fed the crossover trend to pop, with his 1975 hit "Blue Eyes Cryin' in the Rain." Two other Nelson hits, "Always on My Mind," and "On the Road Again," even nourished the Urban Cowboy movement. Other recordings have found him touching on gospel, jazz, and mainstream (in the 1993 *Across the Borderline*, with Bob Dylan and Paul Simon).

Johnny Cash was born in Arkansas, in 1932. He was self-taught on the guitar and in song composition. In 1954, he moved to Memphis, where he met guitarist Luther Perkins and bassist Marshall Grant and began performing with them gratis on station KWEM. After a while, Sam Phillips caught his performance, was impressed, and gave him a contract with Sun Records. Early recordings like "Hey Porter," "Cry, Cry, Cry," and "Folsom

Prison Blues" were so successful that station KWKH invited him to join the *Louisiana Hayride* show, in 1955. He toured ceaselessly, and when his "I Walk the Line" registered as a crossover hit followed by another 1956 victory, "There You Go," he graduated to the Grand Ole Opry.

He experimented with rockabilly. Drug taking got in his way. Yet, through the sixties and early seventies he added several hits to his Outlaw output. His musically half-declaimed "Understand Your Man," from 1964, is a fine instance of Cash's "outlaw" vocabulary. In typical "outlaw" fashion, the singer ends a love affair expressing not regret but defiance and refusing to take disrespectful talk from anyone. He tells her he is leaving and doesn't want to hear her calling after him from the window and giving him her usual "cryin' cussin' moan." She needs to clean up her foul mouth and try to understand her man.[9]

Cash's career goes from the 1950s until his death in 2004. After several years of contentment with past achievements, he returned in 1994 with *American Recordings*, which introduced new Cash songs and proved his creativity had not dried up.

One of country's most famous celebrities, Merle Haggard, did not start life auspiciously. He robbed people and burglarized homes. In 1957, he was sentenced to San Quentin Prison. While imprisoned he heard Johnny Cash give a prison concert and began to try his hand at guitar playing and song composing. Like most country musicians, he was self-taught but had studied the notable musicians who had come before. He pays tribute to Bob Wills, Jimmie Rodgers, Buck Owens, Lefty Frizzell, and "that ol' boy from Alabama who sang as though he knew every teardrop and felt every pain—Hank Williams."[10] Released in 1960, Haggard embarked on a musical career, aided by a loyal manager, Fuzzy Owen. In 1963, Merle turned country heads for the first time with "Sing a Sad Song," done in a honky-tonk vein. Two years later, "(My Friends Are Gonna Be) Strangers" climbed close to the top of the country chart. Other honky-tonk specials followed: "Swinging Doors," "The Bottle Let Me Down," and "I'm a Lonesome Fugitive." In 1969, a song that he claimed he had written as a joke, "Okie from Muskogee," became a favorite among soldiers and the "silent majority." He explained his song by stating, "My father worked hard on his farm, was proud of it, and got called white trash once he took to the road as an Okie. . . . There were a lot of other Okies from around there, proud people whose farms and homes were foreclosed . . . and who got treated like dirt. Listen to that line: 'I'm proud to be an Okie from Muskogee.' Nobody has ever said that before in a song."[11]

Joke or not, "Okie from Muskogee" struck many Northern urbanites of progressive bent as being an outright reactionary redneck song at a time of civil rights and anti-Vietnam turmoil. At the same time, conservative country people detested the nationwide upheavals and what they saw as the undermining of morality that was going on without pause. They helped elect Richard Nixon in the same year the song came out, after he persistently wooed this "moral majority" with his "Southern" strategy. However it was understood, the song became very popular. The people in Muskogee don't smoke marijuana, take trips on LSD, or burn draft cards. They are proud of living right and being free, of being an "Okie from Muskogee."[12] The music is completely diatonic (devoid of accidentals), and the melody jogs along jauntily, with a rather swaggering kind of brashness. Haggard achieved further triumphs through the early eighties, but after that his popularity began to subside a little. However, at the turn of the century, he continued to hold on to a substantial body of admirers in mainstream country music.

Country music encountered some disturbing problems when the Urban Cowboy development of the late seventies and early eighties directed it further away from its true character. It was a giant move toward popular culture, helped forward by John Travolta's film *Urban Cowboy* (1980), with its pseudo-honky-tonk ambiance of abandoned women and aggressively virile men. The effort to cross over and attract a cautious pop audience with country music modified to exhibit conventional melodic features resulted sometimes in weak music, despite the high popularity of a few songs. The Outlaw celebrities of the 1970s, like Nelson, Jennings, Cash, and Haggard, would dominate the country landscape less. Scoring large were crossover compositions from the Urban Cowboy camp, including several from the Oak Ridge Boys and John Conlee, who certainly possessed one of the gloomiest voices in the country world. Beginning with "Rose Colored Glasses," in 1978, Kentucky-born Conlee produced a series of hits, several of which sided with the ordinary laborer—"Busted," "Common Man," and "Working Man." During the nineties, Conlee still engaged in concert tours, often to benefit charitable institutions.

Glen Campbell, who could eventually be considered an urban cowboy, came out of Arkansas to become a highly esteemed country-pop singer and guitarist. In 1960, he migrated to Los Angeles, where he played behind Sinatra, Rick Nelson, Johnny Cash, Dean Martin, the Mamas and the Papas, Gene Clark, and the Beach Boys. Striking out on his own, Campbell registered his first success in 1967 with his recording of songwriter

John Hartford's "Gentle on My Mind," a song so pleasing to the public that over 100 other competing singers recorded it. Again in 1968 he triumphed with Jimmy Webb's "By the Time I Get to Phoenix," also in 1968 with Webb's "Wichita Lineman," and in 1969 with Webb's "Galveston." He said that when he made a recording, he toured without stop in order to promote it. The public had to be wooed. Campbell explained, "The ugly part of being a singer is that you have to work a record as hard as you can while you can, because there are plenty of other artists vying for your spot on the charts."[13] However, first the singer had to sense what might please listeners: "Some people have said that I can 'hear' a hit song, meaning that I can tell the first time a song is played for me if it has hit potential. I have been able to hear some of the hits that way, but I also can 'feel' one. There is a special feeling that falls over a studio and its musicians when a hit is being created. . . . That's the feeling I got during the recording of 'Phoenix,'"[14] a song about a wanderer reflecting on love that he has just discarded. Campbell sang it less like a country singer and more like a Tin Pan Alley crooner. The melody lent itself to this treatment since it does not sound very country, with its phrases ending agreeably on the third of the scale, and secondary-seventh harmonies resonating beneath.

In the seventies, he moved to Nashville and recorded his greatest Urban Cowboy hit, the 1975 "Rhinestone Cowboy," words and music by Larry Weiss. He made the disc by first taping himself singing the tune, and then overdubbing his vocal so as to harmonize with himself. He later called it an ironic ditty meant to describe the cowboy suits that singers like him wore at the time and to portray the life that they led. To a comfortably flowing melody were set words about a man trying to make it in an urban world where corruption is rife, people swindle each other, and acting decently leads to downfall. Performing it, he said, was a journey into his own past. It also, however indirectly, took cognizance of the prevalent mood after Nixon's impeachment and resignation, and of the materialism and self-seeking amoralism that was taking over the nation. One way or another, this cowboy is determined to achieve success. He's broke and willing to make whatever the compromises to advance his career to the status of a rhinestone-clad cowboy riding his horse under the glowing lights of a gleaming rodeo.[15]

As early as the sixties, country music was receiving an input that would lead to country-rock. By the next decade, a clear rock beat was appearing in songs like Parton's "Coat of Many Colors" (1971). Country-rock would not embrace all of the principles of authentic rock 'n' roll. It was a deliberate introduction of the rock manner into country, augmented by elements of pop, folk, gospel, and jazz. One heard a powerful increase in the sound level of the guitars, in particular the bass guitar, and in the drums playing rock-generated rhythmic patterns. The lead guitarist's style was more rock than country. The sung lyrics, unlike those of traditional country, could show political and social awareness. They did not avoid references to drugs, environmental issues, and the plight of the downtrodden.

In California were many resettled Southerners who regularly listened to country music. There were also a host of young people living informally and unconventionally who were aware of the Southerners and their music. Many of them found they liked the idea of country music but thought it too traditional. They wanted also the visceral stimulation of rock music. To satisfy their needs they helped create another new category of country music, country-rock. The emerging country-rock musicians, like their audience, tended toward keeping their hair long, their faces bearded, and their image craggy, rough, and countrified. One California country-rock band, the Flying Burrito Brothers, sparked their vocals with the sound of electric and acoustic guitars and keyboards, bass, and drums. Occasionally they added a banjo, Dobro, harmonica, or fiddle. It was bluegrasslike music with a decided rock accent.

Several singers from all over the United States traveled in this new direction and sought to enlarge the audience for it. Gram Parsons, born in Florida in 1946 and raised in Georgia, turned to country-rock in an attempt to bring country music to rock 'n' roll audiences. Participating in music groups like New York's International Submarine Band, and California's Flying Burrito Brothers and the Byrds, he went on to try promoting the genre with young listeners during the sixties and early seventies. He participated in the California lifestyle and would die in 1973 through an overdose of morphine combined with tequila. Preserved on records, his tortured and emotional vocals (as in "Song for You," "Love Hurts," and "In My Hour of Darkness") and the oftentimes spirited music he made were key influences on an array of performers, among them Emmylou Harris, the Eagles, Wilco, the Rolling Stones, and Elvis Costello. Combining a sense of anomie with mystification and a dollop of disconnect, his "Song for You" tells us that Jesus built a ship for singing, and that some friends do not know to whom they belong and fail to make anything "work inside."[16]

Emmylou Harris, who toured and recorded with Parsons, carried on after his death with her Hot Band, cutting a debut album, *Pieces of the Sky*, in 1975. Since then she has maintained a steady flow of albums, starting with *Elite Hotel* (1976), *Luxury Liner* (1977), and *Quarter Moon in a Ten-Cent Town* (1978), which earned her the title "queen of country-rock." In 1987, she made an album, *Trio*, with Linda Ronstadt and Dolly Parton, which received an extraordinary response from fans. In over twenty-five years of singing she has displayed a talent for integrating different styles into her repertoire and achieving popularity with the pop, folk, and country crowds. Whatever music she attempts, she delivers with an appealing vocal manner and an interpretation that conveys the central feeling of the music. Top hits include "If I Could Only Win Your Love," "Making Believe," and "Heartbreak Hill." She once spoke of an Indian saying: "The best way to catch a horse is to build a fence around it. I like to build fences around feeling and capture them with music."[17]

In 2001, Harris was still attracting huge crowds. On the Fourth of July she and a trio on guitar, bass, and drums performed at New York's Battery Park to a throng of 15,000. She did songs "stretching across her multifaceted career, moving through haunting a cappella, driving rock, heart-stilling country, telltale folk and her more atmospheric recent work." Fifty-four years of age at the time, she was still able to connect with her enthusiastic followers.[18]

The Eagles were a California country-rock band whose members had come together as the backup ensemble for Linda Ronstadt's album *Silk Purse* (1970). They were soon appearing on their own, taking up where the Flying Burrito Brothers and the Byrds had left off. This meant increasing the sound level and the driving beats that characterized Parson's country-rock. In 1972, they gained national prominence with the popular "Take It Easy." Their performances and recordings were commercially successful and highly profitable, from 1971 to their breakup in 1980. The Eagles were responsible for skillfully written songs performed with country-flavored vocal harmonizations to which were added the loud, strong propulsion of guitars. The lyrics sometimes reflected world-weariness over life and love ("Life in the Fast Lane" and "Hotel California"); at other times longing for an end to inner emptiness ("One of These Nights" and "Best of My Love"); and still other times a roistering sensibility ("Midnight Flyer" and "Witchy Woman").

Another splinter off country and western and a big selling country-rock group was the Allman Brothers, whose beginnings were in Florida and Georgia. Their initial recording of 1969 sold poorly but did establish their presence in the Southern rock scene. In many ways they were more rock than country, as can be heard in the song "Stormy Monday," from their 1971 album *At Fillmore East*. It is a T. Bone Walker blues number given country plus rhythm-and-blues treatment, with thunderous, animated rhythms throughout. Alongside the Allman Brothers belong Lynyrd Skynyrd. This band followed the Allman road map and drew heavily on Southern themes that showed sympathy with Southern white positions— not excluding George Wallace—and to Richard Nixon. Their 1974 song "Sweet Home Alabama," from *Second Helping*, for example, rebuts Neil Young's "Southern Man," which had talked of lawless Confederate violence. "Southern Man" was one of many country songs bolstering the South, among them Charles Daniels's "The South's Gonna Do It Again" (1974), John Denver's "Thank God I'm a Country Boy" (1975), and Hank Williams's "The South's Gonna Rattle Again" (1977).

Also to be mentioned is the group Alabama, whose first great success was "I Want to Be with You," in 1977. This was followed by two more hits, "I Wanna Come Over" and "My Home's in Alabama." The four musicians displayed the requisite beards and long hair and wore the usual casual attire. Their country-rock music was lighter than that of the Californians but proved popular to Southerners. During the eighties, Alabama were the top country-rock performers in the South.

THE RISE OF THE SINGER–SONGWRITER

Singer–songwriters were survivors from the conflicts of the sixties and the violent confrontations that stained the early seventies. Most of them performed alone with an acoustic guitar or piano. These musicians no longer tried to reach out and build coalitions with others in order to combat social inequities. Feeling pressured by the turn of events and the intractable problems crowding upon them, most of them withdrew into themselves. They were descended mostly from the folk and country-music camps—musicians like Leonard Cohen, Carole King, Jim Croce, Neil Young, Laura Nyro, Jackson Browne, James Taylor, and Joni Mitchell. They left off the criticism of society and turned to personal concerns. Normally they abandoned strident rock and sang to individual guitar or soft-rock accompaniments. Their instrumentation might include a trio or quintet or something larger, or it could just as easily be stripped down to just an acoustic guitar or piano.

The chief interest of every singer–songwriter centered on the music and lyric more than on the performance. Quite a few songs had a similar sound, and were typically straightforward, lean, and thoughtful. The lyrics in their songs focused intimately on their own failings, yearnings, regrets, and relations to others. Meaning was often obscured by metaphoric references and recondite concepts. By the seventies, several musicians from the folk and country ranks were plunging into personal waters—Paul Simon, Linda Ronstadt, and Neil Diamond, to name three. It was a time, too, when some record companies were dismissing their in-house songwriting and production teams. Authenticity had become a watchword. Audiences were insisting more and more that performers produce musical material that was generated by their own feelings and needs. Singer–songwriters waxed strong through the seventies and then faded in the eighties, although they would continue to occupy major positions throughout the century.

Carole King had already made a name for herself in the sixties as a versatile professional songwriter working in the Brill Building, and a creator of hits like the Shirilles' "Will You Still Love Me Tomorrow," the Drifters' "Up on the Roof," the Byrds' "Wasn't Born to Follow," and the Cookies' "Chains." She would supply James Taylor with "You've Got a Friend," and Aretha Franklin with "A Natural Woman." Taylor made a strong impression with his rendition of King's moving "You've Got a Friend." It is a muted, comforting ballad for people whose marriages have failed and for others who live alone and stand in need of reassurance. The listener is assured that he has a friend ready to help when things go wrong.[19] The melody soothes; the plain harmonies give unobtrusive background support.

In the late sixties, she began appearing with Taylor. Audiences discovered her warm likable contralto voice, which sometimes sounded as if weighted down and weary of struggling. Emboldened to go out on her own, she recorded the album *Tapestry*, in 1971, which went on to sell over 20 million copies before the century's end. The subject matter was autobiographical, related to her divorce from Gerry Goffin, who had been her cowriter. With desolation in her voice and melancholy in her music, she included "It's Too Late." She remains in bed after dawn, wasting time for hours, feeling that something has died inside her.[20] Pensively yet urgently, she introduced "I Feel the Earth Move," where the ground seems to move, the sky to topple, and her heart to quiver whenever near the man she loves.[21]

Through the seventies King continued to communicate with listeners with her personal messages. After that listeners turned away to other singers and she was unable to come up with many big numbers. Perhaps they had wearied of her approach and wanted something fresh.

Another resourceful professional songwriter who had worked in the Brill Building and then branched out on his own as a singer–songwriter was Neil Diamond. He went from writing to order for others to writing for himself, with the 1969 "Sweet Caroline." He said that he took to performing because he was desperate to get his songs heard and he loved singing before an audience. He said, "Performing is the most joyful thing I do. It's also the happiest thing I do. The bigger the audience, the more anticipated, the more excitement. When you're writing, it's a solitary profession, and you wonder about people's reactions. . . . For what other reasons am I going on stage than to please my audience. I have never understood the kind of artist who thinks he has some kind of divine right to play, and the audience has to work to get inside what he's trying to communicate."[22]

Other songs followed that achieved wide circulation, like the early "Holly Holy," "Cracklin' Rosie," "I Am . . . I Said," and "Song Sung Blue." They move within a soft-rock style that gives ample hints of country-rock. A 1978 duet with Barbra Streisand, "You Don't Bring Me Flowers," demonstrated Diamond's flexibility. He continued achieving hits in the eighties, even with the music to a film failure, the remake of *The Jazz Singer*, in 1980. A country-music flavoring was more noticeable in the 1996 *Tennessee Moon*. At all times, versions of his songs covered by other performers keep on appearing.

The *New York Times Magazine*, 22 July 2001, had a picture of him at sixty, holding an acoustic guitar. In the accompanying article, Diamond said that incessant touring had unfortunate consequences—it cost him his two marriages. He added that he and Bob Dylan had based their careers on the strength of their songwriting, "so we have a lot to talk about. Same with Paul Simon or James Brown—we talk about all we've been through, how our children are doing, how we compensate for not being with our children, our guilt, et cetera."[23] Nevertheless, he was still holding forth with new songs for new generations.

James Taylor was the model singer–songwriter dedicated to exposing his personal feelings in songs. These he wrote and sang from the early seventies to century's end. His early compositions dwelt on interior anguish communicated through understated melodies. He brought his music forward and caught the audience's attention through a relaxed tenor voice and expert acoustic-guitar accompaniments. He came across as friendly and with nothing to hide in songs that were both folklike and countrylike. Born in Boston, he grew up in Chapel Hill, North Carolina, where his father was

dean of the medical school. James suffered a nervous breakdown, and, after self-commitment in McLean Psychiatric Hospital in Belmont, Massachusetts, started up his singing career in earnest. However, it would be a
while before he could leave behind his alcohol and heroin habits. As he
was to say later, "When you give somebody millions of dollars and millions of fans, and amazing press, and incredible support from all areas,
when you're twenty years old [his age in 1968], you feel as though you can
have everything you want. It is never about finding peace of mind, or
serenity, or finding your proper place in your own skin. All that takes time.
. . . So it's easy to want to buy a pill or a vial or a syringe, or twist up a
joint. At that age, you're looking for instant gratification, instant life, instant arrival, instant feelings. You're out there thinking, 'I can buy it
all.'"[24]

As with Carole King, 1971 was the year Taylor achieved major status
with the songs he had composed for his soft-rock album *Sweet Baby
James*, which he accompanied with guitars, bass, drums, and King at the
piano. The title song has a gently rocking tune in triple-time. The prayer-
fully tender words allude to his babyhood, but they touched off sympathetic feelings in countless listeners, when he begs moonlight ladies to
comfort and gently rock him to sleep.[25]

In the same album, "Carolina on My Mind" refers back to his childhood
home, which assumes an idyllic image. It is one of hundreds of "going-
back" songs, usually to an idealized southland; these were bread-and-butter items to 19th-century songwriters like Stephen Foster and were still
finding a responsive chord in 1971. Here, he returns in his imagination to
a place of warm sunshine and soothing moonlight.[26]

"Fire and Rain" has a different impact than the previous two. No comforting sounds or words come through to ease the despair. Here is Taylor
standing emotionally naked before his listeners. In it, he has just learned
that the Susanne he loves is gone. He now remains utterly friendless, des-
titute of companionship, where once he thought he had at least her he
could turn to when in need.[27] He prays to Jesus to see him through the day
without her; otherwise he won't make it. He cannot understand how things
have come to pass. All kinds of good and bad experiences have come his
way but his aloneness grows excruciating—the one he loves has vanished,
although he had hoped to see her at least one more time.

Taylor has had his ups and downs. For years personal instability has in-
truded to temporarily interrupt his calling. His first marriage was to Carly
Simon, but no marriage of his stayed permanent. Yet, well-loved songs

have kept on coming out, his audiences continued large, and several younger singers have felt his influence. Fortunately, his erratic behavior seems to have gradually subsided. He has continued to think of himself as a combination of folk and pop musician with a touch of country and a product of all that he has heard. Experimentation is kept on a backburner; consideration of his audience is to the fore.

Recently, he has married Carolyn Smedvig and come to live in the Boston area. When he appeared at the Tweeter Center, in Boston, in June 2001, Jonathan Perry heard him "fusing pleasant soft-rock melodies around often darker, more emotionally complex sentiments—rueful longing and troubled solitude among them." Taylor's solid craftsmanship was always apparent, Perry said.[28]

In July 2002, he sang at Tanglewood, the summer home of the Boston Symphony, and included all three songs cited above, three new ones, and a traditional song. One of his songs, "Mean Old Man" was filled with absurdist wit about an old codger whose fate it is to be reborn as a golden retriever puppy. Richard Dyer, music critic of the *Boston Globe*, described Taylor as immediately appealing and musically sophisticated, adding, "Taylor's voice, like his lyrics and music, is unvarnished but complex in grain; he creates the impression of unpretentious sincerity and artlessness by knowing exactly what he is doing. He's got a long breath that lets him phrase meaningfully; he can rock a beat or swing around it like a jazz singer; his vocal range is wide enough to match his emotional range."[29]

Carly Simon was married to Taylor from 1972 to 1983, and they had two children together. She was born in New York City, her father being a founder of the publishing house Simon & Schuster. She entered her music career as a folk singer in the sixties, but went over to folk-rock beginning in the seventies. Quickly she earned her reputation as an introspective singer–songwriter, especially with her 1971 success, "That's the Way I've Always Heard It Should Be," which she wrote with Jacob Brackman. Backed by a small combo, she sang affectingly about parents not communicating with each other, about married but unhappy friends whose children hate them, and about couples who live together only to tear each other apart, and she wonders if marriage is worth it. Despite all of the negatives, and she knows them all, she decides on marriage and raising a family because she has always understood that is what people should do.[30] An out-of-the-ordinary tune helps the words go down.

Like the above, her songs rocked nicely. At the same time, they met head-on the questions of love and family with an honesty that was ingratiating.

Her highly personal lyrics were later wedded to a variety of styles, including blues and pop.

In 1972 she wrote "You're So Vain," which was her biggest triumph. She insisted that the song was not about James Taylor, as acquaintances claimed. Egotism is pilloried with a sharp eye for detail. She describes a person full of himself and dashingly dressed so that people will notice. A mocking refrain with a twist in meaning enters after every verse telling him he is so vain he believes what she says is about him.[31]

She went on to record almost two dozen albums and to write music for films. Several of her songs are memorable, like "Anticipation," "Haven't Got Time for the Pain," and "You Belong to Me." Simon has continued to explore with sensitivity the inner workings of the individual. "Letter Never Sent," written in collaboration with Jacob Brackman, came out in 1995. She sings of a suitcase on a closet shelf hidden from her that contains "fits of madness, pool of grief, fevers of desire." Here are found letters she never mailed, "never sent to you."[32]

In addition to her music, Simon has authored four children's books and an opera for children. She married poet and author James Hart in 1987.

Canadian-born Joni Mitchell has been one of music's most esteemed singer–songwriters, in a career that began in the late sixties and has continued into the 21st century. Although she started as a folk-rocker, she has constantly made trial of other musical styles—whether as a partner of the former Byrds member, David Crosby, or as an associate of James Taylor, or as a collaborator with the jazz musician Charlie Mingus. Her first big album, *Blue* (1971), with Taylor on it, I find to be an utterly lovely and gloomy album. On fine pieces like "Casey," "My Old Man," and "The Last Time I Saw You" she makes her intimate feelings known with a voice that aches and breaks with emotion. Her singing has a kinship with that of Judy Collins and Joan Baez. The title song, "Blue," took a frank look at Taylor and his problems of that time. She sees him going under weighted by "acid, booze, and ass." She worries about him and despite all still loves him.[33]

Between the confessional *Blue* and the attractive pop album *Court and Spark* came the 1972 *For the Roses*. It caught Mitchell in a subdued mood. Although her performance is simple and direct, she dips a little into blues and tries out some jazz-based harmony ("Barangrill"). The musical settings stress sadness, as in the resolute "Cold Blue Steel and Sweet Fire" and somber "Woman of Heart and Mind." "You Turn Me On, I'm a Radio," a bow to country-rock, was the set's hit. If her lover is driving and feeling depressed, he can just dial her in like a radio and hear someone who loves him. "I'm a radio . . . a country station," she says.[34]

Mitchell moved to a smooth pop style enriched with jazz components in *Court and Spark*. She had caught up with the times and had replaced the country girl with the contemporary woman. Acutely loving, always inquiring, pieces like the title song, "Help Me," "Free Man in Paris," and "Same Situation" put a more freethinking Mitchell on show.

She went on to record albums with a jazz-fusion band (for example, *The Hissing of Summer Lawns*, 1975). The public gave them a mixed reception, while her fellow musicians offered them praise. Critics puzzled over her new freedom with song structures and her knotty lyrics. During the eighties she returned to a more popular style (*Wild Things Run Fast*, 1982), including some social commentary in the lyrics (*Dog Eat Dog*, 1985). At the turn of the century, she recorded *Both Sides Now* using a large ensemble to back her. The lush arrangements that appear are like the ones Nelson Riddle used to do. Among the tracks were torchy-song classics ("Stormy Weather," "At Last") and two Mitchell songs from an earlier time—"A Case of You" and the title track. Her voice sounds lower and smokier than before.

Joni Mitchell spoke for serious singer–songwriters in a *Rolling Stone* interview published 32 October 2002. Of herself, she said, "I'm just a spirit with a mouth." She lumped *Rolling Stone* magazine with the music industry, when she commented, "This is not a classy business that we're in. And I think that the men who run it—and, in general, the spirit of rock & roll—are more comfortable with the vulgar. . . . I hope it all goes down the crapper. . . . Now, this is all calculated music. It's calculated for sales, it's sonically calculated, it's rudely calculated. . . . You know, I just think it's a cesspool." Asked about the teenyboppers Britney Spears and Christina Aguilera, she became personal: "What can you say? I mean, that's what they've chosen. God, my granddaughter is three, and she's really rhythmic. And already she's grabbing her crotch and dancing. It's really tragic what MTV has done to the world."[35]

More the rough-and-ready singer–songwriter than any musician already mentioned, Bruce Springsteen is noted for his individual blend of folk-rock, rockabilly, and rhythm and blues. His songs afford an understanding of the everyday American working-class experience and have affected millions of Americans. He started as a lyrical storyteller of youthful hopes and frustrations. Gradually, along with their patriotic surface, his songs gave mournful recognition of urban ruin and dreamt of something better in the future. However, he remained a realist who admitted that immediate prospects for improvement were rather bleak.

Springsteen was born in Freehold, New Jersey, son of a bus driver who was often without work. His secretary-mother needed to work in order to keep heads above the water. Bruce knew firsthand the joys and frustrations of life among people on the lower rungs of the economic ladder. John Hammond hoped he would be a younger version of Bob Dylan, but Springsteen had his own ideas about where he wanted to head. His constituency was not the college crowd, but the millions of neglected laboring families, trying to carry on however they could.

He began to record in 1972 with his group, called the E. Street Band (guitars, keyboards, bass, drums, and tenor sax). His songs challenged the "promise of America" by giving a picture of youths as they made their way with effort through the rot of small industrial towns. He rose to the top of the *Billboard* chart in 1975, when Columbia issued his album *Born to Run*, which found a ready reception throughout the land. The title track and "Thunder Road" met with special favor. Here were stories of stifled young men longing to escape their blue-collar surroundings performed in a hard-rocking manner. The music was arranged for maximum drama and assigned a strong, even violent, beat. The lyric of the title song is forthright—entirely bitter and without sugar coating. It talks of young people sweating it out on the streets in pursuit of an American dream. At night they drive recklessly about in a town that is tearing them apart. The advice is to flee from this death trap of a place while one is still young. The lyric concludes that "tramps like us, baby, we were born to run."[36]

He never sings sweetly; he often sings raucously. Around the time of this album, Springsteen tried to explain himself: "I felt I saw nobility in people, the kind where people go to work every day, they come home every day, and dinner's on the table every day. There's people doing this in little ways every day all the time. . . . That's what moves me. That's what makes me want to sing my song."[37]

For three years Springsteen stopped recording as a management dispute was fought out in the courts. He did continue to tour and several of his songs were raised to hit status via the recordings of other performers ("Sandy," "Blinded by the Light," "Fire," and "Because the Night"). He finally came out with the album *Darkness on the Edge of Town*, in 1978, but it proved too dismal and brutal to have a huge sale. Nevertheless, the songs added deeper meaning to Springsteen's offerings. His voice could sound weighted down with concern or ring out like an evangelical preacher as he sang of blue-collar predicaments and aspirations (as in the title track, "Promised Land," and "Adam Raised Cain"). Next, he went from relatively smooth compositions, in *The River* (1980), to more acute and caustic, in *Nebraska* (1982). The former with its shorter and more standard verse-refrain construction was deftly composed to have surface appeal, though some lyrics were more about submission to one's fate than struggling against it. The latter was more folk-influenced; its subject the social failings of the Reagan administration.

Over the next two years, Springsteen started to long more for mass admiration than for critical esteem. He left real despair behind him in the 1984 *Born in the U.S.A.* The result was that the album had a sale of around two million copies. Simple, compact pop-leaning songs tell you to make the most out of the cards you are dealt and find surcease from reality if you can, as in "Dancing in the Dark," whose message goes: one must cease mooning over a broken heart and a world falling apart. Instead, one must pull himself together and keep going even if it may be just dancing in the dark.[38] In "Cover Me," he is tired of everyone trying to take advantage of him. He wants out and instead searches for someone who will love, unite with, and protect him.[39]

Even conservative politicians, recognizing Springsteen's popularity and finding nothing threatening in the lyrics, snuggled up to "The Boss" and his album. The title song is not as accepting as the two songs mentioned above. In it, a veteran returns from the killings of Vietnam, finds no job, gets short shrift from the Veterans Administration, and loses his lover. He has "nowhere to run; ain't got nowhere to go." Ironically, he concludes, "I'm a cool rocking Daddy in the U.S.A." Possibly not truly understanding the message, President Reagan quoted the song in order to serve his own interests in a speech before voters. According to Paul Friedlander, "Springteen was forced to rebut Reagan from the stage. He backed up his actions by donating money from concert proceeds to local food banks, veterans groups, the homeless, and activist trade-union groups."[40]

Other albums came out that met with an excellent reception. One of them, the 1987 *Tunnel of Love*, was extremely personal—about his marital problems and love coming apart. "Brilliant Disguises" and "One Step Up," in particular, look despondently at his disintegrating marriage. In 1993, the nervously unfolding "Streets of Philadelphia," designed for the film *Philadelphia*, shot up to top position on the charts. Not for him the myopic vision of a number of rock stars of the time, who seemed totally preoccupied with their appalling childhoods, sexual skills, and accumulating possessions.

After the 9/11 tragedy that traumatized the country, Springsteen wrote "The Rising" and sang it everywhere in the fall of 2001 and throughout 2002. He told audiences of a "sky of blackness and sorrow, sky of love, sky of tears; sky of glory and sadness, sky of mercy, sky of fear," and stirred people's emotions mightily. Do not feel overcome and despondent, he urged, but "come on up for the rising." The music at one point reaches a high degree of emotional intensity, carrying listeners with it.

A final singer–songwriter, Bronx-born Billy Joel, released his first solo album, *Cold Spring Harbor*, in 1972 but had to wait until 1978 to win real recognition with the singles "Just the Way You Are," "Movin' Out," "Only the Good Die Young," and "She's Always a Woman." In 1980 he reached pop heights with the single "It's Still Rock and Roll to Me," again in 1983 with "Tell Her about It," and still again in 1989 with "We Didn't Start the Fire." He in no way cultivated an untamed personality during perform-ance. His music normally retained its connection with classical pop and never went wild, and his lyrics had an autobiographical character—which caused some critics to try to belittle him by labeling him a crooner. These critics began to favor him only after his albums *The Nylon Curtain* (1982) and *An Innocent Man* (1983) came out. The songs in his several albums drew on the fantasies, delusions, and defeats of suburbanites and the col-lege-educated—these were his principal fans. His 1993 *River of Dreams* album went over well, and seven years later he was still gaining new fol-lowers with albums like *The Millenium Concert* (2000).

REGGAE MIGRATES TO THE UNITED STATES

I have referred to white Americans as savoring their traditional popular ballads, country-and-western music, and songs of singer–songwriters in the 1970s. Black Americans discovered reggae in the same decade. Reg-gae was a style that the musically diverse and politically impassioned Ja-maicans generated during the last half of the sixties. It synthesized time-honored African rhythms and home-grown Jamaican folk practices with the American rhythm and blues that came to the island over the radio from New Orleans. By the seventies, it was an international style that was find-ing acceptance in the United States. Some writers identified it as an ex-pression of a burdened people. Ordinary young people found in it a new vehicle for dancing. It was music built on ska, Jamaican popular music in quadruple-time rhythms (with a strong backbeat on 2 and 4) that was powered by acoustic and electric guitars, drums, and a scrapper—a regular stick wiping across a ridged one. The sharp sound of a rhythm guitar was heard regularly, measure after measure, to underscore the basic beat. The songs were given vivid lyrics that transmitted antiwhite and pro-indigenous cultural themes. In the midsixties, some musicians developed a slower version of ska, given the name "rock-steady." Alongside ska appeared the Rastafarian religious movement, a form of black Christianity propounded by Marcus Garvey, a Jamaican who preached a return to Africa and Ethiopia in particular. The followers grew dreadlocks (long, ropelike strands of hair) and smoked marijuana out of religious conviction.

Reggae emerged out of ska and introduced an even greater input of the rhythm and blues that Jamaican musicians were learning from American radio broadcasts. Many of its adherents were also Rastafarians. Promoters like Duke Reid and Clement Dodd earned names for themselves for using immense sound systems to play recorded reggae at outdoor dance parties. As more Jamaican disc jockeys took over this approach, they added "toasting," speaking along with the music. The term "reggae" is said to come from a 1968 Jamaican song, "Do the Regay," of Toots and the Maytals. This band was heard along with the Jamaican singer–songwriter Jimmy Cliff in a 1972 film, *The Harder They Come*, which introduced reggae to the United States. However, when Toots and the Maytals toured the United States with the Who, in 1975, they were not greeted with much enthusiasm.

Bob Marley (a musician, songwriter, and Rastafarian) and his Wailers toured Europe and America with more success. He also made records. In sympathy with black culture, gospel, and funk, Marley wrote "Exodus," in 1977, taking a leaf from the Old Testament. Like the Exodus, he states, black people have experienced "great tribulation" and are on the move. They will allow no one to fight them to a standstill. They are going to walk through the "roads of creation" to achieve their liberty.[41]

He could also give a reggae context to lines like those resembling soul, as in "Waiting in Vain," which is about unreciprocated love. Both this and the previous song found a big response in Britain; a limited one in America. Interestingly, the biggest responses in Britain came from out-and-out dance songs like "Jamming" and "Punky Reggae Party." Helping also to advance the cause of reggae were the covers sung by rock stars like Eric Clapton and the Stones. Only one of Marley's songs became in any way truly popular in the United States. It was "Roots, Rock, Reggae," actually by Vincent Ford and designed musically and verbally as an open invitation to dance, and that is all. Toward the song's conclusion, there is a direct reference to rhythm and blues.[42]

The last song is an example of the songs that Marley fashioned to suit the American rock market and the DJs spinning records in dance halls. Acceptance among black Americans also grew. New York's Caribbean community, in particular, brought major elements from Jamaican dance hall practices into their neighborhood dance parties, which were soon added to American popular music—the powerful sound systems, the pounding prominence of bass and drums, the use of the drum machine, the "dub" remixing of popular songs, and the practice of rapping over rhythm tracks. It influenced the various hard-core American rock styles and presaged the surfacing of hip-hop. It also aided in enlarging reggae's acceptance in African-American quarters.

"Dance hall reggae" has prospered from its very beginning. Like disco, it allowed dance lovers to put aside their concerns and fall into rhythmic revelry. It proved again that a market always exists for dance songs that promote partying. Its later Jamaican practitioners in the United States, like Shaggy (Orville Richard Burrell), have worked to create danceable reggae that can more easily cross over to the white market, by blending it with pop and hip-hop. Shaggy, whose pop reggae won him a 1995 Grammy Award, defended his courting of the mainstream audience by saying, "You've got to do that at some point. If you're not a force to be reckoned with, you're not a force at all."[43] Kelefa Sanneh, writing in the *New York Times*, describes reggae in 2002 as going generally at a fast pace, and capable of existing with other types of music. Ideas are constantly exchanged with hip-hop. Its leaders at the beginning of the 21st century were Beanie Boy, Bounty Killer, and Elephant Man.[44]

DISCO AND THE URGE TO DANCE

In every decade when music seemed to be getting rhythmically flabby, people have come along to reclaim their right to dance. In the earliest years of the 20th century one-step, two-step, and animal dances culminating in the fox trot came to the fore. In the twenties it was the Charleston. In the Swing Era it was the jitterbug. In the sixties, reggae entered the picture. Also, there was the "twist," said to have originated in Georgia when a bandleader and the rest of his band improvised twisting movements while playing music. Chubby Checkers attained countrywide prominence in

1960 with "The Twist." He started people frantically twisting on the dance floor. The twist remained popular for a while and gave a foretaste of disco. Discotheques had started in occupied Paris during World War II. The Nazis had shut down many dance nightspots, and driven devotees into hideaway cellars to hear swing and dance to it. One site on the rue Huchette called itself La Discothèque. Later Paul Pacine opened the Whiskey a Go-Go, where disc jockeys were employed to select and play records for dancers. Elmer Valentine visited this Paris club and observed girls dancing in cages as a spur to dance-floor activity. On his return to America, he and two partners opened the Whisky a Go-Go in Los Angeles in 1964, and then started other discotheques in San Francisco, Atlanta, and elsewhere. "Go-go girls" were soon swiveling on television for the rest of America to see. They promoted energetic dancing that allowed everyone to invent their own body motions and engage in elaborate footwork. The new dance fashion gradually caught on throughout the country.

Disco promoted the expansion of its own dance-based popular music that attracted a following of millions of men and women. The term gave a new meaning to discotheque. At the same time, the music owed a large debt to black dance pieces that had evolved into a style of popular music for dancing at black nightclubs. Disco provided almost complete escapism for its devotees. As a rule, the music was recorded and featured a great deal of electronic instrumentation. Repetitive lyrics usually of utmost simplicity, sometimes making little sense, were attached to a heavy, pulsating, rhythmic beat. The rhythm resembled that of funk, but simplified. The words were normally exhortations to dance, often shaded with sexual meaning. The beat was emphasized above everything else, including the singer and the song. The resultant music was frequently mesmerizing but sometimes sterile and rigid. Systematically computerized beats could come to sound overly mechanical. Quite a few contemporary rock musicians and their followers detested disco. They said the music was clichéd, contained no surprises, and was calculatingly made more exciting.

Several New York discos started as clubs primarily for homosexuals, in which the DJs played soul and funk recordings that had a loud and strong pulse. Sad to say, cocaine taking crept in as part of the disco scene. Shortly disco was getting bigger radio exposure and increased public attention. Almost immediately, record companies started producing records purposely for disco dancing. To maximize sales, the music featured persuasive pop devices that caught the attention, so that recordings could achieve crossover acceptance. Disco albums regularly had a limited number of

tracks—only a few lengthy songs featuring solid beats. Record companies
also issued singles in order to facilitate remixes. By means of singles discs,
DJs could more easily mix tracks together. Before long, unrelentingly
hammering disco rhythms dominated the pop chart, and all sorts of performers entered the market with their own disco records. In most instances,
the music remained a producer's vehicle, since he supervised the songwriting and doctored the tracks. Disco would reinforce the supremacy of
the producer over songwriter and performer.

Disco dancing had several roots—fox trot, tango, swing, samba, cha
cha, mambo, and meringue. The hustle, the dance par excellence for disco,
probably began in New York around 1970. The International Hustle Dance
Association defined it as "a dance form using and combining the creative
elements of circular rotation, slotted movement, elliptical rotation, traveling movement, visual lead and follow within the rhythm and timing of the
dance." It came in three variants, as a line dance, a couples exercise, or a
freewheeling solo activity. On the whole, the last two were done at high
speed, with much posturing, spinning about, and, in couples dancing, with
partners closing together then bursting apart. The dancing could be pat-
terned on a basic hustle, Latin American hustle, or the trendy California
street hustle that had originated with skaters in Venice and Malibu.

In 1973, a number undoubtedly intended for disco managed to rise high
in the charts, the Love Unlimited Orchestra's "Love's Theme." The next
year disco fever began to grow with Gloria Gaynor's "Never Can Say
Goodbye," and Donna Summer's "Lady of the Night." By this year, New
York had disco establishments to suit every taste. West Village catered to
homosexuals; Studio 54 and Zenon were for the "jet set" (the fashionable
social set composed of wealthy well-traveled people); Leviticus and Oth-
ello's attracted affluent black Americans; Charles's Gallery was for poorer
black people. A few Italian DJs opened places for white people of limited
means in Brooklyn and Queens. *Rolling Stone* magazine at the end of the
year estimated that the United States had 2000 disco halls, of which the
New York City area had 200 to 300.[45] Disco was having an impact on very
popular performers like the Jackson 5. They did not desire to be left behind. The Jacksons wanted to turn out their own songs with the new electronic beat. In 1974, they recorded "Dancing Machine," produced by Hal
Davis for Motown. It sold over 2 million copies. Its sound forecast the
electronic manipulations of '80s "techno-pop."[46]

In 1975, Summers became the darling of the disco world with "Love to
Love You Baby." It was a huge radio hit, writes David Bowman, "a *disco*

song by Donna Summer—'Love to Love You Baby' was definitely mini-
mal. All you hear on the track are the mechanistic duo sounds of a great
robotic fucking machine . . . mounting Donna Summers. Her repeated
moans of pleasure. Who said minimalism had to be boring."[47] This 17-
minute piece crossed over into pop and rhythm and blues.

The essence of crude but flashy disco music was contained in Van Mc-
Coy's "The Hustle," which also was out in 1975. It was an immediate international triumph and sold over 8 million copies. When interviewed a
year later, McCoy admitted that he had no idea what the hustle dance was
all about. The lyric calls it "trash disco," "seventies cool," and a "walk on
the wild side."[48] At any rate, the piece illustrated the self-indulgence in
disco and its obsession with dancing.

A host of performers were turning to disco and recorded hits, among
them Diana Ross, ABBA, KC & the Sunshine Band, Barbra Streisand,
Cher, Rod Stewart, and Tina Charles. Every singer came out with recordings of his or her disco songs.

Saturday Night Fever (1977) filmed John Travolta radiating sexuality
as he strutted on the streets and cavorted on the dance floors. The film
made disco dancing fashionable for people in general. Playing in this
film, the Bee Gees became the principal disco band anywhere with the
conspicuously successful "Stayin' Alive," "How Deep Is Your Love," and
"Night Fever." Thousands of Travolta emulators suddenly materialized
from coast to coast. I confess to having enjoyed the music of the Bee Gees
and trying to "disco," however awkwardly, to the rhythms. The film
seemed to reinforce among the chic set the idea that disco was meant for
people who wore dressy clothes and enjoyed showing themselves off. To
some critics it illustrated the meaningless pleasure-seeking way of thinking infecting the seventies. They neglected to note that the disco dancing
in the film was a release from the depressing existence of Travolta's Tony
Manero, whose work offered no hope of improvement and whose father
was jobless. In addition, the Bee Gees were one of the more interesting
disco bands, despite the inanity of some of their lyrics, as in the 1977
"You Should Be Dancing." Somewhat disconnectedly it describes "my
baby" who stays in motion from midnight to dawn. She also keeps him
warm. Suddenly it darts off on a tangent, asking why someone is on his
back when he should be dancing.[49]

Disco was a billion-dollar industry in 1979, and around 15,000 discotheques operated nationwide. At the same time, the seeds for disco's de-
mise were being planted. Studio 54, an exclusive Manhattan club, was

opened in 1977 for "the beautiful people" (trendsetting members of glamorous social circles). Here they could "prove their superiority to the unfashionable" and render the realities of the outside world "magically irrelevant." The more dynamic earlier disco music gave way to a "standardized studio production style that started to give disco a bad name." Much of the music grew increasingly boring and merely commercial. Particularly among the straitlaced, disapproval arose over its affiliation with the militant gay movement, drugs, and sex.[50]

Counterattacks against disco from dedicated rock aficionados were bound to happen. Antidisco gatherings took place. One was held at a baseball game at Chicago's Comiskey Park, when rock devotees made a bonfire of 10,000 disco records. Disco lost potency when the '70s changed to the '80s, but it did not disappear. It metamorphosed into several different dance-based genres, like dance-pop, hip-hop, and techno. Moreover, it served to encourage the New Wave punk development in rock. Rock magnets like Michael Jackson, Madonna, Christina Aguilera, 'NSync, and Britney Spears fed off disco. During the nineties a revival of disco started up, nourished with contributions like Cher's "Strong Enough" and the Spice Girls' "Never Give Up on the Good Times."

THE REBELLIOUS POSTURE: HEAVY METAL

Several sources are cited for the origin of the term "heavy metal." Some writers claim that a *Rolling Stone* magazine reviewer invented it in 1968 by stating that the music of Jimi Hendrix was "like heavy metal falling from the sky." Others point to the words "heavy metal thunder" in the Steppenwolf song "Born to be Wild." One frequently mentioned source was the opening of chapter 14 of *The Soft Machine* (1961), from the novelist and former heroin addict William Seward Burroughs. Timothy White writes that in this example of psycho-sexual science fiction, the phrase was invented to represent a young hooligan, Uranian Willy the Heavy Metal Kid. By the next chapter in the book, the term was representing a violent storm in an imaginary war-torn world.[51] Robert Walser disputes the Burroughs origin and writes that the term "heavy metal" has a lengthy history going back into the 19th century, where it has meant large guns or people wielding great power. In music it came to signify the evoking of images and experiences of power. In the early 1970s, it was Lester Bangs and David Marsh who put it to musical use in their writing for *Creem*.[52]

Heavy metal began, in some measure, as a youthful emotional explosion against the mayhem and malaise of the early seventies and the indifference or incapacity of social and political leaders to supply a corrective. The music commanded attention with its strong, forceful expressiveness and vehement interpretation of the rhythm-and-blues musical style alongside pop gestures. As a rule, it conveyed a picture of darkness and mystery. Generally described as a form of hard rock (anticipating "New Wave" and "punk"), heavy metal encompassed an exceedingly amplified and ear-shattering rock music marked by a heavy beat and occasionally prolonged guitar solos. Manipulation of electronic devices produced distortion, noise, muddled sound, and a feeling of overwhelming power. A resultant thickness of sound, though having a peculiar richness, affected the vocals, which were more hidden than not at first. The American bands, more than the British, brought melody out in each piece.

Contributing to heavy metal's emergence in the late sixties were the dynamic guitar style of Jimi Hendrix and also Led Zeppelin's rather muffled, pounding percussion, and tunes and vocals that emerged as if out of a narcotic-induced trance. Starting in 1969, Britain's Led Zeppelin had helped pioneer the heavy-metal sound by recasting the blues of Howlin' Wolf and Willie Dixon and giving it a defiantly provocative format. They took advantage of amplification devices to manufacture feedback, reverberation, and noise. They created electronic distortion by presenting signals inaccurately through shifting the frequencies or unequally altering the delay or amplitude of the output wave. They explored mythology and occultism for their lyrics. In "Stairway to Heaven" (1971), their most popular song, they sang of a lady buying herself a stairway to heaven, and added the commentary that if everyone takes control for themselves, then "the piper" will guide them to wisdom and usher in a new day filled with joy.[53]

Also contributing from Britain were the Kinks' exemplary performances, the Rolling Stones' irreverent manner and arrogant delivery, the Who's unpredictable stage behavior and the electronic distortion added to their music in order to build tension, and Eric Clapton and Cream's jamming and bouncy delivery. In the United States, Alice Cooper and a form of shock rock arose—Cooper being the offensively dressed and genderless persona invented by Vincent Damon Furnier. As if the overly violent rock they played was not enough, Cooper and his band threatened the audience with items like live snakes, mutilated mannequins, guillotines, and electric chairs. It was called "aggro-theater." Fans who were uninterested in or bored with folk, folk-rock, and country were given a mesmerizing alternative. In exaggerated form, Cooper exemplified heavy metal's affinity to menace and provocation.

Shortly after these musicians came Black Sabbath and Deep Purple out of Britain, two bands that directly traded in occultism and Satanic imagery. The boisterous and intemperate AC/DC group, formed in Australia, retailed songs about the pleasures of sex and drinking, and the prospect of damnation. The New York Dolls appeared in 1971 as a rawer American extension of the Rolling Stones and played in an impassioned manner that foreshadowed the punk bands. Aerosmith from Boston was in favor of hard-hitting blues, uninhibited sex, and unrestricted drug usage. These outfits offered rock fans an alternative to the antiseptic disco sound and the soft singer–songwriter offerings.

Originating in Birmingham, England, Black Sabbath marked out the direction heavy metal was heading in their 1970 album *Black Sabbath* and a single, "Paranoid." Tours of the United States began in December 1970. Their name had come from a 1963 film, the atmospheric and menacing *Black Sabbath* in which Boris Karloff appears as a vampire. They used blues and riff formations to produce a sinister, convulsed sound that made major use of riffing. (The rather lunatic thrash rockers of the eighties would study the antics and music of the Black Sabbath members.) Unfortunately, they also indulged in extreme alcohol and drug use. In performance, they put up crosses as stage props and sang about cataclysm, ruin, demons, the occult, and the ending of life. Millions of youngsters were titillated by albums like *Paranoid* (1971) and *We Sold Our Soul for Rock 'n' Roll* (1976). However, starting in 1977 personnel changes started taking place and Black Sabbath's popularity peaked, although one way or another they have managed to keep going to century's end.

The Australians AC/DC, harboring the stentorian-voiced Brian Johnson and his uncontrollable mates, bashed the listening mobs with hard-rock blows, almost bursting eardrums with their stripped-down riffing, and entertained youths with burlesque acts, ribald language, and crazy stage activities. Formed in 1973, they did not win a following in America until 1979 and their album *Highway to Hell*. Owing to the mayhem produced by an AC/DC concert given in Salt Lake City, in 1991, three teenagers were crushed to death. Nevertheless, the band achieved greater popularity in 1995 and has continued to attract the crowds.

Aerosmith, from its formation in 1970 to the end of the century, has been a dominant hard-rock band because the American music public could feel a connection with this odd gang more than with other similar bands.

They were musical descendants of Led Zeppelin, Jimi Hendrix, the Yard-birds, and Cream. Their approach to writing a composition was to start with a guitar riff, add words, and then add the riff over the drum machine (an electronic apparatus including a sequencer that can be manipulated to arrange and alter digitally stored drum sounds), which started them off on their basic song. This furnished a rough mixture out of which the final song could be molded. It also aided in allowing their music to make a fresh impression on listeners, said their guitarist, Joe Perry.[54] Their tours sold out and their albums had huge sales. However, after a while they lost favor owing, in large part, to their drug taking. They then took stock of themselves and came back as "the jam-loving blues band built around the dirty riffs of the guitarist Joe Perry and the bedrock rhythm section of Tom Hamilton and Joe Kramer." They have learned to accommodate themselves to the constraints of MTV television and the requirements of film sound tracks, but they continue to retain their "confident looseness," and the rest of the "authentic core" of their style.[55] Their early "Dream On" (1971), written by Steven Tyler, is musically attractive. Its lyric sends out a message of mortality and despair. It claims that life victimizes everybody. When you see yourself in a mirror, your face gets increasingly lined. The past is irretrievable. At the end everybody must pay their dues in life.[56]

More urgent, but also attractively musical, was "Janie's Got a Gun" (1989), about a sexually abusive father and the daughter who shoots him down. The victim has defended herself from rape by killing him with a bullet to the head.[57] In 1990, its video won two MTV awards, as "Best Metal" and "Viewer's Choice."

The heavy-metal audiences of the seventies were usually estranged white male teenagers from the working class, who welcomed music that gave them some identity and the representations of strength, danger, and emotional excitement that they valued. Around 1985, the listeners had swelled to encompass preteenagers, as well as those in their late twenties. Some adult members of the middle class were also taking an interest.[58] Yet, there was so little scope and depth to some heavy-metal music that one wondered about how they gained prominence. Nevertheless, for left-out segments of society, the interest in heavy metal should be expected given the political crises, up-and-down job situations, policies favoring the wealthy, nasty cutbacks in social services, and a seeping feeling of victimization.

From the late seventies on would arrive bands like Van Halen, White Snake, Anthrax, Megadeth, Deaf Jam, and Motley Crüe. Here, designations break down. Writers have described them variously as hardcore,

New Wave, punk, and thrash. They were all variations on the heavy-metal idea. By the eighties and nineties several new and old bands, two of them being Metallica and Motorhead, had put on the mantle of thrash and others, like Nirvana and Korn, that of grunge, and still others, like Van Halen, were into punk. One band, Bon Jovi, veered toward pop, allowing their music to be evaluated by adolescent jurors and selecting what was voted the most attractive. After such testing they put out the album *Slippery When Wet* (1986) and sold over 12 million copies. Finally there were the outer reaches of heavy metal found in the extremes of thrash and called death metal or grindcore, as with the bands Napalm Death, Carcass, and Obituary.

PROGRESSIVE TO PUNK

Progressive rockers wanted to "progress" rock from what they perceived as simplemindedness to a higher level of musicianship, whether in the quality of the music played, or in the sophistication of the lyrics. Progressive-rock was also called art-rock or symphonic-rock. Some compositions could last as long as 20 minutes; others might be subdivided into linked tracks, like the movements of a symphony or symphonic suite. It was more music for listeners rather than for dancers. Most of its practitioners were British rather than Americans. Progressive outfits often contained virtuoso players like Keith Emerson and Rick Wakeman on keyboard, and Steve Howe and Robert Fripp on guitar. Many of them sought to introduce art ("classical") music's feeling of scale and range of views without reducing rock's rude power and potency. Other styles—art, folk, jazz, and non-Western music— found their way into progressive compositions. John Covach writes that pieces of extended length characterized Jethro Tull; aspects of opera, Peter Gabriel and Genesis; contrapuntal writing, Gentle Giant; complicated meter, atonality, and free-form improvisation, King Crimson.[59]

Emerging in the late sixties, progressive-rock did not achieve its greatest strength until the seventies. It first made headway with bands like the Moody Blues, out of Birmingham, who went over to a lyrical pop-rock style with intricate harmonies, a "symphonic" sound, and "cosmic" lyrics, in 1967. The band was even asked to record a rock version of Dvořák's Symphony No. 9. Moody Blues was known for its use of the Melletron synthesizer, a keyboard apparatus that duplicated the sounds of violins, flutes, and so forth. One 1967 song that was a hit when it came out in Britain and five years later became a hit in the United States was "Nights in White Satin," a ballad written by band member Justin Howard and recorded with the London Festival Orchestra. In a sense, it provided a foil to the angry tones usually emerging from the heavy-metal contingent. The song tells of endless nights like white satin, of never-sent letters and overlooked beauty; about elusive truth but one certainty: "oh, how I love you."[60]

From 1967 through 1972, Moody Blues recorded several albums that were musically enterprising, lyrically aspiring, and contained singles pleasing to a huge number of listeners. They then ceased playing as a group until 1978, when they took up a simpler style and recorded albums that met with wide approval through the eighties. Other British bands took up the cause of progressive-rock: King Crimson, the Soft Machine, Jethro Tull, Yes, Emerson, Lake & Palmer, and Pink Floyd, among others.

In America, the influence of jazz, folk, and non-Western music often took precedence over art music in progressive-rock. Frank Zappa, for one, liked the 20th-century composers Stravinsky and Varèse, and had an impressive knowledge of jazz, rhythm and blues, doo-wop, and rockabilly. He formed his band, the Mothers of Invention, in 1964, and with them he first made a name for himself by traveling along the California hippie route. His songs would always exhibit unexpected twists and traits, whether in music or lyric. In albums like *Absolutely Free* (1967) one could hear flashes of advanced experimentation à la Varèse, plus assorted rock flavorings. In the same year, he employed a large orchestra alongside the Mothers of Invention in *Lumpy Gravy*. His group served mainly as a showcase for his talents, which could dwell on doo-wop at one moment or entertain with weird electronic noises at another. The lyrics vied with each other in their unconventionality. For example, in *Zoot Allures*[61] (1976), Zappa constructed an oddly pessimistic lyric in the track "Wind Up Workin' in the Gas Station." One is admonished to decide. Continue with your job, the lyric warns, and remain stupid. On the other hand, "you oughta know" that all of your education will not help you in any way. He gets bizarre and scary in "The Torture Never Stops," where slime, rot, snot, vomit, and rats cover the floor, weird spear holders are at the door, tools for inflicting pain are plentiful, and a creepy midget mops up the blood. Finally, he became breezily scatological in "Ms. Pinky," who is an artificial rubber-headed girl with whom one can have sex.

To become hits, songs like the above require easily digestible, likable melodies. They were not thus provided as a rule. Not surprisingly, his musical offerings found few takers among the public. In the eighties the Berkeley Symphony did one of his art works, and a recording, *Boulez Conducts Zappa: The Perfect Stranger*, made some headway, but in classical-music circles alone. The closest Zappa ever came to a popular hit was with his disco takeoff "Dancin' Fool," in 1979, and his satire on empty-headed fashion-mad women in "Valley Girl," in 1982. Most songs either offended people or went over their heads or just did not rock enough.

Among the other American progressive bands were the advanced and unconventional-sounding Captain Beefheart and the Magic Band, the jazz-rocking Blood Sweat and Tears, and the intensely rocking Styx, who practiced what was denominated "pomp-rock" for the display that was put on during concerts. The term "pomp-rock" indicated that the musical arrangements also might verge on the bombastic and overblown. Yet, Styx went beyond pomp to successfully woo their 12- to 16-year-old fans via FM radio, offering them melodious and accessible songs. Especially well received were the songs "Lady" (1973 release) and "Babe" (1977 release). Later came two more hits, "The Best of Times" and "Too Much Time on My Hands."

Although progressive-rock never died out, it was supplanted in popularity by New Wave and punk-rock, which grew out of heavy metal and progressive-rock in the latter half of the seventies. The last two also benefited from the burgeoning backlash against disco by offering a dance-floor alternative. "New Wave" is a term used loosely to describe a large number of bands that began to come into prominence in the late seventies. The music made much use of electronic instruments and stressed sophisticated artistry, accessibility, and usually some element of the outrageously theatrical. It presented an ambiance that would go down well in the gay community.

Although its performers were mostly British, New Wave did have a greater American popular success than progressive-rock. Indeed, a few American outfits would structure themselves on the New Wave model—the Cars of Boston, Massachusetts, Devo of Akron, Ohio, and the B-52s of Athens, Georgia. New Wave's particular audience in the United States included many college students from well-to-do families. Several New Wave performers were known for their extraordinary hairdos, platform shoes, distinctive dress, and showy conduct. The aura of a decadent lifestyle hung around them. Usually wearing makeup and sporting "big hair," and clothed in extremely smooth and glossy fashion, neoromantics like David Bowie first ensnared the believer with their invented personae, and then with their music.

Bowie's stage appearance exemplified the efforts that went into the portrayal of a fictional self. In the seventies, he took on the "glitter" character of "Ziggy Stardust." The androgynous Ziggy haircut, orange colored and straight down and long in the back, appealed to both sexes. The makeup was after that of stars in Japan's Kabuki theater. Ziggy's red boots were made of PVC and set on plastic platforms. His costumes were amazing. As Ziggy, he wore a striking jumpsuit, or an outlandish extraterrestrial outfit, or a clown costume of silver metallic net with silver ballet slippers. He would also wear non-Ziggy costumes, like the "thin White Duke" look, the "Union Jack frock coat" look, and the "gold pants and leather jacket plus attached gold wings" look.

New Wavers avoided the sometimes flaccid rhythms that infected many a progressive work in favor of energized dance beats helped along with high-powered guitars and synthesizers. Or they could create strange, brooding, synthesizer-generated sound blends. Or they produced less hurried, more "soulful" songs of some sophistication. Especially in the seventies and eighties, David Bowie, Elton John, the Police, Blondie, the Pretenders, and Elvis Costello blended New Wave into their own individual styles.

At the opening of the seventies, Bowie's "Space Oddity" was about a Major Tom who is shot into space, converses with ground control, and takes a space walk. The song reached a sales peak a few weeks after Neil Armstrong walked on the moon. The music is given a steadily moving staccato shape, like the hectic rhythms in a busy space center. A shuddering dissonance, seven different tones piled one on top of the other, denotes the liftoff. Now the music soars fittingly, as the astronaut hears the peculiar message from ground control that he has succeeded in his flight and been made famous by the media who even inquire about whose shirt he wears. He is told that it is time to step out of the capsule if he dares.[62] A decade later, Bowie wrote "Ashes to Ashes," which hurled sarcasm at Major Tom, calling him a "junky" stupefied on "heaven's high."[63]

Bowie achieved high renown in the United States, especially with two songs, "Fame" (1975) and "Let's Dance" (1983). The first sounds joyful and its rhythms fit well into a disco setting. The second was from the album *Let's Dance*, which he called "the most positive, uplifting album I've made in a long time."[64] Among his strongest albums were *Station to Station* (1976), *Low* and *Heroes* (1977), *Lodger* (1979), *Scary Monsters*

(1980), and *Let's Dance* (1983). Bowie has kept on trying to stay abreast of the pop trends by discarding used-up music styles and stage personalities and restructuring his music and persona. His consistently most reliable period was the seventies and early eighties.

Another British New Wave singer–songwriter, Elton John, achieved British acceptance with the 1970 album *Elton John*, which included the well-received "Border Song." His American debut in Los Angeles came in 1970. He quickly became a superstar in Britain and America, as he issued top-selling albums, one after another. These contained songs often created in joint authorship with lyricist Bernie Taupin. His garish costumes concealed an accomplished musician. Astutely staged shows with his band publicized favorite songs, like "Crocodile Rock" (1973), "Bennie and the Jets" (1974), and "Philadelphia Freedom" and "Island Girl" (1975). A fine pianist, Elton John developed an expressive singing style through which he delivered his persuasive tunes. John was a consummate actor and a performer conversant with the public's changing tastes. Extraordinary sales, with around 25 important song hits, made him a wealthy man. Even in the nineties he and Taupin were turning out notable successes like "Don't Let the Sun Go Down on Me" (1992) and "Something about the Way You Look Tonight" and "Candle in the Wind" (1997). Over 5 million people bought copies of the last song, after it was sung at Princess Diana's funeral. He was also the composer of the music for Disney's successful film *The Lion King*.

The Police could surprise with their subject matter. Their popular "Don't Stand So Close to Me" (1980), by their bassist and vocalist Sting, sings of a young teacher about whom a schoolgirl fantasizes. Overwhelmed by her crush she approaches the teacher only to get a reprimand for standing too close.[65] On the other hand, the surprise in "Every Breath You Take" (1983), also by Sting, is not from the theme, which is a straight affirmation of love. It is in the music's considerable length, its willingness to modulate to distant keys, and its high-reaching melody that features Sting's high-pitched warble.

Blondie looked forward to punk-rock, and the group's "Atomic" (1976), by the keyboardist James Destri and vocalist Deborah Harry, implied more than what was actually said, where apparently a tryst after dark has been arranged during which the singer hopes to engage in fabulous sexual activity.[66]

Elvis Costello in the late seventies was as much into punk as he was into New Wave. He applied a rough forcefulness and disrespectful impudence to the tightly structured songs he wrote and performed. His debut came in 1977 with the heated "Less Than Zero," and the album *My Aim Is True*. He produced even angrier rhythms in 1978 with *This Year's Model*. Belligerence and heavy drinking marred his 1979 tour of America. The adverse criticism caused him to rethink his attitude and behavior and he resumed concertizing in 1981 as a reformed character who had left behind his bad-boy manner. *Imperial Bedroom*, the anger gone and paradoxical and poignant love songs substituting, garnered rave reviews in 1982. From then on he authored polished pop ballads that were carefully formed and had a sophisticated appeal. Around the end of the century, he was collaborating with Burt Bachrach in writing music and also attempting classical composition.

Covach states that the simplicity that seems to invest quite a few of the New Wave pieces is illusory. Whether Elvis Costello, Talking Heads, Joe Jackson, Devo, and other late-1970s New Wavers, their compositions are far more sophisticated than they appear at first. He finds them "carefully written, arranged, and produced, and all this to the highest of pop-music professional standards." The simplicity for some, he explains, is owing to a return to straightforward formal structures, especially the long-standing verse-refrain format. One also can find "a relatively conservative harmonic 'vocabulary.'" Resorting to earlier models of instruments and amplifiers and an apparent return to basics also conveys the idea of directness.[67]

After the early eighties, New Wave commanded less and less of a following and gave way to newer musical modes. Nevertheless, several performers soldiered on. In a June 2002 interview of David Bowie, Jon Pareles described Bowie as an "astute conceptualist" who had turned concerts into theater and fashion spectacles, and who had recharged his song with electronics, dance rhythms, and punk styles. He quotes Bowie as saying, "I'm well past the age where I'm acceptable. You get to a certain age and you are forbidden access. You're not going to get the kind of coverage that you would like in music magazines; you're not going to get played on radio; and you're not going to get played on television. I have to survive on word of mouth."[68]

Punk-rock, which superseded New Wave, started as an intense response to the economic depression affecting the poor and anger at the complacencies of conventional middle-class society. More than was true for heavy metal, its extraordinary rate of growth was attributable to sponsorship by a host of restless, impatient, and obviously irate young people. Predictably, it soon disconcerted the middle-of-the-road majority. It also provoked the public into taking a new look at itself through the eyes of its disgruntled youth.

Evidently conventional society disapproved of what it saw. The middle-class response went from denunciation to rejection, and the young people's response was to aid and abet even more the punk movement and its belligerence. Whatever the reaction, the adult public was witnessing a change in youthful attitudes that left it uncomfortable, and it identified the punk musicians as uncaringly heading the show.

Punk had its antecedents in the Rolling Stones, garage-rock, and the heavy-metal bands. Blondie and the Velvet Underground from New York, and Iggy and the Stooges from Ann Arbor, also carried influence. Like garage musicians, punk-rockers reveled in their musical illiteracy and sneered at the competency of New Wave players. They had no sympathy for the folk people or for the sensitive singer–songwriters. Punk's cultural yardsticks were different. They were, above all, anti-art. Adolescent punksters plucked awkwardly on guitars, banged ferociously on their drum sets, turned the volume up on amplifiers to deafening levels, and sent out a raging howl that was as much a cultural as a musical statement. They took up where guitarist Lenny Kaye left off after he compiled his garage-band *Nugget* album, in 1972, and in the liner notes invented the term "punk-rock" to describe the music.

The adherents to punk detested the direction in which the music world was going. They were especially offended by the boosting of money-hungry musicians to superstar status. They saw center stage occupied by gigantic rock acts, presented by Fleetwood Mac, REO Speedwagon, and Journey, among others. These outsized personalities performed for exorbitant fees and had abandoned the more modest auditoriums and dance halls for arenas and stadiums. Costly stage sets, elaborate props, and laser displays isolated the performers from audiences. Ticket prices went up and up. This trend would be more unmistakable in the eighties and later.

Punk's principal followers were cynics, anarchists, and disillusioned youngsters. They also thought themselves being manipulated by the music industry and society. Some felt betrayed and, even more, questioned why they had to live with the consequences of leaders mouthing ideals, giving excuses as to why hard times continued, and doing nothing. To them, Nixon and Ford were failed leaders. Whether right or wrong, these youngsters believed they existed in the worst of all possible worlds and that all humanity naturally tended to evil. As far as the supporters of punk could see, the sixties struggle for justice had failed. Saving the world was a lie coming from the mouths of hypocrites. In reality, political authority and American society remained essentially reactionary and was intent on enforcing conformity. Boredom, urban violence, and murder exemplified their failed civilization. They themselves felt powerless and frustrated. They convinced themselves that no one would listen to them and no one cared. They could see no way to get out of their predicament. Vulgarity, antisocial behavior, and excitement for excitement's sake gave outward expression to their feelings. They stood for a mode of existence that reflected how civilization was moving rapidly along the path to destruction. Shocking people, grabbing attention, making certain they could not be ignored were their modi operandi. Predictably, the media found that punk was uncouth, of poor quality, and too given to havoc. The denunciation achieved the reverse of its purpose. Punk simply spread.

In 1973, a small Bowery bar called CBGB (Country Bluegrass Blues) opened in New York City. It was here that the early punk-rock bands were allowed to operate and present their primitivistic material—jazz-hued Television, the poetry-inspired Patti Smith Group, the earthy, blues-based Ramones, and the pop-rock Talking Heads. They were quickly joined by the jarring and more openly offensive DNA, Suicide, and Richard Hell and the Voidoids. To all of the musicians, rock music seemed to have gotten too complicated, playing instruments had again become too demanding, and the performers were losing touch with young fans. Tommy Ramone, the first drummer of the Ramones, said, "We were connoisseurs of rock's history and where it should go. We wanted to bring back short songs, pop melodies, things like that. But I think we were the first group to consciously use the fact that we weren't virtuosos, to realize that this was an advantage. We stripped down a lot of things and just put in the gist of what was needed."[69] Richard Hell, who deliberately displayed spiky hair and torn T-shirts, explained that his looks were "a sort of strategy." He wanted the do-it-yourself look. "Everything we were doing at the time had that element, from having ripped up clothes to not knowing how to play instruments. . . . The ripped T-shirts meant that I don't give a fuck about stardom and all that or glamour and going to rock shows to see someone pretend to be perfect. The people wanted to see someone they could identify with. It was saying, 'You could be here, too.'"[70]

The Talking Heads, formed in 1975, were a band of alert, intelligent college-educated performers who abandoned unadulterated New Wave for a sort of artistic punk, in the seventies. They did not completely turn their back on technique. Chris Frantz, their drummer, said about audiences, "When we started, [they] seemed to think that you had to wear platform shoes and tight leather pants and you had to lead a decadent

[New Wave] lifestyle. We came on stage looking like a bunch of Je-suits."[71] The Talking Heads drew on hardcore rock, rhythm and blues, Arabian and African music, and the classical minimalism of Philip Glass. This combination generated compositions that were daring and inventive, and that set feet tapping. Their songs, mostly written by vocalist and gui-tarist David Byrne, were always danceable numbers. Their lyrics and stage antics did not try to alarm people as their first order of business. However, they did sing about estrangement, loneliness, the dreariness of life, and the inability to link with anyone. In their first album, *77* (1977), "No Compassion" concludes that everyone has their difficulties and no one is interested in another's troubles, nor wants to hear about them. It is a world where no one has time for each other.[72]

Another song, "Psycho Killer," explains that the "I" is tense, nervous, and unable to relax. He can't "face up to the facts" and is into denial. When he goes to bed, he is a psychological mess, all afire and "a real live wire" that should not be touched. He thinks it is far better to run away.[73]

By 1985 and the release of *Little Creatures*, the Talking Heads were sounding more cheerful, more melodious, and more suited for a wide pop-ular market. In 2002, Byrne issued the album *Looking into the Eyeball*. The songs were inviting and unruffled and had acquired touches of soul and Latin music. The uncultivated slant and outbursts of emotional excite-ment from twenty years before were no longer in evidence.[74]

The Ramones band, formed in 1974, dressed in leather jackets and ripped jeans. The performers specialized in lean, high-speed music, a thick curtain of guitar sound, and pithy lyrics aspiring to seriousness, yet nonetheless confrontational. Their sound was far more aggressive than that of the Talking Heads; their lyrics were far more uncompromising and un-yielding. Their jointly written first album, *The Ramones* (1976), unveiled items like "Now I Wanna Sniff Some Glue," which repeatedly tells us all youngsters want to sniff glue because they need something to do.[75] Or we are told to "Beat on the Brat," hit the little horror with a baseball bat.[76]

In 1977, they issued "Suzie Is a Headbanger" and "Gimmie Gimmie Shock Treatment," in the album *The Ramones Leave Home*. Joey Ramone claimed the songs described the "sick" adolescents in the audience who were high on LSD and the like. These lyrics were among the most ex-treme in their repertoire. Other songs remained more agreeable, serving fans confident love songs, complaints about life, and satires like the par-ody of California surf music, "Rockaway Beach," from the album *Rocket to Russia*.

Their best-selling album, *End of the Century*, came out in 1980, attracting fans with pieces like "Do You Remember Rock 'n' Roll?" and "Baby, I Love You." Five years later, they were clamoring against what they saw as a smug American society and the witless President Reagan who set it an example, with the song "Bonzo Goes to Bitburg (My Brain Is Hanging Upside Down)." Reagan had gone to Germany and spoke sympathetically of the Nazi dead at the Kolmeshohe Cemetery in Bitburg. The song warned him not to become too sympathetic towards German war criminals and thus appear to be a child of Hitler.[77]

At any rate, they were not bubblegum children doing songs by old men with an eye on making a profit and bent on pleasing boys and girls who were not even 9 years of age. The Ramones, wrote Tim White, gave of themselves "with a kooky totality that [was] strangely moving" to audiences that included "the safety-pin-through-the-nose crowds but also a host of Ivy Leaguers" and some "middle-aged longhairs in down parkas."[78] After the eighties their effectiveness weakened. Too much inner dissension, drug taking, and overexposure lost them their edge.

Not to be outdone, California claimed its own variety of punk-rockers, sparked by X, Black Flag, and the Dead Kennedys. Of the three, X was the most capable musically, the most grown-up in their lyrics, and the most given to arriving at intriguing new harmonizations. The other two were far more inclined to dispense twisted, masochistic, morose versions of punk music. Grueling hardcore rhythms promoted slam dancing (a form of dancing in which dancers smash into one another) in the "mosh pit" (the place in front of the stage where slamming takes place) and had frenzied youths hurling themselves from the stage onto the crowded dance floor — the entire practice called "thrash," to go with a "thrash" sound. Some, among them youths sporting shaved heads and Nazi armbands, also found entertainment attacking helpless derelicts and street beggars. The paradox was that many thrashers were not underprivileged but the bored, overindulged scions of affluent families, looking for something to do and feeling they had to prove to themselves and their associates that they were "punk-tough" by slamming and thrashing during performances, and beating defenseless bums afterwards. On the one hand, the Dead Kennedys incited activity reprehensible to normal society in morbid and unwholesome lyrics propelled by sadistically ferocious music, like "I Kill Children" from the album *Fresh Fruit for Rotten Vegetables*. They love to mash children with cars or feed them poisoned candy in order to see them die and to hear their mothers cry.[79]

On the other hand, taken aback by the thuggish violence they were accused of provoking, they sang "Nazi Punks Fuck Off," from the album *In God We Trust, Inc.* The lyric claimed that punk encouraged thinking for oneself, was not a religious cult, and had nothing to do with hardcore "jocks" prone to violence.[80]

The Talking Heads and the Ramones toured Britain in 1976 and, especially the latter, helped launch the rebel-nihilist Sex Pistols and the militant-activist Clash. Malcolm McLaren had come from London to New York in 1975 to manage the New York Dolls, former Brooklyn gang members, and caught the punk sounds coming out of the CBGB club. By the end of the year, he was back in London and running a nonconformist clothing store called Sex. Determined to promote the store and to put together his own punk group, McLaren established a house group, the Sex Pistols, a band far more nasty and hardcore than the Ramones. The recruits from London's slums immediately won reputations as musical ruffians purveying raw destructive rage in their recordings and offering filth and violence as part of their live performances. The melodic content of their songs was negligible; the shock value was great. Although the British government tried to suppress them, the Sex Pistols found wide support among their country's discontented youth. Too many of them were unemployed, saw no future for themselves, and fumed at Britain's class structure.

The Sex Pistols initiated a substantial music underground of do-it-yourself, would-be musicians. At the same time, contemporary rock musicians boasting some playing ability remained dubious. As Roger Waters, who had been a bassist and vocalist with Pink Floyd, said, "The Sex Pistols were just trying to make noise. It was so clearly contrived. You know, they were managed by a bloke who ran a shop selling silly clothes!"[81]

All the members had grown up in a ramshackle, squalid part of London. The vocalist, John Lydon, took on the alias Johnny Rotten (he had an unwashed, repulsive body odor). The bassist, a street tough known as Sid Vicious (which he was), joined shortly after the band was established. Like the rest of the band, he was an incompetent player. Against a strident, crude instrumental backing, a snarling Rotten sang insolently about English neofascism, revolution, creating chaos, and taking charge of one's body. He tried to be as confrontational and threatening as possible, starting with his first single, "Anarchy in the U.K.," a celebration of chaos and lawlessness.[82] The furor over the recording caused the EMI label to drop the band. The BBC banned their next single, "God Save the Queen," released on a Virgin recording. The queen is a non–human being and heads a fascistic regime that aims to keep everyone stupid.[83]

Denied bookings in Britain, these suspect musicians toured the United States in January 1978, but did not go over nearly as well as they had hoped. Rotten left the band after a San Francisco appearance, calling the group "a farce." He formed his own outfit, Public Image Limited, later that year in New York. Other members departed. Vicious stabbed his girlfriend to death, and then died of a drug overdose. The rest of the band dissolved in 1978. Their legacy (and that of the Clash, also) was to introduce skepticism about the validity of big rock acts and the integrity of major record labels into people's minds and further a noncommercial sound that would lead to "alternative music" and the "grunge" of Nirvana and Kurt Cobain.

The Clash were active, vigorous advocates of social and political causes, not nihilists. Their music was based on funk, reggae, and heavy metal. They saw themselves as rabble-rousers, working-class activists instigating the underclass to war via rock 'n' roll. In "White Riot," they shouted that whites, like blacks, should riot instead of going to schools where they are taught to remain dim-witted.[84] In "Garageland" they declared they were not interested in the activities of the rich, who believe they have a monopoly on wisdom. Instead, they praised the pint-sized hoodlums who alone know what truth is.[85] To some ears the musical coefficient was negligible.

The combative punksters like Sex Pistols and The Clash started no great social conflagrations. Punk, however, would produce a cult of youths unconventional in their dress and behavior. Looming in the near distance were chains, boots, strange clothing, peculiarly colored and bizarrely styled hair (like green Mohawk haircuts), and the piercing of bellybuttons, lips, noses, eyelids, and tongues. Posers saw money to be made from punk, formed bands, and counterfeited the behavior and the manner of playing. The singer–songwriter Joni Mitchell, in September 2001, described overhearing a conversation between a punk musician and his "A&R man," at a café in Santa Monica. The former was a young man displaying tattoos, hair still "spray-netted up," and dog bracelets on his arms and neck. "Basically, he's a Midwestern nerd who's become a yuppie," she said. He was floundering around looking for a new hook to attract fans. He admitted that what he played was "crap" anyway, but he did not want to wake up "flat broke at 48." Rock music, he said, was "supposed to be dumb" and without high standards. Mitchell interrupted their conversation and spoke up for the intelligence and standards of musicians like Chuck Berry and Bob

Dylan, saying, "I'm sitting next to your table, listening to how your head works. I don't even have to hear your musical work to know . . . [it's] crap."[86]

Punk continues to provoke unease. Quite a few of its practitioners behave reprehensibly. Its context can seem irrational; its aim, anarchic. Yet, its oftentimes raucous speech forces society to take a critical look at itself. What the best punk bands have to offer their fans is bare-bones and ruthlessly frank communication, absent of charades or disconcerting ploys. And, after its own fashion, punk can present some interesting music when performed by the more accomplished musicians like the Talking Heads, the Ramones, and Aerosmith.

NOTES

1. John Orman, *The Politics of Rock Music* (Chicago: Nelson-Hall, 1984), 1–17.

2. George Packer, review of Bruce J. Schulman, *The Seventies*, *New York Times*, 10 June 2001, www.nytimes.com.

3. Orman, *Politics of Rock Music*, 175.

4. Bruce J. Schulman, *The Seventies* (New York: Free Press, 2001), 151.

5. Deborah Grace Winer, *The Night and the Music* (New York: Schirmer Books, 1996), 17.

6. Stephen Holden, "Audra McDonald Casts Her Spell on Sadness," *New York Times*, 5 November 2002, www.nytimes.com.

7. Tony Bennett with Will Friedwald, *The Good Life* (New York: Pocket Books, 1998), 204.

8. See, respectively, Ed Siegel, "Despite Some Missed Notes, 'Gershwin' Sings," *Boston Globe*, 21 June 2002, C17–18; Steve Morse, "Cole Sets a Mellow and Romantic Mood," *Boston Globe*, 22 June 2002, C5; Steve Greenlee, "Reeve Sings, Writes 'Music for the Soul,'" *Boston Globe*, 28 June 2002, C11.

9. Los Angeles: Anne-Rachel Music, c1964.

10. Merle Haggard with Peggy Russell, *Sing Me Back Home* (New York: Times Books, 1981), 113.

11. Barbara Ching, *Wrong's What I Do Best* (New York: Oxford University Press, 2001), 42.

12. Nashville, Tennessee: Sony/ATV Music, c1969.

13. Glenn Campbell with Tom Carter, *Rhinestone Cowboy* (New York: Villard Books, 1994), 73.

14. Campbell with Carter, *Rhinestone Cowboy*, 74.

15. New York: EMI Music, c1973.

16. New York: Wait & See Music, c1973.

17. "Biography," posted by Capital International Productions on the web, 25 August 2002.

18. Neil Strauss, "Emmylou Harris: Still Finding Joy in a Broken Heart," *New York Times*, 9 July 2001, www.nytimes.com.

19. New York: Colgems EMI Music, c1971.

20. New York: Colgems EMI Music, c1971.

21. New York: Colgems EMI Music, c1971.

22. Mark White, *"You Must Remember This . . .": Popular Songwriters, 1900–1980* (New York: Scribner's Sons, 1985), 76–77.

23. John Leland, "Questions for Neil Diamond," *New York Times Magazine,* 22 July 2001, www.nytimes.com.

24. James Taylor, "It's Life in Retrospect," posted on *The James Taylor Website.*

25. Los Angeles: Country Road Music, c1970.

26. Los Angeles: Country Road Music, c1970.

27. Los Angeles: Country Road Music, c1970.

28. Jonathan Perry, "Taylor Still Enthralls," *Boston Globe*, 30 June 2001, F2.

29. Richard Dyer, "Taylor Connects with Tanglewood Friends," *Boston Globe*, 19 July 2002, D19.

30. New York: Quackenbush Music, c1971.

31. New York: Quackenbush Music, c1972.

32. New York: C'Est Music, c1995.

33. Nashville: Joni Mitchell Publishing, c1971.

34. Nashville: Crazy Crow Music, c1972.

35. David Wild, "Joni Mitchell," *Rolling Stone*, 31 October 2002, 116.

36. Greenwich, Connecticut: Bruce Springsteen, c/o Jon Landau Management, c1975.

37. Jon Pareles, "Bruce Springsteen: His Kind of Heroes, His Kind of Songs," *New York Times*, 14 July 2002, www.nytimes.com.

38. Greenwich, Connecticut: Bruce Springsteen, c/o Jon Landau Management, c1984.

39. Greenwich, Connecticut: Bruce Springsteen, c/o Jon Landau Management, c1984.

40. Paul Friedlander, "The Revolution Will Be Televised," in James D. Torr, editor, *The 1980s* (San Diego, California: Greenhaven Press, 2000), 194.

41. Bryn Mawr, Pennsylvania: Fifty Six Hope Road, c1977.

42. Los Angeles: Bob Marley Music, c/o Universal Polygram International, c1976.

43. Steve Morse, "Shaggy Won't Let His Hair Down," *Boston Globe*, 1 June 2001, C13–14.

44. Kelefa Sanneh, "The Lords of Reggae Are Rolling," *New York Times*, 28 June 2002, www.nytimes.com.

45. Nelson George, *Hip Hop America* (New York: Viking, 1998), 6.

46. J. Randy Taraborrelli, *Michael Jackson* (New York: Birch Lane Press, 1991), 128.

47. David Bowman, *This Must Be the Place* (New York: Harper Entertainment, 2001), 74.

48. Los Angeles: Warner-Tamerlane Publishing, c1975.

49. Beverly Hills, California: Gibb Brothers Music, c1976.

50. Craig Werner, *A Change Is Gonna Come* (New York: Plume, 1999), 203, 206, 210.

51. Timothy White, *Rock Lives* (New York: Henry Holt, 1990), 288.

52. Robert Walser, *Running with the Devil* (Hanover, New Hampshire: University Press of New England, 1993), 1–2, 8.

53. Los Angeles: Superhype Publishers, c/o WB Music, c1971.

54. Steve Morse, "Aerosmoith Is Right at Home with 'Play,'" *Boston Globe*, 6 March 2001, B14.

55. Ann Powers, "Aerosmith, Relishing the Third Incarnation," *New York Times*, 18 June 2001, www.nytimes.com.

56. Los Angeles: Mosaic Music, c1971.

57. New York: EMI April Music, c/o EMI Music, c1989.

58. Friedlander, "The Revolution Will Be Televised," 197–98.

59. John Covach, "Progressive Rock, 'Close to the Edge,' and the Boundaries of Style," in John Covach and Graeme M. Boone, editors, *Understanding Rock* (New York: Oxford University Press, 1997), 3.

60. New York: Essex Music, c/o The Richmond Organization, c1967.

61. North Hollywood: Munchkin Music, c1976.

62. London, England: Essex Music International, c1969.

63. New York: Screen Gems—EMI Music Publishing, c1980.

64. Fred Bronson, *The Billboard Book of Number One Hits*, 4th ed. (New York: Billboard Books, 1997), 572.

65. New York: EMI Blackwood Music, c1980.

66. Los Angeles: Chrysalis Music, c1976.

67. Covach, "Progressive Rock, 'Close to the Edge,'" 5.

68. Jon Pareles, "David Bowie, 21st-Century Entrepreneur," *New York Times*, 9 June 2002, www.nytimes.com.

69. Jon Pareles, "Then, Now: New York City," *New York Times*, 19 May 2001, www.nytimes.com.

70. David P. Szatmary, *Rockin' in Time*, 2nd ed. (Englewood Cliffs, New Jersey: Prentice-Hall, 1991), 228–29.

71. Schulman, *Seventies*, 154.

72. New York: Bleu Disque Music, c1977.

73. New York: Bleu Disque Music, c1977.

74. Ann Powers, "David Byrne: Same as He Ever Was, but More Appreciated," *New York Times*, 15 May 2001, www.nytimes.com.

75. New York: Bleu Disque Music, c1976.

76. New York: Bleu Disque Music, c1976.

77. Beverly Hills, California: Hot Boy Music, c1985.

78. White, *Rock Lives*, 443.

79. Piedmont, California: Decay Music, c1980.

80. Piedmont, California: Decay Music, c1981.

81. Nathan Brackett, "Q&A," *Rolling Stone*, 14 March 2002, 33.

82. Beverly Hills, California: Careers BMG Music, c1977.

83. Beverly Hills, California: Careers BMG Music, c1977.

84. New York: EMI Virgin Music, c1977.

85. New York: EMI Virgin Music, c1977.

86. Timothy White, "Words from a Woman of Heart and Mind," *Billboard*, 8 September 2001, www.billboard.com.

Chapter Eight

The Eighties and Nineties

What were the conditions that may have had an impact on the popular music of the eighties and nineties? For one, the political face of the United States became decidedly conservative with the election of Ronald Reagan to the presidency, which office he held from 1981 to 1989, and with that of George Bush, from 1989 to 1993. Reagan's administration poured money into an accelerated arms buildup while cutting taxes for the wealthy and cutting welfare payments for the needy. The national infrastructure decayed. Urban areas experienced neglect. Family life suffered defeat from increased divorce, drugs, drinking, and domestic violence. Organized young gangs flourished in the inner cities. The militants of the sixties and early seventies who had advocated revolutionary change had given up. Some of them had joined the new "yuppie" breed, which *Newsweek* described, in 1984, as a pro-Reagan "class of young urban professionals [who] could not get enough of hedonism, mindless or otherwise," and who defined themselves by what they joined or owned—clubs, houses, gourmet food, and designer clothes.[1]

The "trickle-down" benefits that the Republicans predicted for the poorer classes never materialized. In 1982, unemployment grew to around 10½ percent. The next year Reagan plunged into the Star Wars development, again squandering money the country did not have. As the national deficit grew, the government's commitment to social services decreased. Two points of brightness were the Live Aid concerts, organized by Bob Geldof in 1985, and taking place in Philadelphia and London, which raised $70 million for starving Africans. A third benefit, in the same year, was the Farm Aid concert given by Willie Nelson and John Mellencamp to help farmers who were strapped for cash. These concerts were put on by concerned popular musicians and had no help from Washington. On 19 October 1987, Black Monday, the New York stock market plunged 508 points from its August record high of 2,722, further depressing the economy.

Nevertheless, voters were in an anti-Democrat mood and voted in another Republican regime with George Bush. The more affluent Americans had been encouraged to think in terms of self-interest and were intent on keeping what was theirs. Social problems ceased to be of interest. Too many Americans were allowing themselves to be defined by what they owned, not by their ideals. They won the epithet of the "Me" generation. Rude and intolerant talk-show hosts and callers could be heard sounding shrill, irate, coarse, selfish, and prejudiced. They dealt out ugly rumors about anyone of liberal persuasion. Scandal, sex, and sensationalism were their chief topics of conversation. Reactionaries like Rush Limbaugh and Patrick Buchanan held sway over millions.

A Reagan-induced crisis immediately hit the country. Reagan had deregulated the savings and loan industry in 1982. Unsecured loans had been made, fraudulent activity by bank officials had gone on, and vast sums had disappeared. Disaster struck. Where no money could be found for the poor, the federal government, starting in 1989, managed to find $166 billion dollars with which to bail out the banks over the next ten years. Bolstering Reagan's image, Russian communism ended in 1991, as did the Cold War. In addition, political diversion from domestic problems was provided by the Gulf War of 1990.

Yet, Americans had little room for gloating. The social fabric had torn apart and could not be mended. Divisiveness was the order of the day. The sad state of the United States was underlined in 1991 by the controversy over appointing Clarence Thomas to the Supreme Court. He was ideologically to the far right, with an undistinguished track record, and a reputation tainted by scandal. However, he was an African-American and his sponsors "played the black race card." African-Americans rallied to his cause, whether it was to their interests to do so or not. The Republicans won out on his appointment. The next year the Rodney King verdict came in over King's maltreatment by Los Angeles police officers and devastating riots by black Americans took place. In 1995, the race card would be played again at the O. J. Simpson trial and he would be acquitted of murder.

Clinton, a Democrat, assumed the presidency in 1993, but violence and upheaval continued. The terrorist attack on the World Trade Center, in New York, took place in February 1993 and the tragic deaths shook the country. Two months later, the standoff in Waco, federal agents versus a fanatic religious sect, ended violently with more than 80 Branch Davidians dead. The next year, the Republicans commenced the Whitewater investigation of Clinton, stressing the president's sexual activities in order to rouse the public. An impeachment trial, in 1999, would fail to convict. The archconservative Newt Gingrich persuaded 350 Republican candidates for Congress to sign the backward-looking "Contract with America," in 1994. The strategy won them control of both House and Senate. Nobody anticipated that, in 1995, an American, Timothy McVeigh, would murder 168 men, women, and children in the Oklahoma City bombing; nor that in the next year a sixteen-year-old, Luke Woodham, would kill his mother and then 9 schoolmates at Pearl High School, in Rankin County, Mississippi; nor that the next year Eric Harris and Dylan Klebold would murder 13 Columbine High School classmates and then themselves in Littleton, Colorado.

After Reagan had been swept into office, a surprising number of Americans chose to live on the surface. Blandness was delivered to the masses as never before. The Hollywood factory provided them with distractions in abundance—films like *Back to the Future* and *Romancing the Stone*; the publishing business followed suit with *Slaves of New York*, *Less Than Zero*, and *Bright Lights, Big City*, "three hip novels about people with nice clothes, cocaine, and hardly anything to say."[2] Bloodshed was turned to profitable account with brutal Rambo, Conan, Terminator, and mafia films. Language in novels and films sprouted countless obscenities. Men and women, strangers to each other, indulged in single, unrepeated sexual encounters, regarding such intercourse as physical activity of no moral importance. Movies went for computer-generated effects that overwhelmed plot lines and character development. At the same time, the television offerings of NBC, ABC, and CBS aimed at a lower and lower common denominator.

Thus, while fortunate Americans became like lotus-eaters living in suburban lotusland, a sizable number of the less fortunate lived ill housed, hungry, and in constant contact with violence.

COUNTRY AND WESTERN PERSISTS

Country continued to reflect traditional social values, even if with some exceptions. With the nation's turning more and more conservative, country and western gained a prominence it had never had before. A majority, though not all, of its devotees advocated the safeguarding of the established order, inveighed against the decline in "family values" and religion, and viewed attempts at reform critically and more often than not with suspicion.

Some singers resisted the trend and managed to introduce topics at a more contemporary personal level. Reba McEntire, for one, came to the fore a little after the Alabama band. She sang with impudence, emotion, and an Oklahoma twang about the problems of and pressures put upon women, as in "I Don't Want to Be a One Night Stand." The song is unusual in its blunt report on a current predicament faced by women, but in its way also an endorser of country standards. McEntire's early singing idol was Patsy Cline, after whom she modeled herself during her younger years. Her father was a rodeo steer roper, and she herself at first engaged in rodeo barrel racing, together with her singing engagements. (Barrel racing is a rodeo event usually for women, in which horseback riders race in a zigzag around three barrels.) She enrolled in college, planning to become a teacher, but a singing of the national anthem at the National Rodeo Finals, in 1974, resulted in a record contract, a decision to pursue a musical career, and a move to Nashville. In the eighties she achieved hit after hit, among them "Just a Little Love," "He Broke Your Memory Last Night," "Somebody Should Leave," "Whoever's in New England," and "One Promise Too Late." Although she sometimes indulged in complicated staging and calculated costume transformations, she was able to keep audiences at the edge of their seats with the sentiment she incorporated into her tones. She went from singing about crushing grief in "Forever Love" to an exhibit of bright cheekiness in "Take It Back." She also demonstrated how varied her talents were when she acted in films and appeared on television shows.

In 1991, eight members of her band died in a plane crash, and in the same year she issued *For My Broken Heart*, an unrelentingly bleak album and a popular success. Revealing an undaunted spirit, she struggled on and coped with difficulty after difficulty in her private and professional life. At the turn of the century, she released *Greatest Hits Volume III*, which contained the song "I'm a Survivor" (also the theme of her television series *Reba* on the WB). She sang: "A single mom who works two jobs, who loves her kids and never stops . . . with gentle hand and the heart of a fighter . . . I'm a survivor."

Shania Twain and the Dixie Chicks (Natalie Maines, lead vocalist; Martie Seidel, fiddler; Emily Erwin, on Dobro, banjo, or guitar) have continued the connection between women performers and country-rock into the 21st century. Starting in the nineties both Twain and the Chicks have offered music to appreciative audiences, via sold-out performances and through highly popular recordings, which reject country conservatism and overproduced Nashville slickness (which they called "pretty darn cookie-cutter and fake"). Twain's singing usually was given a delightfully likable swing that attracted the listener no matter what the song. Especially with the Chicks, the music may take on a hard-hitting "Outlaw" quality to lyrics from a feminist viewpoint, which they articulate with exuberance. They appeared for the first time on a Dallas street corner, in 1989, and were soon making their way upward with their blend of bluegrass, Western swing, and cowgirl music. Over 60 percent of the fans they attracted were under the age of 25. When interviewed, Martie Seidel said, "Just about everyone can relate to songs about needing the freedom to chase your dreams or dealing with a broken heart or falling in love or even just wanting to be a little wild and crazy every now and then."[3]

They got into political trouble after a March 10, 2003, concert in London, England, when Maines told the audience of her opposition to the war in Iraq: "Just so you know, we're ashamed the president of the United States is from Texas." (The group, like President George W. Bush, came from Texas.) The country-and-western conservative majority went into an uproar, denouncing the Chicks as traitors and even worse. Other Americans came to their defense. Interestingly, domestic and international record sales and youthful attendance at their concerts did not suffer.

Other performers, not as outspoken as Maines, have remained more in the mainstream and gone along to make their own well-received country-rock recordings, among them Bonnie Raitt, Melissa Etheridge, Jerry Garcia, Stephen Stills, Buffalo Springfield, the Outlaws, Joe Ely, and the New Riders of the Purple Sage. Country-rock has remained a profitable vein to mine.

As country-rock retained its popularity, some musicians, breathing the atmosphere of the times, began to look again at traditional country music, feeling that its fundamental nature had been compromised. Among them were a few performers who thought the country had met with ruination and that a conservative agenda should be reinstated. Others were in search of an authenticity not far removed from that sought by the folk crowd of the fifties and sixties. Conservative or liberal, they revived the country songs from before the 1960s and created new ones that respected time-honored styles. They reserved the right to sing accompanied only by acoustic guitar or by various combinations of acoustic and electric instruments—guitars, Dobro, banjo, harmonica, accordion, strings, keyboards, and percussion. A few also reserved the right to make occasional excursions into pop and rock. George Strait, Ricky Skaggs, the Judds, Randy Travis, Ricky Van Shelton, Alan Jackson, Brad Paisley, and Lee Ann Womack were some who sought to bring traditional country back to its roots and tried to show young men and women what had made the music meaningful. Folk song, bluegrass instrumental colorings, and sometimes Cajun music were included in performances. The performers quickly were given the title of New Traditionalists (or Neo-Traditionalists).

George Strait, born in Texas in 1952, came before the public in the '80s as a performer of plain and unambiguous country music plus the sort of honky-tonk and Western swing that would fit in with America's attempt to rediscover customary values. He conveyed the impression of a genuine, not a puffed-up, country singer. Strait said in a 1981 *Billboard* magazine interview that he "wanted to get to the point where people hear [his] name and immediately think of real country music." After Strait and his Ace in the Hole Band won over numerous Texas fans in the seventies, they went national with the recording of the popular single "Unwound." Strait remained at the top of the country chart during the eighties with singles like "Fool Hearted Memory" (1982), "A Fire I Can't Put Out" (1983), "Does Fort Worth Ever Cross Your Mind" (1984), and "The Chair" (1985). Durable and dependable, George Strait forged on calmly and with no concern over the newest developments in mainstream country music. The country swing of "Ace in the Hole," the melodiously tender parental affection of "Love without End, Amen," and the uproarious "All My Ex's Live in Texas," three of the tracks contained in the 2002 album *The Best of George Strait*, show him performing his country music without adulteration, without a power-driven instrumental ensemble, and without technical overproduction. What comes through is a fine singer, a skilled handful of instrumentalists, an attractive offering of swinging country and western music, and lyrics that mirror the values of rural people.

The Oklahoman Garth Brooks was a country superstar of the nineties and to some extent a New Traditionalist. At first he was one of the "cowboys" busily merging rock with honky-tonk and Western swing. He became nationally known in 1989, with his *Garth Brooks* album, on which he sang to the accompaniment of steel, acoustic, and electric guitars, strings, keyboard, and drums. For at least half of the numbers, Brooks discontinued his purely cowboy stance, appeared as a New Traditionalist, and did quite well projecting a honky-tonk country ambiance in a song like "Not Counting You." In pieces like "The Dance" and "If Tomorrow Never Comes" he added more contemporary flavorings. In Brooks's next album, the 1991 *No Fences*, he still sounded at times like a New Traditionalist, as in "Friends in Low Places," but he also used an electric piano and added brief melodic enticements for young listeners. In other songs, his music recalls folk-rock.

Brooks came along at a time when the country movement seemed to be faltering and helped propel it forward with renewed energy. Unquestionably, he succeeded in becoming the most popular country musician known up to the nineties and built up an international body of admirers.

By 1995 and *Fresh Horses*, he had abandoned the new traditionalism. For a brief period, around 1999, he went further and assumed an out-and-out rock alias, "Chris Gaines," in his album *In the Life of Chris Gaines*. However, this artificial stance ceased when critics criticized vigorously the Gaines character and the album. He went into temporary retirement until late 2001, when he recorded *Scarecrow*, to the accompaniment of strings, bass, Dobro, banjo, acoustic and electric guitars, harmonica, accordion. Folk-rock is present in numbers like "Don't Cross the River." Nevertheless, one could see elements of mainstream modern country hinted at. Indeed, he emerges with a strong blend of country by way of the Eagles in the alcoholically exuberant "Beer Run" and the melodramatic "The Storm." "Big Money" revels in Western swing as he interprets the song in a jolly unbuttoned manner. The album ends with the upbeat "When You Come Back to Me Again," which reports on the coming together again of separated but faithful lovers.

More faithfully a New Traditionalist, Alan Jackson has made a name for himself as one of the finest singers of traditional country and honky-tonk to emerge in the nineties, though he does use electronic instruments—as in *Alan Jackson* (1996), *High Mileage* (1998), and *When Somebody Loves You* (2000). He sturdily holds forth in praise of noticeably Southern ways of life and the merits of simple folk, as in "Meat and Potato Man." Southern swagger invests the honky-tonk blustering of "It's Alright to Be a Redneck." "When Somebody Loves You" is a warm, lightly tripping promise of loving commitment.

Coming on the music scene at the turn of the century are other New Traditionalists, like Brad Paisley, a follower of George Strait, in his debut album *Who Needs Pictures* (1999), and like Lee Ann Womack, first influenced by Conway Twitty, in her album *I Hope to Dance* (2000). They sing warmly, sincerely, and convincingly whether it is an extant song or a new one they have had a hand in creating. Country music has commenced a new century and thrives in its several manifestations—traditional, new traditional, Nashville, country-pop, cowboy-inflected country-pop, and country-rock.

Although the country audience is now national, care must still be taken to keep the country in country music. Singers like Shania Twain and Lee Ann Rimes are now trying to market to pop radio with music more in a popular than a country vein. On supposedly country radio stations, "roots" or traditional country music is barely aired. Talented "roots" singers like Rhonda Vincent and Jim Lauderdale are ignored, save for the handful of "roots" radio stations. Even Dolly Parton's songs are scarcely heard. Billy Block, radio producer, says, "I think a lot of the music that's being played on the radio sounds more like '70s pop than it does country music. There's room for that, but if you're going to call it country music, for God's sake, let's hear some country." As luck would have it, one of the biggest-selling albums just after the turn of the century was the sound track of the film *O Brother Where Art Thou?* Radio had no share in boosting it into popularity. Instead, Americans on their own came to love the wholesome, unaffected traditional songs. Even when the album sold in the millions, country radio stations ignored it. From the evidence of the film and the best-selling CD accompanying it, the genuine country genre still benefits from extensive and diverse support from fans to whom country radio pays scant attention.[4]

CHANGES IN THE MUSICAL LANDSCAPE

The popular-music world would reflect the segmented American public. One segment, Christian rock, attempted to satisfy those looking for release through religious entertainment. A second segment, ostentatious arena rock, appeased the politically uncommitted and unthinking Americans who desired "bread-and-circus" entertainments. At the same time, hardcore, grunge, and indie-rock cultivated musical primitivism and tried to generate rage against what their adherents described as their phony and imprisoning society. Hip-hop and rap gave voice and more to disaffected inner-city black youths. Black and white young people found attraction in one or another style. They came to concerts and normally bought the records primarily for the music's entertainment value, not necessarily because of any message.

Women increasingly appeared as singers, instrumentalists, and songwriters. They would no longer willingly take second place to men. In the summer of 1997, the concerts given by Lilith Fair would make rock 'n' roll history when presented during the first all-female music tour. Sold-out performances turned Lilith Fair into an annual touring event. Sarah McLachlan, the founder of Lilith Fair, has said that Lilith Fair is not about attacking men, who are welcome at the concerts, but it is a celebration of women. She felt that women needed to establish their place solidly beside men in the music world, and women artists wanted a chance to prove that they, too, could have sold-out concerts without the help of male-dominated bands included in the acts. The stellar casts at Lilith Fair have included Emmylou Harris, Bonnie Raitt, Sheryl Crow, Whitney Houston, Sinead O'Connor, Meredith Brooks, Celine Dion, the Indigo Girls, Jewel, Shawn Colvin, and Erykah Badu. Their offerings have gone from folk and country to hardcore and rap.

There was also an increase of rock groups not from the United States, Canada, and England. Two of the most popular were U2 of Ireland and ABBA of Sweden. Over the last two decades, multiculturalism and cultural fragmentation have been forces in the popular world. Music native to nations from around the world is regularly performed in American concert halls, theaters, and clubs. For example, Misia, the Portuguese popular singer of fado, has met with American approval. Miho Hatori, born in Brazil but with Japanese antecedents, has made a name for herself singing in Portuguese, Japanese, and English. Salif Keita of Mali, the Gipsy Kings of the French gypsies, the Buena Vista Social Club of Cuba, Fateh Ali Khan of Pakistan, Ayumi Hamasaki of Japan, and Suman Chatterjee of India all have their American followers. Timothy Taylor, in his book *Global Pop*, gives a very long list of popular world-music groups that have been high on the *Billboard* charts.[5] Latin-American pop has always been big in the United States. One of the most popular Latin-pop singers, Gloria Estefan, was born in Havana, Cuba, and entered the American pop mainstream with the album *Eyes of Innocence*, in 1984. Her dance songs, like "Dr. Beat," "Conga," "1-2-3," and "Rhythm Is Gonna Get You," have grown into American favorites. Touring with her group, the Miami Sound Machine, she slipped as easily into English as into Spanish-language numbers. Another Latin star, Shakira, has held Latin and more than a few American young people in the palm of her hand. She is Colombian but half Lebanese by birth and has performed songs in a variety of styles—mainstream rock, tango, disco, Colombian, Mexican, Brazilian, and Middle Eastern.

With the purpose of stimulating a sensation of personal tranquility, New Age music came forward as an adjunct to reflection and to the idea that the world had to be sensed in its entirety rather than its parts. Soothing and psychologically sheltering musical compositions were meant to aid listeners in rising above earthly matters and in promoting mental health. New Age, therefore, could be understood as more a state of mind than a musical genre. The musical compositions it generated were insubstantial on the whole and were supposed to be tools for realizing a version of nirvana. The genre grew popular in the eighties as a music to accompany meditative groups who were deep into unconventional spiritual explorations, Jungian psychology, paranormal experiences, and environmental concerns. The sound was unintrusive and could utilize either acoustic or electronic instruments, or both. The piece might be improvised, consist of ambient sounds, turn impressionistic à la Debussy, minimalist à la Glass, atmospheric à la Sakamoto, or easy-listening à la Kitoro and Yanni. Little of it was song that was actually to be sung. The important thing was to establish an atmosphere of thoughtful calmness or to stimulate profound contemplative states.

California's Windham Hill label, started by Will Ackerman and his wife, Anne Robinson, became known for its sumptuously recorded New Age sounds that earned its products the name "Muzak for yuppies." This label put out George Winston's *Autumn*, in 1980, which went on to sell around a million copies. As might be expected, the music presented a serene landscape, clear and unruffled. In 1987, New Age reached greater prominence when the Swiss harpist Andreas Vollenweider won the first Grammy Award[6] for a New Age composition.

He showed no great musical endowment, but New Agers approved his sounds. As long as significant numbers of people are willing to purchase New Age albums, the music industry will continue to put them out. The huge Sony Corporation happily issued several Vollenweider albums because they helped strengthen its bottom line. When they cease to do so, Vollenweider will be dropped. To find new potential moneymakers, Sony, like all large record labels, watched the performers on small independent labels, who at best controlled 5 to 10 percent of the market. As Sanjek writes, "The A&R staffs of the major labels appeared to treat the 'indies' as farm teams, waiting to see which of their artists found a constituency and then offering them lucrative contracts, to which a number succumbed."[7] The same holds true for producers and songwriters. The producer/writer/performer Kenneth "Babyface" Edmonds was sought after because he has generated hits for Whitney Houston, Paula Abdul, Bobby Brown, and Toni Braxton. The songwriter Diane Warren was in demand because her compositions, sung on albums and in films, usually produced high profits. She was 45 in the year 2002 and already had over 80 "Top 10" hits recognized in *Billboard* that she had written in a variety of styles. Her clients included Mary Bilge, Reba McIntire, Celine Dion, Toni Braxton, Cher, 'NSync, and Aerosmith.

Because of the "authenticity" factor and the desire to boost salability, many performers put their names to songs as cowriters, when in reality much of the music was owing to professional songwriters. The practice is an old one. Stephen Foster and George Gershwin in the early stage of their careers allowed well-liked performers to put their names down as cowriters of songs. In recent times, record labels have connived at the practice because it enhances their profit line. When performers were evoking strong enthusiasm and releasing songs that they had ostensibly written, they made the most of the potential to generate immense sales. If these sales materialized, a performer could command an astronomical figure when signing a contract with a record label.

Celebrated performers received dazzling payments from record companies, while most second-tier performers got along as best they could. Thirty million dollars induced the extremely successful Janet Jackson to leave A&M for Virgin Records in 1991. In the same year, Aerosmith, with a run of winning albums, signed with Columbia for around $30 million. The Rolling Stones, reliable sellers for record companies, received $40 million for recording three albums for Virgin. Madonna, Michael Jackson, and Prince could exact guarantees on future recordings worth more than $60 million each.[8] On the other hand, a slump on the sales chart immediately caused companies to discard a performer. Mariah Carey, who had earned millions for herself and Columbia Records, went over to Virgin Records. Her new album *Glitter* failed to please her public. Without hesitation, Virgin Records, a subsidiary of EMI, ended their affiliation by buying out her contract for $28 million in January 2002. The contract would have paid Carey a reported $100 million.

However qualitatively excellent the song or singer, the test question was always, "Will it sell?" regardless of the purported excellence of the music or the voice. As rock music aged, so did the performers. From the eighties on, aging bands found it less and less easy to connect with the new crop of young. For most of them, their hope for survival depended on retaining their original fans, who were also growing older, plus winning over what existing youngsters they could. James Taylor and the Rolling Stones had this talent. On the other hand, however popular most groups might have been, their usual lifespan amounted only to about a dozen years. After that their music was deemed to lack freshness. They lost the ability to thrill the music public. Record companies knew this. They also knew that with the eighties, different forms of rock music were so abundant that anyone not liking one type had many alternatives. The same thing applied to bands and their vocalists. Enthusiasts were inclined to be devoted to one form and shun anything different. Accordingly, different record labels saw to it that their albums offered an assortment of rock styles together with examples of classical pop, country music, traditional rhythm and blues, disco, and reggae.[9] Normally, the less well a style sold, the smaller the companies that purveyed it.

A case in point is Christian pop, which comes in various country and rock mixes. It raised its head in the eighties and grew in popularity in the nineties with performing groups like Audio Adrenaline, MxPx, the Danielson Family, Whiteheart, and Jars of Clay. Despite the opposition of conservative Christians, blues and country-rock versions of Christian pop grew. Small, independent labels issued the music, but the big companies watched to see if the movement would continue to gather strength. Gary Chapman, starting in the eighties, recorded several country-pop Christian albums that gradually caught on with the public. It was to be expected that in 2002, *Circles and Seasons* would come out on the Word label, which had become a subsidiary of Warner Brothers in 2001.

Petra, a Christian country-rock group, put out its first album in 1974 and achieved a popular breakthrough in 1979 with *Washes Whiter Than*, which included the favorite "Why Should the Father Bother?" Noting the success of some heavy-metal bands, Petra went more heavily into the style in 1988. By the nineties, Sony had decided they were worth taking a chance on and gave them exposure with music like the 1992 *Petra Praise: The Rock Cries Out* and the 2000 *Double Take*. Creed, starting as an unknown Florida grunge band, was soon commanding young listeners' attention with their aggressive beat, and went on to sell millions of recorded copies of *My Own Prison* (1997), *Human Clay* (1999), and *Weathered* (2001) for New York's Wind-Up Entertainment. Their style borrowed from Led Zeppelin and Metallica; their vocalist Scott Stapp sang unabashedly about moving up higher and reaching for God, with music provided by guitarist Mark Tremonti. Also there was the vehement rap-metal California band P.O.D. (Payable on Death). Their spiritual devotion was fierce, their sound was overpowering. Thundering instrumentalists, screaming singers, and frenzied fans contributed to the uproar. What was most important to the Atlantic label was that P.O.D. has an excellent sales record. They sang of thinking they could fly and for the first time feeling so alive that they had to say yes to God.[10] Not surprisingly, a P.O.D. singer rapt with excitement and singing the words "I think I can fly" might fly off the stage into the mosh pit. Many concert attendees were present for the excitement as much as, if not more than, for the non-denominational religious message.

An interesting new development was Muslim rap, with performers like Native Deen, formed in 2000 and urging an end to violence, promiscuity, alcohol, and drugs, and a turning to Allah. Because Muslims believe that Mohammedan teachings prohibit the playing of most musical instruments, Native Deen used only traditional drums in its live performances. A typical number, "Hellfire," started with synthesized bangs, which would, under different circumstances, have gone well with any diatribe against "whitey" or in favor of some form of violence. The message that followed was unexpected. The student listener is advised to steal quietly into a bathroom or empty classroom in school "or even at home," whenever it was time to pray. Great effort was necessary to avoid conflict. Indeed, to be a Muslim, "the stress is double."[11]

Significantly, white and black youngsters who were not Muslims attended Native Deen's concerts. One can be sure that the big labels will watch to see how the public takes to Deen's recent offering, *For the Cause of Allah*. Also watching will be MTV, the dominant cable-television music network, which at the turn of the century had already begun to show videos of Christian bands.

MTV began its existence on 1 August 1981, and in the beginning had to make an effort to find enough rock-music videos and advertisers to sustain it. At first, the videos were straight presentations of performers in concert. Gradually they changed to become vivid telling of musical stories to sell albums and performers. Masters of such musical narrations have been singers like Michael Jackson and Madonna, who were expert at drawing viewers visually into their songs. By the end of the century, MTV claimed it had grown to become the world's largest TV network, reaching more than 75 million homes in the United States, and 342 million homes worldwide. The 12-to-32 age group provided its most devoted viewers. Owing to MTV, the production of music videos has grown to the extent that for many adolescents they are musts for a band's and a recording's acceptance.

To them, how the performer looks and sells the song on cable television has become as important as how the music sounds. Lip synchronization, which was debated when the Monkees and Milli Vanilli used it, was more frequently practiced at century's end and, what is more, the fans mostly did not care any longer. Madonna, Janet Jackson, the Backstreet Boys, and Britney Spears were among those who have pretended to sing during concerts and video productions.[12]

MTV was the first of several cable music networks. In December 1984, MTV helped organize VH1, which was intended to address the over-25 age group. Later there came BET (Black Entertainment Television), and the Nashville Network aimed at country-music viewers. Soon after the turn of the century, problems arose. MTV increased its nonmusical programming and found that its viewership dropped. VH1 did not always seem certain of its identity. In the new century, rock-music lovers were coming in a broad range of ages. There were still the teenagers, of course. However, the teenagers of the fifties were now into their sixties and did not usually share the same tastes as those of current adolescents. In July 2002, Jason Gay reported: "VH1's relatively wide audience has occasionally posed conflicts for executives, who fretted that rockumentaries about Fleetwood Mac turned off viewers in their twenties, while programs about rap and teen pop might alienate the older *Behind the Music* loyalists."[13] It may portend the introduction of several cable music networks to satisfy several different age groups.

A most significant change in the music world took place with the advent of the Internet. It had been developed in the sixties and early seventies. The term "Internet" was first used in 1974 in a paper on Transmission Control Protocol, by Vint Cerf and Bob Kahn. Its impact on music really began in 1999, when Shawn Fanning developed Napster and offered a means for exchanging music files over the Internet. Music lovers were delighted because, for one, they could choose from a wide spectrum of songs and download what they liked, without the limited offerings and restrictions imposed by large commercial interests. Battles over copyright infringement ensued and about two years later Napster ceased offering a free exchange of musical numbers. However, other similar Internet websites sprang up—Open Nap, Napigator, Gnutella, and Freenet, to name four. The battles have continued into the 21st century; the big music business has tried to move aggressively to put the genie back into the bottle.

CELEBRITIES IN THE ADOLESCENT ARENA

Arena rock is meant here to include music personalities inflated to appear bigger than life who presented elaborate stage shows before huge crowds of adoring teenagers. In many instances, arena rock presented a glittery exterior concealing an empty interior. Outsized showy devices in the music and theatrical action were meant to catch attention, galvanize the immature, and cause the singer to be accepted. As one young wag commented to me, "When you see three trailer trucks rolling up to the back entrance to drop off the paraphernalia—and find it takes two days to set the stuff up and one day to milk the kiddies—then it's arena rock."

Arena rock held major sway, beginning in the late seventies, with New Wave among its antecedents. Only after the end of the century did it somewhat lose its hold, probably temporarily, on the young public. Behind the rise of arena rock was the music industry's desire to sell to an enormous but clearly defined market that would generate the most profits. It opted for boys and girls in their teens and preteens, seeing them as renewable customers with huge funds at their disposal. What a performer achieved hinged on how readily salable he or she was, and much of the selling took place by means of dazzling shows or videos shown on a music television channel. A person with marginal talent was potentially marketable if possessed of a good-looking face and body, capable of making a communicable fashion statement, and possessing a contagious stage presence. Some, like the nimble-footed Michael Jackson and the manipulative Madonna, did have a considerable degree of substance behind them and excelled as performance artists. Others were less talented. 'NSync was a group of good-looking boys who utilized their appeal to teenyboppers for profit and occasionally came out with a substantively interesting number. New Kids on the Block danced cleverly and clutched their crotches in ways to send girls shrieking. Britney Spears set the fashion for adolescents with her exposed belly button, snug tube-top, hip-hugging pants, and "virginal" sexuality. A songwriting committee knew in depth what sort of songs to write in order to suit their often meager talents, and how singer and songs might sell, and to what audience.

The truly talented Michael Jackson left his family group, the Jackson 5, and tried to make his independent way in the music world during the late seventies. His imaginative exploitation of video film, showing him singing and dancing within a highly inventive story format, made him a superstar in the eighties. In concert, he put on a remarkable show abounding in pageantry, dancing, and action. A shrewd showman, he wooed the public with sensuous ballads, vivacious disco morsels, and hard-rocking, techno-pop rhythms involving electronic synthesizers. He found an extraordinarily able producer/arranger in Quincy Jones, who supervised the making of two very well-received albums, the good-timing, funky-pop album *Off the Wall*, in 1979, and the glossy *Thriller*, in 1982, which became the biggest-selling album in history when more than 45 million copies were snapped up. Jackson had made video presentations of songs on the album, featuring his graceful break dancing and intriguing baby voice within a multifaceted spectacle. *Thriller* was a triumph that the pop superstar never achieved again, though he tried repeatedly to achieve as high a success again. In the 1982 album, a Jackson approach to songwriting and performance was evident that aimed to please pop lovers and the disco crowd with admirable rhythmic songs like the catchy "Billy Jean," a youth's denial of begetting an illegitimate child, and the rocking "Beat It" (with Eddie Van Halen's guitar driving the rhythm), which promoted nonviolence. The first song was built on an uncomplicated but individual drum-machine design, a constantly recurring melodic fragment in the bass, and a straightforward chord sequence. The second also made use of a drum-machine rhythm and a recurring melodic fragment heard in the bass and guitar.

His main audiences were the preteens and teenagers who delighted in the musical confections that he and Jones put together. They also went for his glittery stage conduct, polished dancing, and colorful theatricalness. Without question, the video-musical *Thriller* had a major impact on the music world. For one, it broke through the color barrier of MTV. The film pioneered new ways of scenic depiction, which would influence Hollywood and television drama. It also encouraged the formation of juvenile bands that wooed their cohorts with elaborate staged spectacles illustrative of the songs performed, often taking dramatic form and usually supported with eye-catching props—and videos of the same. Soon after the album's release, Jackson was asked if he was now happy. His reply was surprising: "I do not think I am ever totally happy. . . . What really makes me happy, what I love is performing and creating. I really do not care about all the material trappings. I love to put my soul into something and have people accept it. That's a wonderful feeling."[14]

In 1985, troubled by the hunger in Africa, he with the help of Lionel Ritchie wrote "We Are the World," which became the central number in the video and album that he and Quincy Jones made featuring the many stars gathered at the American Music Awards ceremony in Los Angeles. The proceeds from the sales went to African relief.

By the nineties, Quincy Jones no longer was participating in Jackson's professional life. This was a decade when public attention turned from Jackson's music to gossip about his bodily appearance and actions—the surgical treatments to modify his Negroid looks, his unisex characteristics, his sunglasses and white sequined glove, his fondness for animals and children, his increasingly weird behavior, accusations of homosexual relationships with boys, and his marriage to and divorce from Elvis Presley's daughter Lisa Marie. No longer did fans rush to buy up his albums as they had. After the turn of the century, he had a run-down, tired look, perhaps the result of his frustrations at getting back to a top spot on the pop chart.

Michael's sister Janet also emerged from the Jackson-family pack and realized several big hits beginning in 1986 with the album *Control*. Like her brother, she skillfully planned and directed music videos and arena displays, singing danceable songs that dealt with questions of love, sex, and female power. Her voice was not the equal of her brother's, but she polished her dance skills and enhanced her performances with throbbing rhythms, contagious tunes, and smart displays. She experienced a run of pop and rhythm-and-blues successes—"Miss You Much," "Escapade," "Love Will Never Do (Without You)," "Again," "Together Again," and "All for You" being six of her top singles.

A third black musician, who was extremely popular for a while, was Prince Rogers Nelson—gaudily costumed, widely and oftentimes unfavorably discussed, and gifted. Like Jackson, he developed his own contagious version of pop, rock, and funk and made astute use of video films to promote himself and his music. Far more than in Jackson's songs, Prince's songs purveyed eroticism even when seemingly clean.

He started as a musical prodigy in Minneapolis, teaching himself to play several instruments, forming his own band while attending junior high school, and acquiring knowledge of the use of electronics. Later he formed his own band, the Revolution. Two songs from 1979, "I Wanna Be Your Lover" and "Why You Wanna Treat Me So Bad?" were early rhythm-and-blues successes. However, it was not until 1982, and the double album *1999,* that he actually began to attract a large following, with pieces like "1999," "Little Red Corvette," and "Delirious." Then, in 1984, he reached a peak of popularity with *Purple Rain,* an ostensibly autobiographical film set in a Minneapolis club and furnished with top-quality material—"When Doves Cry," "Let's Go Crazy," "Purple Rain," and "I Would Die 4 U."

Both film and music won awards—an Oscar for the score, and Grammys for the songs.

One song on the album, the scorching "Darlin Nikki," upset Al Gore's wife, Tipper, because of its casual references to masturbation and blatant sex. Nikki is described as a nymphomaniac who, when first sighted, is engaged in masturbation with a magazine. When she rotated her hips suggestively at him, he had to accept her invitation.[15] The lyric caused Tipper Gore to start the Parents Music Resource Center and incited a congressional investigation of repulsive rock lyrics. No bona fide cleanup of lyrics resulted.

A second important album-cum-video came out in 1987, *Sign 'O' the Times*. This rambling, insanely diverse and continuously imaginative double set demonstrated that *Purple Rain* was not necessarily Prince's highest creative achievement. The songs were tributes to his unquiet creative gifts. The title song alluded bleakly to crack, AIDS, and nuclear bombs. In the next piece, Prince assumed a cheery, dancing pose, as he rollicked about in "Play in the Sunshine" and wiped out the previous gloom. A strong sex-laden tone sounded in "Slow Love" and "Hot Thing." Contrasting with these songs, "Forever in My Life" and "Adore" were affecting ballads for lovers that extolled faithfulness and commitment.

In 1989, he achieved a further success with the *Batman* sound track. However, four years later, Prince officially changed his name to an unpronounceable glyph combining male and female attributes, and opened himself to ridicule. His action struck the music public as overly bizarre and provoked laughter. He received the sobriquet "the Artist Formerly Known as Prince," of which he could never rid himself. Prince did have a triumph in 1991 with "Cream," and in 1994 with "The Most Beautiful Girl in the World." However, he could not attain again to the heights he had reached with the songs of *Purple Rain*, despite his continuing to command a cult following.

Like the phoenix, the mythical bird that burned itself on a funeral pyre only to ascend from its ashes in youthful freshness, the Italian-American pop singer and dancer Madonna Louise Veronica Ciccone has had the extraordinary ability to burn away old selves and assume new identities that have kept her in the popular-music limelight over the years. Born in Michigan in 1958 and moving to New York in 1977, she hoped to become a ballet dancer. Instead, she found work with pop-disco outfits before cutting her first album, *Madonna*, in 1983.

She has had a string of hits since then and has become an international celebrity. When she started her singing career, she tried to make the most of her twangy but engaging girl-like warble, so suited to dance songs, whether of the disco or techno-rock (more deeply into using synthesizers) variety. She said of her modest musical talents, "I've always been into rhythmic music, party music. . . . Soul was my main influence, and I wanted my sound to be the kind of music I'd always liked. I wanted to approach it from a very simple point of view because I wasn't an incredible musician. I wanted to be direct. I still love to dance, and all I wanted to do was to make a record that I would want to dance to, and would want to listen to on the radio."[16]

Madonna's ability to endure and thrive owed plenty to her having a feel for, and oftentimes generating, trends. Her exceptional business shrewdness, her knack for shocking people, and her forward-looking videos have made her the most noticed female singer of the eighties and nineties. She has also had starring roles in Hollywood movies, including *Desperately Seeking Susan* (1985), *Dick Tracy* (1990), and *Evita* (1996). With Mark Kamins, a New York disc jockey, as producer, she recorded "Everybody" (1982), which brought her into public notice. Madonna entered the major pop field with "Holiday," written and produced by John "Jellybean" Benitez. It was one of the top hits in America and Europe, in 1984. At the same time, her rowdy, earthy, and sexy nature was clearly recognizable, especially with the 1984 album *Like a Virgin*, featuring the attractive title song by Tom Kelly and Billy Steinberg. She parlayed the song into a number one hit, claiming she felt like a virgin, shiny and new, when touched and embraced by her lover.[17] She described herself in a Peter Brown and Robert Rans song, "Material Girl." It's okay for boys to kiss and hug her, but if she doesn't get "proper credit," she just drops them. However much they plead with her, they will fail, because "Mister Right" for her is the one who comes up with "cold hard cash." After all, the world we live in is completely materialistic and so must she be.[18] The video for "Material Girl" initiated one of her most typical impersonations, her masquerade as the "blonde bombshell" Marilyn Monroe.

With this album, she became celebrated musically as a reliable source for attention-commanding technodance numbers that used synthesizers to produce thumping basses, computerized riffs, and strongly emphasized dance beats. This identity helped keep her in the spotlight year after year.

In addition, the album contained "Love Don't Live Here Anymore," by Miles Gregory. It suggested that Madonna had more than one arrow in her quiver. Putting hurt in her voice, she sang of being abandoned, of being emptied of love.[19]

A year after *Like a Virgin* was offered to the public, Madonna had developed into a globally acknowledged luminary, familiar even to the multitudes reading newspapers who took less notice of her music than of her antics. Her fans loved her outrageousness and the genuinely interesting music she was responsible for. She was an example particularly to adolescent girls, the so-called Madonna wannabes, who fought parental control and claimed indifference to what others thought of them.

Madonna knew it was good for business when she caused an uproar, in 1989, over the music video of "Like a Prayer," which merged religion with eroticism. The Catholic Church swiftly denounced the video, and Pepsi-Cola called off an advertising sponsorship of Madonna. Nevertheless, the fevered media exposure promoted the album of the same title so that it turned into a runaway success worldwide. She went on to exploit off-color verbiage in *Exotica* (1992), with words like those of "Waiting," a song she and André Betts wrote: Desert me and you will break my heart, she admits. However, when again "you want pussy," she won't be available. Instead you'll just have to gaze into a mirror.[20]

In addition, remixes became a Madonna specialty—selling her favorite songs over and over again in re-recorded albums, especially those made more amenable for dancing, as with the *You Can Dance* (1987) that John "Jellybean" Benitez and Shep Pettibone pulled together for her.[21]

She continued to appeal to a vast public over the next dozen years, with hits like "Vogue," coauthored by Madonna and Shep Pettibone, which set off a brief dance fad, "Justify My Love" (cowritten with Lenny Kravitz), which provoked a storm for its unambiguous portrayal of different kinds of sexual practices; also there were "Rescue Me," created by Madonna and Shep Pettibone, "Take a Bow," which came from her and Kenneth Edmonds, and "Music," the creation of Madonna and Mirwais Ahmadzai.

The female performer who sold the most records in the 1990s was Mariah Carey. She achieved the heights of stardom owing to her astonishing five-octave vocal range and a flexibility that allowed her to go from pop ballad to rhythm and blues, dance-rock, and hip-hop. She also had a hand in composing many of the songs she sang.

Born in 1970, Carey was brought up and coached by her mother, an Irish-American opera singer, who had divorced her father, a black Venezuelan engineer. In New York at the end of the eighties, Mariah Carey had her start as backup vocalist for the dancer-singer Brenda Starr. Starr admired Carey's voice and gave Tommy Mottola of Columbia Records a demo tape of Carey's singing. He listened, was flabbergasted by the talent she showed, and immediately signed her for her first album. He also married her. Suddenly zooming into the limelight in 1990, Mariah Carey caused a sensation with this first album, *Mariah Carey*, which contained four top singles, "Vision of Love," "I Don't Wanna Cry," "Someday," and "Love Takes Time." It won her Grammy Awards for best new artist and best female vocalist. She quickly gained a reputation for having a beautiful voice that was comfortable in all parts of its uncommonly wide range. She projected a wholesome image and favored evocative ballads that touched her fans deeply. *Emotions*, in 1993, continued her winning streak, with three top singles, "Emotions," "Can't Let Go," and "Make It Happen." By the end of the century, she had become the most successful female vocalist of all time, selling more than 140 million albums and singles worldwide, and recording more number-one hits that stayed for more weeks at the top of the *Billboard* chart than the songs of any other singer in history. Gospel and rhythm and blues occupied the background; pop dance songs the foreground of her music. (Later, hip-hop components would enter her recordings.) Other top albums were *Music Box* (1993) and *Daydream* (1995). The single "One Sweet Day," which she coauthored and then sang with Boyz II Men, in *Daydream*, took possession of the top position on the charts for an unprecedented 16 weeks. The song pleased as no other recent pop song had, and awakened the tender emotions of love, nostalgia, and regret. A person dear to her has died and it is now too late to embrace and tell all that she wanted to say to her friend. Nevertheless, like other friends who have died, "you're shining down on me from heaven." She knows that in the end they will meet again "one sweet day."[22]

Until the end of the century, her uppermost position was unassailable. Her creation of acclaimed albums, which she cowrote and coproduced, continued to 1999, with *Rainbow*. Here, the range of styles passed through pop, gospel, soul, and hip-hop. One of its songs, "Heartbreaker," was her fourteenth number-one single.

She divorced Mottola in 1997. Regrettably, she had also begun to cultivate a sexy image and introduce more and more hip-hop and funk into her offerings. Soon she was losing the adult segment of her audience. She came out with the film and sound track album *Glitter*, in 2001, and failed ignominiously. The songs in the album tried to exploit the rhythmic style of disco-funk but came off as tiresome. She tried again in late 2002 with *Charmbracelet*. With the media hype accompanying this song collection, one would have thought that a major comeback was being staged. However, for the most part the songs lack variety and real vitality. This album was not likely to return her to her former high rank.

Close behind her were the bubblegum groups—those extremely popular human concoctions contrived by the music industry to capture the fancy of the immature. Foremost among these were the flashy and good-looking boy bands 'NSync and Backstreet Boys and the nubile girl acts of Christina Aguilera and Britney Spears. Prefabricated and spoon-fed to teenagers, they achieved instant fame even as they substituted spectacle for music. They were primarily entertainers, and excellent as such, who performed in arenas and stadiums that would seat thousands. They presented gaudy acts complete with eye-grabbing attire, glittering scenery, awesome props, light shows, ramps extending everywhere, cables ready to lift and deposit performers where desired, and huge video screens to promote them still further. If pompous dance rhythms or overly sentimental ditties were the vogue, that was what they delivered. If the latest taste was for rhythm-and-blues or choppy beats, they switched their style. They filched ideas from Michael and Janet Jackson, Prince, Madonna, and Carey. What they produced was usually secondhand, factory-assembled, and packaged by technicians in the hidden recesses of corporate offices. They might change but they found it difficult to grow as artists. They combined mostly disco-club pop with suggestive choreography to foster a state of extreme excitement in their preteen audience wherever they played.

When Britney Spears, a former Mouseketeer, appeared at Boston's Fleet Center, in December 2001, as elsewhere, she was given the finest stage production that money could buy and backed by a band that played "so loudly (and so rotely) that Spears [was] routinely drowned out." The result was: "a) much ado about nothing; b) a night of agony; c) a sad triumph of marketing over music; d) a ripoff since many tickets cost $75." Fans numbering 17,000 attended to witness her go through a vigorous workout executed to nonstop pop-disco music.[23] She performed disposable songs suited to the short attention spans of preteens and to her own vocal limitations.

Heading the list of bubblegum performers, Spears helped initiate a major rise to popularity in music for juveniles during the late '90s. She became a genuine marvel in the popular-music world. Newspapers, magazines, and television constantly put her before the public and were awed by the millions of records she sold. Her sex appeal was exploited from the beginning, with her initial video for ". . . Baby One More Time," which was filmed when she was 17 years of age. Spears's managers, especially Max Martin, deliberately cultivated a dual image both in her appearances and songs: the innocent girl and the sexually inviting woman who proved so fascinating to her followers. The dichotomy provoked continuous public discussion of her impact on impressionable adolescent girls. Martin, in particular, was also responsible for her effective dance songs and sentimental pop ballads.

It is impossible to predict how long she, like others of her kind, can continue to command a market. It could be six years or ten years. What is certain is that after she loses her attractiveness, there will be others who will take her place as purveyors to the bubblegum crowd.

NEW OPTIONS: GRUNGE, ALTERNATIVE, AND INDIE

Hardcore had already been around for some time, when it received further expansion with the grunge musicians and their followers, beginning in the mideighties. The music of grunge had features drawn from heavy metal, thrash styles, and punk. It would soon attract a new generation of youngsters, some of them consciously cultivating long matted hair and wearing dirty acid-washed pants with duct-tape patches and jackets that flamboyantly displayed skulls of people and animals. Others resembled punksters, with repellent haircuts, torn clothing, and antisocial behavior. They would acknowledge scarcely any duty or obligation to society and scorn mainstream pop music and the slick enticements of the huge music corporations. In short, if this hardcore genre was to attain prominence it had to make its own way.

Grunge's music combined intense riffing with angry or gloomy lyrics. The music was intended to be a direct opposite to much of the pop of the time. Before long it occupied a major position of its own, as it attracted those youngsters who found their feelings of personal disorientation, isolation, and vulnerability reflected in the music. By the mideighties, to be sure, these had become recurring sentiments in the young, continuing from one decade to the next and demanding a fresh musical expression every few years. Since the fifties, American society had continued to have no basis for stability, and nobody was certain of their position in the social order. As before, lip service was paid to moral values but in actuality amoral business decisions, self-interested personal dealings, and swiftly changing technology were affecting the public. As children grew into adolescents and then into young adults, a number of them could not help but be influenced by what was going on around them.

Grunge, also known as alternative rock or as indie (independent) rock, emerged in Seattle, Washington, with the appearance of Andrew Wood and his band, Mother Love Bone, which began life toward the end of 1984 and functioned until 1990, when Wood died of a drug overdose. Most of the bands that followed, as with several earlier hardcore outfits, came out of the suburbs and moved into the urban centers. Quickly, the independent Sub Pop Records, founded by Bruce Pavitt, took up the cause. The members of Mudhoney, also initiators of grunge, supplied the first break for Sub Pop Records. The band and its locally popular recordings provided the basis for the splinter groups that would make a keen impression on the rock world with their mix of heavy-metal sludge, a modified punk outlook, and garage's self-taught primitivism. Mudhoney sounded deafening, resolutely slapdash, and a little scary. Their essential nature was revealed on their first single, "Touch Me I'm Sick" (1988), a frantic musical shriek loaded with defeat and self-disgust, as the singer tells us that he feels terrible and declares himself a "creep" and "jerk."[24]

Death, despair, and drug addiction set to grinding dark-colored riffs became standard fare for the Seattle musicians. Layne Staley, vocalist for Alice in Chains, later had second thoughts about the message grunge was delivering. In 1996, he admitted to writing and singing about drugs, and then commented, "I didn't want fans to think heroin was cool. But then I've had fans come up to me and give me the thumbs up, telling me they're high. That's exactly what I didn't want to happen."[25]

The Seattle area, in the nineties, was paying attention to bands like Soundgarden, Alice in Chains, Stone Temple Pilots, and Pearl Jam. In early 1991, the album *Temple of the Dog* brought together Chris Cornell and Matt Cameron of Soundgarden with Jeff Ament and Stone Gossard, the surviving members of Mother Love Bone, and Eddie Vedder, later with Pearl Jam. It was the first grunge recording to have a national distribution, then an international one. Another important advance for grunge came with the 1992 movie *Singles*, which brought forward Soundgarden, Alice in Chains, and Pearl Jam. In early 1990, another band, Nirvana, had signed up with Sub Pop. Led by the tormented but magnetic Kurt Cobain, talented songwriter, guitarist, and vocalist, early on the band issued *Bleach* (1989), which had a tepid reception, and then followed it with the release of a favorably received second album, *Nevermind* (1991). Their recordings had poor sound production. Their playing was just adequate. However, their music attracted listeners with its unique resonance. Their concert appearances were without clever ploys meant for amusement, without eye-catching costumes, and without showy splendor.

The corrosive *Nevermind* sound has become fairly ubiquitous because all sorts of rock groups that came after have helped themselves to its approach. Its punk-styled riffing, from "Smells Like Teen Spirit" to the album's ending with "Something in the Way," enlarged on and concentrated the anger of the rock underground with what sounds like a loud, passionate howl. The colossal buildup of Kurt Cobain's shrieks remains devastating even today. This album is unrelenting and sounds somewhat under the influence of drugs. "Smells Like Teen Spirit," created by Cobain, runs along a familiar punk road, telling its listeners to supply themselves abundantly with weapons and bring friends. They will find it amusing to make believe and fail.[26] Alongside this number, the odd "In Bloom," and the eerie "Come as You Are," we hear the tuneful clamor of "Breed" and "Territorial Pissings," the black noise of "Drain You," the raw anxiety in "Lounge Act," the distorted pop of "Stay Away," the glum melodiousness of "On a Plain," and the hauntingly simple "Something in the Way." The language of the last song is disjointed—a collection of one-liners having little to no connection with each other. One line tells you a tarpaulin is leaking; another that trapped animals are now pets; another that eating fish is approved since they lack feeling; and so forth.[27] They are absurd songs to go with an absurd "trickle-down" economy, hypocritical shows of sorrow over the plight of the poor, and the bizarreness of the first Gulf War.

Writing in 2001 about Kurt Cobain's iconic image and the album *Nevermind*, Robert Christgau opined that Cobain "seemed like every born loser . . . a geek you could get wasted with, a shy guy whose cuteness cried out for mothering, an arty wierdo with a common touch. . . . He gave a generation of losers a hero who felt like a loser himself."[28]

Nirvana was the first of the Seattle hardcore outfits to reach a widespread public. Radio stations played their songs, and MTV gave them airings. The growing number of grunge fans celebrated. The larger record industry seeking to profit from grunge signed up Seattle's superior bands. By 1992, the sounds of grunge were heard on radio stations everywhere, on MTV, and on a proliferating number of recordings. Nirvana, Soundgarden, and Pearl Jam experienced breakthroughs to a huge public and their albums promoted them to international recognition. Outstanding recordings included Nirvana's *Nevermind* (1991), MTV *Unplugged in New York (Live)* (1994), and *From the Muddy Banks of Wishkah* (1996); Soundgarden's *Superunknown* (1994) and *Down on the Upside* (1996); Pearl Jam's

Ten (1991) and *Vs.* (1993); and Alice in Chains's *Dirt* (1992), *Jar of Flies* (1994), and *Alice in Chains* (1995).

Cobain committed suicide in 1994 and, by the end of 1995, grunge was moribund. Nevertheless, hardcore as reconstituted grunge, heavy metal, and thrash, or as affiliated with hip-hop, continued into the next century. Alternative rock emerged in the late nineties as an umbrella term for young rockers who damned the commercial character and flashy practices of conventional pop. They preferred their music to sound coarse and exploratory; their lyrics to speak truthfully, if morosely, of their chaotic inner state and of the ennui that infected modern living. Nirvana had presented harsh grunge. R.E.M. gave out tidy guitar-rock. Belligerent industrial-weight metal music came from Ministry and Nine Inch Nails. The Red Hot Chili Peppers and Fishbone delivered gang-inspired punk-funk. The emo or emocore that Rites of Spring and Promise Ring produced went to the opposite extreme, with their sensitive, poetic lyrics and resonant harmonies.

Various parts of the United States had their own grunge bands, whatever the particular stylistic inclination. For example, Pavement, established in California in 1988 and destructing in 2000, dispensed sophistication and angst. The metal-leaning Korn, filled out with California musicians, was formed in 1993 and had its debut release in *Korn* (1994). In 2002, the band came out with the album *Untouchables*. Its guitarist Munky Shaffer explained its angry rock, saying, "We are people who grew up feeling out of place. We were misfits, and we went through adolescence feeling awkward. That's where we write from and find our inspiration." In one song, "Here to Stay," the vocalist Jonathan Davis screamed, "I take my face and bash it in a mirror so I won't have to see my pain." Davis in a calmer moment spoke of "the buzz-saw rhythm section" of bass and drums and "the savage roar of down-tuned guitars" that saturated the album.[29]

The all-female Babes in Toyland started in Minneapolis in 1987 and emitted bottomless rage in their music. Sonic Youth, from New York's clamorous antiestablishment sphere, won importance in 1990 with *Goo*. Everclear, formed in Portland, Oregon, hit its stride with the 1995 *Sparkle and Fade*. The grunge movement got a foothold in Australia when Silverchair debuted with the album *frogstomp*, recorded in 1995. It was caustic alternative rock and won followers throughout the world.

Interestingly, a large portion of the post-turn-of-the-century adherents of hardcore are young white males who reside in affluent suburbia and are college-bound. They define the United States as two-faced, grasping, and suffocatingly standardized. They aim to break out of the mold that they find themselves in. These youths prefer bands with irreverent titles. Paul Zielbauer writes, "Dismay comes from Danbury, and Sicboy from Stamford [both towns in Connecticut]. But members of lurid-sounding Late Night Revenge reside in leafy Simsbury. And in Greenwich, home of dog salons and Ferrari dealerships, there is . . . a quartet called Pray for Death." They, like their music, screamed forth in gut-wrenching fashion to accompany flying fists, body slams, and dives into the mosh pit—anything to keep boredom in abeyance.[30]

HIP-HOP AND RAP TAKE OVER

The background to hip-hop involved the black middle class fleeing the ghettos, leaving behind them inner-city poverty, crime, prostitution, heavy drinking, and drug addiction (angel dust, crack, and cocaine). With the return of black soldiers from Vietnam also came the anger at second-class citizenship and, unfortunately, the familiarity with heroin, which exacerbated the ghetto situation. At the same time President Nixon curtailed the antipoverty and urban-development programs. Nelson George writes that with Reagan's administration, tragedy hit the ghettos even more, especially among the children of cocaine users: "Hope became a very hollow word. The world became defined by the 'hood, the block, or the corner where" drugs were sold. In the eighties, "the physical and moral decay begun by heroin was accelerated by angel dust and then the McDonaldization of crack." Consequently, greed ruled over ideals "as a definer of life's worth." Sex displaced romantic love; the begetting of throwaway children replaced child rearing.[31] This was the milieu for the parties featuring hip-hop's DJs and their turntables and speakers in playgrounds, community centers, clubs, gyms, and the streets.

Hip-hop and rap first appeared not among white, relatively affluent suburban youths but among black, mostly poor, inner-city youths. Quite a few of those involved with hip-hop had belonged to street gangs and been involved in crime. The terms "hip-hop" and "rap" were frequently used to mean the same thing. To speak more accurately, hip-hop described rap's cultural environment, including break dancing, dressing in an idiosyncratic manner, and graffiti slogans and drawings. (The expression "B-boy" included youths who break-danced, dressed in hip-hop fashion, and used macho body language.) Hip-hop also encompassed the DJ's artful management of records and turntables to generate new musical assemblages. He did this by merging preselected musical fragments with a decided dance beat from older recordings and adding striking "scratch" and dropped-needle effects. Rap directed attention toward the skill involved in rhythmic vocal rhyming of a rapper, as the DJ spun the music.

Fueled by the rise of adolescent gangs, prevalent in places like the South Bronx, the teenagers who were into hip-hop united in "posses." They supplied the pattern for this fresh category of pop group and supported the rappers who slung rhythmic patter at the audience. Rapping frontmen added rapid, slangy, and occasionally boastful social commentary that mirrored the experience of the African-American community. Simultaneously and behind them, the DJs offered fascinating "samplings" of rhythms, breaks (all sounds dropped except drums), and musical fragments through the clever manipulation of record discs and turntables. Some performers included a second DJ—one to lead and the other to supply the beat.

Funk and disco were antecedents of hip-hop. So also were the toasting and dub talks of reggae. Kool Herc (Clive Campbell) came to the Bronx from Kingston, Jamaica, in 1967, when he was thirteen. In the seventies, he floated the Jamaican idea of delivering improvised lines over the dub adaptations of his reggae records at block parties and clubs. However, he had few takers. In order to enhance acceptability, he started to recite over instrumental, or just percussive, slices of popular music. The emphasis was on danceability. By means of an audio mixer, he went on to lengthen his recitation without letup or interruption. He used two copies of the same record on two turntables, which enabled him to continuously reinstate the chosen section. At first, the patter involved someone like Kool Herc acknowledging people present in the audience. He might chant over the instrumental break: "Yo this is Kool Herc in the joint-ski saying my mellowski Marky D is in the house." This would regularly stir up the listeners to respond with their own names and sayings.[32] The rapid speech of the emcee gradually became more involved and rhyming was added. Eventually, it got to be too much for him alone. He turned over the "emceeing" talk to friends while he DJ'd at the turntables. He had arrived at rap.

Along with Kool Herc, other early DJs included Grand Wizard Theodore, Grandmaster Flash, and Afrika Bambaataa. "Grandmaster" as a designation came from Bruce Lee's kung fu movies honoring the martial arts. Grandmaster Flash popularized scratching on records and spinning them backwards. He also developed a drum machine to add emphatic percussion beats. Afrika Bambaataa was a former gang member and a follower of Malcolm X. He believed that hip-hop was valuable for fighting the unchecked street violence in the Bronx. In 1973, he initiated the Youth Organization, shortly renamed the Zulu Nation, which exerted a pull on young adults who wished to take part in Bambaataa's pursuit of the street arts, among them break dancing, graffiti drawing, disc jockeying, and rapping. He is supposed to have been the first to apply the term "hip-hop" to the South Bronx street culture after he heard a rapper at a party chant, "Hip-hop, you don't stop/That makes your body rock."[33] At this point in its development, rap was good-time dance music and repartee.

An inevitable corollary to hip-hop was the later introduction of bubblegum-rap for the kiddies: rap-prattle about dating problems, parental discipline, partying, and deciding what to wear. DJ Jazzy Jeff, Nelly, and Lil' Bow Wow were three successful performers of this repertoire. To enhance sales, their recordings came out in two versions, explicit and cleaned up—a practice that was pursued by other rappers, too. In addition there was a variety of rap some have called "feel-good music," purveyed at times by people like M. C. Hammer, Will Smith, Young MC, and Puff Daddy. The goal was to have their music cross over to white audiences by emphasizing danceability over rhyme and aiming the discourse to please white adolescent tastes.[34]

Rap (emceeing) grew popular because it was open to all young urban African-Americans and permitted them to talk uncensored, and to say what was on their minds. What would make it more popular was the Sugar Hill Gang's album *Rapper's Delight*, which sold half a million copies in 1979, and rap's inclusion in the 1983 film *Flashdance*. National and European tours of rap groups ensued. By the mideighties, hip-hop was a national phenomenon; local DJs and rappers were appearing nationwide. With the success of Run-DMC's *Run-DMC* (1984) and *Raising Hell*, in 1986, rap was big business. By then, rap had achieved a handful of highly admired frontrunners. However, it was still seen as a passing fancy. Yet, this opinion had begun to change with Run-DMC's rise to popularity. "It's Like That" and "Sucker MCs" from the 1984 album were put together by cleverly inserting riff samples, jiggling vinyl recordings under the needle to produce scratching effects, and creating "breakbeats" (managed through going back and forth between two copies of the same record). This last was the foundation for the break dancing of the "B-boys." The usual melodic phrasing was displaced by jagged rhythms and sounds that symbolized the noisy urban environment of traffic in the streets, the loud talk of pedestrians, and the screech from playground games. In *Raising Hell* was "Walk This Way," in which Aerosmith participated and by so doing helped bolster the career of the rappers. Run-DMC were responsible for a new hip-hop look—track suits, leather jackets, jeans, black felt hats, and Adidas sneakers.

The widely known rap star M. C. Hammer emerged, in 1988, with his million-copy sale of *Let's Get It Started*. Women's groups like Queen Latifah and Salt 'N' Pepa joined the male groups, as did white outfits like Vanilla Ice, the Beastie Boys, and Eminem. The Beastie Boys' *License to Ill* became a best-seller in 1987, Vanilla Ice's *To the Extreme*, in 1990, and Eminem's *The Slim Shady EP*, in 1999. They encouraged other white hip-hop "crews" to enter the market.

Hip-hop found room for individual personalities who might otherwise never have come to view. When rap started, it was inappropriate to read from a paper. If rhymes were prewritten, they had to be memorized, so as to give the impression of legitimacy, that is to say, of extemporaneous speech. Conveyed were black-power harangues, exaggerated boasts, talking blues, larger-than-life stories, and "the Dozens," a prescribed procedure for exchanging insults. It was not long before "message" raps, commentaries about current conditions and events, were being heard, alongside the lighter versification. Jollification ceased; serious talk entered. The bitter talk of Gil Scott-Heron, emceeing in the seventies, came forth to touch black nerves. He hears that "Whitey is on the moon." Yet, at the same time a rat has sunk its teeth into his sister Nell, causing her face and arms to swell. He can scarcely afford to get her a doctor. Bitterly he says that ten years from today he will still be paying off his debt, "while Whitey's on the moon."[35]

Grandmaster Flash and the Furious Five recorded Ed Fletcher's "The Message" (1983). More than did Scott-Heron, they told listeners what daily life was like in the black slums, with no hope for relief. Such songs also reached the poor white boys living in projects, who also were confronting the bleakness of their existence and seeing daily crime and drug activity. Grandmaster Flash complained rhythmically to the pulse of rap music about endless broken glass and persons urinating on stairways. Rats infested his front room and junkies with baseball bats lurked in the alley. The constant stink, noise, and danger was unbearable, but he couldn't afford to move. He once had tried to escape without avail, because a guy in a tow truck repossessed his car.[36] In conclusion, he rapped about being close to losing his mind and being overwhelmed or destroyed by what was going on, living as he did in an urban jungle.

Pieces like the above described the consequences of Reaganomics and "benign neglect" in a way that hit home. The music became a catalyst in the examination of American issues like violence, racism, sexism, morality, and the excessive devotion to materialism, writes Tricia Rose. "Rap music," she continued, "brings together a tangle of some of the most complex social, cultural, and political issues in contemporary American society."[37]

Although many musicians admitted to the power of hip-hop and rap, they were not convinced that it was actually music they were listening to. Teo Macero, a record and film-sound-track producer who had worked with Duke Ellington, Miles Davis, and Charles Mingus, said of rap, "It's all right, but it isn't really music. It's like a run-on sentence; how long can you keep it going without really saying anything."[38] He was by no means alone in this judgment. To listen to Run-DMC, two rappers, and another DJ let go with their rough voices and booming drum-machine-generated rhythms, sans band, sans melody, simply words and the beat, can make one wonder.[39] In addition, rap had not endeared itself to involuntary listeners who hear it blaring at them at top volume from boom boxes on public transportation and cars with windows open and get a defiant "finger" from the young perpetrators when they complain.

There was also another disturbing edge to some hip-hop—an attitude and a way of life that promoted a love of material goods, anti-intellectualism, sexism, anti-Semitism, hatred of white people, viciousness, violence, and the use of guns. In December 2001, Jon Pareles complained in the *New York Times*, "Through most of the year, best-selling hip-hop acts competed to depict the most garish visions of hedonism: designer labels, call-brand drinks, easy women. They celebrated Mercedes-Benzes and platinum-and-diamond jewelry. . . . Rappers . . . also escalated the rhetoric of self-adoration; recently Jay-Z, the year's dominant rapper, renamed himself Jay-hova." Rappers have been absorbed "with the fantasy lives of gun-toting playboys, pop for teenagers . . . which is now more blatantly artificial than it was in the days before the Beatles."[40]

When underground hip-hoppers turned professional, tension developed between the need to maintain authenticity and the craving for commercial success, especially when recordings began to be made. Thus, Ice-T claimed he made an attempt "not to go pop . . . and get on radio"; yet, he also quoted Dr. Dre, who said that for him it was not about making the best record but "about who sells the most records."[41] Selling more records meant you had gained an advantage over your competitors and proved you were a person of importance. It also earned you money, so that you could indulge yourself as you pleased.

As poverty and despair gathered strength in the cities, and dead bodies due to gang violence piled up, the subject matter of the music changed. Desperation in the late eighties gave rise to "gangsta rap," which was a response to exacerbated urban violence and often an exploiter of the degenerating conditions in the ghettos. Philadelphia's Schoolly D and his single "PSK—What Does It Mean?" of 1985 was one of its earliest manifestations. On the West Coast, the Ice-T album *Rhyme Pays* came out in 1987. The next year, a Los Angeles group, N.W.A., recorded *Straight Outta Compton*, a hardheaded picture of slum life. The Geto Boys, from Houston, starting in 1988, delivered some of gangsta rap's most gruesome and obscene accounts of rape and murder, provoking censure from citizens' groups.[42] According to Robin Kelley, gangsta rap's violent lyrics were not intended to be taken literally. They were to be interpreted as "boasting raps" to establish who is the "baddest motherfucker around." Kelley writes, "Their standpoint is that of the ghetto dweller, the criminal, the victim of police repression, the teenage father, the crack slanger, the gang banger, and the female dominator."[43]

When the record industry realized that gangsta rap was incredibly popular in suburbia and was giving the white kids a frisson of living dangerously, it boosted this music commercially and publicized it to the limit. Producer Hank Shocklee said that for whites gangsta rap allowed a sort of voyeurism, like getting on a roller coaster ride. To listen on records was safe, the fear was controlled, and the patter could be turned off at will. Several critics, like Jay Cocks, worried that it reinforced the negative image of blacks as "murderous thugs."[44]

Whether through Run-DMC, Public Enemy, Dr. Dre, or Ice-T, a black message of violence was carried to "whitey." What they had to say was of doubtful propriety but it was undoubtedly potent. Typical was Ice-T's "Home Invasion" (1993), where foul language dominated the proceedings, and a gang is after the "motherfuckin' kids" and the parents are to have their "goddamn" heads busted.[45] He was far more compelling in "Race War" (1993), about people getting killed on the streets and blaming it on the media, police, and television—"anybody but yourself."[46]

Much less acceptable to whites was "Cop Killer," which caused a nationwide furor when it came out the year before. The words declare him a "cop killer" with a "long-assed knife," which he bought "to kill me sumthin."[47] It was the voice of inner-city black rage over police brutality and over a white society that oppressed the poor and suppressed any criticism of its oppression. The beating of Rodney King and the Los Angeles black riots were part of the background. Ice-T claimed, "The song was written from the perspective of a black man who becomes so enraged at his mistreatment by the police that he goes out with a gun to kill cops."[48] However, whites took it as a threat. President Bush, Vice President Quayle, actor Charlton Heston, and police everywhere inveighed against the piece. Ice-T retired the composition.

Gangsta rap could get quite mean, even vicious. In 2002, the wildly popular white rapper Eminem (Marshall Bruce Mathers) came out with *The Eminem Show*. On one track, "White America," he wants to urinate on the White House, burn the American flag, and insult Mrs. Cheney and Mrs. Gore. On another, "Without Me," he boasts, "Though I'm not the first king of controversy, I am the worst thing since Elvis Presley / To do Black Music so selfishly and use it to get myself wealthy (Hey)." Elsewhere, he speaks of his hatred of his mother and ex-wife. "Drips" is designed to be especially offensive, with its reference to "last night's tunk" and "pussy residue on my penis."[49]

People ready to accept rap were repelled by gangsta rap's foul language and gross subject matter, as in the above, much of which was there because offensiveness sold well to the young, not because it had anything to do with inner-city realities. Touré, writing in the *New York Times*, has tried to explain rap's deliberate setting out to offend in an article on the notorious Sean "Puff Daddy" Combs. He writes: "It has long been an article of faith in hip-hop that if you are not upsetting white people, then you are not doing your job. This merely restates an old belief held by many blacks that if you're upsetting white people, then you must be doing something right. Such thinking explains part of the appeal of activist preachers like Rev. Adam Clayton Powell, Jr., Louis Farrakhan and the Rev. Al Sharpton, firebrands like Mohammed Ali and Tupac Shakur and scoundrels like O. J. Simpson. . . . A man so seemingly grating to white people has tremendous cathartic value to black people."[50]

Dionne Warwick, on the other hand, said that she, an African-American singer, had at first enjoyed and loved dancing to the hip-hop emanating from performers like M. C. Hammer. But her ears were assaulted and insulted by gangsta rap, with its chauvinistic garbage about women and prurient drivel about sex. Echoing what Teo Macero had said, she concluded, "I don't think that rap has become the new black American music at all. I don't consider rap music. I consider it as a form of communication.

When you talk about American black music, you talk about Ray Charles and Gladys Knight and Aretha Franklin. You talk about those who are making music."[51] Indeed, gangsta rapper Ja Rule admits what he does is not music: "I don't sing, let's get that straight. I'm soulful on those tracks [of *Pain in Love* and *Down 4 You*], but it's not quite singing." He acknowledges being angry and aggressive in "songs," but he confesses, "Success helped me understand life more. I'm not all that angry, and I have another side of my life now."[52]

Sad to say, a number of hip-hoppers have engaged in crime, overdosed on drugs, been involved in assaults, or gotten themselves murdered. Numerous rap verbiage portrays a society of cold-blooded, trigger-happy individuals. Some rappers have proved less than law-abiding in real life— Slick Rick's attempt at murder; Suge Knight jailed for a violent attack; Shyne (Jamal Borrow) serving a sentence for a shooting. Among those murdered were Tupac Shakur, Biggie Smalls, and Jam Master Jay (of Run-DMC). Grammy-winning hip-hop artist Sean Combs (a.k.a. Puff Daddy, a.k.a. P. Diddy) has acted as a hip-hop promoter, record producer, songwriter, and performer. He has also been in court for a New York nightclub shooting and was accused of complicity, along with his friend, rapper Notorious B.I.G., in the murder of Tupac Shakur. Notorious B.I.G. was himself gunned down a few months after Tupac's death.

Yet, for all its black marks, rap has been a significant performance genre. When, in 1990, some critics accused rap of being unoriginal and only a recycling of works of others by means of sampling, defenders like Gene Santoro quickly pointed out that it was a "startling new way to imagine sound." He added, "Lopping, defacing and recontextualizing isolated snippets ('samples') from old records," the rappers mold "shredded musical history into new shapes within a single tune behind a singsong, usually macho, deep-vices, street-style poetry."[53]

Several subdivisions had appeared by the turn of the century—jazz rap, feminine rap, Muslim rap, Christian rap, and gay rap. It has gone international, with rappers in Europe, Asia, Africa, and Australia.[54] Rap has also been modified by increasing injections of hardcore, soul, and pop. Originating in racial and lower-class areas, it was a demonstration of acute discontent (oftentimes accompanied by disquiet and despair), which arose from unanswered needs and continuing social and personal problems. At its best, it gave honest, factual sketches of inner-city existence. This truth about rap was frequently forgotten because the public only remembered rap's inflammatory communiqués.

NOTES

1. Walter LaFaber, Richard Polemberg, and Nancy Woloch, *The American Century*, 3rd ed. (New York: Knopf, 1986), 545.

2. Pat Blashill, "Anthems of Alternative Music," in Stuart A. Kallen, editor, *The 1990s* (San Diego, California: Greenhaven Press, 2000), 137.

3. "Dixie Chicks," posted on *CountryStars.com*, 13 July 2001.

4. "Country Music Has Changed Their Tune," *ABC News.com*, 20 October 2002.

5. Timothy D. Taylor, *Global Pop* (New York: Routledge, 1997), 7–9.

6. The annual Grammy Award was established by the record industry in 1958 in order to give recognition of noteworthy recordings. The first award was granted in 1959.

7. Russell Sanjek, updated by David Sanjek, *Pennies from Heaven* (New York: Da Capo, 1996), 657.

8. Reebee Garofalo, "From Music Publishing to MP3: Music and Industry in the Twentieth Century," *American Music* 17 (1999): 347.

9. See Myron A. Marty, "Pop Culture in the '80s," in James D. Torr, editor, *The 1980s* (San Diego, California: Greenhaven Press, 2000), 184.

10. New York: Famous Music Corp., c2001.

11. David Cho, "Rap with Religion," *Boston Globe*, 25 February 2002, A2.

12. Thor Christensen, "Old Singers, New Dilemma," *Boston Globe*, 15 September 2001, E2.

13. Jason Gay, "VH1: Behind the Shake-Up," *Rolling Stone*, 4–11 July 2002, 31.

14. Lois P. Nicholson, *Michael Jackson* (New York: Chelsea House, 1994), 72.

15. Los Angeles: Controversy Music, c/o University Music Publishing Group, c1984.

16. J. Randy Taraborelli, *Madonna* (New York: Simon & Schuster, 2001), 67.

17. New York: Sony Tunes Inc., c1984.

18. Los Angeles: Candy Castle Music, c1984.

19. Los Angeles: May Twelfth Music, c1984.

20. Los Angeles: Nuff Loot Inc., c1992.

21. Taraborelli, *Madonna*, 128–29.

22. Nashville: Sony/ATV Songs, c1995.

23. Steve Morse, "Spears Is Déjà Vu of the Worst Repetitive Sort," *Boston Globe*, 10 December 2001, B8. I did not attend the show but did see an extraordinary number of mothers holding the hands of children, who seemed no older than seven or eight, crossing the street to enter the Center.

24. Seattle: Better Than Your Music, c1988.

25. John Pareles, "Layne Staley, Singer for Leading Grunge Band, Dies at 34," *New York Times*, 22 April 2002, www.nytimes.com.

26. New York: EMI Virgin Songs, c1991.

27. New York: EMI Virgin Songs, c1991.

28. Robert Christgau, "Nevermore," *New Yorker*, 20 and 27 August 2001, www.newyorker.com/critics/books/?010820crbo_books.

29. Steve Morse, "Anger's Here to Stay: Korn Still Has Some Issues," *Boston Globe*, 16 June 2002, 24.

30. Paul Zielbauer, "Musical Angst Prospers in Tranquil Connecticut," *New York Times*, 24 August 2001, www.nytimes.com.

31. Nelson George, *Hip Hop America* (New York: Viking, 1998), 41.

32. David "Davey D" Cook, "Hip Hop Started in the Bronx with DJ Kool Herc," from http://www.daveyd.com/raphist2.html, accessed 12 December 2002. Mr. Cook is a chronicler of hip-hop and has appeared on Radio 94.1 FM, KPFA, in the San Francisco area.

33. Eileen Southern, *The Music of Black Americans*, 3rd ed. (New York: Norton, 1997), 578–79.

34. Jennifer Keeley, *Rap Music* (San Diego, California: Lucent Books, 2001), 27–29.

35. Amy Waldman, "A Ravaged Musical Prodigy at a Crossroads with Drugs," *New York Times*, 10 July 2001, www.nytimes.com.

36. Englewood, New Jersey: Sugar Hill Music, c1983.

37. Tricia Rose, *Black Noise* (Middletown, Connecticut: Wesleyan University Press, 1994), 2.

38. Bella English, "Teo Macero," *Boston Globe*, 5 December 2001, D6.

39. Robert Palmer, *Rock & Roll: An Unruly History* (New York: Harmony Books, 1995), 283.

40. Jon Pareles, "Blasted from Its Self-Absorption at Least for Now," *New York Times*, 30 December 2001, www.nytimes.com.

41. Theodore Gracyk, *Rhythm and Noise: An Aesthetic of Rock* (Durham, North Carolina: Duke University Press, 1996), 182.

42. For an examination of the beginning of gangsta rap, see Robin D. G. Kelley, *Race Rebels* (New York: Free Press, 1994), 187–88.

43. Kelley, *Race Rebels*, 189–91.

44. Keeley, *Rap Music*, 33–34.

45. Burlington, Vermont: Bridgeport Music, c1993.

46. Los Angeles: Warner/Chappell Music, c1993.

47. Los Angeles: Ernkneesea Music/Polygram Intl., c1992.

48. Keeley, *Rap Music*, 87.

49. The lyrics are transcribed from the album *The Eminem Show* (Interscope B00006690G).

50. Touré, "Sean Combs: Unstoppable, Whatever His Guise," *New York Times*, 8 April 2001, www.nytimes.com.

51. Alex Ogg with David Upshal, *The Hip Hop Years* (New York: Fromm International, 2001), 145–46.

52. Ken Capobianco, "Family, Music Rule for Rapper," *Boston Globe*, 28 June 2002, C10.

53. Gene Santoro, "Public Enemy," *Nation*, 25 June 1990, 90.

54. Tony Mitchell, editor, *Global Noise: Rap and Hip-Hop outside the USA* (Middletown, Connecticut: Wesleyan University Press, 2001), introduction, 10.

Chapter Nine

A Temporary Ending

Obviously, whatever the form it takes, music has been and will always be essential to the public. Through a song and singer, listeners can summon feelings, recollections, and significant moments in time. Some may find popular music to be a diversion, a means for getting away from boredom or the more pressing problems of the present. Others may find in it an expression, whether emotional or thoughtful, of matters important to them. Still others revel in the sheer sound of melody, rhythm, and harmony. Music can encapsulate personal meaning for the listener that is not easy to put into words.

The evaluation of the significance of melody, harmony, rhythm, and their presentation, and why in one instance they have proved attractive and in another unattractive, is always a difficult proposition for the writer. To talk technically about how a song is put together does not necessarily tell us why it is loved by a body of listeners. Nor does such analysis mean much to the reader with no musical training. Admittedly, I have dwelt more on the lyrics than on the music in songs.

In the 21st century, even more than at any time in the past, popular song means different things to different people and different things to the same person at different times. Arriving at an all-embracing characterization is unachievable. Nor is it desirable. The categorizations given today's music can never be clear-cut—genres run into and through each other at will. We have seen that, since the fifties, popular music has seemingly turned out to be more and more divided. Combining, recombining, metamorphosing, and constantly susceptible to new technologies, popular music does try to sound fresh, though not always with success. One reason is that inevitably today's songs must be constructed on yesterday's foundations—whether traditional pop, folk, blues, country, or earlier rock. In short, popular music is permanently in a state of reinventing itself while looking over the past. Closing off one approach necessitates opening up another. All endings are transitory, therefore temporary.

In 1841, Emerson gave advice that included the arts: "No man can quite emancipate himself from his age and country, or produce a model in which the education, the religion, the politics, usages, and arts of his times shall have no share. Though he was never so original, never so willful and fantastic, he cannot wipe out of his work every trace of the thoughts amidst which it grew. The very avoidance betrays the usage he avoids."[1]

Popular song responds profoundly to its age and country. In the twenties, it reflected the push for personal liberation and for being happy no matter what of the Jazz Age, a drive energized by the college generation. "Ain't We Got Fun," "The Black Bottom," and "Let's Misbehave" captured the generation's thoughts. Jumping to the sixties, music reproduced the contentiousness and social and political advocacy of militant black and white youths, among them many college students, in folklike protest ballads, folk-rock, soul, and funk. At the beginning of the 21st century, college students no longer made as public a display of their disagreements or acted as forcefully to become part of a political or social movement. Most were at ease with the institutions that had power over them. They were self-centeredly getting an education in order to reap the financial rewards that it promised. If education also stretched their minds, then well and good. A 1998 poll asked students what they saw as the major problems facing America. They replied, "Selfishness, people who don't respect law and the authorities, wrongdoing by politicians, lack of parental discipline, and courts that care too much about criminals' rights."[2] Few of them were ready to cope with these challenges; more of them were part of the problem.

POPULAR CULTURE AT THE TURN OF THE CENTURY

Young people, whether attending college or high school, were inundated with the mediocrity produced by the commercial world surrounding them. It is a wonder that many of them did not succumb completely to it. By the 21st century, the young men and women of the United States were buried in cheap, trashy goods. Newspaper reporting came in the form of narrative accounts that colored the facts. Television "news" embroidered, sentimentalized, or fictionalized the news. Movies and television shows served up nonstop sensationalism, sex, sadism, and vulgar language to accommodate short attention spans, lack of intellectual curiosity, and desire for titillation. Leonard Maltin, movie critic, complained that the worst films of all time were appearing after the turn of the century. The cheapest standards imaginable prevailed. He warned, "The danger is that young people weaned on these mediocre films will have no yardstick for measuring a good movie. If a kid has eaten nothing but fast-food hamburgers his whole life, how is he to recognize the quality of filet mignon? When virtually every comedy . . . is awash in crudity, an entire generation may come to believe this is the norm."[3]

A glance at the entertainment and lifestyle section of newspapers showed them feeding the same dumbed-down message to the young. They assumed of course that the young had limited capacity for thinking. To sustain their profits, newspaper pages placated advertisers who wanted to channel their goods-for-sale at the 9-to-29 age groups. The media was cultivating a human sector that was perceived as able to gobble text in only nibble bits and at the most superficial grade. Some newspapers were better than most. Certainly the *New York Times*, the *Washington Post*, and the *Boston Globe*—three newspapers I regularly read[4]—do have thoughtful "arts" pages. However, they also include information apparently aimed at stunted minds. Writing in and about the *Boston Globe*, Hayley Kaufman remarked, "'Go!' [a feature of the *Globe*] spends an inordinate amount of time immersed in pop culture's lowbrow depths. Places where intellect gets checked at the door and glossy image is all. Now, we're not complaining . . . but sometimes it's nice to check in with our higher brain functions, just to see if our cerebrum is still spongy and vital or if it has hardened like a day-old baguette."[5] The *Globe Calendar* pullout has suffered from the same malady.

These were the conditions that also prevailed in the popular-music community. One might expect vital news items and informative articles on popular music in the issues of *Rolling Stone*. Looking through the magazine for the year 2002,[6] one found a few informative items and longer articles, and huge numbers of photos of performers' belly buttons, bared breasts and buttocks, closeups of crotches, and couples in provocative positions. The language almost throughout was of the prurient adolescent sort. Titillating gossip and smutty commentary substituted for information on most pages. The back matter of the 17 January publication was also typical. Under "Announcements" was an advertisement, "Get New ID. College Degrees by

Mail. Secret Loans." Under "Clothing" was "Rotton Cotton! Twisted T-Shirts! Horror, Sleaze, Filth, Exploitation." Under "Health" were advertisements of Viagra, herpes cures, and ointments for penis enlargement. "Bizarre Sex Videos" were offered as well as invitations to phone "Adultery Wives," "Daddy's Lil' Teen Sluts," and "Horny Gay Boyz." Apparently *Rolling Stone* editors assumed that the intellectual attainments of its wide readership were mired at bog level. They pandered to young people's lowest impulses. It took a mighty effort for adolescents to keep their heads above the sewage. Fortunately, more than a few succeeded in doing so.

The commercial music executives, hungry for profits, played on youth's emotionally undeveloped state. In the year 2000, André Schiffrin wrote that more than ever money ruled everything. Doctors, lawyers, academics, authors, and artists were subject to market criteria: "The idea that our society has been fundamentally affected by the importance of money is widely recognized. Other values that have been looked to as countervailing forces are fast disappearing. Not only our belongings, but our jobs and, indeed, our selves have become commodities to be bought and sold to the highest bidder. There have been other times in history when such changes have taken place. But now, linked to globalization and to the industrialization of the media, the effects are all the more staggering."[7] The same logistics have affected the music business. The industry made small effort, as in the fifties, to take an interest in a musician, say a Chuck Berry or Elvis Presley, whose first records might sell modestly but who would nonetheless give performances that a producer could take pride in sponsoring and who might in the future become popular. Record companies issuing rock, country, and rhythm and blues were once predominantly small, one-man shows, happy to make a moderate profit but still linked to the musical life of the communities they served. Now they were mammoth firms whose directors evaluated a song and singer least for quality but most for salability to the far-flung and faceless millions. So important was profit that to obtain permission to quote even two lines of a lyric for discussion in a book such as this one might incur a prohibitive charge.[8] Universal Music and Video Distribution, Sony Corporation of America, Time Warner, EMI Music Distribution, and Bertelsmann Music Group (BMG) were the five largest controllers of recorded music, who sold approximately 85 percent of all recordings purchased in the United States.

The reality was that, although independent companies did exist that would take chances on presenting many dissimilar musical styles and interesting performers, the dominant presences were these multinational corporations who pursued the same teenage audience with their artificially built-up celebrities and lavishly produced albums. If albums are never recorded and offered to the public because corporate officials decide they will not sell quickly and in quantity, the result is cultural dictatorship by a commercial oligarchy. This unquestionably undermines the potential for really fresh popular music by diminishing the fund of themes and views that can be examined for new ideas. In May 2001, Steve Morse interviewed the independent rocker Ike Reilly and asked, "Is there still room for smart, witty garage-pop during this increasingly corporate era of the arts?" Reilly replied, "Wouldn't it be great if that was true. It's such a strange time right now. Pop music is so brainless. We're in one of the worst periods in American history."[9] The accusation of brainlessness was not completely fair and to a large extent was owing to Reilly's exclusion from the circle of most highly touted performers. Nevertheless, under the tight control of commercial interests, music did seem to be heading in a discomforting direction.

There were also reports on the rising unhappiness over commercial radio. After 1996, when deregulation of ownership took place, a few business interests bought up large numbers of stations. Largest of all, San Antonio's Clear Channel soon owned 1,200 stations throughout the country. It and a few other group owners have been accused of limiting the airing of new artists, of having cozy relations with large record companies, and of allowing little choice of repertoire to their disc jockeys. Big names backed by big money are featured. Absent are variety, risk taking, and the bringing to light of local or little-known artists.[10] Directors meeting in corporate offices decide on the preferences of music listeners. Sometimes political ideology, which is usually conservative, influences who is put on the air. Whether rightly or not, they pare down the choices, and channel their music according to these decisions.

COUNTERTHRUST

Fortunately, among the adolescents and young adults will continue to be many who have far more discrimination in taste than they are given credit for and who resist the barrage of inanities that assail them daily. The lack of variety on radio turns off such listeners. The predominance of bubblegum in the record-store racks discourages these more critical record purchasers.[11] They rebel when tickets for concerts and club admission increase rapidly. A few leading performers have tried to impose exorbitant prices for tickets, and fans have balked at paying out the ransom. By August 2001, *MSNBC* was reporting a 15.5% drop in the concert business among the top 50 touring acts, according to *Pollstar*. Madonna, who got $250 each for the best seats and $128 each for one-half of the rest, still waxed strong, but most found at least one-third of their seats empty—among them Janet Jackson and Destiny's Child.[12] Several of the rock, rap, and rhythm-and-blues entertainers were descending into irrelevance for all their flashiness, because young people would not pay the price for admission to their concerts. To add to the disillusionment of serious music lovers, an increasing number of them were getting impatient with what they saw as the influence of affluent, indulged suburban adolescents, their punk bands and their "spoiled-brat" anger. "What are they so darned angry about?" asked one person. "Did Dad borrow their bong and forget to return it?"[13]

The most revered symbols of the past were debauched. A "Woodstock Festival" was held in an air force base in Rome, New York, in 1999. Thirty years before, the acclaimed first festival was a peaceful witnessing for love and peace and an end to the Vietnam War. At century's end it was a greedy and shoddy money-making event that angered the young crowds, who resorted to burning the booths that gouged them for bagels and bottled water.[14]

After the 9/11 terrorist attack, music-business officials and their stable of compliant performers realized they were having less and less impact on the public. A few days after the tragedy, Antonio Reed, head of Arista Records, said that music had been "in a very stagnant place before the attack," and now records were no longer meaningful.[15] A deepening recession was setting in and there was less and less money to throw around. Many of the huge stage productions were being eliminated—to save money and lower ticket prices. For example, in the summer of 2002, the Goo Goo Dolls decided to appear without staged antics, light shows, and a calculated working of the audience. Instead they sang normal rock songs with emotional meaning, which would show off their musical strengths, amidst a simple stage setting.

Hip-hop and rap also came under increasing criticism. Nine Inch Nails (Trent Reznor) was praised in the nineties for his pieces that enthusiastic fans claimed contained the quintessence of angst, alienation, and pain encapsulated in artistically gripping pop. Others were less enthusiastic, seeing self-indulgence and sensation seeking rather than expressions of ghetto rage in the profanity and violence of the words. In 1994, he recorded *The Downward Spiral*, which dispensed vitriol, pop hooks, harsh percussion, and hard-hitting guitars. It became a frequent offering of dance clubs. In it is the track "Big Man with a Gun." It pleased the young followers of Nine Inch Nails; it struck others as disgusting. In the song, he boasts about his "big old Dick" and a victim who will have to suck it or maybe find a hole blasted in his head, "just for the fuck of it."[16]

It was one of several pieces cited by Dr. Frank Palumbo, on behalf of the American Academy of Pediatrics, before a Senate subcommittee in 1997. He insisted that songs like this affected adolescent minds and led to moral decay, especially when part of a video shown on MTV and VH1.[17] Soon, even one or two rappers were agreeing.

In October 2000, *Newsweek* quoted the acclaimed rapper Mos Def as saying, "In terms of what certain media outlets show you, it's very one-dimensional. It's not just hip-hop music—TV and movies in general are very narrow. Sex, violence, the underbelly, with junkies, prostitutes, alcoholics, gamblers. The new trend today is depravity." This quotation is reprinted in Steve Allen's *Vulgarians at the Gate*. Allen, who himself was an entertainment personality, denounced rap music's murder-boosting lyrics, Madonna's brazen furthering of herself through sensual arousal, Howard Stern's relentless pursuit of sordidness, and cable television's "adult-oriented" shows, one of them HBO's "Sex and the City," in which thirtysomething women's attitudes toward sex resemble that of teenagers. He found no redeeming value in the Geto Boys' "Mind of a Lunatic," which graphically describes a girl's rape—the slitting of her throat and sexual intercourse with the corpse. A growing number of voices were raised in agreement.[18]

In 2002, although the white rapper Eminem reached the top of the *Billboard* charts, he and other rappers were already fashioning less-edgy images for themselves. They were perhaps hearing the rumble of criticism advancing toward them that complained about how so much of what they performed sounded tired, dated, played out, and forced. He and other white rappers were also involved in an argument with black rappers over rap— whether it was a craft open to all or a black cultural expression. To most young fans the argumentation was of little interest. They wanted their listening, whether from a black or a white musician, to continue offering a stimulating experience. In an attempt to keep hold of supporters, an increasing number of tracks combined rap with other genres—among them, soul, heavy metal, and punk.

In the new century, the rap mixtures were part of a confusion of styles, a result of the splintering of tastes and audiences who wanted to scan the various pathways along which popular music had traveled. A sampling of the weekend concerts in any of America's larger cities would reveal an extraordinary number of very different-sounding groups appearing at the same time—rap and country in their several manifestations, bubblegum, disco, reggae, swing-pop, traditional pop, art-rock, techno-rock, heavy metal, punk, New Wave, Latin bands and singers, singer–songwriters, soul, funk, rockabilly, folk, and folk-rock. For example, on the weekend of 17 March 2001 almost every one of these genres was represented in local Boston clubs and concert halls.[19] Writing in the *New York Times*, Joe Hagan said, in August 2001, that music had "broken down into a zillion niches, from clichéd acts like Bush and Matchbox 20 to arch nerd-rockers like Weezer and Ben Folds Five. There's been a little something for everyone but no longer one big thing for all."[20]

Hogan saw the situation as one that weakened the force of rock, because it could no longer speak with one voice. One could conclude, on the other hand, that from the divisions would come the renewal of popular music, perhaps through a new synthesis. At the least, the stylistic sharing-out that goes on corrects the homogenization that the huge music corporations have been promoting. It counters the sameness centered on the least creative and most brainless part of the musical spectrum. Further, it lays the groundwork on which a renewed, viable integration of musical styles can take place—a tendency that has always been a characteristic of popular music and that has become more and more in evidence in recent years. What is more, after the turn of the century, a significant segment of popular music's devotees welcomed the attempts at blending. For example, to the delight of hipsters, the Chicago rock band Tortoise launched itself into unusual experimentation, fusing rock, jazz, funk, and electronica, and without concessions to immature tastes.[21] The "Three Mo' Tenors" tours, featuring three talented African-American singers, thrilled audiences with a mix of popular and classical music—opera, jazz, folk, blues, soul, gospel, and Broadway. Analyzing their audiences, reviewers found oldsters and adolescents, whites and blacks, Asians and Hispanics, all having a wonderful time.[22] Then there was Nelly Furtado, born in Victoria, British Columbia, whose every performance was a sellout. Her concerts had a certain glossiness about them. However, her songs were "full of unexpected combinations: singing pop hooks and generous melodies, speedy rapping and brisk scat-singing, terse hip-hop rhythms and broad guitar chords, with bossa nova, Jamaican danceable syncopations and a few Portuguese lyrics on the side."[23] Her ethnic roots are Portuguese; her tastes are wide ranging; her willingness to bundle different styles together may help point popular music toward renewal.

Another reason for optimism is the proliferation of festivals throughout the country whose main purpose is not to make money and showcase celebrated performers but to present popular music in its several varieties. Music lovers who came to listen to one genre ended up listening to quite a few. Interests were broadened and music lovers were encouraged to break out of the narrow channels they might have been pursuing. One instance is provided by the Berkfest, a three-day festival held yearly, starting in 1999, in the Berkshire Hills of western Massachusetts. Its directors wanted to avoid the conditions that took down Woodstock '99, so kept away from expensive performers, costly stage productions, overpriced food, and the pricey tickets to pay for it all. They wanted to draw on as wide an audience as possible—young and old. Represented among the outfits appearing at the festival were blues, rhythm and blues, bluegrass, jazz, electronica, folk, folk-rock, rockabilly, other more mainstream rock, and some world music. Discouraged was abrasive, belligerent music in the manner of heavy-metal groups. It was striking that most Berkfest bands were not on major record labels, MTV, or radio. Also striking was the absence of drugs, and the moderation in drinking alcoholic beverages. The Berkfest was "a community gathered for music's sake," according to Seth Rogovoy, the reviewer of the 2001 festival.[24]

On the opposite coast, an annual Live Oak Music Festival has been held every Father's Day weekend since 1988, in the Santa Ynez Valley, California. Yearly, thousands have gathered here to take in music representative of a wide range of styles, going from traditional, folk, bluegrass, and gospel to blues, jazz, classical, and world music. The festival was a family event, designed for parents and their children. In addition to the main-stage performances, attendees could enjoy visiting art and craft booths and music workshops, or engage in barn dancing. Various activities for small children were also provided. Bands were encouraged to perform music with perceptible melodies and to observe civility rather than presenting rants against everything and everyone but themselves. These two festivals are grassroots events, each having a different emphasis.

Repeatedly among groups performing at festivals like these we find greater flexibility, less submission to the domination of the huge music-business interests, and more music selected from a variegated range of sounds and textures. The independent musicians have made genre divisions more easily crossable. They may enter as adherents to one style, but come away borrowing from an array of practices like the ones named above plus surf music, psychedelia, reggae, or New Wave. Improvisation may break out with some songs, while other songs reveal a complete dedication to careful craftsmanship. Receptive listeners encourage the performance groups in these pursuits. Again, all of these festival activities aid in the freshening of popular music. As for those critics who would like to keep a genre pure and unbastardized, they face a losing battle. It is in the nature of popular music to go on constantly to the next new thing, whether for good or bad, if only to court and retain an audience of some dimensions. Sometimes nostalgia prevails and aspects of the musical past achieve prominence. However, in the long run musical reminiscence becomes part of the foundation on which a vital new art can be built.

Talented young musicians with a fresh take on their material also encourage hope. Among the women is the sassy Klea Blackhurst, who first came into notice in 1999. She has been busy reinterpreting Ethel Merman's repertoire and carving out a place for herself in classical pop. The soul singer–songwriter India.Arie achieved a breakthrough in 2001 with her album *Acousic Soul*. She is obviously unafraid to mine the riches of Stevie Wonder and various Motown artists and fashion from them her own pleasing, approachable, straightforward style. We have another soul singer–songwriter, Alicia Keys, whose album *Songs in A Minor* was such a hit in January 2002. She was a Hell's Kitchen alumna, who grew up with rock and hip-hop, yet trained as a classical pianist and learned to love Chopin. At 13 years of age, she heard Marvin Gaye's soul-music album *What's Going On*. Keys said, "It hit me like a rock over the head. I had never heard a body of music like that, so in tune with people and reality and consciousness, socially and politically, and in love with stillness and then turmoil. It was like everything that you ever have felt at one point or another all in one, bam!"[25] Rock, hip-hop, Chopin, and Gaye have all had an input into her album. Finally, there is Neko Case, born in Virginia, growing up mostly in Tacoma, Washington, and starting her music career as a drummer in punk bands. Her first album, *The Virginian*, was in a cautious traditional country style. After that she blossomed out as a country singer–songwriter. In 2000, she recorded *Furnace Room Lullaby*, backing supplied by "Her Boyfriends." In 2002, she and a fine backup crew issued *Blacklisted*. The songs she wrote and delivered, often with a haunting melancholy, unfolded naturally and not to a "retro" sound. Folk-rock and punk had tempered her country manner, and her lyrics, those of an independent woman living in a rough present-day world, breaking away from tradition. Depending on what she is singing, her magnificent voice can sound like a torch singer's or like a singer of soul music.

These four gifted women are cited, not because they are likely to become superstars, but because they bring with them the breakaway outlooks needed to rejuvenate popular music. They provide a third reason for optimism. Whenever popular music arrives at an impasse, musicians like these women help push it forward.

Last but not least are the options offered by the Internet. KaZaA and other sites like it offer fans thousands of unauthorized copies of songs to download at will. In addition, owing to sites like Apple's iTunes and Buy.com's buymusic.com, inexpensive downloads of individual songs also obviate the need to purchase albums. Listeners can sort through the Web for specific styles or compositions that they like without being limited by what monopolistic commercial interests decide to feed them. Room is found for compositions and performances by little-known or unknown musicians. Indeed, more and more lesser-known performers are offering their songs free for the sampling. The listener can appraise them without restriction. Album sales may be more profitable for record companies and major performers, but demand may sink owing to the Internet. The danger, of course, exists that in refusing an album purchase, the fan may never discover the fresh, innovative, but unknown piece that an album might include with a favorite one. Metallica, Radiohead, Led Zeppelin, the Beastie Boys, and others have tried to stop the availability of singles from their albums at the click of a computer mouse. They have not succeeded as well as they would have liked.[26]

THE ONSET OF THE OLDER FAN

In the late fifties and sixties a decided break had taken place in popular-music culture. On the one hand, there were the urban adults who preferred the traditional pop of Broadway and Tin Pan Alley, the rural adults who prized the conventional figurations of country and western, and the African-Americans who looked to the established formats for the blues; on the other hand, the young people who prized rock, folk-rock, country-rock, and soul music.

A half century later, those who were in their fifties and sixties had been the youngsters who participated in the earlier changeover. They continued to cherish the styles that were radical during their youth and that had inspired the musical procedures that came after. By century's end, they were asserting themselves in order to support their own musical preferences. Among them were former president Clinton and Tony Blair, a one-time rocker who became English prime minister in 1997.

David Brooks took note of this aging process, saw adults and adolescents as closer in tastes than they were fifty years before, and claimed that in the 21st century rebellion and alienation were a thing of the past. "The counterculture and the mainstream culture have merged with, and co-opted, each other. For [college students] it's natural that one of the top administrators at Princeton has a poster of the Beatles album *Revolver* framed on her office wall. It's natural that hippies work at ad agencies and found organic ice-cream companies, and that hi-tech entrepreneurs quote Dylan and wear black jeans to work. For them, it's natural that parents should listen to Led Zeppelin, Jimi Hendrix, and the Doors—just like kids."[27]

Nevertheless, each age group enjoyed most the music that had accompanied their youth. Styx had been a leading band, dispensing pomp with their art-rock, in the late seventies. They fell from favor and disbanded in 1984. They came together again for a single tour in the late nineties, were astonished at their enthusiastic reception, and decided to remain together. They also discovered that the music sold to people over the age of 35 had increased to 44% of total sales, even though the younger market was shrinking.[28] All sorts of older band outfits and singers were coming alive again to satisfy a growing special-appeal market covering the several styles of the last fifty years. Anxious to enhance sales, Shania Twain released *Up* in November 2002. She intended to satisfy as many people as she could by putting out three different versions of each song to cater to different tastes. Country and pop-rock adaptations were offered for sale in the United States; pop-rock and world-music adaptations for international sale. The album had a wide sale in its several versions.

The difficulty for the large music conglomerates was that they were so busy trying to capture the youth trade, they could not pay much attention to the over-35 fans and their desires. It was left mostly to small record labels and independent radio to meet the growing demand from the oldsters.[29]

Real old-timers like Tony Bennett were continuing to pull in adult audiences. The public avidly purchased his traditional pop albums *Playin' with*

My Friends (2001) and *A Wonderful World* (2002). Paul McCartney, one of the former Beatles, was selling out his U.S. concert tours and had issued his album *Back in the U.S. Live 2002* with great success at the beginning of the new century. Although well into their fifties, Elton John and Billy Joel were likewise performing for sold-out engagements, attracting their old devotees back and winning some new fans among younger people. Asked to explain their continued popularity, John said: "All the great songs of the 60's and 50's, you can still sing them now. The lyrics were like poetry, but they weren't overcomplicated. You can't actually think of someone going down the road singing a complete Alanis Morissette lyric—it's impossible. . . . You're not going to be singing Ja Rule in five years. Or Jennifer Lopez or any of it."[30] Why, asked Bob Sheffield, was the music of 2000–2001 insipid to him and missing true "pop passion?" Because, he replied, "the American pop scene is grottier [of poorer quality] than it was back in 1963. . . . The fluent energy and urgent emotion of this music are exactly what we pop fans have been starved for lately."[31] Some truth lies in these observations, although we must keep in mind that John and Sheffield were lashing out at musicians toward whose styles they were not particularly sympathetic.

Styles of earlier times were again fashionable. Early Beatles songs were gathered into a new album, *The Beatles 1*, at the end of 2000 and by the middle of February 2001 had sold more than 5 million copies. A repackaged Presley album reached the top of the charts in 2002. *Good Rockin' Tonight: The Legacy of Sun Records*, a tribute to Sam Phillips, came out and sold well. *O Brother Where Art Thou?* the traditional-country sound track of the film of the same title, was issued in December 2000, zoomed up to the topmost position in the charts, and stayed there week after week in 2001. This music from the Coen brothers drew on the unadulterated stream of country, blues, bluegrass, folk, and gospel music. The nonpareil singers were Alison Krauss, Gillian Welch, Emmylou Harris, and Ralph Stanley, among others. The sincere articulation of deep feeling in Krauss's "Down to the River to Pray," the unsettling sorrow and melancholy in Stanley's "O Death," and the album's highlight of Krauss, Welch, and Harris harmonizing on the extraordinarily affecting "Didn't Leave Nobody but the Baby" were expressions absolutely unavailable in other current songs. As I have said before, revisiting the past was an important part of eventually going forward with popular music, if only because it proposed alternatives to some of the stultifying commercial nonsense that was prevalent.

What was also significant was that the music critics of newspapers began to notice this trend away from assembly-line pop. Additionally, they also began reviewing promising young musicians who decided their future lay in addressing adults rather than focusing on teenagers. In October 2001, Joan Anderman published an article entitled "Pure Pop for Grown-up People," in the *Boston Globe*, and proceeded to list twelve such performers, one of them Nelly Furtado. They were "making intelligent, inventive, well-crafted music; astonishingly, some of them have record deals. They span the spectrum from folk-influenced to techno-tinged, classic tunesmiths to masters of pastiche."[32] The singers found that the songs most favored by adults were apparently those that sounded less insubstantial and strident than current adolescent pop. These songs contained memorable tunes and salutary messages, and captured cultural times and images that they could relate to. Even the crude rapper Eminem occasionally was trying to get his act together. In *The Eminem Show* (2002) was the track to his baby daughter, "Hailie's Song." Looking at her he finds that life makes sense after all.[33] For a change Eminem was singing a ballad that abandoned his usual profanity.

IN CONCLUSION

Pop is again getting to the point where it would like to reach a much broader age group than it did in previous years. It is also realizing that one style and one kind of performer cannot win over everyone. Today, updated country and a coarse type of rap may have large followings but tomorrow they inevitably will be supplanted by something else. I want to stress, too, that admirable songs have come out over the last couple of decades and have been enthusiastically listened to by countless music lovers.

Millions of music lovers exist who care little for country and rap and have specific musical needs they wish to have met—hence the growth of today's niche markets to meet the various desires of these millions. Among them are adult listeners whose influence on musical developments is increasing. They show a preference for those particular genres of music that strike them as truly melodious and whose singers offer perceptive commentaries that have a relationship to their daily existence. They often show a love for the quieter vocalists and harmonious vocal ensembles and less for the massive sound of guitars, synthesizers, and shouting over the percussion. At the same time, we find among the younger set boys and girls growing up and wondering if all there is to music is the commercial drivel fed them day after day. Bubblegum will not satisfy them at the end. More and more of them may soon be in revolt, refusing to follow the narrow pathways the commercial world is making them travel. In the years that I have studied and written about American popular music that was published from the end of the 18th century to the present time I have found that quality has a way of reasserting itself, given time.

As always is true of popular music, change is in the offing. Every decade of the 20th century has produced songs that I and others have relished. This will continue. Whatever the change will be, we can expect to discover future songs that will give us as great a pleasure as those of the present or past.

NOTES

1. Ralph Waldo Emerson, "Arts," in *The Essential Writings of Ralph Waldo Emerson*, edited by Brooks Atkinson (New York: Modern Library, 2000), 275.

2. David Brooks, "The Organization Kid," *Atlantic Monthly*, April 2001, 42.

3. Leonard Maltin, *Movie and Video Guide, 2002 Edition* (New York: Signet, 2001), xiii.

4. The *Boston Globe* is delivered to me; the other two are read on the Internet.

5. Hayley Kaufman, "Go! Thursday," *Boston Globe*, 28 June 2001, E2.

6. My subscription ran through December 2002. I decided not to renew.

7. André Schiffrin, *The Business of Books* (London: Verso, 2000), 170–71.

8. Several publishers refused me permission altogether. Others failed to answer my letters or telephone calls. One actually demanded $1,300 for quoting two lines. Scarcely any allowed quotation on a gratis basis.

9. Steve Morse, "Irreverent Ike Reilly Hits the Road in Earnest," *Boston Globe*, 10 May 2001, C16.

10. Clea Simeon, "Taking Back the Airwaves?" *Boston Globe*, 27 June 2001, C16.

11. "Linkin Park has 2001's Bestseller in Down Year," *CNN.com*, 6 January 2002.

12. Phil Gallo and Justin Oppelaar, "Tour Tumult in the Concert Business," *MSNBC.com*, 29 August 2001. In the summer of 2003, Madonna would have the unusual experience of bombing with a new recording.

13. Jim Washburn, "Bored Bands? Sullen Audiences?" *MSNBC.com*, 16 May 2001.

14. James Caryn, "Woodstock Just Isn't What It Used to Be," *New York Times*, 16 August 2001, www.nytimes.com.

15. John Leland and Peter Marks, "New Look for Entertainment in a Terror-Conscious World," *New York Times*, 24 September 2001, www.nytimes.com.

16. New York: TVT Music Inc., c1994.

17. "The Social Impact of Music Violence," testimony of the American Academy of Pediatrics, before the Senate Subcommittee on Oversight of Government Management, Restructuring, and the District of Columbia, 6 November 1997, presented by Dr. Frank Palumbo.

18. Steve Allen, *Vulgarians at the Gate* (Amherst, New York: Prometheus Books, 2001), 243, 348.

19. According to the *Boston Globe Calendar* for 15 March 2001.

20. Joe Hagan, "The White Stripes: Hurling Your Basic Rock at the Arty Crowd," *New York Times*, 12 August 2001, www.nytimes.com.

21. Ben Sisario, "Tortoise: 'Post Rock' Hipsters Look Back to Fusion," *New York Times*, 18 March 2001, www.nytimes.com.

22. Nekusa Mumbi Moody, "Three Mo' Tenors Celebrate Talents," *Washington Post*, 5 August 2001, www.washingtonpost.com.

23. Jon Pareles, "A Singer Who Puts Herself before Her Dates," *New York Times*, 9 March 2002, www.nytimes.com.

24. Seth Rogovoy, "Berkfest: A Three-Day Community," *Berkshire Week*, 9 August 2001, 30–31.

25. Jon Pareles, "To Be Alicia Keys," *New York Times*, 27 January 2002, www.nytimes.com.

26. Jon Pareles, "What Albums Join Together, Everyone Tears Asunder," *New York Times*, 20 June 2003, www.nytimes.com.

27. Brooks, "Organization Kid," 49.

28. *The Rolling Stone Encyclopedia of Rock & Roll*, 3rd ed., edited by Holly George-Warren and Patricia Romanowski (New York: Rolling Stone Press Book, 2001), s.v. "Styx"; David Lieberman, "Musicmakers Lure Grown-ups," *USA Today*, 18 February 2002, B1–2.

29. Lieberman, "Musicmakers Lure Grown-ups," B2.

30. Anthony DeCurtis, "Elton John and Billy Joel, Talking about Songs," *New York Times*, 10 March 2002, www.nytimes.com.

31. Bob Sheffield, "Beatles Save World for Second Time," *Rolling Stone*, 15 February 2001, 28.

32. Joan Anderman, "Pure Pop for Grown-up People," *Boston Globe*, 28 October 2001, N1, 5.

33. Los Angeles: Ensign Music, c/o Famous Music Publishing, c2002.

Selected Bibliography

Allen, Frederick Lewis, *Only Yesterday*. New York: Harper & Row, 1964.

Allen, Steve, *Vulgarians at the Gate*. Amherst, New York: Prometheus Books, 2001.

Amburn, Ellis, *Buddy Holly*. New York: Martin's Griffin, 1996.

Anderson, Terry H., *The Movement and the Sixties*. New York: Oxford University Press, 1995.

Atkins, John, *The Who on Record*. Jefferson, North Carolina: McFarland, 2000.

Bach, Steven, *Dazzler: The Life and Times of Moss Hart*. New York: Knopf, 2001.

Bailey, Pearl, *Between You and Me*. New York: Doubleday, 1989.

——, *Talking to Myself*. New York: Harcourt Brace Jovanovich, 1971.

Barlow, William, *Looking Up and Down: The Emergence of Blues Culture*. Philadelphia: Temple University Press, 1989.

Barlow, William, and Cheryl Finley, *From Swing to Soul*. Washington, D.C.: Elliott & Clark, 1994.

Barrett, Mary Ellin, *Irving Berlin*. New York: Simon & Schuster, 1994.

Barzun, Jacques, *The Culture We Deserve*. Middletown, Connecticut: Wesleyan University Press, 1989.

——, *From Dawn to Decadence*. New York: Harper Collins, 2000.

Bashe, Philip, *Heavy Metal Thunder*. Garden City, New York: Doubleday, 1985.

Bego, Mark, *Aretha Franklin*. New York: St. Martin's Press, 1989.

Belz, Carl, *The Story of Rock*, 2nd ed. New York: Oxford University Press, 1972.

Bennett, Betty, *The Ladies Who Sing with the Band*. Lanham, Maryland: Scarecrow Press, 2000.

Bennett, Tony, with Will Friedwald, *The Good Life*. New York: Pocket Books, 1998.

Bergreen, Laurence, *As Thousands Cheer: The Life of Irving Berlin*. New York: Penguin, 1990.

Berry, Chuck, *Chuck Berry*. New York: Harmony Books, 1987.

The Billboard Illustrated Encyclopedia of Rock, edited by Lucinda Hawksley. New York: Billboard Books, 1998.

Block, Geoffrey, *Enchanted Evenings: The Broadway Musical from Show Boat to Sondheim*. New York: Oxford University Press, 1997.

Bloom, Allan, *The Closing of the American Mind*. New York: Simon & Schuster, 1987.

Blume, Jason, *6 Steps to Songwriting Success*. New York: Billboard Books, 1999.

Boardman, Gerald, *Jerome Kern*. New York: Oxford University Press, 1980.

Boyer, Horace Clarence, *How Sweet the Sound: The Golden Age of Gospel*. Washington, D.C.: Elliott & Clark, 1995.

Bowers, Dwight Blocker, *American Musical Theater*. Washington, D.C.: Smithsonian Collection of Records, 1989.

Bowman, David, *This Must Be the Place*. New York: Harper Entertainment, 2001.

Brackett, David, *Interpreting Popular Music*. Berkeley, California: University of California Press, 2000.

Bronson, Fred, *The Billboard Book of Number One Hits*, revised and updated 4th ed. New York: Billboard Books, 1997.

Brooks, David, "The Organization Kid." *Atlantic Monthly*, April 2001, 40–54.

Brown, Charles T., *The Art of Rock and Roll*, 2nd ed. Englewood Cliffs, New Jersey: Prentice-Hall, 1987.

Cahn, Sammy, *I Should Care*. New York: Arbor House, 1974.

Campbell, Glenn, with Tom Carter, *Rhinestone Cowboy*. New York: Villard Books, 1994.

Cantwell, Robert, *Bluegrass Breakdown*. New York: Da Capo, 1992.

———, *When We Were Good: The Folk Revival*. Cambridge: Harvard University Press, 1996.

Carmichael, Hoagy, *The Stardust Road*. Bloomington, Indiana: Indiana University Press, 1983.

Carmichael, Hoagy, with Stephen Longstreet, *Sometimes I Wonder*. New York: Farrar, Strauss & Giroux, 1965.

Chapple, Steve, and Reebee Garofalo, *Rock 'n' Roll Is Here to Pay*. Chicago: Nelson-Hall, 1977.

Charles, Ray, and David Ritz, *Brother Ray*. New York: Dial, 1978.

Chilton, John. *Let the Good Times Roll: The Story of Louis Jordan and His Music*. Ann Arbor, Michigan: University of Michigan Press, 1994.

Ching, Barbara, *Wrong's What I Do Best*. New York: Oxford University Press, 2001.

Citron, Stephen, *The Wordsmiths*. New York: Oxford University Press, 1995.

Clark, Dick, and Richard Robinson, *Rock, Roll and Remember*. New York: Crowell, 1976.

Clarke, Donald, *The Rise and Fall of Popular Music*. New York: St. Martin's Press, 1995.

Clarke, Gerald, *Get Happy: The Life of Judy Garland*. New York: Random House, 2000.

Collier, James Lincoln, *Benny Goodman and the Swing Era*. New York: Oxford University Press, 1989.

Covach, John, and Graeme M. Boone, editors, *Understanding Rock*. New York: Oxford University Press, 1997.

Crawford, Richard, *America's Musical Life*. New York: Norton, 2001.

Croce, Arlene, *The Fred Astaire and Ginger Rogers Book*. New York: Vintage Books, 1972.

Crosby, Bing, as told to Pete Martin, *Call Me Lucky*. New York: Simon & Schuster, 1953.

DeLong, Thomas A., *Pop: Paul Whiteman, King of Jazz*. Piscataway, New Jersey: New Century, 1983.

Denisoff, R. Serge, *Sing a Song of Social Significance*. Bowling Green, Ohio: Bowling Green State University Popular Press, 1983.

Dickstein, Morris, *Gates of Eden: American Culture in the Sixties*. New York: Basic Books, 1977.

Dunaway, David King, *How Can I Keep from Singing: Pete Seeger*. New York: McGraw-Hill, 1981.

Edwards, Anne, *Streisand*. Boston: Little, Brown, 1997.

Eells, George, *The Life That Late He Led*. New York: Putnam's Sons, 1967.

Ellison, Curtis W., *Country Music Culture*. Jackson, Mississippi: University Press of Mississippi, 1995.

Ewen, David, *All the Years of American Popular Music*. Englewood Cliffs, New Jersey: Prentice-Hall, 1977.

———, *The Life and Death of Tin Pan Alley*. New York: Funk & Wagnalls, 1964.

———, editor, *American Popular Songs*. New York: Random House, 1966.

Filene, Benjamin, *Romancing the Folk*. Chapel Hill, North Carolina: University of North Carolina Press, 2000.

Flanagan, Bill, *Written in My Soul*. Chicago: Contemporary Books, 1986.

Fordin, Hugh, *The World of Entertainment*. New York: Avon Books, 1975.

Friedwald, Will, *Sinatra!* New York: Scribner, 1995.

Frith, Simon, *Sound Effects*. New York: Pantheon, 1981.

Furia, Philip, *Ira Gershwin*. New York: Oxford University Press, 1996.

———, *The Poets of Tin Pan Alley*. New York: Oxford University Press, 1990.

Fuss, Charles J., *Joan Baez*. Westport, Connecticut: Greenwood Press, 1996.

Gaines, Steven, *Heroes and Villains: The True Story of the Beach Boys*. New York: New American Library, 1986.

George, Nelson, *The Death of Rhythm and Blues*. New York: Pantheon Books, 1988.

———, *Hip Hop America*. New York: Viking, 1998.

George, Nelson, and Susan Flinker, Patty Romanowski, *Fresh: Hip Hop Don't Stop*. New York: Random House, 1985.

Gershwin, Ira, *Lyrics on Several Occasions*. New York: Knopf, 1959.

Giddins, Gary, *Bing Crosby: A Pocketful of Dreams, The Early Years 1903–1940*. Boston: Little, Brown, 2001.

Gilbert, Steven E., *The Music of Gershwin*. New Haven: Yale University Press, 1995.

Gillett, Charlie, *The Sound of the City: The Rise of Rock and Roll*, 2nd ed. 1983. Reprint, New York: Da Capo Press, 1996.

Goldberg, Isaac, *Tin Pan Alley*. New York: Ungar, 1961.

Goodman, Fred, *The Mansion on the Hill*. New York: Vintage Books, 1998.

Goodwin, Andrew, *Dancing in the Distraction Factory*. Minneapolis, Minnesota: University of Minnesota, 1992.

Gracyk, Theodore, *Rhythm and Noise: An Aesthetic of Rock*. Durham, North Carolina: Duke University Press, 1996.

Greenberg, Clement, *Homemade Esthetics*. New York: Oxford University Press, 1999.

Greenfield, Robert, *Dark Star: An Oral Biography of Jerry Garcia*. New York: William Morrow, 1996.

Guralnick, Peter, *Last Train to Memphis*. Boston: Little, Brown, 1994.

———, *Lost Highway*. New York: Perennial Library, Harper & Row, 1989.

Haggard, Merle, with Peggy Russell, *Sing Me Back Home*. New York: Times Books, 1981.

Hajdu, David, *Positively 4th Street*. New York: Farrar, Straus & Giroux, 2001.

Halberstam, David, *The Fifties*. New York: Fawcett Columbine, 1993.

Hamil, Pete, *Why Sinatra Matters*. Thorndike, Maine: Thorndike Press, 1998.

Hamm, Charles, *Yesterdays*. New York: Norton, 1979.

Hammerstein, Oscar, II, *Lyrics*. Milwaukee, Wisconsin: Hal Leonard Books, 1985.

Handy, W. C., *Father of the Blues*, edited by Arna Bontemps. New York: Macmillan, 1941.

Hanson, Erica, *The 1920s*. San Diego, California: Lucent Books, 1999.

Haskins, James, with Kathleen Benson, *Nat King Cole*. New York: Stein & Day, 1984.

Heilbut, Anthony, *The Gospel Sound*, rev. ed. New York: Limelight Editions, 1985.

Helander, Brock, *The Rockin' '50s*. New York: Schirmer Books, 1998.

——, *The Rockin' '60s*. New York: Schirmer Books, 1999.

Heylin, Clinton, *Bob Dylan: Behind the Shades Revisited*. New York: Morrow, 2001.

Holland, Gini, *The 1960s*. San Diego, California: Lucent Books, 1999.

Hyland, William G., *The Song Is Ended*. New York: Oxford University Press, 1995.

Jablonski, Edward, *Alan Jay Lerner*. New York: Holt, 1996.

——, *Gershwin*. Boston: Northeastern University Press, 1990.

——, *Harold Arlen*. New York: Da Capo, Press, 1986.

——, *Irving Berlin*. New York: Holt, 1999.

Jasen, David A., and Gene Jones, *Spreadin' Rhythm Around: Black Popular Songwriters, 1880–1930*. New York: Schirmer Books, 1998.

Kallen, Stuart A., editor, *The 1980s*. San Diego, California: Lucent Books, 1989.

——, editor, *The 1950s*. San Diego, California: Lucent Books, 2000.

——, editor, *The 1990s*. San Diego, California: Greenhaven Press, 2000.

Keeley, Jennifer, *Rap Music*. San Diego, California: Lucent Books, 2001.

Keil, Charles, *Urban Blues*. Chicago: University of Chicago Press, 1991.

Kelley, Robin D. G., *Race Rebels: Culture, Politics, and the Black Working Class*. New York: Free Press, 1994.

Kislan, Richard, *The Musical*. Englewood Cliffs, New Jersey: Prentice-Hall, 1980.

LaFaber, Walter, and Richard Polenberg, Nancy Woloch, *The American Century*, 3rd ed. New York: Knopf, 1986.

Lees, Gene, *Inventing Champagne*. New York: St. Martin's Press, 1990.

Lerner, Alan Jay, *The Street Where I Live*. New York: Norton, 1978.

Lewis, Lisa A., *Gender Politics and MTV*. Philadelphia: Temple University Press, 1990.

Lynes, Russell, *The Lively Audience*. New York: Harper & Row, 1985.

Lynn, Loretta, with Patsi Bale Cox, *Still Woman Enough*. Waterville Valley, Maine: Thorndike Press, 2002.

——, with George Vecsey, *Coal Miner's Daughter*. Chicago: Regency, 1976.

McBrien, William, *Cole Porter*. New York: Knopf, 1998.

McElroy, John Harmon, *Finding Freedom*. Carbondale, Illinois: Southern Illinois University Press, 1989.

Malnig, Julie, *Dancing till Dawn: A Century of Exhibition Ballroom Dance*. New York: New York University Press, 1992.

Malone, Bill C., *Country Music, U.S.A*. Austin, Texas: University of Texas Press, 1985.

——, *Singing Cowboys and Musical Mountaineers*. Athens, Georgia: University of Georgia Press, 1993.

Marks, Edward B., as told to Abbott J. Liebling, *They All Sang*. New York: Viking, 1935.

Marsh, David, *The Heart of Rock and Roll*. New York: New American Library, 1989.

Mattfeld, Julius, *Variety Music Cavalcade, 1620–1969*, 3rd ed. Englewood Cliffs, New Jersey: Prentice-Hall, 1971.

Meyerson, Harold, and Ernie Harburg, with the assistance of Arthur Perlman, *Who Put the Rainbow in the Wizard of Oz?* Ann Arbor, Michigan: University of Michigan Press, 1993.

Miller, James, *Flowers in the Dustbin: The Rise of Rock and Roll, 1947–1977*. New York: Simon & Schuster, 1999.

Mitchell, Tony, editor, *Global Noise: Rap and Hip-Hop outside the USA*. Middletown, Connecticut: Wesleyan University Press, 2001.

Morrison, Joan, and Robert K. Morrison, *From Camelot to Kent State*. New York: Oxford University Press, 1987.

The New Rolling Stone Encyclopedia of Rock & Roll, rev. and updated, edited by Patricia Romanowski and Holly George-Warren. New York: Fireside, 1995.

Nicholson, Lois P., *Michael Jackson*. New York: Chelsea House, 1994.

Norman, Philip, *Shout!* New York: Simon & Schuster, 1981.

Ogg, Alex, with David Upshal, *The Hip Hop Years*. New York: Fromm International, 2001.

Okun, Milton, editor, *Great Songs of the Eighties*, rev. ed. New York: Cherry Lane Music, 1999.

——, editor, *Great Songs of the Nineties*. New York: Cherry Lane Music, 1999.

——, editor, *The New York Times Great Songs of the Sixties*. New York: Quadrangle Books, 1970.

——, editor, *The New York Times Great Songs of the Seventies*. New York: Times Books, 1978.

Oldham, Andrew Loog, *Stoned*, edited by Ron Ross. New York: St. Martin's Press, 2001.

Orman, John, *The Politics of Rock Music*. Chicago: Nelson-Hall, 1984.

Palmer, Robert, *Rock & Roll: An Unruly History*. New York: Harmony Books, 1995.

Palmer, Tony, *All You Need Is Love*, edited by Paul Medlecott. New York: Grossman Publishers, 1976.

Perris, Arnold, *Music as Propaganda*. Westport, Connecticut: Greenwood, 1985.

Pessen, Edward, "The Great Songwriters of Tin Pan Alley's Golden Age." *American Music* 3 (1985): 180–97.

Pleasants, Henry, *The Great American Popular Singers*. New York: Simon & Schuster, 1974.

Potash, Chris, editor, *Reggae, Rasta, Revolution: Jamaican Music from Ska to Dub*. New York: Schirmer Books, 1997.

Press, Petra, *The 1930s*. San Diego, California: Lucent Books, 1999.

Price, Charles Gower, "Sources of American Styles in the Music of the Beatles." *American Music* 15 (1997): 208–32.

Ritz, David, *Divided Soul: The Life of Marvin Gaye*. New York: McGraw-Hill, 1985.

Roberts, John Storm, *The Latin Tinge: The Impact of Latin American Music on the United States*. New York: Oxford University Press, 1979.

Rodgers, Richard, *Musical Stages*. New York: Random House, 1975.

The Rolling Stone Encyclopedia of Rock & Roll, 3rd ed., edited by Holly George-Warren and Patricia Romanowski. New York: Rolling Stone Press Book, 2001.

Rose, Tricia, *Black Noise*. Hanover, New Hampshire: Wesleyan University Press, 1994.

Sanjek, Russell, updated by David Sanjek, *Pennies from Heaven*. New York: Da Capo, 1996.

Schuller, Gunther, *The Swing Era*. New York: Oxford University Press, 1989.

Schulman, Bruce J., *The Seventies*. New York: Free Press, 2001.

Schwartz, Charles, *Gershwin: His Life and Music*. Indianapolis, Indiana: Bobbs-Merrill, 1973.

Seabrook, John, *Nobrow*. New York: Knopf, 2000.

Secrest, Meryle, *Leonard Bernstein*. New York: Knopf, 1994.

——, *Stephen Sondheim*. New York: Knopf, 1998.

Shapiro, Harry, and Caesar Glebbeek, *Jimi Hendrix, Electric Gypsy*. New York: St. Martin's Press, 1990.

Shaw, Arnold, *Black Popular Music in America*. New York: Schirmer Books, 1986.

——, *Honkers and Shouters*. New York: Collier Books, 1978.

——, *The Jazz Age*. New York: Oxford University Press, 1987.

——, *The Rockin' '50s*. New York: Hawthorn Books, 1974.

——, *The Rock Revolution*. Toronto: Crowell-Collier Press, 1969.

——, *Sinatra: Twentieth-Century Romantic*. New York: Holt, Rinehart & Winston, 1968.

Simon, George T., *The Big Bands*, rev. ed. New York: Collier Books, 1974.

Small, Christopher, *Music of the Common Tongue*. New York: Riverrun Press, 1994.

Sounes, Howard, *Down the Highway: The Life of Bob Dylan*. New York: Grove Press, 2001.

Southern, Eileen, *The Music of Black Americans*, 3rd ed. New York: Norton, 1997.

Spaeth, Sigmund, *Read 'Em and Weep*. New York: Arco, 1945.

Spitz, Bob, *Dylan*. New York: Norton, 1989.

Stephenson, Richard M., and Joseph Iaccarino, *The Complete Book of Ballroom Dancing*. Garden City, New York: Doubleday, 1980.

Stewart, Gail B., *The 1970s*. San Diego, California: Lucent Books, 1999.

Szatmary, David P., *Rockin' in Time*, 2nd ed. Englewood Cliffs, New Jersey: Prentice-Hall, 1991.

Taraborrelli, J. Randy, *Call Her Miss Ross*. New York: Carol Publishing Group, 1989.

——, *Madonna*. New York: Simon & Schuster, 2001.

——, *Michael Jackson*. New York: Birch Lane Press, 1991.

Taylor, Timothy D., *Global Pop*. New York: Routledge, 1997.

Tichi, Cecelia, *High Lonesome*. Chapel Hill, North Carolina: University of North Carolina Press, 1994.

Titon, Jeff Todd, *Early Downhome Blues*, 2nd ed. Chapel Hill, North Carolina: University of North Carolina Press, 1994.

Torr, James D., editor, *The 1980s*. San Diego, California: Greenhaven Press, 2000.

Uschan, Michael V., *The 1940s*. San Diego, California: Lucent Books, 1999.

Vallée, Rudy, *Let the Chips Fall*. Harrisburg, Pennsylvania: Stackpole Books, 1975.

Waller, Don, *The Motown Story*. New York: Scribner's Sons, 1985.

Walser, Robert, *Running with the Devil: Power, Gender, and Madness in Heavy Metal Music*. Hanover, New Hampshire: University Press of New England, 1993.

Ward, Brian, *Just My Soul Responding: Rhythm and Blues, Black Consciousness, and Race Relations*. Berkeley, California: University of California Press, 1998.

Waters, Ethel, with Charles Samuels, *His Eye Is on the Sparrow*. Garden City, New York: Doubleday, 1952.

Weinstein, Deena, *Heavy Metal: The Music and Its Culture*. Boulder, Colorado: Da Capo Press, 2000.

Werner, Craig, *A Change Is Gonna Come: Music, Race and the Soul of America*. New York: Plume, 1999.

White, Charles, *The Life and Times of Little Richard*. New York: Harmony Books, 1984.

White, David Manning, editor, *Pop Culture in America*. Chicago: Quadrangle Books, 1970.

White, Mark, *'You Must Remember This . . .': Popular Songwriters, 1900–1980*. New York: Scribner's Sons, 1985.

White, Timothy, *Rock Lives*. New York: Holt, 1990.

Whiteman, Paul, and Mary Margaret McBride, *Jazz*. 1926. Reprint, New York: Ayer Co., 1974.

Whittcomb, Ian, *Tin Pan Alley*. London: Paddington Press, 1975.

Wilder, Alec, *American Popular Song*. New York: Oxford University Press, 1972.

Wilk, Max, *They're Playing Our Song*. New York: Atheneum, 1973.

Wilson, Earl, *Sinatra*. New York: Macmillan, 1976.

Winer, Deborah Grace, *The Night and the Music*. New York: Schirmer Books, 1996.

Wolff, Daniel, with S. R. Crain, Clifton White, and G. David Tenenbaum, *You Send Me: The Life of Sam Cooke*. New York: Morrow, 1995.

Zadan, Craig, *Sondheim & Co.*, 2nd ed. New York: Harper & Row, 1986.

Index

About the Author

Nicholas Tawa is professor emeritus at the University of Massachusetts, Boston. He is the author of numerous articles and books on American music history and the place of music in American culture, the latest being *From Psalm to Symphony: A History of Music in New England* (2001); *High-Minded and Low-Down: Music in the Lives of Americans, 1800–1861* (2000); and *Arthur Foote* (1997). American popular music prior to the years covered by this book is explored in his *Sweet Songs for Gentle Americans: The Parlor Song in America, 1790–1860*; *A Music for the Millions: Antebellum Democratic Attitudes and the Birth of American Popular Music* (a Julliard performance guide, 1984); *The Way to Tin Pan Alley: American Popular Song, 1866–1910*; and the previously mentioned *High-Minded and Low-Down*. His writings chronicle musical developments within the context of the prevailing geographic, economic, political, and artistic directions that influenced and defined the nation's musical experiences.